# MANUFACTURING SOVEREIGNTY

This book delves into the legal and labour history of the Hashemite Kingdom of Iraq to explore the role international law and its institutions played in Iraq's state formation.

Focusing on a turbulent period in global and Middle East history, it shows how the case of Iraq became a laboratory for experimentation with the concept of sovereignty by the Permanent Mandates Commission of the League of Nations in Geneva. This resulted in the development of a doctrine of 'semi-peripheral sovereignty' to justify Iraq's independence from the Mandate process. This novel doctrine and its operation within the provisions of the 1930 Anglo-Iraq Treaty ensured the maintenance of British dominance over Iraq, especially to safeguard the extraction and transportation of its valuable oil resources to Western markets.

The book traces how this legal doctrine impacted the everyday lives of working class Iraqis. It explores the governance of the extraterritorial spaces of capitalist accumulation and labour exploitation, in particular the Iraq Petroleum Company oil fields, the Iraq State Railways and the Port of Basra. It goes on to detail how the oil, railway and port workers led by the Iraqi Communist Party effectively organised themselves into a nationalist revolutionary labour movement. They waged an anti-colonial struggle against these imperial legal structures to improve their lot, leading up to the 1948 Wathba, the 1953 Intifada, and ultimately the July Revolution of 1958, which upended the British-sponsored monarchy.

Spanning various international archives and Arabic primary source materials, this book offers an example of a social, legal and labour history written from below, centering ordinary working peoples' agency in the historiography of international law. Drawing on Third World Approaches to International Law (TWAIL) and Marxist methodologies, it emphasises the significance of the semi-periphery in the making of the international legal order.

**Volume 15 in the series Hart Monographs in Transnational and International Law**

**Hart Monographs in Transnational and International Law**

Series Editor: Craig Martin Scott, Professor of Law, Osgoode Hall Law School of York University, Toronto

The objective of this series is to publish high-quality scholarship in public international law and private international law, as well as work that adopts "transnational law" as its thematic, theoretical or doctrinal focus. The series strives to be a leading venue for work of the following sort:

* critical reappraisals of foundational concepts and core doctrinal principles of both public and private international law, and their operation in practice, including insights drawn from general legal theory;
* analysis and development of conceptions of 'transnational law', including in relation to the role of unofficial law and informal processes in transnational regulation and in relation to theories and studies of 'governance' in transnational spheres; and
* empirical studies of the emergence, evolution and transformation of international and/or transnational legal orders, including accounts and explanations of how law is constructed within different communities of interpretation and practice.

In relation to the first of these categories, the series especially welcomes monographs that explore the interactions between the ever-integrating fields of public and private international law. Of special interest are explorations of the extent to which these interactions are structured by higher-order principles and policies, on the one hand, and by politics and the exercise of various forms of power, on the other hand.

The series is open to work not only by law scholars but also by scholars from cognate disciplines.

**Recent titles in this series**

Transconstitutionalism
Marcelo Neves translated by Kevin Mundy

The Institutional Problem in Modern International Law
Richard Collins

Liability for Transboundary Pollution at the Intersection of Public and Private International Law
Guillaume Laganière

Faith in Courts: Human Rights Advocacy and the Transnational Regulation of Religion
Lisa Harms

The Law's Last Frontier: The Private Dimension of International Law
Horatia Muir Watt

Manufacturing Sovereignty: International Law, Labour Struggle, and the Making of Iraq
Ali Hammoudi

# Manufacturing Sovereignty

## *International Law, Labour Struggle, and the Making of Iraq*

Ali Hammoudi

•HART•

OXFORD • LONDON • NEW YORK • NEW DELHI • SYDNEY

HART PUBLISHING

Bloomsbury Publishing Plc

Kemp House, Chawley Park, Cumnor Hill, Oxford, OX2 9PH, UK

1385 Broadway, New York, NY 10018, USA

Bloomsbury Publishing Ireland Limited, 29 Earlsfort Terrace, Dublin 2, D02 AY28, Ireland

HART PUBLISHING, the Hart/Stag logo, BLOOMSBURY and the Diana logo are trademarks of Bloomsbury Publishing Plc

First published in Great Britain 2026



A catalogue record for this book is available from the British Library.

A catalogue record for this book is available from the Library of Congress.

Library of Congress Control Number: 2025934347

ISBN: HB: 978-1-50995-287-8
ePDF: 978-1-50995-289-2
ePub: 978-1-50995-288-5

Typeset by Compuscript Ltd, Shannon

For product safety related questions contact productsafety@bloomsbury.com

To find out more about our authors and books visit www.hartpublishing.co.uk. Here you will find extracts, author information, details of forthcoming events and the option to sign up for our newsletters.

*To the memory of Zahra Kubba*

# Acknowledgements

IT GOES WITHOUT saying that my long journey in the making of this book, which has taken over a decade, would have been inconceivable without the help, support and encouragement of so many people.

This book began as an idea I had for my doctoral project at Osgoode Hall Law School of York University in Toronto after reading Hanna Batatu's magnum opus, *The Old Social Classes and the Revolutionary Movements of Iraq*, to revisit the history of pre-revolutionary Iraq from the perspective of international law and labour struggle. My doctoral advisor, Susan Drummond, from our first meetings encouraged me to follow through with this idea despite my initial doubts of its feasibility. I am indebted to her for her belief in this project, and very much grateful for all her support. I am also deeply indebted to Thabit A. Abdullah, for playing an instrumental role of getting this project on its feet, and reassuring me of its importance despite its unchartered nature. Our long conversations on Iraqi history had a great impact on my thinking and on this book. I am very much grateful to Doug Hay for his close readings and invaluable feedback, which improved this work immensely. Last but not least, I am thankful to Sabah al-Nasseri, Patrick Macklem, Raju Das, and Obi Okafor for providing constructive feedback on how to take this project forward.

My initial thoughts on this project – in particular on the *Wathba* uprising and the 1948 Portsmouth Treaty – were presented as a short paper at the Third World Approaches to International Law (TWAIL) Conference at the American University of Cairo in 2015, and was later published in a special TWAIL issue of *Third World Quarterly* (2016, Vol. 37, No. 11, pp.2028–2046). My ideas were shaped by the discussions I had with the TWAIL community, and I am thankful for having had the opportunity to engage with this growing vibrant intellectual network.

I spent a couple of years rethinking many aspects of this manuscript during my time as a postdoctoral fellow at the National University of Singapore Faculty of Law at the peak of the global pandemic, which also allowed me to publish several articles on related topics, such as semi-colonialism, unfree labour, and treaty-making in the Middle East. I would like to express my gratitude to the NUS law faculty, colleagues and friends in Singapore for creating a positive intellectual environment and community despite the circumstances, especially Antony Anghie, Damian Chalmers, Simon Chesterman, Victor Kattan, Michael Grainger, Jan Mihal, James Penner, Eugénie Mérieau, Alastair Cook, M. Sornarajah, and Fanar Haddad. I would like to acknowledge the support of all my wonderful colleagues at the University of Windsor Faculty of Law, in particular Reem Bahdi, Sujith Xavier, Claire Mumme, Vasanthi Venkatesh,

Joshua Sealy-Harrington, Irina Ceric, Jillian Rogan, Tess Sheldon, Shanthi Senthe, Beverly Jacobs, and Vincent Wong. I could not have asked for a better intellectual home. I would also like to thank many friends and colleagues far and wide who have in one way or another played a role in the making of this book, whether it was with their mentorship, feedback, encouragement and/or inspiration, in particular Antony Anghie, Adrian A. Smith, John Reynolds, Rob Knox, Ntina Tzouvala, Mai Taha, Amar Bhatia, Mazen Masri, Abdel Razzaq al-Tikriti, Victor Kattan, Konstantin Kilibarda, Sara Farhan, Sune Sandbeck and Usha Natarajan.

The research for this book would not have been possible without the tireless assistance of the archivists, librarians, and staff of the British National Archives at Kew, Osgoode Hall Law Library, the Yale University Library, the British Library, the Nami Yafet Memorial Library of the American University of Beirut, and the United Nations Office at Geneva Library. I would like to thank Peter Housego, chief archivist of the British Petroleum Archive at The Modern Records Centre in Coventry. I would also like to thank Jacques Oberson of the League of Nations Archives, as well as, Remo Becci and Jacques Rodriguez of the International Labour Organization Archives in Geneva for their generosity.

Closer to home, I would like to express my appreciation to my dear uncle, Dr. Khalil al-Ghazali for providing me with pages upon pages of valuable feedback on my work based on his lived experience with the Iraqi left. I also want to thank my relative, the late Shamil al-Nahir, who was kind enough to connect me with several veteran Iraqi communists, particularly the late renowned labour leader Ara' Khājādor. I will ever be grateful for his assistance. I want to express my thanks to my cousin, Hussein al-Ghazali for providing me with much-needed books from Iraq. Finally, I could not have done any of this without the unconditional love and support of my parents, Nada and Imad, and my siblings, Zaid and Rusul.

It should be mentioned that this work was written in the spirit of remembrance of the lives of my grandmother, Zahra Kubba, a feminist educator and school principal in Baghdad, who had a great influence on me in my formative years and in many ways was the embodiment of the Iraq that I came to know as a child growing up in the diaspora; and to my grandfather, *Muqaddam* [Lt. Col.] Ibrahim al-Ghazali, a revolutionary, judge and poet, and to their lost generation, who struggled for and dreamed of not only a free sovereign Iraq, but also a free Palestine, which they saw as a necessary prerequisite for the liberation of the entire region from Western colonialism and imperialism.

Ali Hammoudi
*Windsor*
*October 2024*

# Contents

# *List of Abbreviations and Acronyms*

| | |
|---|---|
| APOC | Anglo-Persian Oil Company |
| ARAMCO | Arabian American Oil Company |
| BMEO | British Middle East Office (Cairo) |
| BP | British Petroleum |
| BPA | British Petroleum Archives |
| BAPCO | Bahrain Petroleum Company |
| BPC | Basra Petroleum Company (subsidiary of IPC) |
| BPD | Basra Port Directorate |
| BPWU | Basra Port Workers' Union |
| CID | Criminal Investigation Department |
| CLN | Council of the League of Nations |
| CO | Colonial Office (UK) |
| CPGBA | Communist Party of Great Britain Archives |
| FCR | Frontiers Crimes Regulation |
| FO | Foreign Office (UK) |
| FOWU | Federation of Oil Workers Union |
| GFTU | General Federation of Trade Unions |
| GOC | General Officer Commanding (UK) |
| HC | House of Commons (UK) |
| HMG | His/Her Majesty's Government (UK) |
| ICP | The Iraqi Communist Party (*al-Hizb al-Shīū ʿi al-ʿIraqī*) |
| IDB | Iraq Development Board |
| ILC | International Labour Conference |
| ILO | International Labour Organization |
| ILOA | International Labour Organization Archives |

| | |
|---|---|
| INA | Iraq National Archives |
| IO | India Office (UK) |
| IOWU | Iraqi Oil Workers' Union |
| IPC | Iraq Petroleum Company |
| ISR | Iraqi State Railways |
| JAS | *Jamʿīyat aṣḥāb al-ṣināʿa* (Association of Craftsmen) |
| JDB | Joint Defense Board |
| KPC | Kuwait Petroleum Company |
| MAC | Mesopotamian Administration Committee |
| MESC | Middle East Supply Centre |
| MPC | Mosul Petroleum Company (subsidiary of IPC) |
| O.J. | Official Journal of the League of Nations |
| PMC | Permanent Mandates Commission |
| RAF | Royal Air Force (UK) |
| ROC | Royal Observer Force (UK) |
| RWO | Railway Workers' Union (Baghdad) |
| SOCAL | Standard Oil of California |
| TCCDR | Tribal Criminal & Civil Disputes Regulation |
| TNA | The National Archives of the United Kingdom |
| TPC | Turkish Petroleum Company |
| TWAIL | Third World Approaches to International Law |
| UNGAD | United Nations General Assembly Documentation |

# *List of Figures*

# *Note on Transliteration and Translation*

THIS BOOK FOLLOWS the transliteration guidelines of the *International Journal of Middle East Studies*. All translations in this book are my own unless otherwise indicated.

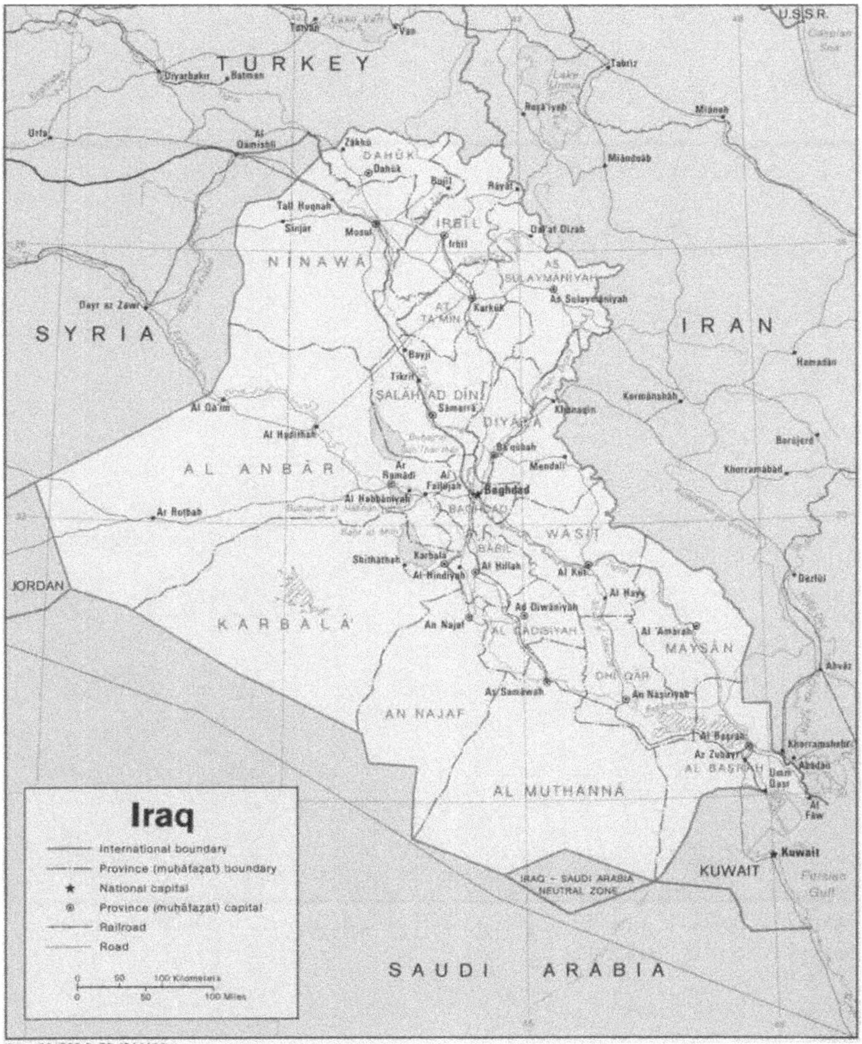


**Figure 1** United States Central Intelligence Agency. *Iraq* [Washington, D.C.: Central Intelligence Agency, 2008] Location Map https://www.cia.gov/resources/map/iraq/

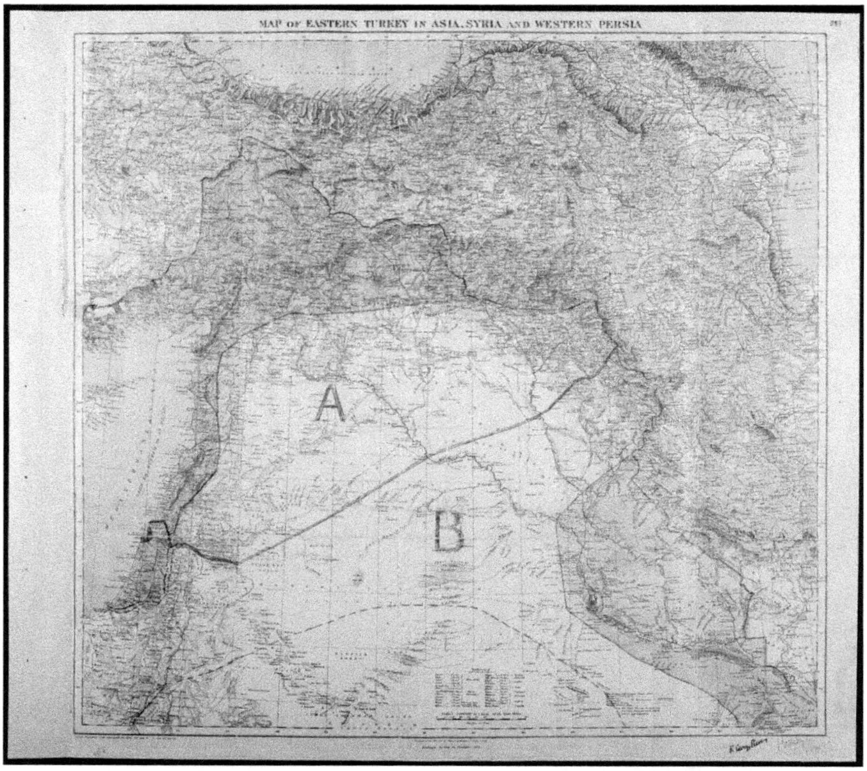


**Figure 2** Sykes-Picot Agreement, Eastern Turkey in Asia, Syria and Western Persia, signed 8 May 1916. MPK1-426

# Introduction

In a meeting in 10 Downing Street in 1915, a young mid-level British officer and advisor to the War Office, Sir Mark Sykes was asked by the Foreign Secretary Arthur Balfour what kind of arrangement he envisaged with the French in the Arab territories of the Ottoman Empire at the Great War's end. He responded by pointing at a map he had brought with him, 'I should like to draw a line from the "e" in Acre to the last "k" in Kirkuk'.[1] Herbert Kitchener, the secretary of state, who was present, intervened, 'I think that what Sir Mark Sykes means is that the line will commence at the sea-coast of Haifa'.[2] In less than twenty years, analogous lines would demarcate the oil pipelines of the British-owned Iraq Petroleum Company (IPC), which originated in Kirkuk, that transported Iraqi oil westward through Syria, Lebanon and Palestine and ending at the ports of the Mediterranean in Haifa and Tripoli. The drawing up of 'lines' on maps and the 'carving up' of territories by European powers and oil cartels is a powerful image that is commonly evoked when one thinks of the Middle East. It could be said that the modern history of the geopolitical region known as the 'Middle East' is a history of various 'lines' – straight lines drawn on maps by Europeans. Such a statement would not necessarily be a truism if it did not intentionally disregard other types of 'lines' in the history of the region – the *organic lines* of *agency*, working-class *movements*, organized anti-colonial *struggles*, and revolutionary *actions*.

This book is essentially an attempt to rewrite the history of the region by examining the international and transnational history of Iraq in two interconnected ways: first, by revealing how this act of imperial 'line-drawing' and state-making is a juridical act *par excellence*. The law can be found to parallel these imperial lines drawn on the maps of the region and must therefore be (re) traced in detail. In fact, my underlying claim is that the materialization of imperialism and semi-colonialism on the ground, and their operation within this geopolitical space, could not have been possible without international law and juridical arrangements being assembled in certain ways. The law, therefore, played a significant role in the production of unique geopolitical and economic spaces for imperialism to function in the Middle East. Moreover, the

[1] TNA, CAB 24/1, "Meeting held at 10 Downing Street, on Thursday, 16 December at 11:30am, Evidence of Lieutenant-Colonel Sir Mark Sykes, Bart, MP, on the Arab Question," as quoted in J Barr. *A Line in the Sand: The Anglo-French Struggle for the Middle East*, (W.W. Norton & Co, 2012), 7.

[2] *Ibid*.

contribution of international law to the formation of the Iraqi state itself had wide repercussions for the entire region.

Second, this book endeavors to retrace the hidden *lines* of (nationalist and labour) resistance and anti-colonial struggle in the region (specifically that of Iraq), and to demonstrate that these living lines of revolutionary action, movement and agency, and their conjunctures, had a lasting role not only on the history of Iraq and the region, but also on the larger Third World, and ultimately on international law itself. This study is, therefore, one that endeavors to use Iraqi history as a lens to understand the role of international law in the region. It is hoped that by situating the history of Iraq in such a way, one would in turn better grasp how the agency of Third World peoples could be written into the historiography of international law.

## I. THE SPECIFICITY OF THE GEO-POLITICAL REGION OF THE MIDDLE EAST, THE LOGIC OF SYKES-PICOT AND THE MAKING OF IRAQ

Soon after his visit to London, Mark Sykes met with his French counterpart Georges Picot in secret to negotiate and draft the Sykes-Picot Agreement (May 1916) between Great Britain and France, which divided the region into spheres of influence.[3] This document, made public by the Bolsheviks in *Izvestia* and *Pravda* soon after they came to power in 1917, included a map, which showed the French portion marked as 'A' and the British marked as 'B'.[4] Although the agreement envisioned the existence of a Confederation of Arab states within its spheres of influence, it was in direct contradiction with British assurances to the Sharif of Mecca, Hussein Bin Ali in the Hussein-McMahon Correspondence (1915–1916), which promised Arab independence in return for the Arabs waging a revolt against the Ottoman Empire.[5]

The Sykes-Picot Agreement ultimately failed to materialise as it had been envisioned as the borders of the newly emerging states that were settled after the war were different and were in fact shaped by political compromises and unpredictable post-war changes, such as the rising unformidable Arab nationalism across the region, the discussions at the (more transparent) conferences in Paris (1919), San Remo (1920) and Cairo (1921), and with the emergent Turkish state. The discourse surrounding Sykes-Picot, however, is alive and well and continues to creep into the historical narrative of the region, presented as a kind of 'originary moment' of imperial intervention in the region and its corresponding post-war

[3] See *The Sykes-Picot Agreement May 1916*, Oxford Public International Law, and U Özsu, Sykes-Picot: the treaty that carved up the Middle East, *OUPBLOG* (May, 2016).

[4] See Figure 2. Britain's sphere of influence included Basra and Baghdad in Mesopotamia, while France included Syria, Southern Anatolia and Mosul. Palestine was designated as an international zone.

[5] *See* E Kedourie. *In the Anglo-Arab Labyrinth: the McMahon-Husayn Correspondence and its Interpretations, 1914–1939* (Routledge, 2000).

state formation.[6] It is especially evoked to further the argument that Iraq and Syria are artificial creations of European powers.[7] One need not mention how such an orientalist narrative of 'line-drawing' by Europeans on 'empty maps' ultimately takes away the agency of the local population and erases all traces of resistance. Sara Pursley has already showed how this 'artificiality thesis' was a narrative concocted by the British in the 1920s to legitimise their continued control of Iraq, and the reality was that both the Cairo and San Remo conferences were *responses* to nationalist demands by the local inhabitants of Iraq and Syria for independence, expressed in popular uprisings and armed resistance.[8] Iraq therefore, 'is no more artificial that any other country with borders drawn as a result of a variety of reasons including wars, treaties, compromises, backroom deals, internal and external pressures, and plain chance'.[9]

The Sykes-Picot Agreement would be more accurately perceived as one that denotes the *specificity* of the geopolitical space of the Middle East as a whole. It was accordingly not necessarily about the actual carving up of the region, but rather about the economic exploitation of the *entire* Middle East by the West. In this way, it remains relevant to the subsequent Mandate period in question. In fact, the concept of the 'Middle East' was itself constructed as a geopolitical term in the context of great power competition.[10] Consequently, although it was decided that the Mandate system would be the manner by which these territories would be disposed of, the nineteenth century imperialist spirit of Sykes-Picot – including the old practices of annexation, colonial plunder and secret diplomacy – was far from over. As this study of Iraq will show, the imperialist logic of Sykes-Picot continued to permeate deep within the impetus of the Mandate system and Article 22 of the *Covenant of the League of* Nations,[11] except that now it was legal, transparent and governed by the novel principles of international law. Karin Loevy has aptly made the point that Sykes-Picot comprised new imperial imaginings of a regional 'geospace' of economic development. It evoked, she writes, 'a powerful imperial image of a region that is opening up for innumerable future possibilities for development and for the management of broad strategic concerns'.[12] These economic concerns were reflected in its provisions that covered the infrastructures of extractivism, trade and exploitation, including the erection of 'free ports', the establishment of

[6] S Pursley. 'Lines Drawn on an Empty Map': Iraq's Borders and the Legend of the Artificial State', *Jadaliyya*, June 2 2015.

[7] *Ibid*.

[8] *Ibid*.

[9] T Abdullah. *Dictatorship, Imperialism & Chaos: Iraq since 1989*, (Zed Books, 2006), 2.

[10] See ME Bonnie, A Amanat, ME Gasper (eds), *Is there a Middle East? The Evolution of a Geopolitical Concept*, (Stanford University Press, 2012).

[11] Article 22 of the Covenant of the League of the Nations was the legal basis of the mandate system.

[12] K Loevy, 'The Sykes-Picot Agreement's Regional Moment: Drawing Lines of Development in a New and Open Space' Symposium on the Many Lives and Legacies of Sykes-Picot, *AJIL Unbound*, Vol.110, 2016, 122.

norms for free trade, the transfer of water, as well as, the organisation of imperial lines of communication and transportation, such as railroads.[13]

In his introduction to the *American Journal of International Law* Symposium on the centenary of Sykes-Picot, Antony Anghie emphasises these continuities when he makes the point that inter-imperial arrangements were always concerned with free trade and navigational rights and that therefore this illustrates that, 'questions of governance and sovereignty … were inextricably *linked* in such agreements with trade and commerce'.[14] Edward Said analysed Sykes-Picot by reference to its 'peculiar epistemological framework,' one whereby, 'the Orient was seen … as a geographical … entity over whose destiny they [i.e. the European powers] believed themselves to have traditional entitlement'.[15] Such ideological frameworks to the study of the Orient, and its corresponding economic logic went hand in hand with the 'civilizing mission' of European imperialism in the Third World, and they were re-conceptualized and translated into the language of international law and its new post-war institutions. As this book will show, despite the novel realignments occurring in the international legal order at the time, these conceptual frameworks with their economic linkages continued unabated in the semi-periphery. In fact, the same economic preoccupations of free trade that imperial powers were concerned with in The Treaty of Berlin of 1885, and which emanated in the spirit of Sykes-Picot, in many ways continued in the Mandate system albeit in a subtle way. It is these intricacies that this study is concerned with.

## II. THE SEMI-PERIPHERY IN THE MAKING OF INTERNATIONAL LAW

There are four major interventions that run throughout this book. The first intervention is that critical international legal scholars, especially those who study the Third World, have generally overlooked the semi-periphery and its significance in the history of international law and its institutions. The TWAIL literature, for example, has for the most part maintained a strict dichotomy between the periphery and the core, while the semi-periphery, which has a unique history, with the exception of a handful of studies has generally not been studied in much detail.[16] The semi-periphery from the perspective of international legal discourse could be understood as including weak Third World states with an 'intermediate' status, which were given provisional sovereignty, and so

[13] *Ibid.*

[14] A Anghie, 'Introduction to Symposium on the Many Lives and Legacies of Sykes-Picot', September 28, 2016, *AJIL Unbound*, https://www.asil.org/blogs/introduction-symposium-many-lives-and-legacies-sykes-picot, 106, emphasis added.

[15] EW Said, *Orientalism.* (Vintage, 1978), 221.

[16] Anghie for instance relies on a dichotomy of the periphery and the core in his history of international law without any specific reference to the semi-periphery. See A Anghie, *Imperialism, Sovereignty and the Making of International Law*, (CUP, 2004), 314.

technically had a certain amount of agency on the world stage. The 'A' Mandates of Iraq, Syria [which includes Lebanon], and Palestine, were, therefore, regarded in various degrees as being a part of the semi-periphery. This book will illustrate that it is only by deconstructing the concept of the 'semi-periphery' in detail as it relates to the Middle East that its specificity becomes clear and, in turn, the operation of international law in the region can be fully understood.[17] The permanent analytic ambiguity associated with the definition of the region demonstrates how the law – a combination of international, transnational and imperial law – often operated in a manner that obscured the realities on the ground. The Western powers, ultimately through the Permanent Mandates Commission (PMC) in Geneva, experimented with the concept of sovereignty in Iraq. This was meant to allow for the making of a unique form of non-European sovereignty in international law – what I refer to as 'semi-peripheral sovereignty' – which was specifically manufactured with the geopolitics of the Middle East in mind to make it compatible with plans for the political domination and economic exploitation not only of Iraq, but the entire region. Iraqi oil – the jewel in the crown of the Middle East – could only be exploited in this manner. In this sense, a focus on the geopolitical characteristics of the semi-periphery makes it easier to understand why it was necessary from an imperial viewpoint to designate the 'A' Mandates, where 'independence' was provisionally recognised, as such.

The semi-periphery was therefore a laboratory for juridical and legal experimentation with the notoriously abstruse concept of sovereignty with the aim that the advent of 'independence' in the region, as upheld by the new post-war international legal order and based on Wilsonian notions of self-determination, would continue to allow a (legal) licence for imperialism to function through the uninterrupted flow of capital and oil extraction, ensuring its continued operation in a subtle but (doctrinally) legitimate manner. International law was, therefore, deployed in the region for specific geopolitical purposes, in particular the maintenance of European influence, imperial control and access to oil. Iraq, as we shall see, was at the heart of this experiment. The non-European sovereignty that emerged was not only meant to be a model for the entire region, but also was arguably the precursor for the neo-colonial governance of post-colonial

[17] The literature on the role of the semi-periphery in the history of international law has slowly begun to emerge: *See* U Özsu, *Formalizing Displacement: International Law and Population Transfers* (OUP, 2015); AB Lorca. *Mestizo International Law* (Cambridge University Press, 2014); M Taha. 'Nation and Class Subjectivity in International Law and its Institutions in the Middle East (1919–1939),' SJD Dissertation, University of Toronto, 2015; P Singh. 'Of International Law, Semi-colonial Thailand, and Imperial Ghosts' (2019) 9 *Asian Journal of International Law* 46; D Margolies, U Özsu, M Pal & N Tzouvala (eds.), *The Extraterritoriality of Law: History, Theory, Politics* (Routledge, 2019); A Hammoudi. 'The International Law of Informal Empire and the "Question of Oman"' *TWAIL Review*, Issue 1 (2020) 121–151; YY Zhu. 'Suzerainty, Semi-Sovereignty, and International Law, *Asian Journal of International Law* 10/2 (2020), 293–320.

and newly independent states of the Third World and their resources.[18] Iraq was ultimately to become the only mandated territory that was proclaimed as sovereign and independent under the Mandate process of international law. As this book will show, this 'independence' was a sham – a mere figment that was maintained through the law. Only a deep historical analysis of the law and its manifestation in the semi-periphery can reveal how this legal fiction was maintained, its exploitative effects on the peoples of the region established, as well as its implications for the future of international law.

## III. A MARXIST ANALYSIS OF INTERNATIONAL LAW

The second intervention of this book is that the history of international law – and law in general – must be analysed from a historical materialist perspective if one wants to uncover its constitutive and structural connections with racial capitalism and imperialism. Luis Eslava and Sundhya Pahuja have emphasised the need for a new 'methodological turn' towards an understanding of how international law operates in everyday life.[19] The aim of this book is not merely to do just that, but also to grasp international law's interconnected role to the making and furtherance of the capitalist modes of production, which has had an effect on the material lives of the peoples of the Third World. The importance of analysing how international law's formation was historically and structurally developed in conjuncture with capitalism and its relations is the main contention of those who adhere to Marxist approaches to international law.[20] It also emphasises that it is necessary to incorporate the category and lens of class and its formation in one's legal analysis. This book, therefore, engages with the 'historical turn' in international legal scholarship to argue that a broader conception of historiography is needed to seriously take into account the agency of the colonised peoples of the Third World, and that such an approach is necessary if one is to truly understand how transformation of law and legality occurs on a global scale. Furthermore, this study is simultaneously a critique of the 'cultural turn' in critical international legal scholarship, which mirrors the direction taken by historians of the Subaltern Studies School in particular and scholars of late post-colonialism in general.[21]

[18] P Menon, 'Negotiating Subjection: The Political Economy of Protection in the Iraq Mandate (1914–1932)' *TWAIL Review*, Issue2, (2021), 193.

[19] L Eslava, S Pahuja, "Beyond the (Post)Colonial: TWAIL and the Everyday Life of International Law", *Journal of Law and Politics in Africa, Asia and Latin America – Verfassung und Recht in Übersee (VRÜ)*, Vol. 45(2), 2012, at 195–221.

[20] For an overview of Marxist approaches to international law and legality see P O'Connell, U Özsu (eds.), *Research Handbook on Law and Marxism* (Edward Elgar, 2021).

[21] See N Berman, *Passion and Ambivalence: Colonialism, Nationalism, and International Law* (Leiden: Martinus Nijhoff Publishers, 2011), 404; M Koskenniemi. *From Apology to Utopia: The Structure of International Legal Argument* (Cambridge University Press, 2006), 7, 12.

A focus on the materiality of international law emphasises the manner in which the peoples of the Third World were not only directly affected by the imperialism of international law and its institutions, but also sought to transform it from the ground up. It connects international law to the everyday lives of the colonised. It stresses how the uses of international law and its institutions by imperial powers certainly contributed not only to state formation, but also to the capitalist modes of production, which, in turn, structured class formation and social relations in the (semi-) periphery.[22]

Consequently, by inserting class as an analytic lens to understand the materiality of international law, this book elucidates *how* the unique capitalist spaces of production that were produced through international legal mechanisms in Iraq (such as, the Mandate, the Anglo-Iraq treaties, and the doctrine of semi-peripheral sovereignty) violently impacted the Iraqi working class. Iraqi workers eventually organised against the violent effects of the structural constraints that they experienced directly in their workplaces and everyday lives. My focus on labour as a site of agency is useful for several reasons, one of which is that the Iraqi worker, similar to his or her counterparts in the region, at the specific conjuncture of (early) decolonisation experienced the violent *contradictions* of capitalism, semi-colonialism and imperialism within these colonial and semi-colonial spaces from a distinctive location. This consequently gave the worker (in particular the advanced sectors of the working class) a unique vantage point for conscious anti-colonial struggle, which connected his or her material conditions to the legal and structural workings of imperialism in the region. Tracing agency through the site of labour relations, therefore, allows this study not to lose track of how agency moved from the seemingly confined spaces of capitalist production to the wider spaces of anti-colonial nationalist struggle, and eventually became a total rejection of the international legal order that was imposed on Iraq. It also illustrates how the Iraqi working class created anti-hegemonic spaces with their organised actions, and as a result attempted to work out a more just and emancipatory alternative social and legal order for their country and for the region. The manifestation of the imperialism of international law in Iraq certainly had material effects on certain classes more than others. In other words, the unique sovereignty granted to Iraq by the Mandate process was itself a limited and constricted sovereignty granted to a minority ruling class to govern and suppress the masses, and to prevent revolution. A serious focus on class and labour as sites of agency, then, can shine a light on this constitutive connection between international law, imperialism, and capitalism in a more grounded way.

[22] Materialist and Marxist studies of international law have been undertaken by several scholars, such as BS Chimni, Rose Parfitt, Rob Knox, and Susan Marks. An influential work was China Mieville's reinterpretation of Bolshevik legal theorist Evgeny Pashukanis. See in particular, C Mieville. *Between Equal Rights: A Marxist Theory of International Law* (Haymarket Books, 2006).

Finally, considering that this study is not only a history of the role of international law in the making of the Iraqi state, but simultaneously a labour history of Iraq (as it aims to connect the histories of labour/anti-colonial agency to that of international law), my arguments above are not only aimed at critical international legal scholars who prioritise culture over social relations and the capitalist modes of production, but are also a response to the principal arguments of the Subaltern Studies historians[23] in their analyses of labour in the history of India and Eastern societies in general. The history of the Iraqi working class as presented in this book will demonstrate the continuing relevance of the concept of 'class' and will show that despite their tribal and peasant backgrounds, Iraqi workers in fact formed (at certain critical conjunctures) a unique class-consciousness and bonds of class solidarity in waging their united struggles against semi-colonialism and Western imperialism. The subaltern approach, which tends to discard Marxist categories (such as class), and prefers a post-structuralist – cultural – notion of *difference* will be shown to be quite unsuitable for understanding the history of Iraq, for culture *on its own* should never be the underpinnings of any analyses of Iraqi, Arab or Near Eastern societies.

## IV. AN INFRASTRUCTURAL HISTORY OF INTERNATIONAL LAW IN THE MIDDLE EAST

The third underlying intervention of the book is that the imperialism of international law would be better grasped by emphasising its spatiality, especially considering that the semi-periphery has generally been viewed as a set of highly geo-strategic locations for the imperial powers.[24] Iraq's unique geo-strategic location was one reason for the emergence of capitalist enclaves that were essentially severed from the governing capacity of the Iraqi state. It was in a way the existence of these de facto extraterritorialised enclaves that characterised Iraqi semi-peripheral sovereignty, which was developed and arranged to govern these important sites of production, accumulation and the capitalist infrastructures of the Iraqi state, not to mention, the region as a whole. This book will not only explore these enclaves – namely the IPC oil fields in Kirkuk, the Iraq State Railways and the Port of Basra – how they were managed and governed, but also most significantly, it will detail how Iraqi workers and their

[23] The Subaltern Studies group came together in the 1970s and consisted of Partha Chatterjee, David Hardiman, Gyanendra Pandey, Sumit Sarkar, and Dipesh Chakrabarty. *See* R Guha, "Introduction," *Selected Subaltern Studies* (Oxford University Press, 1988); D Chakrabarty, "Subaltern Studies and Postcolonial Historiography," Nepantla: Views from South 1:1 (2000), 9–32; D Ludden, "A Brief History of Subalternity," in Ludden, ed., *Reading Subaltern Studies* (Anthem Press, 2002), 1–39.

[24] See M Bell, R Butlin, M Heffernan (eds.), *Geography and Imperialism 1820–1940*, (Manchester University Press, 1994), 4.

trade unions organised against these legal structures of exploitation by using these infrastructures 'against the grain,' in turn, producing their own alternative counter-hegemonic emancipatory spaces. This particular argument relies not only on the Marxist scholars who have developed analyses on the spatiality of capitalism to argue that space is a social construct that contributes to the production of capitalist structures and as such acts as a means of political and economic domination,[25] but it also relies on those legal scholars who have emphasised the need to explore international law's relation to infrastructure – or how international law and its governing arrangements produced global capitalist infrastructures.[26]

The point here is to maintain the interconnections between international law, capitalism, the spatiality of infrastructures, and the workers materially affected by these processes. As Tayyab Mahmud has clarified in his work on indentured labour, '... international law [is] unavoidably entangled with hierarchal positionings of bodies and spaces by global operations of capitalism.'[27] It is, however, the specificity of the semi-peripheral Middle East that is of interest to our study as the region was itself constructed to further the geopolitical aims of the Western powers, as we have seen above with the framework used to draft Sykes-Picot with its underlying imperial logic. It is consequently the semi-peripheral Middle East's unique geopolitical spatiality that made it vital for imperialism. For the British, the Middle East was the route to India, which included the essential lines of imperial communications and trade that needed to be secured for the maintenance of its hegemony over other great powers. Its waterways, straits and vast desert landmass has a significant geopolitical value as it connects the continents of Asia, Africa and Europe. It is these geographic characteristics of the region that made it important as a vital infrastructural node in the security of the British Empire, which will be examined in the context of Iraq.

The Iraqi state emerged out of the Mandate process as an 'independent' sovereign state in 1932. However, this independence was not based on the principle of self-determination but rather on the doctrine of semi-peripheral sovereignty, which was implicitly manufactured by League functionaries and European jurists in the rooms of the Peace Palace in Geneva. The doctrine of semi-peripheral sovereignty in conjuncture with other legal instruments, such as the 1930 Anglo-Iraq Treaty and the 1925 IPC Oil Concessionary agreement,

[25] See D Harvey, *The Limits of Capital*, (Verso, 1999); Harvey. *Spaces of Global Capitalism: A Theory of Uneven Geographical Development* (Verso, 2006); and H Lefebvre, *The Production of Space*, (London: Blackwell, 1978). Harvey spatialises Marx and demonstrates how space is produced by and also shaped by capitalism. See "David Harvey and Dialectical SpaceTime", in N Castree, D Gregory (eds), *David Harvey: A Critical Reader*, (Blackwell, 2006).

[26] See B Kingsbury, 'Introduction to the Symposium on the Infrastructuring of International Law' 117 *AJIL Unboud* (2023).

[27] T Mahmud, "Cheaper than a Slave: Indenture Labor, Colonialism, and Capitalism", *Whittier Law Review*, (2013), Vol. 34.2, 215–243; 216.

as well as the agreements that governed the Railway system and the Port of Basra, effectively maintained the imperial domination over the country, and more importantly, secured the legal extraction and transportation of petroleum from Mosul to the West. The way in which these legal doctrines and instruments were developed and how they manifested on the ground is the main focus of this study. It will become clear by the end of our analysis how international and transnational law played a fundamental role in the production and governance of the infrastructures of imperialism in Iraq and of the region at large.

## V. SUBALTERN AGENCY AND CONJUNCTURAL ANALYSIS

The final argument of the book is a methodological one – it concerns the question of agency and how it should be approached in its relation to international legal history. In a word, it is an attempt to answer the following question: how could one write the history of the agency of the ordinary peoples of the Third World into the historiography of international law? It will be argued that a methodological approach borrowed from Marxist theory of the (international) conjuncture[28] is necessary to properly assess the question of agency in relation to international legal transformation. This approach takes the 'conjuncture' as the starting point of any analysis of agency, emphasising that acts of resistance, especially revolutionary action aimed at the overthrow of any social order, are contingent to the international legal structures in question. The concept of the conjuncture refers to the potentialities of action in the historical arena; it analyses agency in relation to the *structures* of political and economic forces in question rather than in isolation. The point is to focus on certain conjunctures in history, wherein the specific alignment of political (domestic and international) forces and structures creates counter-hegemonic spaces allows for effective action to become possible and where agency is more conducive to historical transformation and social development. Action and agency are more effective in these specific situations. By making the correct determinations, agency can be analysed in relation to these historical conjunctures and grasped more fully, while keeping the *present* conjuncture in mind so as to determine the praxis that is required today.

This argument is in response to how some streams of critical and TWAIL scholarship have theorised subaltern agency in isolation from the wider conjuncture, especially by romanticising the plurality of law, its spontaneity and its non-violence.[29] This is not merely a manifestation of the limits of the current

[28] See Chapter 7.

[29] B Rajagopal, *International Law from Below: Development, Social Movements and Third World Resistance* (CUP, 2007); V Nesiah. 'Resistance in the Age of Empire: occupied discourse pending investigation' *Third World Quarterly*, Vol. 27, No. 5, pp. 903–922, (2006); R Buchanan. "Writing Resistance Into Law" *International Community Law Review* 10 (2008) 445–454.

'historical turn' in international law scholarship, but also illustrates the dominance of notions of culture in critical legal approaches as mentioned earlier. TWAIL analyses of anti-colonial subaltern agency or their preferred notion of 'resistance', discards its wide-ranging influence, considering it has more often been violent, organised and party-oriented.[30] The sanitisation of this history of revolutionary agency completely ignores the fact that not every anti-colonial or anti-imperial action or subaltern resistance is effective as it depends on its contingent relation to the structures in question. The assumption that *any* creative, pluralist anti-hegemonic uses of law by a movement could turn into an effective struggle against imperialism and its manifestations in international law is problematic. The following study of Iraqi subaltern (labour) agency shows how structure and agency are in fact interconnected, and so one must understand how a conjuncture brings about the possibilities of revolutionary action in the first place by giving social movements room to wage an effective organised struggle. To do this, a much wider international perspective of subaltern agency is needed – one that is situated more broadly in opposition to the (international, legal and natural) unity of imperialism to understand why it is that targeting *one* localised or regional location on the global imperial map at a particular *time* is effective, while another is not.

A conjunctural analysis is therefore undertaken to illustrate how Iraqi anti-colonial subaltern agency ultimately contributed to the decolonisation of international law. This analysis reveals how the various labour strikes transformed into wider revolutionary anti-colonial struggles at particular points of Iraqi history leading up to and culminating in the massive *Wathba* uprising of 1948, which was waged against the imposition of yet another unequal treaty, and which ultimately led to the overthrow of the British-sponsored Hashemite monarchy in 1958. The Iraqi subaltern masses and working class will be situated in a broader regional and international context, and will elucidate how they were in fact quite cognisant of the intricate ways that Britain were controlling their lives through legal techniques. Moreover, it will become clear how through their organised actions, the Iraqi subaltern and working classes envisioned an alternative social and legal order in Iraq and the region at large that was completely free from semi-colonial domination and imperial rule. Iraqi nationalists, anti-colonial activists and Marxist intellectuals amongst others, who led the labour movement were, therefore, in the words of Adom Getachew, 'worldmakers,' undertaking a 'project of anti-colonial worldmaking,' *from below*, which sought to transform the structures of the international legal order, and to constitute the right of self-determination in international law and in praxis.[31]

[30] See O Taylor, *International Law and Revolution* (Routledge, 2019).

[31] A Getachew, *Worldmaking after Empire: The Rise and Fall of Self-Determination* (Princeton University Press, 2019), 9.

## VI. CHAPTERS OUTLINE AND THE STRUCTURE OF THE BOOK

It is now appropriate to briefly outline the chapters of the book. Chapter 1 begins in rural Iraq and describes how a system of semi-feudal capitalist production was established and structured through the operations of British administrative techniques and imperial law. It explores two interrelated narratives: the invention of tribal customary law and its uses in the enclosure of tribal land, and the role of property law in the entrenchment of capitalist relations in Iraq. It illustrates how the law played a significant role in the formation of capitalist relations and in the structuring of underdevelopment and inequality in Iraq.

Chapter 2 explores the role of international law in the making of the Iraqi state and reveals how a unique doctrine of sovereignty was developed by the PMC in Geneva – what I refer to as 'semi-peripheral sovereignty' – a sovereignty that was constructed to further the geopolitical aims of the great powers with interests in the Middle East, especially its economic exploitation and to legally extract and transport Iraqi oil to the Mediterranean and to the West. The chapter analyses how members of the PMC in Geneva concluded that Iraq was ready for independence. I explore the contradictions in their reasoning, especially concerning the principle of economic equality, also known as the 'open door' principle, which was in theory meant to prevent monopolisation and exploitation. The Iraqi oil concessions, however, were intentionally differentiated and separated from the discussion of political sovereignty. The chapter ultimately reveals how economic considerations pertaining to the extraction of oil were at the heart of the development of a non-European sovereignty for Iraq and the semi-peripheral Middle East. Moreover, it examines the oil concessionary agreements in detail to illustrate how it was connected to the question of Iraq's independence. Iraqi semi-peripheral sovereignty was accepted as being a legitimate part of international law until the unremitting struggle waged by the Iraqi masses (which first emerged with the 1948 *Wathba* uprising) overthrew its logic and legitimacy after the 1958 July Revolution, leading up to the unequivocal rejection of veiled forms of semi-colonialism through the Iraqi contribution to the drafting of the 1960 *Declaration on the Granting of Independence to Colonial Countries and Peoples*.

Chapter 3 examines the early history of the urban labour movement in Baghdad, in particular its first organisation: the *Jamʿīyat aṣḥāb al- ṣināʿa* (JAS). It goes on to explore how the International Labour Organization (ILO) contributed to the drafting of the first labour legislation in Iraq, thereby playing a significant role in the structuring of what it deemed 'civilized' labour relations in Iraq. The chapter illustrates how, despite the fact that the 1936 Labour Law was to become merely black ink on paper, not to be applied by the state for the next 22 years until after the July Revolution, the labour movement consistently appropriated its language and used it as a reference point in making their demands in nearly every strike to come. The law was, therefore, a useful (but limited) tool of counter-hegemonic struggle as it provided a language for workers to advance their demands for social justice and national liberation.

Chapters 4 and 5 are micro-histories that describe the infrastructural spaces that were juridically linked to foreign capitalism and its modes of production in Iraq, namely the IPC oil fields of Kirkuk, the Iraq State Railways, and the Port of Basra. Describing the wretched conditions of the workers who lived and toiled there, the chapters highlights how these semi-colonial extraterritorialised enclaves were central to the operations of capitalism and imperialism in Iraq.

Chapter 4 closely analyses the legal structures that governed the IPC enclave and the city of Kirkuk – in particular through the IPC Concessionary Agreements. The IPC was allotted wide discretionary powers to govern the oil fields and its company town, which also had a significant economic impact on the city of Kirkuk and its surroundings as a whole. Similarly, Chapter 5 reveals how the Railway and the Port Directorates were also governed through separate agreements that institutionalised their semi-autonomous status. In the end, the chapters show how international law, transnational law and imperial law produced these spaces and it shows how they directly affected the lives of ordinary Iraqis and workers, while also describing how labour agency organised strikes to free the workers from these socio-economic constraints. Finally, the chapter ends by analysing how British labour advisors and so-called experts responded to strike actions, undermined the workers' efforts, and promoted certain social and labour reforms with the aim of upholding British semi-colonial hegemony rather than allowing for real structural change. It ultimately becomes clear that Iraqi workers used the law inventively as a rhetorical and tactical tool to undermine the legitimacy of the social order, while British experts devised legal reforms as a way to undercut any real structural change in Iraqi society.

Chapter 6 examines the violence underlying the doctrine of semi-peripheral sovereignty by recounting how the Iraqi state used criminal law, martial law and the doctrine of emergency to crush any form of political dissent. It argues that the Iraqi state used this tried and tested colonial method of repression to institute a de facto permanent state of emergency after the 1952 *Intifāda* to maintain its hegemony. The doctrine of emergency was to become a predominant technique of semi-colonial governance in Iraq, which was ingrained into the institutions of the Iraqi state and even into the Constitution. The military courts relied on the 1938 amendment to the *Baghdad Penal Code* to imprison thousands of protestors and strikers, while communist leaders were executed after the *Wathba* uprising. It is made apparent how semi-peripheral sovereignty and the doctrine of emergency in fact operated as two sides of the same coin.

The book ends with Chapter 7, which recounts the massive 1948 *Wathba* uprising, initiated by workers and students and a wide stratum of Iraqi society, who came out to the streets of Baghdad to protest the imposition of a revised treaty between Iraq and Britain. The proposed revision of the 1930 Anglo-Iraq Treaty was aimed at reasserting Britain's relationship with Iraq to supposedly make it consistent with the UN Charter. However, the provisions of the revised Portsmouth Treaty in reality entrenched Iraq further into imperialist control. After analysing the contents of the Treaty, the chapter explains how workers and students organised in just over three weeks to prevent the imposition of this treaty before the uprising was violently crushed. The *Wathba* will be shown to be a manifestation of the conjuncture of decolonisation against the imperialism of international law. This event will be situated within the wider history of early decolonisation in the Third World. The argument of this chapter, therefore, brings the entire historical narrative of this book together. The oil, port and railway workers utilised their previous experiences in strike action and sabotage within their confined workplaces for a wider anti-colonial nationalist struggle. Organised people's coordination committees sprang up. The workers' consciousness of the connection between their material conditions and imperialism was conveyed by the Iraqi masses during the *Wathba*, who displayed a clear understanding of how imperialism operates through law and how law obscures reality. Through their very actions, the Iraqi urban poor, workers, students and peasants came together to reject the entirety of the social order, and in particular the doctrine of semi-peripheral sovereignty, denoting their demand to control their own destinies. The *Wathba* became the seed through which the July Revolution of 1958 sprung, as every uprising after it would call for its renewal until the revolutionary overthrow of the Hashemite monarchy by the Free Officers a decade later.

## VII. A NOTE ON PRIMARY SOURCES

It should be mentioned that this book was the product of the painstaking weaving together of the fragmented primary sources on Iraq. It was the best that could be done considering the circumstances, and so a lot of questions remain. The extensive archival research that was conducted for this legal and labour history of Iraq include the following: British records from the National Archives at Kew; the company records of the Iraq Petroleum Company (IPC) located in the BP Archive of the Modern Records Centre in the UK; ILO records in Geneva; the Reports of the Permanent Mandates Commission (PMC) of the League of Nations; and the *Muḥātharāt Majlis al-Nuwāb* [Records of the Council of Representatives – the lower house of the Iraqi Parliament] held at the Nami Yafet Memorial Library of the American University of Beirut in Lebanon. Despite visiting the US National Archives, I did not end up using these records for various reasons. To reconstruct Iraqi labour history, I relied on a variety of sources, in particular the memoirs of communist, nationalist and labour leaders; working class, nationalist and communist newspapers (especially the communist *al-Qā'ida* and the social democratic *Ṣawt al-Ahālī*); communist pamphlets; Iraqi Marxist journals, primarily the cultural ICP journal, *al-Thaqāfa al-Jadīda* ('The New Culture'); and selected records from the British Communist Party Archives.

It is unfortunate that I was unable to travel to Baghdad to delve into the Iraqi National Archives due to the security situation at the time and the difficulty of gaining access to the archives in the first place. The possibility of conducting oral interviews was also regrettably grim, since a significant number of the participants in the labour and communist movements of the period (if not executed by the Ba'ath party in 1963) have either long passed or were unable to meet for health reasons. I did, however, get a chance to correspond with several old Iraqi communists, including, Ara' Khājādor, 'Azīz Sbāhī, Shāmil al-Nahir and Ghānim Ḥamdūn. They have all since passed. I am ever so grateful for their input and generous guidance. Turning from the historiography of international law to that of labour, it has been said that 'it is nearly impossible' to find the necessary primary sources to build a labour history of Iraq.[32] Although it has certainly been quite difficult to write this history, I do not think that the mere fragmentation of primary sources should prevent scholars from at least attempting to weave together a labour history of the region. Although this study is not a typical labour study, its focus on international law and institutions allows Iraqi labour history to be situated in a novel way. Such a shift in the study of labour could be argued to be in itself an original contribution to the literature and the labour historiography of Iraq and the Middle East. Still, I hope that I have contributed in some small way or form in weaving together a historical study of labour and law in Iraq for future generations of scholars to build on.

[32] KM Jones, "Unmaking the Middle Eastern working classes: labour and the politics of historiography", *Social History*, 2015, Vol. 40, No. 2, 145–156; 150.

# 1

# *Enclosing Mesopotamia: Frontier Governmentality, The Rule of Property and the Origins of Underdevelopment in Hashemite Iraq*

## I. INTRODUCTION

How was a system of 'semi-feudal' capitalist production established in mandatory Iraq?[1] This chapter will analyse the role of property law and British tribal legal administration in the establishment of capitalist relations and, in turn, the establishment of underdevelopment in mandatory Iraq. The history of Iraq and its colonisation has generally been approached under the guise of different broad economic theories, while the role of law in the historical narrative has been marginalised or entirely ignored. The law, however, was a crucial imperial instrument in the structuring and institutionalisation of the economic, social and power relations that emerged to constitute the modern Iraqi state. The underlying claim here is, therefore, to emphasise that the law is not merely a 'superstructure' that should not be taken as seriously as the economic 'base', to use Marxist terminology. Although it is not my claim that law determines these economic relations, I do contend that law played an essential role in the overall process that tends to be overlooked. My argument concerning the law in the colonies will be made in the context of two interrelated historical narratives in Iraq: the British tribal policy and the invention of customary law on the one hand, and the uses of property law in the land tenure system on the other.

The British and the Iraqi state deployed property law and certain imperial legal techniques of tribal administration – or 'frontier governmentality'– into their practices of indirect rule eventually bringing about a modern 'semi-feudal' system in Iraq, which served British imperial interests and the capitalist world

[1] The concept of 'semi-feudalism' illustrates that certain characteristics of feudalism, such as unfree labour relations, could still exist in harmony with capitalism. See J Banaji, "Capitalist Domination and the Small Peasantry: The Deccan Districts in the Late Nineteenth Century", in *Theory As History: Essays on Modes of Production and Exploitation*, (Haymarket, 2010), 282.

economy at large. This process led to a significant rearrangement of the socio-economic structures of Iraqi society, as well as its tribal composition. Traditional property relations were drastically transformed, which in turn destabilised the socio-economic structures of tribal society, while the 'invention' of customary law through the institutionalisation of a separate tribal legal system ensured the imperial control over the tribes of Iraq, all of which contributed to the deep entrenchment of capitalism in the region.

British tribal administration in the Middle East revolved around the management of communications, trade, movement, raiding and trafficking between tribes in the vast 'desert corridors' of the Empire. British officials improvised with various legal techniques to develop a unique space of tribal administration within these inter-imperial spaces that spread across (and at times connected) the deserts of Egypt, Trans-Jordan and Iraq, where nomadic Bedouin tribes roamed.[2] A certain flexible form of 'Desert Law' emerged across the region – amounting to a patchwork of customary laws made for British administrative purposes and which were relied on to govern the geopolitical corridors of the desserts of the region. On the other hand, an interrelated land tenure process of enclosure, which was specifically a *legal* one, produced not only private landed property, but also constructed the peasant/native as a legal and governable subject. Enclosure involved turning landscapes into 'exclusionary spaces' of private individual property, and the destruction of the traditional rights of the tribal commons and the social relationships that were attached to it. As we shall see, enclosure as a *structure*, whether it was in eighteenth century England or twentieth century Iraq, revolved around similar processes of 'improving' the land through its cultivation for surplus value, dispossessing the indigenous peoples of the tribal commons, and ultimately establishing 'a new agrarian order' based on capitalist relations.[3]

## II. BRITISH TRIBAL ADMINISTRATION AND THE INVENTION OF CUSTOMARY LAW IN IRAQ

The tribes of Mesopotamia have been the source of romantic fascination of many a European traveller at least since the nineteenth century. It is no doubt that the orientalist views chronicled by these travellers of the Bedouin influenced the formation of tribal administrative policies when the British found themselves in control of this region in 1916-1917. Furthermore, the British had to improvise in circumstances of limited financial assistance from London, while considering

[2] For a detailed study of British tribal administration across the region, *See* RSG Fletcher, *British Imperialism and 'The Tribal Question': Desert Administration and Nomadic Societies in the Middle East, 1919-1936* (OUP, 2015).

[3] For a theoretical study of enclosure as a *structure* that connects the history of Palestine, North America and England, *See* G Fields, *Enclosure: Palestinian Landscapes in a Historical Mirror* (University of California Press, 2017), 26.

the military weakness of the new Iraqi state that was run by a small number of *ex-Sharifian*[4] officers with the newly selected King Faisal in Baghdad.[5] The British administration and later the Iraqi state had no real control over its rural areas, which made up the majority of the country – its borders and frontiers controlled by heavily armed tribes. These multitudes of nomadic and semi-nomadic tribal sections and confederations, which previously had an almost fluid character in that they had been in constant movement throughout their existence, needed to be brought under the purview of British administrative control and eventually Iraqi state control in an efficient but inexpensive manner. As will be shown, this was done through several approaches and strategies whereby the law played a significant role. Although it is important to realise that the 'tribes' were not homogenous in any way, but rather made up of a diverse nomadic, semi-nomadic and settled groups that lived in differing topologies and environments – whether it was in Kūt and ʿAmārah on the Tigris river to Muntafiq, or Dīwānīyah and Hillah in the central and lower Euphrates. In that sense, one must avoid essentialising the 'tribe' qua tribe as they were quite diverse. So, although it would be wiser to study the specificity of a particular tribe in question before making any broad generalisations, it is still necessary to make some useful general observations about tribal organisation for the sake of analytic argument, while recognising their heterogeneity and avoiding essentialism.[6]

Samira Haj has argued that the very dichotomy between the urban townsmen and rural tribesmen that is so prevalent in Iraqi historiography was in itself an essentialism that is misleading as the two have always overlapped and interacted throughout their existence.[7] In fact, the tension between tribal and state organisation was much more intricate and dynamic than is generally perceived; this has previously been understood by Ibn Khaldūn who emphasised the cyclical character of early Islamic history, whereby tribalisation and settlement were processes in constant alternation and flux.[8] As Richard Tapper has explained, (centralised) 'government control is clearly an important determinant of tribal political organisation, but it is not simply an external force; its impact depends on how it is internalised by the tribespeople and how they react to it.'[9] The tribe

[4] The *ex-Sharifian Officers* were former Ottoman military officers who participated in the Arab Revolt against the Ottoman Empire during World War I (1916-1918), and were led by the Sharif Husayn ibn Ali. They would later play a prominent role in the establishment of the Iraqi state. A 'Sharif' is one who claims descendance from the Prophet Mohammad and holds a position in society on this basis. The term commonly used in Iraq is 'Sayyid'.

[5] H Batatu. *The Old Social Classes and the Revolutionary Movements of Iraq: A Study of Iraq's Old Landed and Commercial Classes and of its Communists, Baʿthists and Free Officers*, (Saqi, 2004), 88.

[6] S Haj, *The Making of Iraq* 1900-1963, (SUNY Press, 1997), 13.

[7] *See* S Haj. "The problems of tribalism: the case of nineteenth-century Iraqi history," *Social History*, (1991) Vol. 16: No. 1, 45–58.

[8] See S Haider, "Land Problems of Iraq", (PhD Thesis, University of London, 1942), 22.

[9] R Tapper, "Anthropologists, Historians, and Tribespeople on Tribe and State Formation in the Middle East," in P Khoury and J Kostiner (eds.), *Tribes and State Formation in the Middle East* (University of California Press, 1990), 67.

may for example internalise certain aspects of state centralization – 'elements of state could be found within every tribe' and vice versa.[10] This, as we shall see, was precisely what happened with the tribal policy that was institutionalised by the British administration. Ironically, despite its intention of 'preserving' customary laws and tribal traditions, this British policy ended up inventing something unique instead through its construction of a separate tribal legal system excluded from and yet sanctioned by the state and its institutions.

Before embarking on a detailed analysis of the British tribal policy and its implications, it is necessary to briefly explain the character of tribal organisation – its basic structures and institutions. The tribe, as the only socially organised unit in the desert and rural countryside, functioned as a necessary safeguard for the nomad-tribesmen and the settled cultivator-peasant alike. This was generally the case before the Ottomans attempted to strengthen the central government based in the cities, intentionally breaking down the power of the tribes and their cohesion in the late nineteenth century. Generally, under the tribal system the tribe held land communally and although the Shaikh divided parts of the tribal land provisionally among the families of the tribe, private ownership was *not* absolute.[11] The division of land was done according to certain principles and criteria that ensured that the land would always remain within the tribal *dīrah*.[12] Therefore, despite the existence of certain forms of private property, depending on the shaikh's (provisional and rotating) assignment of land, and although the tribesman's attachment to his tribal *dīrah* was strong enough that he was willing to die to defend it, he lacked any sense of *individual* ownership of any *particular* plot of land in the *dīrah*.[13] It is in this way that the idea of absolute private property, including profit, was alien to the tribe.[14] I will return to the complicated question of land later.

An important point that needs to be emphasised early on is that the migration of tribes from Northern Central Arabia (Najd) in present-day Saudi Arabia eastward or southward into Iraq and the coastal Arabian Gulf was a relatively recent phenomenon that could be traced to the late seventeenth and eighteenth centuries. As Hala Fattah has shown, certain clans and tribes dissociated themselves from their traditional tribal confederations whether it was a result of force or for political or socioeconomic circumstances.[15] Migrating, they re-formed themselves anew and regrouped into more powerful tribal configurations in Iraq. It should therefore be kept in mind that tribal custom in Iraq was certainly

[10] *Ibid*, 68.

[11] Haider, *supra*, 88.

[12] D Warriner. *Land and Poverty in the Middle East*, (Royal Institute of International Affairs, 1948), 18. The *dīrah* was an area of land which was 'habitually occupied' by the tribe or which was 'its preserve' as long as it could militarily defend it.

[13] Haider, *supra*, 316. Batatu, *supra*, 71.

[14] Batatu, *supra*, 73.

[15] H Fattah, *The Politics of Regional Trade in Iraq, Arabia, and the Gulf 1745-1900*, (SUNY, 1997), 28-29.

not in any way an 'ancient' tradition as the British believed it to be, but rather partly formed out of a modern historical process of tribal reconfigurations and movements. It was no wonder that the renowned Iraqi sociologist ʿAlī al-Wardī argued that this historical process was the root of a 'cultural paradox' that shaped the Iraqi personality, and explained the common Iraqi's general ambivalence to state authority.[16] al-Wardī argued that the Iraqi psyche contained an internalised tension between tribal and urban modes that produced a 'schism of the Iraqi personality'.[17] This 'schism' would operate depending on the circumstances – in times of war, Iraqi society reverted to tribal values of *ʿasabīyya*,[18] while in times of peace sedentary values prevailed. As I will detail below, it could be argued that the British, consequently, took advantage of this 'schism' in the 'nature' of Iraqi society, and it was for this reason somewhat an effective strategy of colonial and semi-colonial control.

The position of the shaikh of a tribe was attached to his office rather than his person. In other words, the shaikh himself was merely considered *primus inter pares* ('the first among equals') with neither privileges nor authority.[19] The shaikh's responsibility was vast and included conducting the tribe's relations with outsiders, the declaration of war, and dealings with (central) governments. He was also responsible for the maintenance of social functions within the tribe, including the extension of hospitality in his *mudhif* (guesthouse), which is considered the centre of political deliberations, where he exercised his judicial function of resolving disputes amongst his tribespeople.[20] Robert Fernea has characterised the tribe as a 'jural community,' whereby the *mudhif* of the shaikh is the 'centre of jural activities' and where, '[i]ndividual crimes which conspicuously violated the moral code of all tribesmen … might result in physical punishment as described by the shaykh and *ajāwīd* (or elders) of the tribe, or in banishment of the defendant and the kinsmen who supported him'.[21]

The notion of justice for the Bedouin is consequently one that emphasises the concept of 'right' as one of entitlement. When an injustice occurred a tribesman generally had a right to rectify that injustice within the context of his tribe's customary law. So, if murder was committed, for instance, the

[16] A al-Wardī, *Shakhṣīyat al-Fard al-ʿIraqi* [The Nature of the Iraqi Personality]. (Dar al-Warrāq, 2009), 44–45. Originally published in 1965.

[17] *Ibid.*

[18] *ʿAsabīyya* is a term that refers to 'social solidarity with an emphasis on group consciousness, cohesiveness and unity'. It was first coined and popularised by Ibn Khaldun in his *Muqaddimah*.

[19] C Bailey, *Bedouin Law from Sinai & the Negev: Justice without Government*. (2009) (Yale University Press) 14.

[20] K Mahdi. *State and Agriculture in Iraq: modern development, stagnation and the impact of oil* (2000), 73. Shakir Salim writes that the *mudhif* serves as a 'social centre, political conference chamber, and a court of justice'. Salim. *Marsh Dwellers of the Euphrates Delta* (1962) (Athlon Press), 72-82. It has been described elsewhere as akin to a 'parliament' for tribesmen. NK al-Barāzī. *al-Badāwa wa al-Istiqrār fī al-ʿIraq* [The Bedouin and Settlement in Iraq], (Mʿahad Bihūth wa al-Dirāsāt al-ʿArabīya, 1969), 100.

[21] R Fernea. *Shaykh and Effendi: Changing Patterns of Authority Among El Shabana of Southern Iraq*, (1970) (Harvard University Press), 93.

victim could enforce his right by killing the murderer or the murderer's clansmen with impunity.[22] In bedouin eyes, the restoration of justice could only occur in this way in the difficult and dangerous environment of the desert where there is no central authority to protect him. As for the settled tribesman not living in a desert environment, it was the restoration of the honour of his tribe that remained the paramount function of a vendetta. The bedouin concept of justice, therefore, should be understood in relation to both the importance of security and deterrence in a desert environment, and the importance of honour in tribal culture. It is in this way that 'bedouin law … seeks to deter violations by endorsing the principle of mutual liability, according to which every man is accountable for the actions of his clansmen and is subject to punishment for them.'[23]

The perfect example of this is the settlement of a blood-feud by giving a woman of one tribe to another, what is referred to as *faṣl*. Although a cash payment is sometimes permitted, it is the former that is usually what 'herald(s) real peace between the disputing segments' as the offspring of these marriages is real proof that the feud has truly been settled.[24] The point here is that while certain actions of tribesmen could be conceived as evidence of 'lawlessness' in the deserts, this is an oversimplification and an incorrect characterisation, as the traditional tribal system of organisation in fact comprised an intricate and effective system of customary law that performed specific social and political functions. Here, one could also refer to the practice of raiding in the desert, which should not be confused with theft, for the bedouin resorts to the collective act of raiding only as a means of sustenance in an environment that ordinarily lacks rainfall, drinking wells and pastures. Raiding is therefore not equivalent to thieving or even war, but rather is a part of the bedouin's traditional way of life.[25]

## III. THE TRIBAL CRIMINAL & CIVIL DISPUTES REGULATION (TCCDR): ITS ORIGINS, JURIDICAL CHARACTERISTICS AND WIDE IMPLICATIONS

The British approach to dealing with the tribes of Iraq was the complete reversal of the Ottoman detribalisation policy that was aimed at the destruction of the cohesiveness of the tribes, with an attempt to render them under the control of the Ottoman state.[26] The British Political Officers sought to find the appropriate balance of 'internal political forces' by consolidating a firm connection between the *ex-Sharīfian* officers running the state and certain selected tribal

[22] Bailey, *supra*, 16, 17.
[23] *Ibid*, 18.
[24] Fernea, *supra*, 112.
[25] F Baali., *Relation of the People to the Land in Southern Iraq*, (University of Florida Press, 1966), 5.
[26] A Jwaideh, "Tribalism and Modern Society: Iraq, a Case Study" in RM Savory, ed., *Introduction to Islamic Civilization*, (Cambridge University Press, 1976), 165.

shaikhs.[27] They therefore began rebuilding the tribal system from the outset of their occupation, selecting 'official' shaikhs, who were made responsible for 'law and order' in relation to their tribe to ensure the protection of British interests, lines of communication and property.[28] This strategy was based on the notion that entire tribes could be controlled through the influence of their shaikhs. As Ghassan Attiyah illustrates,

> '[i]n the long run, both policies [British and Ottoman] had similar consequences – a schism in tribal institutions – but they arose from different sources: the British alienated the Shaykh from his tribe, while the Turks multiplied the number of Shaykhs to the detriment of tribal unity and solidarity … the Turks … tried to alleviate the position of his tribesmen as against that of his Shaykh, but the British reversed the emphasis by upholding the Shaykh's interest against those of his tribesmen'.[29]

To institutionalise their policy, the British drafted and imposed the (legal) instrument of the *Tribal Criminal and Civil Disputes Regulation* (TCCDR), extending it into ordinary state law in 1925, and enshrining it in the constitution. The TCCDR was first issued during the British occupation of southern Iraq in 1916. It was, in other words, initially drawn up as an instrument of colonial administration and pacification, yet ultimately, 'what may have begun as an administrative expedient ended as political necessity'.[30] The TCCDR constructed a separate tribal legal system that was severed from civil and criminal courts of the state. The jurisdiction of the national courts was therefore institutionally restricted. The TCCDR guaranteed that the selected shaikh would dispense the administration of justice on his tribespeople according to customary law and tribal tradition. It therefore maintained 'the tribal law as the law of the tribal land,' while 'enhancing the jural role of the shaikh,' reinforcing primacy in his person rather than his office.[31] The TCCDR defined a tribesman broadly as, 'a member of a generally recognised tribe or tribal section which has been accustomed to settle its dispute by recourse to the arbitration of elders or shaikhs and not by recourse to the Courts of the land as ordinarily constituted.'[32] The authority of the selected shaikh (who gained political and economic power through tax subsides, land and seats in parliament) was now dependent on British patronage and particularly the Iraqi state rather than his fellow tribesmen. This had a tremendous transformative effect on the social and economic relations between the shaikhs and their tribesmen, eventually opening the door for the institutionalization of extreme capitalistic exploitation and accumulation in rural Iraq

[27] See D Pool. "From Elite to Class: The Transformation of Iraqi Political Leadership," in A Kelidar (ed.), *The Integration of Modern Iraq* (Croom Helm, 1979), 63–87. Batatu, *supra*, 88, 91.

[28] P Ireland, *Iraq: A Study in Political Development* (The McMillian Co, 1938), 94.

[29] G Atiyyah, *Iraq: 1908-1921. A Socio-Political Study*, (The Arab Institute for Research and Publishing, 1973), 235.

[30] Batatu, *supra*, 88.

[31] Pool, *supra*, 78.

[32] TNA. Lt. Col. EB Howell, Revenue Secretary to the Civil Commissioner, "Land Revenue Demand: Theory and Practice," Administrative Report on the working of the Revenue Dept. for the year 1919; CO 696/2, Iraq Administrative Reports, 1919.

and, as will be shown, the TCCDR transformed the very customary laws that were intended to be 'preserved'.

Before turning to the wide implications of the TCCDR in Iraq in more detail, it is important for this analysis to trace the origins of this piece of legislation and imperial instrument. The TCCDR could be directly traced to the administrative methods developed by Sir Robert Sandeman in the North-West provinces (present-day Baluchistan – in Pakistan – as well as, Afghanistan) in the late nineteenth century, which were aimed at the pacification of the tribes and in turn the protection of British interests in the frontiers surrounding India.[33] Sandeman's methods (which were first successfully used in 1876) were not necessarily unprecedented, but were still a unique synthesis of approaches of indirect rule applied elsewhere in the British Empire.[34] These were based on some basic premises: first, know and befriend the tribes. Second, adhere to tribal custom as much as possible and work with tribal leaders and chiefs. Third, bind the tribe to the government by payment for tribal service. Finally, peaceful methods must prevail, although overwhelming force must be used when necessary.[35]

In this way, Sandeman hoped, in his words, to 'knit the frontier tribes into our [British] imperial system and make their interests as ours … [so as to] certainly depend upon them being on our side'.[36] He, therefore, believed in preserving and rebuilding the tribal system that he saw as being in decay. The aim was that by appealing to the tribes' own customs and traditions, they would perceive themselves to be under their own rule, and as long as this served British imperial interests, this administrative system would cheaply run itself.[37]

In general, at the heart of this strategy was a part of the 'promise of protection' that was prevalent in many parts of the British Empire.[38] The basic principles of protection were considered to be so useful that they were circulated and diffused in various local contexts. The Sandeman method was therefore a re-articulation of protection in the context of the localised governance of the imperial frontier. In a lecture given to The Royal Central Asian Society in 1932, Colonel C.E. Bruce, a British colonial administrator and the Chief Commissioner of Baluchistan, argued for the universalisation of Sandeman's policy, which he saw as a method that should be put into practice around the world as it was '… equally applicable to every tribesman whether Baluch, Pathan, Arab, Kurd, or African; whether he lives in Indo-China, Burma, Morocco, Tripoli,

[33] *See* TH Thorton, *Col. Sir Robert Sandeman: His Life and Work on Our Indian Frontier. A Memoir, with Selections from His Correspondence and Official Writings* (John Murray, 1895).

[34] Approaches of 'indirect rule' include that of Joseph Gallieni in Senegal, Tonkin and Madagascar, and Fredrick Lugard in Asia and Africa.

[35] C Tripodi. *Edge of Empire: The British Political Officer and Tribal Administration on the North-West Frontier 1877-1947* (Ashgate, 2011), 57-58.

[36] RG Sandeman, Memorandum entitled *Relations with Frontiers Tribes*. *See* Thorton, *supra*, 356-359.

[37] Tripodi, *supra*, 58.

[38] See L Benton and L Ford, *Rage for Order: The British Empire and the Origins of International Law 1800–1850* (Harvard University Press, 2016).

Aden, the Sudan, or East West, South Africa, [...] [and this was] absolutely proved from the fact that every colonial administrator has, wittingly or unwittingly, taken him as their example or followed in his footsteps.'[39]

The pillar of Sandeman's system was based on the development and reliance on certain customary legal structures and institutions, namely the tribal councils (also known as 'council of elders') or *jirgas*. These *jirgas*, which were institutionalised in law under the *Frontier Crimes Regulation* of 1887 (and later revised in 1901),[40] ensured that the tribes were governed under the tribe's own legal customs (or 'tribal usage'). Moreover, the *jirgas* did not apply the rules of evidence of a colonial court (generally derived from British law), and were completely separated from the general legal system of the colonial state.[41] The *Regulation* reserved the Deputy Commissioner's power to overturn a decision issued by a *jirga*, retaining the colonial administrator as 'ultimate arbiters of tribal tradition'.[42] Nevertheless, almost all decisions of the *jirgas* were beyond the right of appeal to ordinary courts.[43]

Marsden and Hopkins have argued that the Sandeman system and its implications shaped a 'traditionalising modernity,' which rather than integrate and 'civilise' the tribesman of the frontiers as their imperial Indian counterparts, sought to 'contain, conserve and traditionalise' them in separation of the colonial state.[44] Their argument goes on to describe these methods as a form of 'frontier governmentality,' which created order by excluding the tribesman from the laws and norms of the colonial state; administrating rather than enforcing difference as defined by the colonial state. Rather than undertaking colonial state control through mere division, 'frontier governmentality was about order through exclusion' from the state.[45] What is interesting for our purposes is the fact that these administrative and colonial methods that were devised specifically for the frontiers, rather than an actual system of government per se, were later on used in a variety of contexts. The essence of the Sandeman system of frontier administration and governance as institutionalised by the *Frontiers Crimes Regulation* (FCR) was flexible enough to be diffused and implanted into other parts of the Empire, extending well beyond its original intent of mere frontier administration.[46] In fact, as Hopkins has recently shown, this practice

[39] Colonel CE Bruce. "The Sandeman Policy as Applied to Tribal Problems of To-day," (1932) in *Journal of the Royal Central Asian Society*, 19:1, 45-67, 60.

[40] This regulation was amended several times 1887 and 1901.

[41] W Barton. *India's North-West Frontier*, (John Murray, 1939), 59.

[42] *See* M Marsden, and B Hopkins. *Fragments of the Afghan Frontier* (Columbia University Press, 2011) 69–70.

[43] W Berry. *Aspects of the Frontiers Crimes Regulation in Pakistan*, (Duke University Commonwealth-studies Center, Monograph number three, 1966), 40.

[44] Marsden and Hopkins, *supra*, 63. The ideological underpinnings of the preservation of tribal custom could be found in the works of Henry Main. *See* K Mantena. *Alibis of Empire: Henry Main and the Ends of Liberal Imperialism*, (Princeton University Press, 2010).

[45] *Ibid*, 64.

[46] Berry, *supra*, 8.

of 'frontier governmentality' was used as a method of imperial control in every corner of the periphery, whether it was in the North-West Frontier of British India, the Northern Frontier Province of colonial Kenya, the San Carlos Apache reservation of southern Arizona, or at the edge of the Argentine Pampas.[47] It was, therefore, an integral part of state making, and so it could be argued that its fragmentary effects were in fact a constitutive part of the process of modern state formation in the Global South.[48]

The practices of frontier governmentality, then, allowed the Iraqi state to gain political control over the countryside despite having the appearance of being technically constricted in its legal jurisdiction over the tribal areas. It, therefore, maintained a juridically weak Iraqi state with a certain measure of political control despite theoretically being unable to enforce its legal hegemony throughout the land. Such fragmentation occurred in the context of a semi-colonial legal order that was clearly Western in character despite the appearance of such a traditional form. In other words, the fragmentation of the law occurred *within* an all-encompassing semi-colonial and imperial order and was a part of the making of the Iraqi state.

Most historians of Iraq tend to focus on the manner in which this dual legal system allowed for a political bond to be established between the state and the tribes, while the British were able to extend its control. The juridical implications of the TCCDR are not dealt with in proper detail. My argument entails that the juridical implications of the TCCDR and the fragmented and dual legal system that emerged in Iraq must be explored in detail to understand how it was in fact an *illusory* fragmentation that was both central to the making of the modern Iraqi state, and a part of the imperial administration of the 'borderlands' and frontiers of the region as a whole. In addition, it was this inability to completely sever the townsmen and the tribesmen that led to the political and economic tensions that would eventually explode in the form of unrest. The legal fragmentation that was the effect of the TCCDR was a form of frontier governmentality, which was used by the British to maintain its indirect control of the Iraqi state and its imperial influence over the desert corridors of the region. In the end, it was neither successful nor efficient.

Sir Henry Dobbs, the High Commissioner in Iraq at the time, who himself served in the Northwestern frontiers (namely Baluchistan) between 1909 and 1911 under the Agent-General A.H. McMahon, was a firm advocate of the Sandeman system of tribal administration, and so strongly supported the application of the TCCDR that he sent Edwin Drower, the Advisor to the Ministry of Justice, a circular on Baluchistan written in 1907 to 'explain his point of view'.[49]

[47] BD Hopkins, *Ruling the Savage Periphery: Frontier Governance and the Making of the Modern State* (Harvard University Press, 2020), 6.

[48] Ibid, 7.

[49] TNA. CO 730/103, Iraq 1926, vol. 12. Residency, Baghdad, 18 October 1923 to EM Drower, Advisor to the Ministry of Justice, Baghdad.

Dobbs quoted directly from the circular the words of McMahon, who emphasised the efficiency of the use of customary and tribal law as an

> ... instrument for the suppression of crime which in its simplicity and effectiveness can be surpassed by no other legal system which we can invent, for the simple reason that it is based on the character, idiosyncrasies and prejudices of the people among whom it has originated and by whom it has been evolved during long periods of time to meet their own requirements and remedy their failings.[50]

Therefore, on the one hand, a tested strategy in the Northwestern frontiers was brought into the Iraqi frame for the same intended purpose of pacification, and on the other hand, British officials believed that they were in fact preserving a deteriorating 'ancient' legal tradition that was a 'natural' part of the tribes in Iraq.

It was also the idea that Western standards of justice could not be imposed on native tribes in any direct manner that warranted the emergence of this separate tribal legal system. Here, one is reminded of Arnold Wilson's claim of the difficulty of imposing any notion of the rule of (Western) law on the tribes of southern Iraq when he first arrived in Basra: '[t]o impose the rule of law upon these dissonant and intractable elements was by far the most difficult of the many problems of civil administration in Basra wilayat.'[51] Of course, this process of legal transformation must be understood within the broader historical context of the previous Ottoman order, which the local population was accustomed to, for the tribesman did not find the duality of law as a foreign construct. There was already a 'duality' during the Ottoman period between *Shari'a* (religious) law and *Kanūn* (secular state) law for instance. Competing legal systems, including tribal custom, co-existed with other legalities before the arrival of the British and so one should not exaggerate the British role in bringing about a dual or plural legal order. For this reason, the tribesmen considered some form of duality and plurality as a natural part of the order of things and therein lies the British ingenuity in imperial control: the British built on what was already there – infusing their own notions of justice and in particular legal positivism. Nonetheless, the British strategy of duality was still an invention, but it was melded in a seemingly organic manner onto the layers of the preceding Ottoman order. In the end, however, the intention of keeping state law based on 'British ideas of justice' removed from tribal customary law did not actually work as the tribal legal order itself not only turned out to be a hybrid creation of the very hegemonic British legal tradition that it was meant to be severed from, but it was constitutive of the modern Iraqi state itself.

[50] TNA. Dobbs to Pulley (Interior) D.O., S.O. 2140 of 28 September 1924. Delhi, British High Commissioner Files, as quoted in P Sluglett, *Britain in Iraq: Contriving King and Country,* (Columbia University Press, 2007), 171.

[51] A Wilson. *Loyalties, Mesopotamia 1914-1917*, (Oxford University Press, 1930), 294.

A closer look at the provisions of the TCCDR illustrates how this piece of legislation led to a significant amount of abuse. It was drafted in a way that ensured that the shaikh had wide discretionary powers that were unchecked and provided no safeguard. Just like its archetype in the Northwestern frontiers, there was no recourse to or due process to appeal an order made under the TCCDR. Nor was there *habeas corpus*. Furthermore, although the finality of any decision under the TCCDR could be brought into question and revisited under sections 11 and 50 for up to two years after it was made, the Political Officers responsible for the administration of the district, and later the *mutassarifs* (governors) had very wide discretion under section 40 to elect to try a citizen under the tribal system rather than the national courts.[52] It was this infamous provision that led to considerable injustice and arbitrary effects. For example, dissident (non-tribal) townsmen were occasionally tried under tribal law rather than state law, and subsequently put into a form of 'internal exile' by an administrative order specifying where one was to reside.[53] It is not merely the trying of a townsman under tribal law that was arbitrary and unjust, but even the removal of a tribesman or an entire tribe[54] from a specified district as a form of punishment. The role of the administrative official was to affirm a TCCDR order and to ensure that it was enforced. However, the fact that these officials had such wide discretion made them susceptible to bribery from shaikhs who wanted to influence a certain outcome.[55] It is for this reason that Batatu fittingly referred to the TCCDR as more of an 'arbitrary administrative regulation' in the context of its uses and interpretation, especially in relation to the cities.[56] The TCCDR was criticised, even at times by some shaikhs, for giving too much discretion in the hands of administrators, who were neither trained in Iraqi law nor tribal law and custom.[57] In that sense, the TCCDR was, to use the words of Mahmood Mamdani when referring to the customary legal institutions enforced by the British in Nigeria, 'the triumph of techno-administration under the guise of indirect rule through customary law … [That is,] a retreat into legal administration'.[58] The rule of law turns into the rule of legal administration (i.e. a concern for 'law and order' in the tribal area) as the whole purpose of such structures was the administration of imperial power *through* the enforcement of so-called tribal custom and tradition.

[52] Batatu, *supra*, 93.

[53] The TCCDR was also used in this manner to deal with the anti-Zionist demonstrators against General Maude, as well as, the strikers of the 1931 General Strike, *Ibid.*

[54] This could be compared to the *Bengal Criminal Tribes Act* of 1871 that had the same function in India.

[55] MT Husayn. *Nihāyat al-Iqtā' fi al-'Iraq* (The End of Feudalism in Iraq: *A study of the conditions of the Iraqi peasant & the Agrarian Reform Law*), (Dar al-'lim lil-malayeen, 1958), 79.

[56] *Ibid.*

[57] Jamali, *supra*, 144.

[58] M Mamdani. *Citizen and Subject: Contemporary Africa and the Legacy of Late Colonialism*, (Princeton University Press, 1996), 125.

## IV. LEGAL FRAGMENTATION AND THE PLASTICITY OF TRIBAL LAW

My main argument in this part of the chapter is that the legal fragmentation that was created by the British was not only illusory, because it was incomplete or that it did not reflect reality on the ground, but that it was also a constitutive part of the making of the Iraqi state as much as it was useful in the imperial control of the desert routes of empire. The executive conveniently used the tribal system for its own advantage, often to avoid the implications of Iraqi (state) law. I have already shown how the TCCDR was used as an imperial instrument of administrative control and oppression by the Iraqi state. What is also interesting is that tribesmen did not hesitate to use the national courts when it was in their interest to do so. According to one shaikh, the only reason why a tribesman preferred the tribal courts was that he hoped to receive the monetary remedy that was owed to him under customary law.[59] In reality, however, not unlike the preceding Ottoman order, the tribesman found strategic ways to exercise his rights under state law by disguising himself as a townsman when it was to his advantage to do so. M.N. Kadhim (who started out his career as a deputy prosecutor, becoming a criminal court judge and eventually a member of the Court of Sessions) argued that Iraqi state law was continuously encroaching into the tribal legal system.[60] Kadhim had the following to say from his experience as a long-standing member of the bench:

> '[t]he author in his career has seen tribesmen living in towns or near towns sue one another in civil as well as in criminal courts in towns. When some of them raised the question of tribal customs for one reason or another and asked that the case should be referred to the Administrator, the opponent would immediately reject the suggestion and say that they had nothing to do with tribal customs: they had become "civilized townsmen" and they wanted the "Government" to give them their "rights" or to punish their opponents.'[61]

In the reverse situation, powerful townsmen would claim to have tribal roots to get away with certain crimes, in particular murder.[62] These instances are quite revealing as they illustrate that the 'dichotomy' between the tribesman and the townsman in Iraq that was constructed in law was misleading as, in reality, both were encroaching into each other. It shows that the tribesman was not 'primitive' or 'uncivilised' as the British believed, in the sense that he was too attached to his tribal roots to rely on the rule of (state) law rather than his tribal customs. The fact was that the tribal structures not only existed *in tandem* with the state, but were also a part of it. One reinforced the other (as they were interdependent) *within* an overarching semi-colonial Iraqi order. It was therefore the

[59] Jamali, *supra*, 144.

[60] MN Kadhim, *Reaction to Crime Under Tribal Law and Modern Codification in Iraq*, (D.Phil. Thesis, Oxford University, 1961).

[61] *Ibid*, 317-318.

[62] *See* Sluglett, *supra*, 172.

function of such a positivist duality and fragmentation to further and strengthen certain aspects of the Iraqi state, especially in relation to its role in the protection of British imperial interests.

To what extent then was customary and tribal law 'invented' in Iraq? The literature on the 'invention of tradition' and customary law is vast, especially in the context of the history of colonial Africa.[63] Terence Ranger, who was the first to develop this analysis, argued that what was referred to as 'customary' tradition (including *customary* law) was an invention devised by Europeans who believed that they were 'respecting age-old African custom'.[64] This argument was eventually expanded, influencing a plethora of legal scholarship (especially in legal anthropology), in particular the work of Martin Chanock on customary law in Malawi and Zambia; Sally Falk Moore's work on colonial law in Chaggaland, as well as, Sally Engel Merry's study on law and colonialism in the context of the history of Hawaii.[65] The overarching concern in this diverse body of work was the effect that colonialism had on the legal structures of indigenous native societies – the general claim was that the customary law that emerged during these periods of colonisation was not a residue of the past, but rather emerged out of the colonial encounter itself. It was in this manner that it was 'invented' rather than 'discovered'.[66] This line of reasoning was a direct challenge to the dominant (evolutionary) understanding in legal anthropology of what has generally been termed as 'primitive law'.[67] Customary law is not primitive law, but rather modern (semi-) colonial law in customary garb. Chanock for instance has argued that,

> 'the law was the cutting edge of colonialism, an instrument of the power of an alien state and part of the process of coercion. And it also came to be a new way of conceptualizing relationships and power within African communities, which were undergoing basic economic changes … The customary law, far from being a survival, was created by these changes and conflicts. It cannot be understood outside of the impact of the new economy on African communities. Nor can it be understood outside of the peculiar institutional setting in which its creation takes place ….'[68]

[63] T Ranger, "The Invention of Tradition in Colonial Africa," in Ranger (ed.), *The Invention of Tradition*, (Cambridge University Press, 1983).

[64] *Ibid*, 250.

[65] *See* M Chanock. *Law, Custom and Social Order: The Colonial Experience in Malawi and Zambia*, (Cambridge University Press, 1985); SF Moore, *Social Facts and Fabrications: "Customary" law on Kilimanjaro, 1880-1980*, (Cambridge University Press, 1986); SE Merry. *Colonizing Hawaii: The Cultural Power of Law*, (Princeton University Press, 2000); FG Snyder. "Colonialism and Legal Form: The Creation of 'Customary Law' in Senegal", in C Sumner (ed.), *Crime, Justice and Underdevelopment*, (Macmillan & Co, 1982), 90–121.

[66] There are limits to the notion that customary law was 'invented' *tout court*. The word 'invention' should be approached with caution, for customary law was never invented out of thin air. *See* T Spear, "Neo-Traditionalism and the Limits of Invention in British Colonial Africa," *Journal of African History*, 44 (2003), 3–27.

[67] *See* EA Hoebel. *The Law of Primitive Man: A Study in Comparative Legal Dynamics*, (Harvard University Press, 1954).

[68] Chanock, *supra*, 4.

Customary law was therefore a unique product of the colonial encounter itself and cannot be explained otherwise. It must be understood as being moulded by the historical processes of colonialism and capitalism. Nevertheless, it must always be emphasised that this British 'invention' was not applied on a tabula rasa, but rather adapted into a preexisting Ottoman order. The 'customary law' of the tribes of Iraq should be approached in a similar analytic manner, for it emerged out of and was transformed by British colonial policies, rather than being a restoration of an ancient tradition from the past. It is true that the 'corpus of law' that was applied under the jurisdiction of the TCCDR was 'uniquely Arab,'[69] but one would need to explore the underlying changes within the semi-colonial Iraqi order to expose the transformations that these legal processes were both undergoing and stimulating. Historians of Iraq have generally been aware of the fact that the customary and tribal law that was applied under the TCCDR was somewhat different from what was there before the arrival of the British and their institutions. As I have already mentioned, there are limits to the notion that the British 'invented' this customary law tout court, for they contributed to this invention by molding specific features of such law so as to make it compatible with their imperial agenda. By doing so, they created a unique positivist duality and fragmentation in Iraqi law that served their interests.

What was it exactly then that was unique about this fragmentation process in Iraqi law? The law in this narrative has generally been approached in a strictly functionalist manner, and what has generally been said was that tribal institutions and law contained a 'fluidity' that was 'frozen' and which was made 'rigid' by a process of institutionalisation. To a certain extent this was true, but a more in-depth analysis of the law is needed here. One would need to ask more specific questions, for instance: *how* did this process occur, and what does it reveal about the nature of colonial and semi-colonial legality? It was mainly modern legal positivism that the British brought into the fold. It was certainly this *positivist* characteristic of modern (Western) law, and its legal form that brought about a major transformation (or even mutation) in indigenous legal traditions. The positivist semi-colonial legality ensured that the social and political relations that were altered would be reconciled with the capitalist system turning certain *customs* based on practice and *usage* into *systematised formal legal rules backed by a coercive state*. It is in this way that such 'customary law' was in fact a part of modern state law rather than a past (primordial) tribal tradition. Its function was to strengthen the coercive effectiveness of the Iraqi state, especially in suppressing dissent, while furthering British imperial interests. The fragmentation that was imposed on Iraq through these institutions and structures should

[69] *See* H Batatu, "Of the Diversity of Iraqis, the Incohesiveness of their Society and their Progression ..." in A Hourani and PS Khoury (eds.), *The Middle East: A Reader*, (University of California Press, 1993).

therefore be approached in such a rounded manner – the TCCDR (including the corpus of tribal law that was applied and interpreted through this instrument) was itself *entirely* apart of the general institutions of the modern (positivist) law of the state. It did not necessarily bring about a space of suspension of law (through administrative legality) per se, but rather following Samera Esmeir it allowed for 'positivist elasticity'.[70] This positivist character of modern law defined the parameters of the tribal legal system and its institutions, and despite technically having no jurisdiction in tribal matters, the state retained through such elasticity considerable influence.[71] Of course, customary law was 'disaggregated, fragmented and uneven; stronger in certain corridors, conduits, and enclaves, and cautious, conciliatory, or compromised elsewhere'.[72] However, it was this fragmentation and unevenness that served British imperial hegemony over the Iraqi state well, while giving both Iraqi officials and British administrators the ability to improvise and experiment with techniques in governance. Consequently, the fragmentation of law in Iraq recounted above, which has generally been perceived as a characteristic of British indirect rule, turns out to actually contain a certain *pervasiveness* that allowed the Iraqi state and the British room to maneuver, and, in turn, to encroach on and control the social and political spaces of Iraqi townsmen and tribesmen alike.

## V. THE RULE OF PROPERTY, THE DESTRUCTION OF THE TRIBAL COMMONS & THE ORIGINS OF CAPITALIST RELATIONS IN IRAQ

I will now turn to the complex questions of property law and land tenure to explore the socio-economic aspects of this historical narrative. An analysis of land tenure and its legal dimensions is necessary if one is to grasp how the peasant was dispossessed from his tribal land becoming a mere tenant (and later, a bonded serf), and the manner in which the shaikh became an absentee landlord living in the urban cities. In this section, I will briefly narrate this transformative process in the context of property law and land tenure in Iraq, which could be considered as the principal source of injustice and inequality during this period in its history. Before dealing with the approach of the British and the Iraqi state, I will begin by briefly describing the customary law relating to land, and the manner in which the Ottomans intervened, igniting the massive transformative changes to come. I will then turn to an analysis of the significance of law – in particular property law – in these processes and how it has been unfortunately overlooked in the historiography of Iraq, while considering the wider

[70] S Esmeir. "On Coloniality of Modern Law," *Critical Analysis of Law*, 2:1 (2015), 22.

[71] Robert Fletcher has argued that customary law or what he referred to as 'Desert Law' was in fact under the jurisdiction of 'on the spot' British officials who used it in a highly variable and flexible manner giving them a considerable amount of autonomy. *See* RSG Fletcher, *supra*, 165.

[72] *Ibid*, 164.

implications of an approach that would take the role of property law in a colonial and semi-colonial context seriously. It will be clear from this analysis how property law was used to commodify land, enclose landscapes, and dispossess the customary rights of the tribes. With this overall process – wherein the logics of 'abstraction' through title registration, the discourse of the 'improvement' and 'development' of agricultural land, and legal positivist doctrines were put into operation – colonial capitalism was implanted in Iraq.

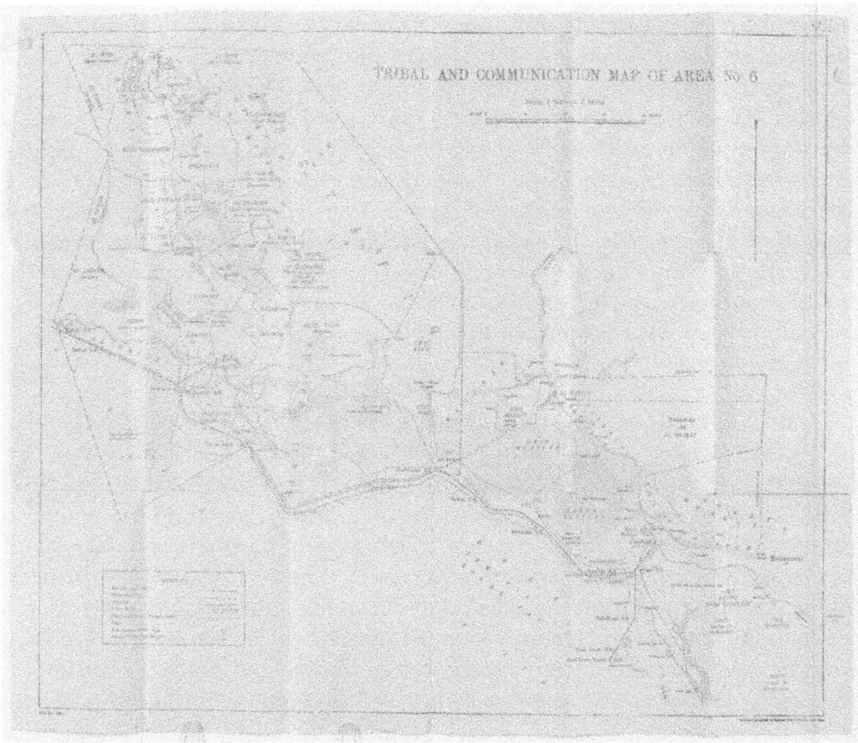


**Figure 3** 'Tribal and Communications Map of Area 6' [222r] (1/2), British Library: India Office Records and Private Papers, IOR/L/MIL/17/15/44, f 222

A tribe's traditional attachment to their land rested on certain customary legal practices that were varied and multiple depending on the region and environment in question. One thing that these varied practices did have in common, however, was that they were based on very distinctive indigenous notions of property. I have already mentioned earlier how land was traditionally held communally by the tribe, and that absolute property was an alien concept to the tribesmen.[73] Instead, it was the tribal *dīrah*, a term that conveyed 'the sense

[73] Haider, *supra*, 316.

of the domain over which the tribe exercised sovereign rights, rather than that of exclusive ownership,' that was so different from Western notions of ownership and yet bore 'a more profound sense of property'.[74] A good example of such tribal customary law relating to land was called the *lazma*, which was a form of corporately held real property by the tribe. It was claimed in perpetuity (as long as the tribe was able to defend it) and did not depend on the continuous maintenance of the land through pasture or cultivation.[75] As long as the land was either initially brought into production by its toil or forcibly taken by conquest, the land became the *communal* property of the tribe.[76] In this manner, tribal *lazma* was 'a form of collective holding paid for by either the toil or the blood expended by the tribe rather than by a purchase price or its equivalent.'[77] Most land in the region was clearly as of yet outside the market and commercial transactions.[78] The shaikh commonly assigned the tribesmen a *saham* (or share) of the cultivated areas of the land in accordance with the tribe's needs, and so land tended to be distributed in a more equitable manner. Furthermore, the rights attached to *lazma* allowed for more freedom of use, as it was not dependent on continuous cultivation and remained valid long after the land was abandoned.[79]

The main policy of the Ottomans towards the tribes from the early nineteenth century onwards was a policy of detribalization as the tribal order was considered as an obstacle to its state authority, especially with regards to tax and revenue collection.[80] Customary laws and practices were never recognised by the Ottoman authorities, which considered all land as being within the domain of the Ottoman state. Nevertheless, Ottoman *wālīs* (governors) based in the towns continuously failed to extend their authority into the rural areas due to vigorous tribal resistance.[81] Hence, Ottoman legal structures continued to coexist with these traditional tribal customs until the Ottoman (administrative, military and legal) reforms or the *Tanzīmāt* were initiated in the mid nineteenth century.

The *Tanzīmāt* began the process of integrating the three provinces of Iraq (Baghdad, Basra, and Mosul) into the purview of centralisation from

[74] A Jwaideh, "Aspects of land tenure and social change in lower Iraq during late ottoman times" in T Khalidi (ed.), *Land Tenure and Social Transformation in the Middle East*, (American University of Beirut, 1984), 334.

[75] *Ibid*, 335.

[76] *Ibid*, 336. Another kind of customary tenure, which was prevalent in the region was the *musha'a* system, which British officials likened to the English commons, and considered as non-productive land. See M Bunton, *Colonial Land Policies in Palestine 1917-1936* (OUP, 2007), 9; JK Irby, "Aspects of *Musha* Land Tenure in Lebanon" *Yearbook of the Association of Pacific Coast Geographers*, Volume 33, 1971, 153–160.

[77] *Ibid*.

[78] Mahdi, *supra*, 73.

[79] Jwaideh, *supra*, 337.

[80] For a recent study on Ottoman tribal policies and land tenure in Iraq, See K Kiyotaki, *Ottoman Land Reform in the Province of Baghdad* (Brill, 2019).

[81] A Jwaideh, 'Midhat Pasha and the Land System of Lower Iraq,' (1963) in St. Antony's Papers Vol. XVI, *Middle Eastern Affairs* No. 3, pp. 106–137, London, 112.

Constantinople. It also intended to modernise the state while reforming the economy in line with expanding international and foreign trade.[82] Part of the reforms included the Ottoman Land Code of 1858, which aimed at strengthening the financial viability and in turn the power of the Ottoman state.[83] This Code categorised landholding into several designations, the two of which concern us here are *mīrī* (state un-alienated land) and *mūlk* (freehold land).[84] The Code provided a framework for the registration of individual land rights, granting taxpayers *tapū sanads* (title deeds), which in turn created a new prescriptive tenure over land (*tapū*). Its main purpose was to weaken tribal institutions by connecting individual cultivators directly to the state, allowing them to obtain rights to usufruct *mīrī* land on the condition of tax payment and cultivation, as well as providing an incentive for higher production.[85]

The Code was in direct contradiction with traditional customary law and tribal principles, which as we saw were based on the notion that a tribe held land communally, rather than dependent on the recognition of the state. The Code expressly forbade communal ownership and only recognised prescriptive rights of individuals who could prove possession and cultivation of a plot for at least ten years. It was therefore generally almost impossible for a semi-settled cultivator (or a customary *lazma* holder) to meet such an evidential threshold and gain a prescriptive (*tapū*) right. Moreover, a tribesman not only saw no reason to pay to gain title to what he saw as his traditional land, but also was highly suspicious of the state, especially due to the high possibility of getting conscripted for its military.

In this way, the application of the Code brought about the unintended consequences of the distribution of *tapū sanads* to city merchants, tax-farmers and a few tribal shaikhs, who went ahead and registered their names to lands (often through fraudulent methods and bribery) as they realised the value of 'the possession of [these] slips of paper'.[86] Most bedouin tribesmen, however, did not understand the value of written law or the power of contractual documents. This is reflected well in one response of a shaikh when asked why he did not obtain *tapū* to formally define the boundary of his land in a legal document, '... he drew his sword and said, "'My sword is my boundary, and I don't want a better one, yes that's it a sword is the thing and no nonsense

[82] *See* E Ceylan. *The Ottoman Origins of Modern Iraq: Political Reform, Modernization and Development in the Nineteenth Century Middle East*, (IB Taurus, 2011).

[83] M Farouk-Sluglet and P Sluglet. "The Transformation of land Tenure and Rural Social Structure in Central and Southern Iraq, c. 1870-1958," *International Journal of Middle East Studies* 15 (1983), 491–505, 493.

[84] The other categories were *waqf* (religious endowments); *metruka* (land for common use and easements, such as roads for example); and *mewat* (uncultivated land, ownership of which was with the government). See HJ Liebesny. *The Law of the Near and Middle East: Readings, Cases and Materials*, (SUNY, 1975).

[85] See M Moosa. "The Land Policy of Midhat Pasha in Iraq, 1869-1872," *Islamic Quarterly*, Jul 1, (1968); 12, 3, 146–159.

[86] Farouk-Sluglet and Sluglet, *supra*, 495.

about writings …"'[87] Although the Code accelerated the already ensuing detribalisation process, it brought about the certain destruction of the military tribal confederations, replacing them with a 'multitude of antagonistic tribal sections,' which created a new socio-economic impetus that altered the traditional tribal structure. In some parts of the country, this occurred in an atmosphere of violent resistance from tribesmen, who were becoming consciously aware of how their ancient landholding customary rights were slowly being taken away from them.[88]

The tribesman was now alienated from his land as this new legal tenure system turned him into a mere tenant (at will) – an agricultural worker cultivating the land for his shaikh, who now became a landlord (or an absentee landlord living in the urban cities).[89] *Tapū* grants were eventually abolished in 1881 as the Ottomans realised the unintended effects of the Code, which merely entrenched the powers of a new class of tapū-holders with no real incentive to pay taxes. It was recognised that granting such documents without an effective system to enforce tax payments would only lead to their loss of control. Hence, although the process described above was interrupted and reversed, it was this Ottoman intervention into the customary legal practices of the tribes of Iraq that initiated the changes in the socio-economic relations of the tribes, creating the advent of the first 'wave of large landlordism', and setting the stage for the impending British colonial intervention to further accelerate such transformation, eventually opening the door for the entrenchment of these exploitative capitalist relations in law.[90]

When the British arrived, the state of land tenure was entirely confusing, contradictory and unsettled. The preceding Ottoman system and its interruption produced a situation whereby only 20 per cent of all the land was *tapū* registered, while the rest of the 80 per cent remained as *mīrī* (state-owned) land.[91] There were many competing claims (between tapū holders and customary lazma holders for example). However, the mandatory administration did not attempt to settle these claims, as there was no general policy that dealt with with land tenure during this transitory period.[92] The British initially approached the tribes based on the region in question, being concerned merely with political and military expediency. Nevertheless, from the outset they realised that supporting one shaikh against his rivals was an efficient way to control the tribes. The selected shaikh would receive financial inducements, favourable land leases and tax breaks as long as he supported the British presence and maintained order in his tribe.[93] As A.T. Wilson recounts in his memoirs,

[87] JS Mann, *An Administrator in the Making* (London, 1921), 202-203.
[88] Batatu, *supra*, 77.
[89] Atiyah, *ibid*, 29.
[90] H Gerber. *The Social Origins of the Modern Middle East*, (Mansell Publishing, 1987), 75.
[91] Warriner, 145.
[92] *Ibid*.
[93] Wilson, *supra*, 77.

'[t]he Shaikhs ... were for the most part reasonable men, of substantial means, with many of the instincts of wealthy country gentlemen. They were in most cases directly dependent on the Civil Administration for the positions they held; realising that their positions entailed corresponding obligations; they co-operated actively with the political officers in suppressing offences against public order.'[94] This method of expedient administrative control, became 'a deliberate scheme of government,' and the tribal policy was clarified further in favour of bolstering the power of collaborative shaikhs.[95] These shaikhs would consequently become government agents, with the principal role of maintaining law and order and collecting tax revenue from their designated tribesmen. This certainly led to the further alienation of the shaikh from his tribe, as his power was now derived not from the respect of his tribespeople but from the imperial British administration.[96]

The British's reversal of the Ottoman policy of detribalisation, strengthened what they saw as decaying tribal institutions. I have already discussed this policy earlier in the context of the TCCDR, and its political and juridical implications. Together with these tribal legal and administrative instruments, the British relied on the shaikh to extract surplus value from agriculture. In the mean time, it was claimed that their intention was to uphold the 'status quo,'[97] supposedly not creating 'new' rights in land where none existed. For this reason, the British administration (temporarily) continued to apply the Ottoman Land Code and the Ottoman legal framework – what was generally referred to in the region as 'Ottoman law in force'.[98] The *Tapū* department was consequently revived to settle title.[99] The result, however, only transformed the so-called status quo into a direr situation. In the Muntafiq region, for example, attempts to settle title strengthened the landowners even further. Although *Tapū sanads* were considered as defective legal documents, they were still, provisionally, taken to be the 'standard' by British Political Officers on the ground, who were left as the final arbiters on the merits of each document, as long as the 'land tenure question' remained unsettled.[100] This temporary arrangement, which 'accepted the legal rights of the landlord against the traditional tribal right to a separate *Dīra* ... perpetuated the injustices done by the Turkish regime to the tribes,' for the real issue was not in the legal interpretation of the *sanad*,

[94] *Ibid*, 95.

[95] Atiyah, *supra*, 234.

[96] *Ibid*, 235.

[97] As Martin Bunton argues in the case of British land policy in Mandatory Palestine, the 'status quo' was itself an invention – it was a 'doctrine of status quo' whereby the British used the Ottoman legal framework to further their imperial interests, while claiming not to have altered the legal status quo. *See* M Bunton, "Inventing the Status Quo: Ottoman Land-Law during the Palestine Mandate, 1917-1936," *The International History Review*, 21:1, 28–56.

[98] Dowson, 'Preliminary Study of Land Tenure in Palestine,' Nov. 1925, CO 733/109, FO 143.

[99] Sluglett, *supra*, 168. See EB Howell. "The Qanun Al Aradhi" (1922) in *Journal of The Royal Central Asian Society*, 9:1, 21–39.

[100] Atiyah, *supra*, 245.

but rather in the complete subjection of the tribes to a small group of 'shaikhly' landlords and the semi-colonial state.[101] In this way, the *tapū* landholders claimed and were successful in gaining settlement of title from the mandatory administration, while they readily used the state to further oust the traditional prescriptive rights of tribesmen.[102] Finally, with rampant absentee landlordism came the widespread use of mechanical pumps as a novel method of irrigation, which despite being meant to increase the crop areas, in reality merely enhanced the ability of pump-owners to claim ownership over large tracts of land, and brought another kind of large landholder into the fold.[103] The government further ingrained these unequal relations when it passed a piece of legislation in 1926, which gave partial tax exemptions to these pump-owners.[104] With these developments, the process of the dispossession of the tribal cultivator-peasant continued unhindered.

It was not until 1932 that a legal framework for land settlement was established after Sir Ernest Dowson was commissioned by the Iraqi government to write a report and make recommendations on land tenure.[105] Dowson, who was considered the most prominent expert of land tenure of the time, started his career as a young engineer with the Egyptian Delta Light Railways, and a few years later was appointed as Director-General of Surveys in 1900. He later served as Under-Secretary of State for Finance and Financial Advisor to the Egyptian Government. From 1923 onwards, he provided advice on land tenure and reform for many British mandated and colonial territories, including Palestine, Trans-Jordan, Zanzibar, Uganda, the Gold Coast, Kenya and Singapore.[106] Dowson's thinking was oriented on the firm belief in the superiority of Western concepts of property law and land tenure, and so his overall goal was to transform native agricultural economies into those that adhered to Western principles of individual property and capitalist relations. Consequently, he regarded 'intensive cultivation of a capitalist agricultural economy as superior to traditional communal forms of tribal or village landholdings, and western concepts of fixed –private land ownership as superior to communal arrangements based on land-use rights'.[107] The implementation of sweeping land reform, for Dowson,

[101] *Ibid*, 246.

[102] D Warriner, *Land Reform and* Development in the Middle East: A study of Egypt, Syria and Iraq, (Oxford University Press), 145.

[103] Mahdi, *supra*, 99. Sassoon. *Economic Policy in Iraq 1932-1950*, (Frank Cass, 1987), 143.

[104] Great Britain, *Special Report on the Progress of Iraq 1920-1930*, 209.

[105] E Dowson. *An Inquiry into Land Tenure and Related Questions: Proposals for the Initiation of Reform,* (Garden City Press, 1931).

[106] M Bunton, 'Dowson, Sir Ernest MacLeod' *Oxford Dictionary of National Biography* (23 September 2004). Egypt would become the model for the British project for 'modernizing' Ottoman land tenure in the Middle East. *See* R Home, "Scientific survey and land settlement in British colonialism, with particular reference to land tenure reform in the Middle East 1920-1950" *Planning Perspectives*, 21:1, 1–22; 11.

[107] G Forman, "Settlement of Title in the Galilee: Dowson's Colonial Guiding Principles" *Israel Studies*, Fall 2002, Vol. 7, No. 3 (Fall, 2002), pp.61–83; 63.

therefore, meant the application of the 'Torrens principle',[108] which required the centralisation of land settlement into definable and fixed units, and relied on precise scientific data based on topographical, cadastral surveys and mapping.[109] In addition, Dowson believed that any reform must be based on the notion of 'revolution through evolution,' meaning that one must employ the concepts and arrangements familiar to the indigenous population to bring about a revolutionary change in land tenure – in the context of the Middle East this meant the preservation of the Ottoman legal framework.[110] Finally, Dowson believed that security of title must improve the conditions of the small peasant farmers, as opposed to the large landowners, if reform was to bring about a healthy agricultural and national economy.[111]

It was on the basis of these principles that Dowson, after visiting Iraq for a period of only five months, drafted a report demonstrating that a settlement of rights to land 'presupposes and requires some stable basis of land law or at least of legalised custom on which such rights can be founded', if the objective of the promotion of agricultural development was to be accomplished.[112] It was for this reason, he wrote, that a proper and clear land survey was required – one that was based on practical policy and 'local knowledge of the land', and that would convert registration of deeds into registration of title.[113] There was no precise or authoritative system of land law in Iraq, for 'four-fifths of the cultivated land ... was not governed by law'.[114] There was hence 'a need to establish security and clarity of tenure everywhere by a general definition and settlement on a clear legal basis of both statutory and equitable rights to land.'[115] Although Dowson was 'baffled' by Iraq's tribal and communal tenure regime that he saw as being 'in various stages of divorce from innumerable primitive practices, but still rarely wedded to law', and although he admitted that it was 'very difficult' to focus 'the whole kaleidoscope panorama into one generally intelligible picture', he insisted that it was necessary to proceed with some form of a generalised plan of diagnosis.[116] He therefore made it clear that the state should make direct connections with the peasant cultivators rather than relying on individual landholders as intermediaries. This, he argued, was what the Ottoman Tapū system was intended to do in the first place – to 'promote a body of industrious peasant proprietors and taxpayers'.[117] He argued that it would be 'dangerous to public peace and contentment' if land were disposed

[108] *See* CK Meek, *Land Law and Custom in the Colonies*, (Frank Cass & Co, 1968), 275.
[109] Forman, *supra*, 63.
[110] *Ibid*, 64.
[111] *Ibid*.
[112] Dowson, *supra*, 6.
[113] *Ibid* 39.
[114] *Ibid*, 5.
[115] *Ibid*, 75.
[116] *Ibid*, 10-11.
[117] *Ibid*, 61-69.

of in an unrestricted manner. The cultivators and small landholders must gain some form of economic stability and experience lest reform turns into merely an 'incitement to the piling up for unproductive debt'.[118] In this way, 'the enormous territories of mīrī [state] land now existing' which constituted the main capital of the nation should not be handed over to individuals unless 'accompanied by equivalent advantages to the public purse'.[119] Taking his cue from his experience in Egypt, Dowson believed that individual legal title must be guaranteed and safeguarded by the state, so that the *fellah* would have the incentive to invest and cultivate his land and improve its productivity.[120] This reflected 'quintessential British colonial thinking' in emphasising that it was insecurity of title to land which retarded agricultural development and that therefore it was the state's role to define and protect individual property rights and to encourage the 'efficient' use of land.[121]

Dowson's final draft report recommended: first, merging all departments relating to land tenure (the Survey Department, the State Domains Department, and Tapū Department) into one so as to better coordinate their efforts; second, the preparation of a digest of existing land law on the model of Goadby and Doukhan's textbook on Palestine; third, the completion of a 'scientifically dependable and functionally suitable survey' of land; fourth, the completion of a systematic land valuation as a basis for taxation; and fifth, the settlement of title on the basis of beneficial occupational use, preceded by 'impartial' local investigations undertaken by officers selected from the community itself. Finally, Dowson insisted that the state should retain its rights of ownership and that land should *not* be registered in freehold ownership, but rather in ten-year leasehold tenancies.[122]

Despite the 'scientific' basis of his report, Dowson's most important recommendations were undermined by Henry Dobbs, the High Commissioner at the time, who had considerable influence on the Iraqi government and who, as we saw earlier, was also the architect of Iraq's tribal policy.[123] Dobbs disagreed with Dowson's analysis as he was of the persuasion that the position of the tribal shaikhs should be further reinforced by allowing them more access to land.[124] Dobbs' goal was clearly to empower a certain class of large landowners to act as a bastion for the newly emerging British semi-colonial state. Dowson, on the other hand, strongly disagreed with Dobbs, stating that, 'I do not myself think either simplification, or public peace or economic advance are to be realised by

[118] *Ibid*.
[119] *Ibid*, 68.
[120] T Dodge, *Inventing Iraq: The Failure of Nation and a History Denied*, (Columbia University Press, 2003), 123.
[121] MR Fischbach, *State, Society and Land in Jordan* (Brill, 2000), 104.
[122] Dowson, *supra*, 76.
[123] *Ibid*.
[124] TNA. Dowson to Humphrys, 15 Jan. 1932. FO 371/16049.

a deliberate policy of establishing a series of large holders as intermediaries in dealing with the mass small holders.'[125] It was ultimately Dobbs' approach that prevailed – it was the most politically expedient one after all.

The two most important pieces of legislation that were subsequently passed were the 1932 *Land Settlement Law*, which gave the government the power to settle land title disputes, and the *Law of Granting Land on Lazma Tenure*, which established a new category of landholding – *mīrī-lazma*. This 'Lazma law' specified that *lazma* tenure could be granted to any person who has enjoyed the usufruct of land if he could prove that the land had been cultivated for over a period of fifteen years preceding the date of settlement.[126] As mentioned earlier, customary *lazma* was a traditional form of customary prescriptive right. The new Lazma law effectively created a rigid positivist 'customary' law that was recognised by the state, and that conferred absolute ownership (*mūlk*), similar to *tapū*.[127] The purpose of passing such a law was to recognise a certain customary law and tribal practice, and to supposedly 'preserve tribal solidarity'.[128] It therefore seemed to be drafted as a compromise, suggesting that certain tribal rights needed to be acknowledged in law. In practice, however, its effects were the complete opposite, as it resulted with what Dowson predicted in his report when he warned against merely 'the passing of bills into law' without ensuring that they were workable on the ground.[129]

The *Lazma* Law and its strict interpretation eventually allowed for the newly emergent stratum of pump-owners to acquire ownership of lands in which they installed pumps, at the expense of the prescriptive rights of tribesmen.[130] According to some, this occurred because of the bias and incompetence of those presiding over settlement courts, which often accepted proof of only one year of cultivation, instead of the expressly requisite fifteen.[131] The president of the Department of Settlements, Hasan Ali, for instance, highlighted that 'with inexperienced land settlement officers, and with the doubtful integrity of the administration, influential people and shaykhs were able to get such grants by presenting even more tenuous evidence as proof of prescriptive claims.'[132] Although this was true, it was in fact the very nature of the Lazma Law that ensured that customary rights would be overridden as it was based on notions of property relations that were completely foreign to tribal customary law. As

[125] *Ibid*.
[126] Warriner, *Land Reform and* Development in the Middle East, *supra*, 148.
[127] *Ibid*, 147.
[128] *Ibid*, 148.
[129] Dowson, *supra*, 57-58.
[130] A very narrow interpretation of the definition of 'usufruct' was accepted by members of settlement courts, which allowed pump-owners to gain title. J Khayyāt. "al-Tatawūr al-Tārīkhi li-Hiyazāt al-Ardh wa ʿAlaqāt al-Mūlkīya fi al-Rīf al-ʿIraqi" [The historical development of landholding and ownership relations in rural Iraq], *Al-Iqtisādi* (1970), Vol. 11, No. 2, 98.
[131] *Ibid*.
[132] HM Ali. *Land Reclamation and Settlement in Iraq* (The Baghdad Printing Press, 1955), 63-65.

mentioned earlier, the traditional customary *lazma* was not only incompatible with such property relations, it did not recognise land as a commodity. It was the insertion of such foreign notions of property into this traditional prescriptive right and its rendering into a positivist form that ensured its use by the pump-owners and capitalist townsmen for their benefit. The law conferred title on whoever was able to make the land in question *productive* (in the context of capitalist relations) rather than as a mere *tribal* customary right per se. It was this fact (and not mere corruption and incompetence that was, as Warriner states, 'not surprising' considering the political circumstances), which ultimately explains the fact that proof of only one year of productive crop cultivation was sufficient evidence for the settlement courts to recognise title (entirely free of charge), while tribesmen whose ancestors lived on their traditional land for hundreds of years were denied any form of ownership or legal rights. In the end, the law imposed *only* obligations on the *fellah*, stripping away all his rights.

A certain understanding of individual property rights and property law relating to land and the importance it attaches to the function of surplus production was reflected in the parliamentary debates on the Lazma Law. The main concern was the definition of 'lazma-holder'. After one member objected to the possibility that this law would override certain customary rights in his region (such as the ancient right of *naqsha*[133]), the member from Hila, Salman al-Barrak, responded by warning against making any peasant (fellah) a lazma-holder. He claimed that, 'if we made each *fellah* a *lazma*-holder, we might as well wish *salam* (peace) upon the land [i.e. wish it farewell] ... and if all Iraqis become *lazma*-holders ... then the land would become a desert. For as long as there is no incentive driving the *fellah*, then he would not cultivate [a thing] ...'[134] It was clear from the these parliamentary debates that the fellah was interpreted as being precluded from the definition of a lazma-holder in law from the very beginning. The law was ultimately passed unanimously in both houses, and this explains the manner in which the commodification of land was primarily contemplated (in the context of 'improvement') as the only way to make land more productive – the application of capital on land was considered a necessary precondition to acquire its ownership.

The property legal framework to settle land was therefore in actuality meant to make permanent a specific understanding of property relations – a 'rule of property' as Ranajit Guha called it[135] – that was not only compatible with but also made to serve the capitalist system in toto. As one African legal scholar

[133] *Naqsha* was an ancient tribal prescriptive right attached to individual plots of land that were originally acquired by means of personal toil or to those who have 'broken the land and developed it'. Jwaideh, *supra*, 338.

[134] As quoted in IA al-Jawāhirī. *Tārīkh Mushkīlat al-Arādi fī al-'Iraq wa Dirāsa fī Tatawurāt al-'Āma* [The history of land problems in Iraq c. 1914-1932], (Baghdad, np), 274.

[135] R Guha, *A Rule of Property for Bengal: An Essay on the Idea of Permanent Settlement*, (Orient Longman, 1982).

suggests, land tenure reform in a colonial context plays a unique role as 'the implication of tenure reform is that it represented a form of progressive transfer from one normative order to another'.[136] In the case of Iraq, a 'semi-feudal' capitalist order displaced a tribal customary one. The law played a significant role in this process, which amounted to a transfer of property rights, ironically and once again with the use of an invented 'customary law'.[137] A specific legal form was evoked that ensured the permanent dispossession of the tribesmen and peasant from his and her traditional land.

It was with such uses of (Western) property law that the process of capitalist accumulation was accelerated, while the logic of 'improvement' and 'development' of the land justified massive transformations in the socio-economic structures of Iraqi society. It is true that it was eventually Dobbs' policy, which was merely concerned with questions of political strategic hegemony and which undercut Dowson's detailed report, that primarily produced the *iqta*ʿ [semi-feudalist] system in Iraq, bringing forth extreme inequality between the landowners and peasants. However, one should keep in mind that both Dowson and Dobbs, not to mention other British experts who were a part of the land reform debate, such as Longrigg, believed in the superiority of Western notions of property law over tribal/communal forms of tenure, and insisted on land reform that would ultimately further capitalist relations and accumulation. From this perspective, the British debate on land reform in Iraq was quite constricted, as it was in fact the infusion of a very specific notion of property law and its positivist framework that transformed the socio-economic structures of Iraq to further British imperial domination and capitalist exploitation. Nevertheless, Dobbs' policy only made things much worse as it enshrined an *extremely* unequal exploitative economic system in Iraq that would last for another two and half decades.

In this way, as Brenna Bhandar has shown, 'property law was a crucial mechanism for the colonial accumulation of capital,' whether it was in the settler colonial context of North America or a semi-colonial one, such as Iraq.[138] Moreover, it was with the uses of 'a panoply of pre-modern and modern property logics' that legal fragmentation became a characteristic of the imposition of capitalist accumulation in the context of (semi-) colonial modernity.[139] The British administration, however, did not consider that this imposed modern European property framework was greatly upsetting to the status quo, for, as one commentator claimed, criticisms of the settlement committees were 'commonly

[136] HWO Okoth-Ogendo, "The Imposition of Property Law in Kenya," in S Burman and B Harrell-Bond (eds). *The Imposition of Law* (Academic Press, 1979), 155.

[137] Jwaideh, *supra*, 350.

[138] B Bhandar. *Colonial Lives of Property: Law, Land, and Racial Regimes of Ownership* (Duke University Press, 2018), 2.

[139] *Ibid*, 81.

exaggerated' as its members 'created no rights, they [merely] recorded what [property] rights they found to exist'.[140] The reality of such meandering in property law nonetheless could not be any different. The new system of land settlement brought about the destruction of an already disintegrating tribal order, and displaced it with a modern capitalist 'semi-feudalism' that endured for another two and half decades until revolution broke.

It is worth quoting Warriner, who similarly refused to hold the British responsible for what occurred in Iraq. She wrote (in the distressing year of 1948): 'land tenure is mainly a controversial subject because it has been linked with British administration, and its abuses attributed to British mistakes. The difficulty has been that the British influence *was only advisory*, and the Government did not control an administration efficient enough to carry out recommendations of expert advisors …'[141] I have already shown how the government did not follow the most important recommendations of the so-called experts, but what is more interesting was the assertion that the British advisory system did not in fact have any influence on realising the intended policies on the ground. The record does not support such a claim. In fact, British advisors to the Ministry of Justice were giving legal advice on how to evict peasants from their lands, as the TCCDR did not contain a provision to allow for such an outright action, and an eviction was only legal under a TCCDR administrative order.[142]

In one instance, a British advisor argued that it was possible to take a peasant to civil court in a situation whereby the provisions of the TCCDR were inadequate to ensure the peasant's eviction from the land. Not only does this contradict the supposed existence of a 'duality' in law and jurisdiction, but it also illustrates that the intention behind this flexible piece of legislation and its subsequent interpretations were clear: to support the landowners against the peasants. This advisor wrote a letter to the ministry of interior where he detailed such legal maneuvering:

> If B wanted to evict G, he had to first make a [TCCDR] application on the basis that the latter has no right [referring to the new lazma law] to reside on the land … and request his eviction. If G did not have a deed to support his presence [on the land], an order would be issued against him. However, if he produced a document to support his presence, then B would have to request [in civil court] for the annulment of the contract [under civil law] presenting his reasons and evidence, and once the deed is annulled, G would be considered as a trespassor on the land.[143]

As Jawāhirī exclaims, a reader would probably be astonished by these instructions, as it plainly shows that British advisors were 'conspiring' with their Iraqi

[140] S Longrigg. *Iraq 1900 to 1950: A Political, Social and Economic History*, (Oxford University Press, 1953), 251.

[141] Warriner, *Land and Poverty*, *supra*,117.

[142] Jawahiri, *supra*, 263.

[143] INA. Advisor to the Ministry of Interior to the Ministry of Justice, No. C/1634, Baghdad, 1 June, 1931, as quoted in *Ibid*.

counterparts against 'the poor peasant' living in his 'miserable hut' to dispossess him from his land, 'in his own country'.[144]

Before moving on, one must mention the one piece of legislation that 'promised genuine serfdom for the peasant,'[145] and which introduced a trend of further concentration of landlordism during the 'independence' era of Iraq – namely, the *Law Governing the Rights and Duties of Cultivators No. 28* of 1933.[146] This law rigidly defined the labour relations between cultivators and the lazma-owners of the farms (whether pump-owners or shaikhs). The fellah had an obligation under severe penalty of law to follow the demands of the landowner relating to the methods of cultivation (whether in the choice of crops, seeds, water supply or harvesting) (Articles 3 and 18). Whatever advances were given to the fellah would be considered 'agricultural debt,' which would incur high interests and penalties if not paid on time (Article 10). If a fellah failed to pay his debt (which was nearly always impossible to repay) he would be prevented from leaving the farm, and could have his crops and hut confiscated and even destroyed by the landowner. Moreover, an indebted fellah was prevented from working elsewhere (Article 15). The fellah was ultimately held negligent under the law for 'virtually every disaster' that might befall the crop – something that cannot be controlled in the unpredictable Iraqi environment.[147]

In this way, the fellah was consequently turned from a tenant-at-will with some freedom of action to a bonded serf tied to the land.[148] One former British official admitted that 'one is obliged to regard the fellah's rights as theoretical only,' and that 'the fellah under the provisions of the present law, is doomed to perpetual indebtedness ... [and is] in reality, reduced to the status of a slave'.[149] The law was drafted to the benefit of the large landholders, who with their political positions and seats in parliament ensured its passage into law, despite the opposition of a few members to it for its clear injustice towards the peasant.[150] It was this law (and its revisions) in combination with the TCCDR that ensured that the *fellah*, now living in extreme poverty, in perpetual debt and enduring serf-like conditions would eventually have no choice but to leave the land and migrate to the cities in search for a better life.[151] It would furthermore contribute to his extreme affliction of a disease-ridden state, conditions that Michael Critchley, a professor of public health and social medicine at the Royal

[144] *Ibid.*

[145] Batatu, *supra*, 133.

[146] *Law Governing the Rights and Duties of Cultivators No. 28 of 1933*, Iraq Government Gazette no. 31(30 July 1933), 315-323.

[147] Sassoon, *supra*,169.

[148] Warriner, *Land Reform*, *supra*,137.

[149] TNA. 'Note on law by Webster, former inspector-general of agriculture,' FO 624/1428/7 (22 Dec. 1933).

[150] See al-Jawahiri, *supra*, 350.

[151] See *Why Labour Leaves the Land: A Comparative Study of the Movement of Labour Out of Agriculture*, (International Labour Office, 1960), 160.

College of Medicine in Baghdad, described in a lecture in March 1954 in the following manner: 'It is not exaggerating to state that the average agricultural worker (*fellah*) is a living pathological specimen as he is probably the victim of ankylostomiasis, ascariasis, malaria, biharzia, trachoma, bejel, and possibly of tuberculosis also'.[152] It should by now be quite clear that this 'pathological specimen' was not only the product of the foreign capitalist forces that swept the country, but was also the embodiment of its unequal relations through the very mechanisms of colonial property law and tribal administration.

## VI. HOW THE 'RULE OF PROPERTY' UNDERDEVELOPED IRAQ: THE NECESSITY OF LAW IN THE HISTORY OF (SEMI) COLONIALISM

The history of property law, land tenure and customary law that I have described above is plainly a narrative about legal transformation as much as it is about political, social and economic changes in the context of colonialism in Iraq. However, historians and scholars of Iraq have never really taken the law seriously. The role of (colonial and semi-colonial) law in the transformation and the imposition of underdevelopment or what has been referred to as 'semi-feudalism' of Iraq is of vital importance to grasp the manner in which it happened, and yet most explanations tend to privilege a *purely* economic or political narrative, whether it is reliance on modernisation theory, dependency theory or its critique of 'Political Marxism' a la Robert Brenner. Let us take one example from the classic Marxist work of Hanna Batatu, who seems to view the law as of mere secondary importance to social and economic 'forces' in understanding the transformations that occurred in Iraq. In referring to the 1932 land policy and the land settlement law, he wrote the following, 'This policy amounted to a legal recognition of a process that had been taking place for a good many decades in Iraq's countryside: the usurpation by the shaikhs and aghas of the communal tribal domain, their disposition of weaker neighbours, and their encroachments on virgin state land.'[153] Considering Law No. 28 of 1933 he wrote, '... fortunately for [the peasant] ... it has never been the custom in Iraq to enforce laws wholeheartedly, and *anyhow legal enactments could not in the long run have checked a movement that social reality itself impelled*'.[154] First, it is clear that Batatu's definition of law is narrowly defined as a 'legal enactment' of certain political and economic processes occurring in social reality that could only be considered effective if properly enforced. Furthermore, law is treated as merely auxiliary to such historical transformation. In other words, his definition is

[152] MA Critchley, "The Health of the Industrial Worker in Iraq," *British Journal of industrial Medicine* 12.1 (January 1955): 73-75.
[153] Batatu, *supra*, 110.
[154] *Ibid*, 133, my emphasis.

confined to an instrumental and functionalist understanding of law.[155] But what is more interesting for our purposes is his suggestion that what happened in rural Iraq could have happened *without the law*. This is an astonishing assertion considering the prevalence of law in the overall historical narrative described above.

Batatu seems to believe that law should be considered as being separate from the social and political processes of transformation in history. However, law is so much more complex and nuanced than he suggests, for as E.P. Thompson emphasised in his study of the *Black Act* in eighteenth century England, 'law was deeply imbricated within the very basis of productive relations, which would have been inoperable without this law'.[156] In the same way, I would argue that the entire transformative process in Iraq described above and the imposition of a semi-feudal system of large landlordism (especially the *iqta*ʿ system concentrated in the South) and the making of the tribesman/fellah as governable legal subject could not have occurred and would have been 'inoperable' without the law – whether through the legal practices of imperial administration and/or the uses of property law to turn land into private property. In fact, the law was a part of the processes of these transformations from the Ottoman period and afterwards, when the British arrived. In this sense, the law is more than an instrument of class (or state) power or mere ideology (which of course it also is), but returning to Thompson, 'class relations were expressed, not in any way one likes, but *through the forms of law*; and the law … [therefore] has its own characteristics, its own independent history and logic of evolution.'[157] The role of law in analysing Iraqi history must therefore not be approached as ancillary to other 'forces', for the fact that law is a part of the superstructure does not preclude its significance in relation to the economic base.

The law might not be determining per se, but it is surely structurally and ideologically pertinent to the transformation in question, especially when it comes to the colonies and I would argue even more so in the semi-colonies, like Iraq. As Peter Fitzpatrick has argued, 'law and state have a role that is more structurally central and structurally enduring in the third world,' that is, in the colonial and semi-colonial context.[158] This is because it is the law that ensures that the traditional mode of production is preserved and kept somewhat intact *within* a capitalist system, which if left to its own devices would completely destroy it. In other words, since these two modes – the traditional and capitalist – cannot be integrated 'naturally,' they must be integrated into 'an operative combination' through the law and the policies of the state.[159]

[155] *See* RW Gordon, "Critical Legal Histories", (1984) *Stanford Law Review*, 36:57.
[156] EP Thompson, *Whigs and Hunters: The Origin of the Black Act* (Penguin Books, 1975), 261.
[157] *Ibid*, 262.
[158] P Fitzpatrick, *Law and State in Papua New Guinea*, (Academic Press, 1980), 36.
[159] *Ibid*.

The Iraqi economist Mohammed Oboosy has argued that the underdevelopment of Iraq emerged from the 'primitive and semi-primitive methods of production', which in turn caused the economic structure to become overly 'inflexible', further afflicting the economy with scarcities, 'bottlenecks', and 'retarding' any development plans.[160] If one were to extend our analysis into this economistic argument, it becomes clear that a study of the law would certainly explain *how* this structural inflexibility and underdevelopment was initiated, extended and maintained in Iraq on the ground. An extensive analysis of law in these circumstances of underdevelopment must be taken more seriously and given its proper due if one intends to get a complete understanding of the transformative nature of (semi-)colonialism and imperialism in the Middle East.

## VII. CONCLUSION

This chapter was an attempt to put law at the centre of the modern history of socio-economic and political transformation of Iraq. The British imported certain colonial administrative and legal techniques from the North-Western Frontiers to secure their imperial interests and produce a semi-colonial Iraqi state. In so doing, they constructed an unstable positivist duality and fragmentation in Iraqi law, which divided the country into two legal jurisdictions: one for the urban townsman and another for the rural tribesman. This in turn brought about the invention of a unique and modern tribal and customary law. Moreover, this fragmentation, alongside the uses of Western and Ottoman property law and the British land tenure policy, institutionalised capitalist relations of production, contributed to enormous transformations in the countryside, structuring deep inequality in Iraqi society. First, it created a specific class of shaikhs who would become dependent on British patronage for their power, while their tribesmen were transformed into bonded serfs. Second, it ensured that land would be concentrated into the hands of a small group of landowners, contributing to the making of a highly exploitative (semi-feudal) capitalist system of production, and eventually forcing many of these miserable peasants to migrate in waves into the slums of the cities, and turning into wage earners. It is therefore quite clear from the narrative above that without the British uses of the law and their development of imperial legal techniques of tribal administration, most of these structural changes would not have emerged in the way that they did.

Considering that this book revolves around the making of Iraqi sovereignty in international law, a note needs to be made on the interconnections between 'sovereignty' and 'property' in the context of colonialism and semi-colonialism.

[160] MJ Oboosy, "A Study in the Theory of Economic Underdevelopment With Special Reference to Iraq" *Middle East Economic Papers*, 15:2 (American University of Beirut, 1958) 136, 148.

What was described in this chapter should be looked at as being part and parcel of the international process of the imperial domination of the Third World – through international law – rather than solely an internal domestic process of land reform. The fact is that internal domestic processes and 'the international' were linked, especially in the context of colonialism and imperialism. Furthermore, the crystallisation of a capitalist agrarian order was pivotal to the making of the semi-colonial Iraqi state. So, rather than being opposites, 'sovereignty' and 'property' were in fact constitutive of each other – the process of enclosure and private property formation was vital to the making of the modern capitalist state. As Martti Koskenniemi has shown, the concept of sovereignty itself in its relation to territory was developed on very specific Western notions of property, and so it is no exaggeration to say that both – sovereignty and property – 'have always operated together so as to create the structure of power that is, at any moment, the real government of the world'.[161] If, as Henry Jones argues, 'colonialism was a necessary condition for enclosure' and experimentation with private property formations, then surely *the history of international law in relation to territory is also the history of property law especially in relation to land*, for both were 'techniques for organising space,' more firmly linked through the processes of colonisation (in all its forms) and imperialism.[162] In tracing the genealogy of the concepts of *terra nullius* and *res nullius*, Anthony Fitzmaurice has shown how the law of occupation was 'a common denominator in European understandings of property, sovereignty and empire'.[163] Despite the early distinction between international law and private law, it was during the nineteenth century that 'state sovereignty over territory' became synonymous with 'acquisition of title to territory,' in particular in the context of colonisation, emphasising the conjunction between sovereignty and property.[164]

Keeping this in mind, the rest of this book will illustrate just how the making of a unique Iraqi semi-peripheral sovereignty and the Iraqi state in international law not only emerged out of, but was also developed to protect the very capitalist structures of property and accumulation that were consolidated in the socio-legal processes described in this chapter.

[161] M Koskenniemi, "Sovereignty, Property and Empire: Early Modern English Contexts" *Theoretical Inquiries in Law*, Vol. 18: 355 (2017); 389.

[162] H Jones, "Property, territory, and colonialism: an international legal history of enclosures," *Legal Studies*, 39 (2) (2019), pp. 187–203; 202, 203.

[163] A Fitzmaurice, *Sovereignty, Property and Empire, 1500-2000* (Cambridge University Press, 2014), 1.

[164] DR Howland, "State Title to Territory – The Historical Conjunction of Sovereignty and Property" *Beijing Law Review*, 11 (2020), 856–878.

# 2

# *Manufacturing Iraqi (Semi-peripheral) Sovereignty in Geneva: Dominance Through* De Jure *'Independence'*

## I. INTRODUCTION

IN A BRITISH Parliamentary debate in 1926 on the ratification of a new treaty with Iraq to fulfil the stipulation made by the Council of the League of Nations in connection to the British government's Mandatory obligations, Major John Hills stated that 'I can imagine no more favourable field for finding [a] common measure of progress and that common civilisation [between the East and West] than the new State of Iraq … [which] … we brought into existence … [and which] starts with a clean sheet,' and that the British would do 'a very great service to the world' by maintaining its presence there.[1] Another MP, Hilton Young, responding to accusations that the British was only in Iraq for its oil, argued that Iraq 'needs [Western] capital for [the] development' of its infrastructure, and its agricultural capacity to feed the world. Young went on to claim that 'for the first time … [the British] have cleared out the way [for] one of the great transport routes of the human species,' ensuring future market connections between East and West through the construction of a 'railway across the desert'.[2] Young further pleaded with his colleagues that what was being conducted in Iraq was an experiment in imperial governance that would transform the British Empire 'from an empire of force to what one might term an advisory empire,' – an experiment conducted 'with the most brilliant success'.[3]

On the other side of the aisle, radical Labour MP and trade unionist, A.A. Purcell, accused the British government of having ulterior motives by pursuing 'capitalist interest[s]' and providing legal cover for oil companies, who, he said, would certainly suppress the Iraqi working class as it had done elsewhere.[4]

[1] HC Debate, 'Anglo-Iraq Treaty,' 18 February 1926, Vol 191 cc2167-289.
[2] *Ibid.*
[3] *Ibid.*
[4] *Ibid.*

His colleague, the anti-colonial communist and the first Indian to be elected to the House of Commons, Shapurji Saklatvala,[5] condemned the Mandate system, referring to the institutions of the League of Nations as amounting to 'an instrument of legalised brigandage,' the only purpose of which was to rob Iraq and the region of its rich mineral resources. Speaking on behalf of his comrades and the colonised peoples of the Third World, Saklatvala stated that, 'We see in [the Mandate and League] the possibility of depriving small nations of their freedom; we see in it the possibility of the powerful armed nations of Europe hypocritically meeting together to talk disarmament [while] contriving plots to extend our British Navy … [and] air bases in Iraq' and the Third World.[6]

This fierce debate at the heart of the imperial metropole illustrates the manner in which certain ideological justifications were used to explain the continuous British presence in Iraq. While Saklatvala and his colleagues were attempting to expose the real economic reasons that Britain was so concerned with Iraq, the imperialists were referring to lofty liberal principles popular at the time, whether it was 'tutelage,' 'protection of minorities,' 'economic development,' or more generally the advancement of 'the commerce of the world'[7] by integrating Iraq into the global economy. However, this was, of course, a strategy of the 'politics of deflection' that was used by liberal imperialists who wanted to 'square the circle between liberal freedom and colonial order, to unbind the liberal empire from its illiberal actions so that no one can ever call its intentions into question'.[8] How did the law allow for such a strategy of deflection? How did legal doctrine and ideology conceal the real aims of British imperialists in Iraq even while claiming that the country was to become a 'sovereign' 'independent' state in 1932? Was the case of Iraq truly an example of an emerging form of 'advisory empire', and if so, how different was it from previous methods of nineteenth century colonial administration and annexation? Or were these justifications, which were often articulated in the language of the principles of the emerging international legal order of the League of Nations, merely, as Saklatvala argued so passionately, in reality a form of 'legalised plunder' aimed at the exploitation of the natural resources of Iraq?

This chapter will address some of these questions by exposing how the uses of international law – whether legal doctrine and/or legal ideology – by the British government and the so-called Geneva 'internationalists,' especially in relation to the Mandate system, structurally concealed the main economic and geopolitical aims of Western interests over Iraq and its people, which was primarily related to the discovery of vast deposits of oil there and its geopolitical importance to the global economy. It therefore attempts to assess

[5] For an interesting account of Saklatvala's life, see P Gopal, *Insurgent Empire: Anticolonial Resistance and British Dissent*, (Verso, 2019).

[6] HC Debate, 'Anglo-Iraq Treaty, *supra.*

[7] Ibid.

[8] J Morefield, *Empire Without Imperialism: Anglo-American Decline and the Politics of Deflection*, (OUP, 2014), 15.

the role of international law and its geopolitical uses in the formation of the institutions of the Iraqi state, the juridical construction of its sovereignty in Geneva and consequent 'independence' in 1932, consolidating its subordination to the global economy. Analysing the unique Iraqi experience with the Mandate process will elucidate more broadly the dialectical relationship between international law, imperialism and sovereignty. Moreover, it could illuminate the legacy of the history of the Mandate system, not only in its relation to the semi-peripheral region of the Middle East, but the entire Third World.

Although some legal scholars have recently engaged in describing and assessing the role of the semi-periphery in international law, it has for the most part been largely neglected within the so-called 'historical turn' in critical international legal scholarship.[9] With the exception of several studies that emphasise the importance of the semi-periphery in the history of international law, in particular, Arnulf Becker Lorca's monograph on the contribution of 'semi-peripheral lawyers' in forging a unique form of 'Mestizo International Law,' Rose Parfitt's rich analysis of the hybridity of international personality,[10] and Ntina Tzouvala's discursive history of the Standard of Civilisation, there has been a 'remarkable' lack of focus on the semi-periphery in international legal scholarship.[11] Even critical scholars affiliated with TWAIL, who have put the role of colonisation and imperialism at the centre stage of the history of international law, have generally kept their analyses within the confines of a strict dichotomy between the core and the periphery. However, this study shows how it was in fact within this nebulous space of the semi-periphery that significant legal experimentation with the concept of sovereignty occurred, eventually ensuring the resumption of certain mechanisms of informal domination, and whose remnants would arguably endure within the structures of the post-war international liberal legal order and the post-colonial state.[12]

Although the League and its Mandatory institutions did technically break from previous aspects of nineteenth century international law, it was simultaneously a reformulation of Western domination of Third World states and

[9] For studies that have engaged with the semi-periphery, semi-colonialism or semi-sovereignty, see P Singh, 'Of International Law, Semi-colonial Thailand, and Imperial Ghosts' (2019) 9 *Asian Journal of International Law* 46; D Margolies, U Özsu, M Pal & N Tzouvala (eds.), *The Extraterritoriality of Law: History, Theory, Politics* (Routledge, 2019). A Hammoudi, 'The Interntional Law of Informal Empire and the "Question of Oman"' *TWAIL Review*, Issue 1 (2020) 121–151. YY Zhu, 'Suzerainty, Semi-Sovereignty, and International Law, *Asian Journal of International Law* 10/2 (2020), 293–320.

[10] AB Lorca, *Mestizo International Law, supra*; R Parfitt. *The Process of International Legal Reproduction* (CUP, 2019).

[11] U Özsu, "From the 'semi-civilized state' to the 'emerging market': remarks on international legal history of the semi-periphery," in U Mattei and J Haskell (eds.) *Research Handbook on Political Economy and Law* (Edward Elgar, 2015), 258.

[12] Despite the uniqueness of the Iraqi semi-peripheral sovereignty that would emerge, it was not only meant to be a model for the region, but also for the control over the resources of Third World states that were seeking independence. *See* P Menon, 'Negotiating Subjection: The Political Economy of Protection in the Iraq Mandate (1914-1932)' *TWAIL Review*, Issue 2, (2021), 193.

its resources through the construction of sophisticated legal doctrines and mechanisms. As Parfitt has correctly elucidated, 'what was revolutionary about the League was … [its] perfecting [of] an international legal process … that concerns the gradual extension, consolidation and reproduction of the very specific constellation of rights and duties which not only create the ideal conditions for unhampered capital accumulation, but also ensure that participation in the market no longer requires coercion, but is, on the contrary, entered into "freely" …' through (seemingly) bilateral treaties.[13] The Mandate System was also an attempt to 'preempt anti-colonialism and its potential destabilisation of the international system'.[14] The main argument of this chapter, consequently, is that a particular kind of non-European semi-peripheral sovereignty emerged in Iraq in 1932 that was manufactured by the Permanent Mandates Commission (PMC) in Geneva to ensure the establishment, disciplining and structuring of a (weak) capitalist state under the hegemony of Western powers and the global economy, which would become a 'model' example of independence for the region, and would also *legally* safeguard capitalist accumulation and the exploitation of its oil resources. I will illustrate the innovative legal reasoning that was developed by British administrators and PMC jurists in its dealings with the Mandatory Iraqi state and its successor state, so as to highlight the continuities and discontinuities of the interwar period, and the post-war liberal international order with the previous international legal order of the nineteenth century. What eventually emerged in 1932 was a curious *de jure* 'independent' Iraqi state *devoid of concrete de facto independence*. Many would refer to it as a kind of 'hollowed out' (political) independence, but it was much more sophisticated than that, as it became part of international law. The Iraqi experience reveals the contradictory features of the international order itself, particularly the complex concept of sovereignty, and the limitations of the principle of 'sovereign equality' in international law as it applies to Third World states that were integrated into the structures of the global capitalist economic system.

I will begin with an overview of the history of British imperial governance and legal techniques of informal domination in the semi-peripheral region of the Middle East through various devices and techniques, such as the 'unequal treaty' and the protectorate before moving to an in-depth analysis of the interwar legal architecture of the League and Mandate system. I will then turn to show exactly how Iraqi semi-peripheral sovereignty was manufactured and justified by members of the PMC in Geneva who made it a part of international law, and in turn, furthered the geopolitical aims of the great powers. This analysis will eventually expose the neglected geopolitical aspects of international law and institutions, especially when it comes to its manifestations in the semi-periphery. I conclude with an examination of the IPC oil concessionary and

[13] Parfitt, *supra*, 219-220.
[14] LV Smith, *Sovereignty at the Paris Peace Conference* (OUP, 2018), 182.

pipeline agreements to show how they were intentionally separated from the question of Iraqi sovereignty to bring to light some important insights on the characteristics of semi-peripheral sovereignty – a sovereignty that turned out to be anything other than granting Iraq its complete independence, but instead about obfuscating its main purpose: the legal safeguarding of the continuous access and exploitation of Iraq's oil resources and its transportation across the region to the Mediterranean and in turn, to the world.

## II. THE GEOPOLITICAL ORIGINS OF THE 'MIDDLE EAST' AND THE LEGAL INSTRUMENTS OF THE BRITISH INFORMAL EMPIRE

To understand the importance of Iraq in Anglo-American geostrategic imperial thinking, one must deconstruct the concept of the 'Middle East'. The 'Middle East' emerged as a geopolitical concept in the late nineteenth century and early twentieth century for the very purpose of dominating this highly strategic location on the world map.[15] This Western process amounted to conceiving an Orientalist category by 're-mapping' the region for imperial ends, and leading to its violent 'dislocation' from its traditional geographical hinterlands, resulting in a massive disruption for its peoples.[16] In fact, the 'Middle East' was made relative to the 'West,' emphasising the cultural differences within the East/West divide – between the (civilised) Christian/Greco-Roman world and the (uncivilised) Islamic world.[17] The American naval officer Alfred Mahan is generally considered to be the first to coin the term in 1902 to argue that Britain needed to establish naval bases in the Persian Gulf to secure its trade and communication lines with India and Egypt, and to counter the growing Russian influence, as well as German expansion through the Berlin-Baghdad railway.[18] The concept of the 'Middle East' was, therefore, developed in the context of great power competition. It should, therefore, not only be seen as a product of geopolitical imperial thought, but also as amounting to a geopolitical category *par excellence*.[19] Its strategic value was due to the fact that it was the point where Asia, Africa and Europe met. Its land and sea routes were interspersed with strategic straits and narrow waterways, such as the Suez Canal and the Strait of Hormuz, the control of which was paramount for imperial powers who wanted to maintain geopolitical advantage on the world stage.[20]

[15] EW Said, *Orientalism* (Vintage, 1978).

[16] D Foliard, *Dislocating the Orient: British Maps and the Making of the Middle East, 1854-1921* (University of Chicago Press, 2017).

[17] R Williams, 'Western' in *Keywords: A Vocabulary of Culture and Society* (OUP, 1983), 333-334.

[18] A Mahan, 'The Persian Gulf and International Relations' (1902) *The National Review*.

[19] W Hazbun, 'The Middle East Through the Lens of Critical Geopolitics' in M Bonine, A Amanat & M Gasper (eds.), *Is there a Middle East? The Evolution of a Geopolitical Concept* (Stanford University Press, 2012), 207.

[20] LC Brown, *Diplomacy in the Middle East: The International Relations of Regional and Outside Powers* (I.B. Taurus, 2001).

For the British, the Middle East was of crucial geopolitical importance initially for the defence and security of the routes to India, as it was considered a part of 'the strategical [Indian] frontier of the British Empire'.[21] The nodal point of the British Empire in the region was of course Egypt, a 'veiled protectorate' at the time, as the Suez Canal Zone was regarded as one of the most important geopolitical locations in the globe – the 'indispensible … life-line of British [imperial] communications' that needed to be protected at all costs.[22] The position of Iraq in this short highway to India in relation to Suez was likewise considered of utmost strategic value. In his report, entitled 'The Future of Mesopotamia,' George Louis Beer, Chief of the Colonial Division of the American Delegation to Negotiate Peace at the Paris Peace Conference, made the following observation:

> [N]ot only is Mesopotamia potentially one of the richest of the world's undeveloped regions, but the head of the Persian Gulf commands a very valuable trade route and is one of the world's chief strategic points. As the outlet for a rich hinterland, it is destined to have the importance of a Trieste or an Odessa and, because of its situation upon a potentially great world route, it may in the distant future rank with a Panama and a Suez.[23]

With the discovery of oil in the early twentieth century, the region would become an even more contested terrain in imperial and geostrategic thought. It is for this reason that one could not fully understand the way international law manifested in the Middle East without taking into account these geopolitical features of the region. The British had a long presence there, especially in the Persian Gulf, where it developed innovative techniques and mechanisms of informal domination.[24] The history and formation of the Arab Gulf states, for instance, emerged out of this development of the British practices of informal empire, and its uses in maintaining selected local rulers in power.[25] From its first arrival in the area, and after the British East India Company's defeat of Portuguese supremacy on the island of Hormuz in 1622, Britain concluded 'friendly treaty relations' with local rulers to ensure its hegemony over the Persian Gulf.[26] It established the first treaty system in the region beginning with the General Maritime Treaty of 1820, which was concluded with the Arab Sheikhs of the Trucial Coast, with the aim of suppressing piracy, trafficking and buccaneering

[21] V Chirol. *The Middle East Question, Or Some Political Problems of Indian Defence* (Murray, 1903), 4.

[22] R Gherson, 'The Anglo-Egyptian Question' *Middle East Journal*, Vol. 7, No. 4 (1953), 456–468, 471.

[23] GL Beer, *African Questions at the Paris Peace Conference with Papers on Egypt, Mesopotamia, and the Colonial Settlement* (Macmillan, 1923), 413.

[24] See G Balfour-Paul, 'Britain's Informal Empire in the Middle East' in J Brown and Wm Roger Louis (eds.), *The Oxford History of the British Empire: Volume IV: The Twentieth Century* (OUP, 1999), 490-514.

[25] RZ Said, *The Making of the Modern Gulf States* (Garnett, 1989).

[26] See P Tuson, E Quick (eds.), *Arabian Treaties 1600-1960 Vols. 1-4* (Archive Editions, 1998).

in the Gulf. This was followed with the Perpetual Treaty of Peace of 1853, which recognised the legitimacy of certain local rulers in exchange for 'cessation of plunder and piracy by land and sea'.[27] The treaty system denied these sheikhs the right of self-defence against external threats, which was allotted exclusively to the British Navy. In 1892, 'Exclusive Treaties' were signed with the Trucial States and other neighbouring states, which ensured that local rulers would make no agreements with any other foreign powers, allowing only the British representatives to reside inside their territories.[28] It was through such informal techniques of semi-colonial governance that the British effectively upheld the informal rule of *Pax Britannica* over the Persian Gulf, and many parts of the Arabian Peninsula, as these Sheikhs would become completely dependent on British power, despite having limited 'internal autonomy' – a semi-colonial relationship that lasted for over a hundred and fifty years.[29]

In addition to the multifaceted notions of 'protection' and its manifestations,[30] which were certainly reflected in the principle of 'trusteeship' of the Mandate System itself,[31] European powers had a long history with the imposition of 'unequal treaties' on African and Asian states.[32] The most famous example was the 'semi-colonial treaty system,' imposed at gunpoint on China after the Opium Wars, which pressured the Chinese to open up their markets to foreign trade (including opium that was cultivated in India), established a regime of extraterritorial jurisdiction in the strategic port cities, and fixed import duties at a significantly low level.[33] The instrument of the 'unequal treaty' was also used to create Indian ('native') princely states, which although were 'independent' of the Indian Raj, were still subject to the doctrine of 'British Paramountcy'.[34] These states were defined as having a unique 'quasi-sovereignty' in a very much similar manner as the Arab Sheikhdoms of the Gulf were designated. British Foreign Office officials interpreted this complicated amalgam of treaty law as being a separate kind of 'imperial law' that should be completely distinguished

[27] See H al-Baharna, *The Legal Status of the Arabian States: A Study of their Treaty Relations and their International Problems* (Manchester University Press, 1961).

[28] JB Kelly, 'The Legal and Historical Basis of the British Position in the Persian Gulf' (1958) 4 *Middle Eastern Affairs, St. Anthony's Papers* (Chatto & Windus, 1958), 119-140.

[29] See M Fitzsimons, *Empire by Treaty: Britain and the Middle East in the Twentieth Century* (The University of Michigan Press, 1964).

[30] See A Clulow, B Attwood and L Benton (eds.), *Protection and Empire: A Global History* (CUP, 2018); A Kamanda, *A Study of the Legal Status of Protectorates in Public International Law* (University of Geneva, Thesis, 1961).

[31] See T Baty, 'Protectorates and Mandates' (1921-1922) *British Yearbook of International Law* 109.

[32] CH Alexandrowicz, *The European-African Confrontation: A Study in Treaty Making* (A.W. Sijthoff, 1973).

[33] D Wang, *China's Unequal Treaties: Narrating National History* (Lexington, 2005).

[34] P Saksena, 'Jousting Over Jurisdiction: Sovereignty and International Law in Late Nineteenth-Century South Asia' *Law and History Review*, Issue 2, May 2020, pp.407–457. 600 princely states covered two-fifths of the area and one-third of the population of South Asia under British rule.

from 'civilised' international law per se.[35] The instrument of the 'unequal treaty,' therefore, excluded (the uncivilised) non-European states from the ambit of (civilised European) international law and the 'society of nations'. As we shall see, these practices of informal empire and indirect rule were inventively repurposed in the context of the Mandate system and especially with the Iraqi state.

## III. THE 'WILSONIAN MOMENT' IN THE MIDDLE EAST, THE LEGAL ARCHITECTURE OF THE MANDATE SYSTEM & THE GEOPOLITICAL SIGNIFICANCE OF THE 'A' MANDATES

With the end of the war in late 1918, negotiations between the Allied Powers for a new international system and a lasting peace began.[36] Although it was V.I. Lenin who laid out the idea of national self-determination in 1914 in the context of the international system, putting it into practice after the Bolshevik Revolution,[37] this post-war shift is generally referred to as the 'Wilsonian Moment,' as it was the ideas behind US President Wilson's 'Fourteen Points' speech, which seemed to have affirmed the principle of self-determination for all peoples, that were ceased and rearticulated by colonised peoples around the world in fulfilling their aspirations for liberation.[38] Wilson declared that 'every people has a right to choose the sovereignty under which they shall live,' and that 'the small states of the world shall enjoy the same respect for their sovereignty and for their territorial integrity'.[39] Despite the fact that Wilson envisioned a new international system that appeared to be a direct challenge to European imperialism, as historian Erez Manela has shown, he ultimately recoiled, since he did not expect that his words would be referred to at length by many colonised peoples around the Third World to affirm their rights for complete independence and to call for a radical transformation of the international system.[40] In fact, it could be argued that Wilson's rhetoric was not only exclusively aimed at European peoples, but was also meant as a convenient phrase and ideological challenge to the spreading influence of the socialistic principles of the Russian Revolution.[41] In the Middle East, as in other parts of the Third World, an eruption of nationalist parties,

[35] L Benton, "From International Law to Imperial Constitutions: The Problem of Quasi-Sovereignty, 1870-1900", *Law and History Review*, Vol. 26, issue 3, 595–619 (2008), 599.

[36] For an overview of the negotiations in relation to the Middle East, see PC Helmreich, *From Paris To Sèvres: The Partition of the Ottoman Empire at the Peace Conference of 1919-1920* (Ohio State University Press, 1974).

[37] B Bowring, 'Marx, Engels, Lenin, and the Right of Peoples to Self-Determination in International Law' in Umut Ozsu and Paul O'Connell (eds.) *Elgar Handbook on Law and Marxism* (Elgar, 2020).

[38] E Manela, *The Wilsonian Moment: Self Determination and the International Origins of Anticolonial Nationalism*. (Oxford University Press), 2007.

[39] *Ibid*, 22.

[40] *Ibid*.

[41] See T Throntveit, *Power Without Victory: Woodrow Wilson and the American Internationalist Experiment* (The University of Chicago Press, 2017), 250, 259.

anti-colonial movements and secret societies sprung out on the international stage from all corners of the Arab World, whether it was in Palestine, Syria or Iraq, to petition the great powers and international institutions for *istiqlāl tāmm* (or 'total independence').[42] The peoples of the region unequivocally rejected the logic of the League and Mandate system that they were 'half-civilised,' and required 'tutelage' of any kind to exercise their rights of self-determination and independence. Before getting to these nationalist responses on the ground, we shall first break down the structures and legal architecture of the League and the Mandate system.

The Mandate System of the League of Nations has its origins in the 1919 Paris Peace Conference, which endeavored to establish a lasting peace, and to settle the 'colonial question' in an orderly manner under the rule of law. The Allied Powers, who at that point occupied all the German colonies in Africa, Asia and Oceana, as well as the Arab provinces of the Ottoman Empire, eventually endorsed the idea of the Mandate system as a compromise between the 'liberal' internationalists and the staunch 'imperialists,' who were still in favour of the old practices of annexation, whereby captured enemy territory was considered as 'booty' or 'legally disposable property to be acquired by victors as spoils of war'.[43] These old colonial practices, which resulted in extreme violent subjugation and exploitation of the Third World, were therefore unequivocally rejected, at least in theory.

It was General Jan Smuts of South Africa, who first put forward a 'practical scheme' for the creation of a Mandate system based on international trusteeship in a pamphlet published in December 1918.[44] Smuts proposed a system of 'trusteeship' based on Wilson's Fourteen Points, specifically the principles of 'non-annexation' and 'self-determination'. He saw the League as the 'reversionary' of these conquered Empires. The main task of the League was 'nursing' the 'destitute' peoples left behind 'towards economic and political independence'.[45] Wilson based his final draft (the 'Hirst-Miller draft') that he submitted to the Conference on Smut's plan, making several adjustments by expanding the mandatory idea. The Conference delegates endorsed Wilson's proposal to create an international organisation that would safeguard peace, adjudicate disputes between the Great Powers, and protect the interests of native peoples. Nevertheless, certain aspects of Wilson's proposal did not come to pass, especially the idea that formerly colonised territories would be subject to international administration, and that its sovereignty would actually reside with the League itself. The US Congress ultimately failed to ratify the peace treaty, and so did not join the League despite Wilson's influence on its inception.

[42] For a detailed history of the role of nationalist movements and local actors in the Middle East during this period, see J Wrytzen. *Worldmaking in the Long Great War: How Local and Colonial Struggles Shaped the Modern Middle East* (Columbia University Press, 2022).

[43] Q Wright, *The League of Nations*, (Greenwood Press, 1930), 24.

[44] J Smuts, *The League of Nations – A practical suggestion*, (Hodder and Stoughton, 1918).

[45] Smuts, *ibid*, 11.

Article 22 of the Covenant of the League of Nations provided that the Mandate system undertook a 'sacred trust of civilisation,' so as to promote the well-being and development of these colonies that were 'inhabited by peoples not yet able to stand by themselves under the strenuous conditions of the modern world'.[46] Its main goal was, therefore, the protection of native populations from abuse, pillage and exploitation, which was the consequence of 'the unfettered discretion of sovereign states'.[47] It was this 'gross disregard of the material and moral welfare of the natives' that supposedly put the old system of formal colonialism in a moral crisis, forcing the Great Powers to re-conceptualise the 'civilising mission' into a new form.[48] Its secondary goal was the promotion of the 'well-being and the development' of the native population.[49]

Aaron Margalith has observed that the term 'mandate' is misleading and was the cause of 'many a misconception'. Some regarded it as a 'new conception of colonial administration and international law'.[50] Alfred Milner, the British statesmen who participated in the drafting of the Covenant, for instance, believed that it was a break from the past when he said, 'we are opening a new chapter in International Law'.[51] Others believed that it was merely British colonial policy and practice and its commonwealth that was 'internationalised' by the Mandate system.[52] All these views if unqualified are doubtless inaccurate, for although the Mandate system was truly an innovation, it certainly did not completely break from past international arrangements either. It was theoretically created as a compromise after all. The three main legal concepts of the Mandate system: the 'trust', 'guardianship/tutelage' and the 'mandate' were technically borrowed from both European private law and British law.[53] Nonetheless, these concepts have much longer histories, especially in the colonies.[54] The political principles that underlie the foundations of Article 22, namely 'non-annexation', 'international supervision', and (economic) 'non-privilege', have also been used in the past in various colonial contexts.[55] Perhaps the best example is the Berlin Conference of 1884-85, which was an attempt by European states to formalise colonial administration, setting down the rules and procedures for 'international

[46] *League of Nations Covenant*, Article 22, para. 1-2.

[47] A Anghie, 'The Heart of My Home: Colonialism, Environmental Damage, and the Nauru Case', (1993) 34 *Harvard International Law Journal* 445–506; 494.

[48] N Bentwich, *The Mandates System* (Longmans 1930), 4.

[49] B Rajagopal, *International Law from Below: Development, Social Movements and Third World Resistance* (CUP, 2007), 54.

[50] A Margalith, *The International Mandates*, (John Hopkins Press, 1930), 35.

[51] See Milner's memorandum of March 8, 1919, Milner papers; as quoted in W R Louis, "Great Britain and International Trusteeship: The Mandates System" in RW Winks (ed.), *The Historiography of the British Empire-Commonwealth: Trends, Interpretations and Resources*, (Duke University Press, 1966), 300.

[52] C Upthegrove, *Empire by Mandate*, (Bookman, 1954), 5.

[53] Margalith, *supra*, 41, 45.

[54] For a historical overview of the evolution of international trusteeship, *See* RN Chowdhuri, *International Mandates and Trusteeship Systems*, (Martinus Nijhoff, 1955), 13–36.

[55] Margalith, *supra*, 46.

administration' (exercised through sovereign rights) of the Congo, under the guise of the 'preservation' and 'well-being and improvement' of native African tribes.[56] The purpose of the arrangement was to minimise European inter-state rivalries, regulate access to navigation of rivers, and allow for freedom of trade. Nevertheless, the resulting agreement, the General Act of Berlin, was, in reality, merely a crude way to provide *legal cover* to legitimise European authority over Africa.[57] It ultimately collapsed, resulting in the violent 'Scramble for Africa'.

If the main concepts and principles underlying the Mandate were not new, then what was it that made the Mandate system an innovation in international administration? It was certainly the profound turn to the 'international institution' as a way to supervise the execution of the mandatory state's obligations.[58] However, it was particularly the addition of the principle of 'international accountability' that differentiated it from its predecessors.[59] The mandatory state was consequently considered 'a protector with a conscience,' which assumed obligations towards the native population and to the 'society of nations'.[60] It acted according to 'definitive principles' that were publicly laid down in the instrument of the mandate, on behalf of and in the name of the League rather than according to its sovereign right, as was the case in the Berlin Act.[61] The organs of the League were the PMC, the League Council and the Permanent Court of International Justice (PCIJ). The PMC, composed of 'experts' with past experiences in colonial administration, was considered the 'centre of mandatory supervision'. This body was tasked with supervision through its scrutiny of the annual reports submitted by the mandatories, advising both the mandatory states and the Council on their international obligations.[62] It is revealing that the majority of the members of the PMC were lawyers and jurists, for they saw their function in 'legalistic terms' and tended to take a 'strictly legal approach', at times fusing the law with their administrative functions.[63] In that sense, the PMC reflected the legal character of the Mandate system, which was entirely based on 'legal norms and gave rise to justiciable legal obligations on the part of the mandatory'.[64] In addition to its emphasis on legalism, the PMC also focused on fact-finding and standard setting.

The Mandate system was classified on the basis of a racialised view of the world as it included evolutionist categories based on various stages of development attributed to each formerly colonised region and peoples as compared

[56] Lindsey, *supra*, 332.

[57] SN Grovogui, *Sovereigns, Quasi-Sovereigns, and Africans: Race and Self-determination in International Law*, (University of Minnesota Press, 1996), 85.

[58] D Kennedy, "A Move to Institutions," (1987) 8 *Cardozo Law Review* 841–988.

[59] D Hall, *Mandates, Dependencies and Trusteeships* (Carnegie Endowment for International Peace, 1948), 12.

[60] Bentwich, *supra*, 5.

[61] *Ibid*. *See* Wright, *supra*, 23.

[62] Wright, *ibid*, 137-138.

[63] Anghie, *Imperialism, supra*, 151.

[64] *Ibid*,153.

to the European 'Standard of Civilisation'. The 'A' Mandates were at the top of this hierarchy, and were designated for the territories of the former Arab provinces of the Turkish Empire, and were said to have 'reached a stage of development where their existence as independent nations can be provisionally recognised, subject to the rendering of administrative advice and assistance by the Mandatory until such time as they are able to stand alone'.[65] The 'B' Mandates were designated for the territories of Central Africa, and were considered as requiring a number of years (perhaps decades) of tutelage under their Mandatories, who were given wider powers for the administration of these territories. Finally, the 'C' Mandates were designated for the 'primitive' peoples of the Pacific, who were to be governed as part of the mandatory territory, considering their remoteness from the metropole and sparseness of their populations.[66] This hierarchal categorisation exemplifies the continuities between the interwar international legal order and the previous nineteenth century international system as it clearly reflected elements of the classical 'standard of civilisation.' As Ntina Tzouvala has argued persuasively, the Mandate system was an attempt to ensure that mandated territories could at least *in theory* attain the Western standard of civilisation. In reality, of course, this meant 'socio-economic transformation with the view to spreading market relations and the capitalist mode of production outside the West'.[67] The very structure of the Mandate implied the 'Eurocentric idea that there was something inherent in Western culture, religion or racial composition … that enabled or even necessitated the transition to capitalism [and] modernity …'[68] The text of Article 22, consequently, reflected these contradictory aspects of the standard of civilisation, a 'historically contingent structure', which was used in the nineteenth century to violently annex territories, and was now being used to integrate formerly colonised territories into the international system and in turn, the global capitalist system.[69] Considering its flexibility as a 'mode of legal argumentation,' the standard was effectively embedded within the text of Article 22.[70] In this way, the novel structures of the Mandate system remained embedded within aspects of the nineteenth century Standard of Civilisation that was used to justify imperialism and conquest in the Third World. It was merely rearticulated and reinterpreted in a manner that was consistent with the emerging international legal order.

Consequently, despite the obvious racial dimensions of these classifications, my argument is that at the heart of these categories, especially the 'A' Mandates' of Palestine, Transjordan, Lebanon, Syria and Mesopotamia (Iraq),

[65] *Covenant of the League of Nations*, 28 April 1919, 13 (1919) *AJIL Sup*. 128.
[66] Margalith, supra, 29.
[67] Tzouvala, *Capitalism as Civilisation*, *supra*,102.
[68] *Ibid*, 98.
[69] *Ibid*.
[70] *Ibid*, 103.

there was more a concern for geopolitics and economic questions of capital accumulation in the Middle East, especially that of oil – its control and extraction from Iraq, and its transportation by pipelines through Palestine, Syria and Lebanon to the ports on the Mediterranean sea. In other words, the 'A' Mandates were classified as such for reasons that were not primarily because Arabs were actually seen as being 'more civilised' or more developed than African peoples but because of the importance of the region's natural resources. The 'A' Mandates were carved out for several reasons unique to the history of the region, such as the performative attempts to fulfil previous promises concerning Arab independence made by the British, but especially for the necessity of *appearing* as though colonial exploitation of the old variety was not continuing there. This was precisely because exploitation of natural resources was expected and plans for these designs were underway. The 'A' Mandates were also meant to be laboratories for legal experimentation in what Lord Cromer called 'administrative internationalism',[71] especially with the concept of sovereignty in international law – searching for the right legal 'ingredients' needed for the construction of a non-European sovereignty that concealed the reality of Western geopolitical designs over the Middle East, ensuring the continuous flow of capital and oil, while *simultaneously* being technically consistent with the new principles of international law of the time.

Many legal scholars have generally avoided an overall analysis of the 'A' Mandates, which tended not only to be differentiated from the 'B' and 'C' Mandates, but also between each other. The 'A' Mandates were generally regarded as 'special cases' that should be studied separately.[72] However, my argument is that the 'A' Mandates were in fact all interconnected and should be so considered, especially if one wants to grasp the political, social and economic background of the Middle East region as a whole. It was how the great powers themselves saw the region after all. Helmut Mejcher's classic study on British imperial oil policy in Iraq has emphasised that, '[a] Model "A" Mandate would provide the guide-lines that could set policy in Iraq on the right path and would help devise a homogeneous administrative system for the entire Middle East'.[73] This experiment with the 'A' Mandates would, in turn, be valuable for devising a model for so-called 'independence' for the 'B' Mandates, and other post-colonial Third World states. Consequently, it is only by understanding the geopolitical elements behind the 'A' Mandate category, while identifying their distinct characteristics as they relate to international law, that one could properly grasp the place of Iraq in the regional and international context of the Mandates system.

[71] Quoted in Beer, *supra*, 423.
[72] Margalith, *supra*, 125.
[73] H Mejcher, *Imperial Quest for Oil: Iraq 1910-1928* (Ithaca Press, 1976), 63.

## IV. THE ARAB PEOPLE'S REJECTION OF THE MANDATE SYSTEM AND THE PRINCIPLE OF TUTELAGE

Article 22 stated that the 'A' Mandates were meant to take the wishes of the peoples of the region into consideration as to the selection of the Mandatory power. However, this principle was completely ignored. The reality on the ground clearly did not reflect the people's wishes. All out revolts broke out, notably in Syria (1919) and Iraq (1920), not only against the Mandatory powers of France and Britain, but against the Mandate system itself, including the very idea of 'tutelage'. This led to the violent repression of these revolts, and the virtual imposition of the mandates over the region.

From the very beginning of the Peace Conference, Arab elites made calls for the complete independence of their emerging states. Prince Faisal's speech to the Supreme Council, introducing himself as 'the [former] commander of the Syrian revolt', declared: 'I base my claims [of self-determination] on the principles enunciated by President Wilson'.[74] Faisal urged the Council that 'the Arabic-speaking peoples of Asia, from the line Alexandretta-Diarbekr southward to the Indian Ocean, be recognised as independent sovereign peoples, under the guarantee of the League of Nations'.[75] Directly challenging the logic of the (Western) Standard of Civilisation, which was the basis of the Mandate system, he retorted to the suggestion that Mandates were necessary in the region with an emphasis on the long history of Arab-Islamic civilisation and its golden age: '[m]y nation has a great civilisation [he said]. When my nation was civilised, the [European] nations you represent were still barbaric and savage. I ask you not to demean this nation that has truly served civilisation'.[76] Speaking in French to the Conference delegates, Faisal's close advisor Rustum Haider questioned the vagueness of the term 'Mandate' in Article 22, implying that it could be manipulated as a tool of domination by Mandatory powers:

> What does the word 'mandate' mean? We do not exactly know. I only wish to say that the nations in whose name I speak intend to remain free to choose the Power whose advice they will ask. Their right to decide their fate in the future has been recognised in principle. Very well! But you will allow me to say, Gentlemen, that a secret agreement to dispose of these nations has been prepared [i.e. the Sykes-Picot Accord], about which we have not been consulted. I ask the Assembly whether this state of [affairs] ought to exist or not.[77]

[74] 'Territorial Claims of the Government of the Hedjaz,' Document 251 in DH Miller. *My Diary at the Conference of Paris: Documents, Volume 4* (Appeal Printing Company, 1924), 297–301.

[75] *Ibid*, 300.

[76] EF Thompson, *How the West Stole Democracy from the Arabs: The Syrian Arab Congress of 1920 and the Destruction of its Historic Liberal-Islamic Alliance* (Atlantic Monthly Press, 2020), 80.

[77] TNA FO 371/4310, Preliminary Peace Conference, Session of Feb. 14, 1919; as quoted in M Provence, *The Last Ottoman Generation and the Making of the Modern Middle East* (CUP, 2017), 69.

Although Haider considered his speech as having had a great appeal, Wilson ignored his reservations, and Clemenceau quickly called the session to a close.[78] Haider clearly grasped the matter at hand: the ambiguity of the concept of the 'Mandate' meant that it was the Mandatory powers that would interpret the meaning of Mandatory rule. He was not wrong in his overall assessment, especially considering that the spirit of Sykes-Picot was reflected in the Mandatory arrangements. In fact, as early as March 1917, the Mesopotamian Administration Committee (MAC), chaired by arch-imperialist Lord Curzon, and which was tasked with developing a strategy for the future governance of Iraq had already devised that it was to be, 'an Arab State with local rule of Government under British protectorate in everything but name'.[79] It was, in other words, to be administered behind 'an Arab façade … by indigenous agency and in accordance with existing laws and institutions as far as possible'.[80] This façade of 'Arab sovereignty', however, needed to be 'something more than [just] a façade';[81] that is, it needed be articulated, legitimised, and concealed even further through the legal principles and ideological labels of the emerging international order. British administrators were, therefore, already aware of the changing winds of the time, and of the necessity of having a collaborator local ruling class, acting behind an 'Arab façade' that concealed the reality of British imperial domination. Even Mark Sykes, himself a member of the MAC, seemed to have renounced the concept of secret diplomacy, which he previously practiced during the war, when he declared that

> we have to look at the problem through entirely new spectacles. Imperialism, annexation, military triumph, prestige, White men's burdens, have been expunged from the popular political vocabulary, consequently, Protectorates, spheres of interest or influence, annexations, bases etc., have to be consigned to the Diplomatic lumber-room … if Britishers are to run Mesopotamia we must find up to date reasons for their doing so and up to date formulae for them to work the country on.[82]

Nevertheless, this technique of obfuscation was already a well-known method in the practices of Britain's informal Empire as detailed earlier, and so it could certainly be repurposed through an 'up to date formulae', such as the manufacturing of a novel non-European sovereignty, to be consistent with Wilsonian principles, the League institutions and the Mandate system.

With the conclusion of the San Remo Conference in 1920, the 'A' Mandates were divided up between the French and British. The conference justified the occupation of Syria by the French, consolidated British mandatory control over Iraq, and allowed for the emergence of a policy of Zionist settler colonial

[78] *Ibid.*
[79] TNA. CAB 24/9, 'Chamberlain to Chelmsford,' 29 March 1917.
[80] *Ibid.* For more on the Mesopotamian Administration Committee see J Fisher, *Curzon and British Imperialism in the Middle East 1916-19* (Frank Cass, 1999).
[81] Mejcher, *supra*, 52.
[82] As quoted in J Fisher, *supra*, 124.

expansion in Palestine by recognising the 1917 Balfour Declaration.[83] It was no wonder that the year 1920 would be known in Arab annals as *ʿAm al-Nakba* ('the Year of Catastrophe').[84] The betrayal of San Remo and the resulting disillusionment of the Arab peoples led to spontaneous outbreaks of mass discontent and uprisings. As historian George Antonius demonstrates, San Remo utterly disregarded the wishes of the Arab peoples and so 'it was regarded ... as a retrograde and wasteful measure which violated not only the promises made but also the principles of decency in the treatment of weaker nations ... the very principles which the mandates were originally created to serve'.[85]

In Iraq, in the summer of 1920, a revolution that united the diverse populace, religious leaders and tribes was launched from the mid-Euphrates region. Like its Syrian counterpart, it was an unequivocal rejection of the mandate and mandatory rule. The British quickly realised the difficulty of directly imposing the mandate instrument on the people and so devised a plan to circumvent the Mandate document, which was never ratified, by replacing it with a 'treaty'. After the Cairo Conference of 1921, which further cemented British arrangements in the region by selecting the demoralised Hejazi Prince Faisal (recently defeated by the French and expelled from Syria) to the throne of the incipient Iraqi state, a British Conference of Legal Advisors prepared a draft treaty that would be put forward to Faisal for approval.[86] Almost immediately, a petition signed by tribal notables of the mid-Euphrates was sent to Parliament and the Royal Palace, which unanimously rejected the treaty and demanded 'a free representative, and democratic government that was responsible before the nation'. It called for an Iraqi government that was, 'completely politically independent, unadulterated, and devoid of any foreign interference'. It further stated unequivocally the people's 'rejection of the English Mandate, and any treaty that impinge on the honour of the Iraqi nation and its complete political independence'.[87] A similar petition was sent to the League of Nations, which stated: '[w]e reject any Mandate, and protest any decision that opposes Iraq's complete independence'.[88] The very term 'Mandate' [*intidāb*] became synonymous with colonisation and imperialism. Iraqis found it 'extremely distasteful, considering it to be a disguise for another form of colonialism'.[89] The general nationalist feeling toward the Mandate and the terminology used by the British

[83] See J Quigley, *Britain and its Mandate over Palestine: Legal Chicanery on a World Stage* (Anthem Press, 2022).

[84] G Antonius, *The Arab Awakening: The Story of the Arab National Movement* (Capricorn Books, 1965), 358.

[85] *Ibid*, 358.

[86] J Franzen, *Pride and Power: A Modern History of Iraq* (Hurst, 2020), 28.

[87] Hasani, *Tarikh al-Wizarat*, Vol. 1-2, *supra*, 71.

[88] The petition sent to the League of Nations stated that 'the Iraqis have proven their desire for complete independence, and their rejection of any mandate whatsoever. Their important movement of 1920 is the greatest evidence of this ... We reject any mandate, and protest against any decision that opposes Iraq's complete independence'. *Al-Istiqlal*, no.102, 6 June 1922, quoted in *Ibid*.

[89] AA Al-Marayati, *A Diplomatic History of Modern Iraq* (Robert Speller & Sons, 1961), 15.

and the League was expressed in the newspaper *al-Istiqlāl*. The Iraqi people were not deceived by legal terminology or labels – they called for nothing less than *Istiqlāl Tāmm* ['Complete Independence']:

> We do not reject the mandate because of its name, but because its meaning is destructive of [complete] independence .... Words like *intidab* ['mandate'], *wusayah* ['guardianship'], *himayah* ['protection'], *itiman* ['affiliation'], *musa'adah* ['aid'], *muhalif* ['ally'], *ishraf* ['supervision'/'guidance'] and *musharafah* ['tutelage'] are used by the colonisers; they all translate [to and are reflected in the international concept of the] "Mandate" and are intended to deceive weak nations. The name only is changed; just in the same way they talk of liberating humanity, helping the weak, etc.[90]

In a popular poem written by Mohammed Habīb al-ʿUbaīdi, the very notion of *wusāyah* [guardianship] was not only challenged with the rhetorical question, 'We accept the English as our guardian?' repeated throughout, but was also rejected as being an insult to the religious sensibilities of the people, in particular the Shiʿa who regarded only Imam Alī bin Abī Tālib, the cousin and son-in-law of the Prophet, as their legitimate guardian:

> O *al-gharb* [the West], you have come with the unprecedented
> We have known no other guardian, but The Guardian[91]
> We swear by the Quraʾan and the Bible
> We will not accept a guardian for any tribe
> Or else blood will flow like the rivers
> [For] is there a guardian after the Husband of the Maiden?[92]
> We accept the English as our guardian?[93]

The 'Great 1920 Revolution' [*Thawrat al-ʿIshrīn al-Kubrā*] as it came to be known in Iraqi historiography was ultimately crushed with overwhelming violence through the decimation of tribes by British-Indian forces, the aerial bombardment of villages, and the use of poisonous gas.[94] Before resuming our narrative to describe the features of the 1922 Anglo-Iraq Treaty and the institutions of the Iraqi state, we will pause for an analytic interlude to deconstruct the concept of the 'semi-periphery' as it goes to the heart of the book's argument.

[90] As quoted in Ireland, *supra*, 285.

[91] Alī bin Abī Tālib, who was also known as, the Commander and Guardian of the Faithful, is revered by Shiʿas.

[92] The 'Husband of the Maiden' is a reference to Alī bin Abī Tālib, who was married to Fātīma, the daughter of the Prophet. Fātīma was referred to by the Prophet as 'a maiden of paradise'.

[93] Ibrahim Harāj al-Waʾili. *Thawarat al-ʿishrin fī al-shʿir al-ʿIraqī* [The 1920 Revolution in Iraqi Poetry] (Baghdad: Al-Iman Press, 1968), 38-9. Al-ʿUbaīdi (1880-1963) was an Islamic scholar and poet from Mosul. He wrote a polemical book detailing the crimes of the British Empire entitled *Janāyāt al-ạnjlyz ʿala ạlbasẖari ʿāmātïa waʿala ạl-mušlimīn kẖāṣātïan* [The Crimes of the English on Humanity in General and the Muslims in Particular] (Baghdad, 1916).

[94] *See* I Rutledge, *Enemy on the Euphrates: The Battle for Iraq, 1914-1921* (Saqi Books, 2015).

## V. THE CONCEPT OF THE 'SEMI-PERIPHERY' AND ITS SIGNIFICANCE IN INTERNATIONAL LAW

The concept of the 'semi-periphery' emerged from historical sociology and was famously coined by world-systems theorist, Immanuel Wallerstein.[95] It is used in this study as an analytic tool to refer to those states that were free from traditional and formal colonialism but that were still subject to informal imperial control. The concept already contains a certain elasticity that may explain why it is difficult to define, but it essentially denotes an 'intermediate' status of economically and politically weak states that nevertheless had a limited amount of agency, and therefore mediated between centres of economic power, production and distribution, and underdeveloped zones that supplied raw materials.[96] The 'intermediate role' of the semi-periphery contains a unique historical specificity that must not be overlooked by international legal scholars. Wallerstein himself emphasised that semi-peripheral states have 'special political properties'.[97] This entails that its juridical and legal properties are likewise unique. What this study seeks to do is to contribute to the emerging literature in international legal scholarship that finds this concept very useful in describing the dynamism and uniqueness of such an 'intermediate' role in international law.[98] The semi-periphery could be found in notions of the 'semi-civilised' in international law for instance, and this suggests that the concept of the semi-periphery has a unique juridical as much as an economic dimension and function. It is this notion of the 'semi-civilised' that was reflected in the 'A' Mandate designation in relation to the 'B' and 'C' Mandates. As Umut Özsu argues, taking the semi-periphery seriously, '… simply forces us to confront the reality that the international legal system is inseparable from a global capitalist order with a largely Euro-American infrastructure …'[99] It is also inseparable from questions of geopolitics. The 'semi-periphery' is, in other words, the perfect analytic tool to elucidate the economic dimensions of certain juridical formations and this is the main task at hand.

We have already noted that there has been a relative lack of focus on the semi-periphery in critical international legal scholarship, which has generally

[95] See I Wallerstein. 'Semi-Peripheral Countries and the Cotemporary World Crises' (1976) 3 *Theory & Society*, 461.

[96] See G Arrighi, *Semiperipheral Development: the politics of Southern Europe in the Twentieth Century*, (Sage, 1985).

[97] I Wallerstein, *World-Systems Analysis: An Introduction*, (Duke University Press, 2004), 29.

[98] See RS Horowitz, 'International Law and State Transformation in China, Siam, and the Ottoman Empire during the Nineteenth Century' (2004) 15 J World Hist 445; L Obregon. 'Completing Civilization: Creole Consciousness and International Law in Nineteenth-Century Latin America' in A Orford (ed.), *International Law and its Others* (Cambridge: CUP, 2006); T Kayaoglu, *Legal Imperialism: Sovereignty and Extraterritoriality in Japan, the Ottoman Empire and China*, (CUP, 2015).

[99] U Özsu, "From the 'semi-civilized state' to the emerging market': remarks on international legal history of the semi-periphery," in U Mattei and J Haskell (eds.) *Research Handbook on Political Economy and Law* (Edward Elgar, 2015), 246–259; 258.

approached international law based on a strict dichotomy between the periphery and the core.[100] Legal scholars have, as a consequence, overlooked the role of the semi-periphery in the development of international law. Moreover, they have failed to make clear distinctions between the periphery and semi-periphery in relation to international law, in particular when it comes to their analyses of the Mandate System. As Duncan Hall has warned, to theorise the Mandatory system in the wrong historical and political context could lead to numerous errors, one of which is 'obscuring' the relationship between the mandate systems to other species of imperial governance.[101] Moreover, to assume that the 'A' Mandates were 'special cases' (i.e. of a *sui generis* nature) that should be distinguished from the overall system 'minimises the great importance of the Near East Mandates'. The 'A' Mandates should not be considered exceptional 'special cases', but rather 'the main range itself,' while 'the African mandates were the lesser ridges branching off from it'.[102] It is in this way that the semi-peripheral region of the Middle East could be considered as a legal laboratory of the time, especially with regards to the concept of sovereignty and how it could be applied to newly emerging Third World states.

Antony Anghie has argued that it was the 'displacement and reconfiguration' of the *location* of sovereignty by international lawyers that allowed for the construction of a novel form of sovereignty situated within the international institution of the mandate and its processes.[103] That is, the characterisation of the mandatory territory as possessing 'latent sovereignty' gave the Mandatory power the space and legitimacy to penetrate the interiority of the territory in question, considerably transforming its character and society.[104] Anghie, however, did not consider how his analysis, which works well for the periphery (the 'B' and 'C' Mandates), works for the semi-periphery (the 'A' Mandate), where sovereignty was *conditional* and expressly *provisional*, rather than (temporarily or permanently) postponed.

In this case the question becomes: why was there a need to have a situation in which sovereignty *appears* to be provisional in the first place? How would the Mandatory power actually have 'complete access' to a territory if sovereignty were not fully suspended[105] as it was in the periphery? The answer I think lies in the necessity for the construction of a flexible space for legal experimentation with this provisional sovereignty for the future geopolitical control of this oil-rich strategic region. That is, the aim of the Iraqi experiment was to manufacture a non-European sovereignty that not only had the *appearance* of being

[100] For a history of the TWAIL network, see J Gathii, "TWAIL: A Brief History of its Origins, its Decentralized Network, and a tentative Bibliography," 3(1) *Trade Law and Development*, (2011): 26.

[101] Hall, *supra*, 12.

[102] *Ibid*.

[103] Anghie, *Heart*, *supra*, 494-495; Quincy, *supra*, 500-08.

[104] Anghie, *Imperialism*, *supra*, 149.

[105] See D Campbell Lee, *The Mandate for Mesopotamia and the Principle of Trusteeship in English Law* (The League of Nations Union, 1921), 19.

unimpaired, but also was technically consistent with international law, while the former mandated territory simultaneously remained under the economic influence of the Western powers. It was consequently an attempt to push the concept of sovereignty to its utmost limits without compromising it under the law, while preserving and serving the (economic and geopolitical) crux of imperialism in the Third World.

I want to, therefore, suggest that this experimentation in Iraq, with the use of certain legal technologies, including plebiscites, treaties, organic laws, and minority protection regimes, as well as legal reasoning and (at times contradictory) arguments developed in Geneva, was essential for the manufacturing of a non-European sovereignty that was not only unique to the Middle East, but that would eventually become a model for the domination of future independent Third World states – a *semi-peripheral sovereignty* that although allowed a newly 'independent' state to join the international society of nations, ensured that its sovereignty remained *both* politically constrained and economically valuable at the same time. It is in this way that what emerged when Iraq became 'independent' was not only a model for other states in the region, reflecting the manner in which imperialism remained embedded within the emergent international legal order, but also it contributed to the structuring of what would later be referred to as 'neo-colonialism' in the context of the post-colonial Third World.

## VI. THE 1922 ANGLO-IRAQ TREATY: ITS FEATURES, CHARACTERISTICS AND RATIFICATION

Following the defeat of the 1920 Revolution, the British were now convinced of the necessity of drafting a new treaty to reflect the Mandatory arrangements with Iraq. To begin formal negotiations, Prince Faisal had to be crowned as King of Iraq so that there was an official party to contract with on behalf of the state. Faisal's ascension to the throne was, therefore, consequently legitimised through a (sham) plebiscite. His coronation took place in Baghdad on 23 August 1921.[106] Although Faisal was unhappy with the restrictive conditions of the new treaty, he thought that, from a pragmatic standpoint, at least the treaty was technically not a mandate (the hated word did not appear in any of the provisions). He was, however, particularly concerned with how his subordination to Britain could injure his prestige amongst the people.[107] He was a Hejazi from present-day Saudi Arabia after all, and so had no social base in Iraq to rely on. 'I am aware,' he wrote, 'that it is not within my power to resist the establishment of the Mandate should Great Britain insist on it'. However, he became convinced

[106] *See* A Klieman, *Foundations of British Policy in the Arab World: The Cairo Conference of 1921* (John Hopkins University Press, 1970).
[107] Franzen, *supra*, 28.

that exchanging the Mandate for a treaty was a favourable outcome, considering that, '[t]he people have acquired a repugnance towards the term "Mandate," its terms, and interpretations, which is a result of what they have observed in the way of abuse by the Mandatory of his Mandate for the realisation of private aims and objects'.[108]

The Anglo-Iraqi Treaty was ultimately signed by Percy Cox and King Faisal on 10 October 1922.[109] It was written in the contractual language of 'mutuality' and 'reciprocity,' skillfully reproducing the Mandatory relationship in a more acceptable form, while deliberately avoiding the use of the term. The cornerstone of 'indirect control' in the Treaty was the requirement that the Iraqi government appoint British advisors at every governmental post. Ministers were required to consult with British advisors on all courses of action before coming to any decision. The High Commissioner himself was the advisor to the King. This parallel British advisory system was considered as the backbone of the Iraqi state. Supplementary agreements ensured that key military, foreign relations, judicial and financial posts were in British hands.

On April 30, 1923, a Protocol to the Treaty was signed as a measure to try to end the boycott of elections to the Constituent Assembly in opposition to the treaty. The Protocol confirmed that 'the present Treaty shall terminate upon Iraq becoming a member of the League of Nations and in any case no later than four years from the ratification of peace with Turkey'.[110] Although the whole point of the treaty arrangement was to avoid the appearance of a mandatory relationship, the Council of the League only approved the 1922 Treaty in September of 1924 after the Assembly was coerced into ratifying it.[111] The treaty maintained British dominance over the Iraqi state and its institutions, limiting the state's constitutional structures. It was ultimately amended to become intertwined with the structures of the 1925 Iraqi Constitution or Organic Law, enshrining wide executive powers and constricting parliamentary sovereignty, so as to allow the King and Cabinet (through the influence of the High Commissioner) to uphold the

[108] TNA. CAB/24/136 CP 3903, 'Translation of a Letter from King Faisal to Cox'. 23 February 1922.

[109] *Anglo-Iraq Treaty of Alliance, 1922, Cmd 2370.*

[110] A revised treaty was signed on January 13, 1926, which accounted for the new circumstances that had come about with the final settlement of the Turco-Iraqi frontier. This treaty merely extended the provisions of the 1922 Treaty for 25 years, unless Iraq was admitted to the League before the end of the period. The 1926 Treaty was presented to the Council and accepted in March 1926. Finally, another revised treaty was signed on December 14, 1927 (Cmd. 2998) with a new proviso that stated that it should not be ratified until the financial and military agreements were revised and approved by the League. It was suggested at the time that Iraq could be considered for League membership by 1928. The 1927 Treaty was never approved as there were disagreements over the revision of the financial and military agreements. There was a deadlock, and negotiations dragged on until September 1929 when the matter was dropped on the understanding that unreserved British support would be given for Iraq's emancipation from the mandate for 1932.

[111] *See* Q Wright, "The Government of Iraq," (1926), 20(4) *The American Political Science Review*, 743, 765. Wright regarded Article 22 of the League of Nations Covenant, the League Mandate and the Treaty *with* the Organic Law, as forming part of the constitutional documents of Iraq; *supra*, 747.

provisions of the treaty.[112] For instance, Article 26(c) gave the King the power to override constitutional procedures the Royal prerogative by dissolving parliament and issuing ordinances that had 'the force of law' for the fulfillment of 'treaty obligations'.[113] Moreover, any measure pertaining to the application of treaty obligations only required the approval of the Cabinet and did not require the approval of parliament. Part X of the Organic Law also provided for the proclamation of martial law in case of disturbances. Finally, the King had an absolute veto over all laws and ministerial orders.[114] The Constitution, therefore, ensured that the entire relationship between the Iraqi state and Britain remained 'outside the constitutional order,' wholly governed by the treaty, which emanated from international law and its order.[115] This arrangement allowed the British wide room to maneuver and influence the King to not deviate from the treaty provisions, and in turn, from British imperial policy. Through these mechanisms the Constitution was essentially turned into 'an instrument of British [imperial] policy', allowing for constitutional maneuverability for the British to 'obtain the necessary legislation to execute treaty obligations and grant concessions to British-backed oil companies'.[116]

The British drew from their past practices and techniques of informal empire, in particular the instrument of the 'unequal treaty' from their experiences in India, the Persian Gulf, Egypt, to the Iraqi plane. The American international lawyer, Quincy Wright illustrated how the British tradition of imperial and informal administration, which allows for the subordination of *form rather than substance*, was developed in Egypt and imported to Iraq: 'If British administrators can make the government run the way they want,' he wrote, 'they are willing to dispense with the appearance of power'.[117] While the instrument of the unequal treaty was historically utilised to *exclude* the non-European from international law in the nineteenth century, in the case of Iraq, the treaty was brought in to do the opposite: to express the Mandatory relationship, and create a 'sovereign Iraqi state' under international law that would eventually join the society of nations. The legal experiment that ensued in Iraq brought about novel legal practices to ensure that Iraq's 'inclusion' into international society remained an exclusionary measure. This exclusion, however, would now occur *within* the ambit of international law and *through* its mechanisms rather than without it, as was the case with the Arab States of the Persian Gulf or the Indian Princely States.

The 1922 Anglo-Iraq Treaty brought about some confusion to the British proposal that the Mandatory relationship was to be expressed in treaty-form

[112] See CA Hooper, *The Constitutional Law of Iraq*, (McKenzie & McKenzie, 1928).

[113] *Anglo-Iraq Treaty, amendment of 1924*.

[114] *Ibid*, Articles 62 and 63.

[115] N Brown., "Constitutionalism, Authoritarianism, and Imperialism in Iraq," *Drake Law Review*, Vol. 53 (2005): 936.

[116] Mejher, *supra*, 78, 88.

[117] Wright, "The Government of Iraq," *supra*, 748.

rather than the document of mandate itself. This was because it created the ambiguous position whereby the British had 'a mandate for Iraq vis-à-vis the League, and not one vis-à-vis Iraq'.[118] This was reflected in Lord Palmer's speech before the Council where he said that,

> We no longer think it practicable to adopt a mandatory form, even to regulate our obligations towards the League. The conception of a mandate is not popular among the people of Iraq. It is held to imply a form of tutelage inconsistent with the facts as they stand to-day and with large measure of independence which the Iraq State actually acquired ... Iraq has advanced too far along the path laid down in Article 22 of the Covenant for the particular form of control contemplated in that article to be any longer appropriate ... [t]he treaty and connected documents place the British government in a position vis-à-vis Iraq to discharge their obligations toward the League ....[119]

The Council approved the Treaty as reflecting the mandatory relationship in substance rather than in form.[120] The decision of the Council stipulated that the purpose of the treaty was 'to ensure the complete observance and execution in Iraq of the principles which the acceptance of the Mandate was intended to secure.'[121] Although the mandate was not ratified, it remained the operative document, defining the obligations of the British government towards the League and its Covenant.[122] The PMC, which also had its doubts, eventually came to the same conclusion that a Mandate existed in Iraq despite this unusual arrangement.[123] Similarly, although certain international lawyers had some misgivings, maintaining that it was possible to argue that a Mandate did not exist in Iraq, most international lawyers and publicists were eventually convinced that not only was there a mandate in Iraq, but that, 'the form of the documents seem to comply more accurately with the terms of Article 22 ... than is the case with any other class 'A' mandate'.[124] Lindley, for instance, went so far as to argue that Iraq was actually a 'sovereign state', subject to treaty conditions and advice from British advisors and experts.[125] Members of the PMC agreed. Van Rees described Iraq as 'a veritable State, an independent kingdom' considering that it concluded a treaty of alliance on a 'footing of equality' with Britian.[126] Rappard observed that Iraq 'could be compared to a two faced Janus – one face, looking towards Geneva, wearing the expression of a mandate, and the other face, looking toward Bagdad [sic], wearing the

[118] Wright, *supra* 60.
[119] *Official Journal*, V, 1314-15.
[120] See "Iraq, Papers Relating to the Application to Iraq of the Principles of Article 22 of the Covenant of the League of Nations, 1925," Great Britain, Cmd. 2317, in Wright, *supra*, Appendix II.
[121] *Ibid.*
[122] O.J., V, 1217.
[123] P.M.C., League of Nations, 7th Session, 10-14, 123.
[124] Margalith, *supra*,; Wright, *supra*, 60.
[125] Lindley, *supra*, 257.
[126] P.M.C., 7th Session, 13.

expression of a treaty … It was quite clear [he said] that Iraq was administered under Article 22 of the Covenant'.[127]

The 1922 Treaty provided that Iraq was to maintain its sovereignty as a constitutional monarchy with a representative government.[128] The instrument of the treaty was, therefore, used in this instance to distance Iraq from the mandate, while at the same time constructing a limited political subjectivity that would give Britain the ability to negotiate with the Iraqi government while maintaining its control and indirect influence over the Iraqi state. The difference with previous legal arrangements of the nineteenth century was that the non-European sovereignty that emerged was not divisible but rather indivisible with constraints imposed by the treaty. The instrument of the unequal treaty remained a subjugating one despite the 'high contracting' parties coming to a seemingly bilateral 'contractual agreement'. The mandatory subjugation over the Iraqi state was not only maintained by the treaty, but also by the newly emerging international legal order itself, which was still receptive to the old instrument of the 'unequal treaty'. So, the Iraqi arrangement should not be merely understood as a pragmatic reaction to a mere coincidence of events. It was no coincidence that the 1922 Anglo-Iraq Treaty was sanctioned by the Council as an alternative international instrument that embodied the principles of the Covenant, in turn, becoming a part of international law rather than differentiated from it as a unique form of imperial law.

The Treaty was stalled in the Constituent Assembly (the body that was tasked to pass the Iraqi constitution – or Organic law – and ratify the treaty). While the Treaty was signed in October 1922, it was only ratified in June 1924. The circumstances of ratification were so tense that opposition to the treaty was building on the streets and amongst nationalist political parties. After the King, who had tried to appeal to public opinion refused British advice to arrest the leaders of the anti-treaty movement, the High Commissioner, Percy Cox decided to take matters into his own hands when the King suddenly fell ill with appendicitis and went into surgery. Cox swiftly declared martial law, arrested and deported nationalists and dissenters, closed down anti-treaty newspapers and banned political parties and trade unions.[129] The Assembly was eventually strong-armed into ratifying the Treaty (by a narrow majority of 13 votes) after it was coerced into forming quorum in the dead of night, and given an ultimatum to either accept the treaty or allow for the possibility of reversion to the

[127] Ibid, 123.

[128] *Treaty with H.M. King Faisal*, 10 October 1922, Cmd 1757, 1922.

[129] For the classic account of this episode see A al-Wardī, *Lamahāt min Tārīkh al-'Iraq*, volume 6:171-208. For a contemporary account, see Ann Wilks, 'The 1922 Anglo-Iraq Treaty: A Moment of Crisis and the Role of Britain's Man on the Ground' *British Journal of Middle Eastern Studies*, Vol. 43, 2016, Issue 3, 342–359.

Mandate, 'in its original form'.[130] The final wording of the resolution that was passed unmistakably demonstrats that the treaty was ratified under protest:

> This Assembly considers that many of the articles of the Treaty and Agreements are *so severe* that Iraq would be unable to discharge the responsibilities of the alliance desired by the people of Iraq. But it relies upon and trusts the honour of the British government … and is confident that it will not agree to burden Iraq nor to prejudice the aspirations of the people. It is only this confidence and trust on the part of Iraq which has *induced* the Assembly to accept the statements which have been received from His Excellency the High Commissioner on behalf of the British Government, to the effect that the British Government, after the ratification of the Treaty, will amend with all possible speed the Financial Agreement ….[131]

It was, therefore, ironically through martial law that the 1922 Anglo-Iraq Treaty and by extension, the provisions of the Mandate, was eventually ratified, and the legal structures that would govern the Iraqi state were legitimised. This fact tends to be overlooked as a mere tactic by the British to enforce the treaty, but there was surely more to it than that. As Chapter 6 will show, this episode reveals how semi-peripheral sovereignty could only be maintained through the violence of emergency law. In other words, these were in fact two sides of the same coin. The imposition of the 1922 Anglo-Iraq Treaty through martial law illustrates that 'civilising' violence remained at the heart of the new international legal order and the Mandate System.[132] In that sense, martial law would reappear throughout the period in question, peaking after Iraqi independence in the 1940s and 1950s. This could be explained by the fact that martial law (and the laws of emergency) were by now a regular feature of the institutions of the new Iraqi state, but were also at the heart of the treaty relationship itself, and in turn, the mechanisms of the international institution of the Mandate and its order.

## VII. MANUFACTURING IRAQI 'INDEPENDENCE': THE 1930 ANGLO-IRAQ TREATY AND THE DOCTRINE OF SEMI-PERIPHERAL SOVEREIGNTY

We can now turn to an analysis of the legal reasoning that was developed by members of the PMC to construe Iraq as having reached 'independence' through the processes of the Mandate system and under international law. This

[130] Main, *supra*, 85.

[131] *Report by His Britannic Majesty's Government on the Administration of Iraq for the period April 1923-December 1924*, 22.

[132] The report submitted by the British government to the PMC did not even mention the violent use of martial law to force the Assembly to ratify the treaty. See *Report by His Britannic Majesty's Government on the Administration of Iraq for the period April 1923-December 1924*, 21, 22.

will allow for the deconstruction of the peculiar doctrine of non-European sovereignty that emerged, identifying its unique features and characteristics in the context of the semi-peripheral Middle East and the Third World. To reiterate, my argument is that the 'semi-peripheral non-European sovereignty' that emerged when Iraq was proclaimed as an independent state was a novel doctrine that was instrumental to the creation of the structures that perpetuated Iraq's subordination to imperialism, and the exploitation of its natural resources for decades to come, including more broadly the hegemonic control of the Middle East and its complete integration into the global capitalist economy. It is for this reason that Iraq was considered as the ideal 'model' mandate for other states in the region, as well as, eventually, for the African 'B' Mandates, and post-colonial Third World states. It also certainly explains the fact that it was considered as the proudest achievement of the Mandate system and the League. The 'A' Mandates were drawn up so as to bring about an *interconnected economic block* in the Middle East, whereby the great powers would have permanent economic influence, specifically through access to and transportation of oil resources. The doctrine of semi-peripheral sovereignty was manufactured to ensure that an 'independent' Iraqi state was legally and 'consensually' providing access to its oil deposits for the global economy. As we shall see, granting Iraq a form of non-European sovereignty, justified under international law, would make this possible as long as the oil concessions and agreements were resolved *separately* in the interests of both the Mandatory power, and the great powers.

Examining the PMC deliberations on the admission of Iraq into the society of nations, in parallel to those related to oil concessions and agreements in the region would clarify how this peculiar arrangement operated in geopolitical terms. The PMC's contradictory arguments on the meaning of independence illustrate that the questions pertaining to the economic implications of 'independence' were so vital that they had to be concealed behind other arguments that concerned the *political* requirements for the emergence of a modern (capitalist) state through the mandate process. By exposing these hidden economic dimensions, it becomes apparent how the question of (political) sovereignty was interconnected to the wider economic principle of 'open door', and how the question of oil concessions was intentionally disembedded from the overall analysis of political 'independence'. The economic dimension of the Mandate system should for this reason be considered as its most significant characteristic. This section will consequently turn to the controversial discussions relating to the oil pipeline agreements that were meant to link Iraq, Palestine and Lebanon (at the time part of Mandate Syria) with the purpose of transporting Iraqi oil to the ports of the Mediterranean, and ultimately to the world, revealing the significance of Iraq's sovereignty to the region as a whole.

In September 1929, Britain agreed to support Iraq's entry to the League of Nations and, in turn, its formal independence by 1932.[133] There was hence the need for a new treaty to detail the arrangements of the relations between the two states after formal independence. The 'Anglo-Iraqi Treaty of Alliance' was ratified in 1930 only after the most trusted and unscrupulous of the King's court, Nurī al-Saīd headed the cabinet and used his infamous firm tactics to stifle any parliamentary opposition. The treaty's contents maintained a 'close' alliance between the two states, providing that the British were bound to assist Iraqi forces when necessary. Although Iraq would finally attain control of its own military, it was obligated to receive training and equipment from Britain, and in return the Royal Air Force (RAF) would maintain two military bases rent-free by the government, while preserving its privileges and immunities.[134] Iraqi sovereignty, according to the treaty, was therefore clearly conditional and riddled with constraints – especially the British right to move troops over Iraqi soil, and the continued employment of some British judges.[135] The treaty stipulated that the British advisory system would remain intact. The economic dimensions of the 1930 Treaty were not only separated from the treaty in a financial annex, but were also vaguely couched in military terms, so as not to excite any suspicion that the British were using their mandatory position for the purpose of capitalist exploitation.[136] The treaty also ensured that all the major national and strategic assets in the country, in particular, the Port of Basra and the railways remained under British administrative control despite partial transfer of legal ownership.[137] In this way, the 1930 Treaty did not merely become the basis for, 'serving Britain's political and military interests in Iraq', it also provided, 'the means for protecting and widening British economic interests there'.[138]

The PMC was convening its Sixteenth Session in Geneva when it received word from the British representative of its intention to recommend Iraq for admission to the League of Nations.[139] At the afternoon meeting, the chairman swiftly invited the PMC to determine the procedure that needed to be followed to determine the emancipation of a Mandated territory from the Mandate, as well as, the independence of the 'A' mandate states in general. He stated that members would need to consider whether Iraq had reached the 'degree of maturity' that was acceptable for its independence.[140] This would also include

[133] See S Pederson, "Getting Out of Iraq – in 1932: The League of Nations and the Road to Normative Statehood," *American Historical Review*, (2010): 975–1000.

[134] *Treaty of Alliance between United Kingdom and Iraq*, PP 1929-1930, Cmd. 3627.

[135] *Ibid.*

[136] Sassoon, *supra*, 15.

[137] Main, *supra*, 110.

[138] Sassoon, *supra*, 16.

[139] Pederson, "Getting Out of Iraq," *supra*, 982.

[140] P.M.C. Minutes, 16th session, November 6-26, 1929, 17-20.

agreeing on the required guarantees to protect the interests of members of the League.[141] The PMC, eventually, decided that it would 'welcome entry of Iraq to the League if and when certain conditions were fulfilled, in particular that it becomes apparent that Iraq was able to *stand alone*, and that effective guarantees be secured for the observance of all treaty obligations in Iraq for the benefit of racial and religious minorities and of the members of the League of Nations'.[142] In the mean time, the PMC would take the opportunity to question the accredited representative regarding Iraq's ability to govern itself. Upon receiving this note from the Commission, the Council adopted a resolution on January 13, 1930, which requested the PMC to submit any suggestions that might assist it in coming to a conclusion.[143]

By the Eighteenth (Extraordinary) Session in June 1930, the PMC appointed a small drafting subcommittee (including members Van Rees, Rappard, Palacios and De Penha Garcia) to study the *general* conditions that would need to be fulfilled rather than merely deal with the particular case of Iraq.[144] De Penha Garcia, who was appointed as *rapporteur*, submitted a preliminary report in which he developed the general principles of law that were needed to determine the conditions of admission to the League.[145] Although the PMC was attempting to move from general principles to the particular case of Iraq, it was impossible to ignore the fact that it was the 'A' Mandate of Iraq in particular that was the reason behind this exercise. In his report, De Penha Garcia emphasised that 'there is one primary and incontestable principle – that a mandate must terminate when certain conditions are fulfilled'.[146] It was the 'maintenance of peace', he said, that was the primary factor in the development and termination of the Mandate.[147] He emphasised that the latter was connected to the preservation of the 'continuing rights' of the Mandatory powers, as '… all State members of the League … were guaranteed by the mandatory power the peaceful enjoyment of a number of rights. Consequently, when a mandate comes to an end this position must be adapted to the new state of affairs'.[148] Furthermore, termination of the Mandate depended on the 'welfare' of the native population as well as the consent of the Mandatory power, which retained a 'moral responsibility' for the consequences of the termination.[149] Finally, it was not enough that the mandate state had all the 'political institutions and administrative machinery of a modern state', it also needed to provide evidence of 'the social conditions and civic spirit that

[141] *Ibid.*
[142] *Ibid*, 203.
[143] League of Nations, *Official Journal*, 1930, 77.
[144] P.M.C., Minutes, 18th session, 43.
[145] P.M.C., Minutes, 19th session, 153-156.
[146] *Ibid*, 155.
[147] *Ibid.*
[148] *Ibid.*
[149] *Ibid.*

would ensure the regular working of these institutions and the effective exercise of the civil and political rights established by law.'[150]

De Penha Garcia went on to list the factors that were needed to determine the extent of the 'maturity of the country judged ... from a technical [and] juridical standpoint'.[151] These factors amounted to the core features of a modern capitalist (welfare) state from the European standpoint, and constituted the elements of the non-European sovereignty that was developed in the context of mandatory emancipation.[152] In brief, these features included the 'territorialisation of relations of power, state monopoly over legitimate violence through the pacification of society, judicialisation of social relations through legal reform and codification so that laws supported core market functions'.[153] Also listed was the need for the new state to make undertakings as to the adequate management of public finances, guarantees for freedom of conscience and religion, the protection of minorities, an adequate judicial system, and finally the adoption of the principle of 'economic equality' to the new situation created by the termination of the mandate.[154] Some of these conditions clearly embodied a welfarist ideology that was a reflection of the international legal order of the time, as it was expected that the new Iraqi state intervened in social and economic issues such as public health, infrastructure development, education, and, as we shall detail in the next chapter, free (wage) labour relations.[155]

De Penha Garcia's preliminary report demonstrates how the PMC were reformulating the concept of sovereignty through the Mandate process that was applied to the case of Iraq. Although it was considered a *purely* legal question, which was distinct from political and economic questions, these legal principles were clearly being developed and 'set', in the words of De Penha Garcia, by and in the interests of, 'the rich and powerful States'.[156] It is consequently by focusing on the economic dimensions of the discussions that the true nature of this novel doctrine of semi-peripheral sovereignty becomes clear. It was no surprise that the principle of 'open door' or 'economic equality' was considered by De Penha Garcia to be the very basis of the mandate system.[157] It was also clear that the mandatory power, including the members of the League, expected the continuation of certain economic rights, and it was on this specific question of 'economic equality' that disagreements arose as it was

[150] See 'Special Report of the Commission to the Council of the Proposal of the British Government with regard to the Emancipation of Iraq', P.M.C. Minutes, 21st Session, 1931, 221.

[151] P.M.C., Minutes, 19th session, 156.

[152] Ibid.

[153] Tzouvala, *supra*, 111.

[154] P.M.C., Minutes, 19th session, 153-156.

[155] See E Jouannet, *The Liberal-Welfarist Law of Nations: A History of International Law* (CUP, 2012).

[156] *Ibid*, 206.

[157] *Ibid*.

questionable how one could resolve an obligatory open door with any form of independence.

By the Twentieth Session, which was held in June-July 1931, three separate memoranda were prepared on the points in question written by Van Rees, Lugard, and De Penha Garcia. These memoranda raised some interesting issues regarding the different interpretations of independence under the Mandate System. Van Rees attempted to make the argument that the readiness of a people for independence, 'is a question of fact and not of principle, and the answer could be found only in local conditions as a whole, connected with political and administrative organisations and their working with the economic and social development of the territory'.[158] Moreover, when the mandate in question lapses, an entirely new state comes into being. For this reason, Van Rees argued that, 'you cannot say that the mandate is abrogated and at the same time use the mandate as the legal basis for the establishment of conditions which must be fulfilled by the emancipated territory'.[159] Although special conditions should be imposed on the new state, these conditions must have their basis on 'considerations foreign to the mandate'. If these conditions, 'which the civilised world have the right to make on the new state', were not accepted, then the mandated state in question would not be worthy to take its place among the society of nations.[160] Van Rees then turned to the principle of 'economic equality' and admitted that to re-establish this obligation would 'gravely impair the sovereignty of the territories declared independent.'[161] So, there must be a way to square this circle as it were, and this was done by emphasising the notion of 'reciprocity'[162] after independence. In other words, the newly 'independent' state should be able to negotiate freely on the basis of reciprocity with the former Mandatory powers on issues relating to the economic sphere, and that would suffice. The reality, of course, was that this resolution did not take into account that the international legal order served the interests of the powerful Western states, and that real 'reciprocity' was hardly possible.

The memorandum issued by Lugard, the British member, dealt with the meaning of the term 'standing alone'.[163] He argued for a liberal interpretation of these words, and expected a slow transition, whereby a state may need to stand alone, 'with the aid of a prop, or buttress to lean on' i.e. the former mandatory power.[164] Lugard ended with a summary of what was essential for the 'internal conditions' of withdrawal of the mandate, reiterating the conditions in De Penha Garcia's report.[165] As for the question of 'external conditions',

[158] P.M.C. Minutes, 20th session, 195-201.
[159] *Ibid*, 198.
[160] *Ibid*.
[161] *Ibid*, 200.
[162] *Ibid*, 185.
[163] *Ibid*, 201.
[164] *Ibid*, 201-203.
[165] *Ibid*.

Lugard argued that the state must accept 'the general principles of international law', the redisposition of the capitulations if stipulated in the mandate, the protection of the rights and religious freedom of foreigners, and finally it must accept that treaties made by the mandatory on behalf of the territory remain in force unless denounced by the new state.[166] Lugard believed that these conditions were necessary and justified, because 'emancipation from a mandate is something *more than independence*, as is shown by the fact that Iraq, though subject to the mandate regime, is already independent.'[167] As for the principle of economic equality, Lugard did not find it as an essential part of the mandate system.[168] This was not surprising considering that Britain's economic interests were already secured in Iraq – there was no need to insist on this point. The notion that 'emancipation' from the mandate process was '*more* than independence' reveals a lot about the characteristics of the emergent semi-peripheral sovereignty – *concrete sovereignty or complete independence was undesirable.* What was required was a circumscribed sovereignty that was incorporated into the international legal order on terms set by the great powers.

Finally, De Penha Garcia's memorandum reiterated that withdrawal from the mandate should not affect the 'maintenance of peace'. He argued that to require an emancipated territory to give equality of economic opportunity to members of the League would be unreasonable, but that this privilege may be granted voluntarily upon condition of reciprocity by the new state.[169] The members subsequently discussed these three memoranda in the Twentieth Session. Orts believed that with the combination of these three reports, one would be able to draft a reply to the Council. The PMC ultimately agreed that the list of obligations to be imposed by the mandated territory at the time of its emancipation from a mandate, as well as the criteria by which independence would be granted, should both be dealt with by the Council. Orts reminded the members that the Commission's job was strictly a legal one – i.e. that of laying down the legal principles for emancipation from the mandate, and it was not its place to address or make political or economic decisions, which was for the Council to do.[170]

A topic discussed at length in the sessions was that of economic equality, and its perpetuation as a guarantee. One argument made by Orts was the impossibility of imposing this principle on a truly independent state, as it would amount to an impairment of sovereignty.[171] The chairman's response was that this principle should be safeguarded as its existence amounted to, 'an acquisition on the part of the League … in that its application could not but

[166] *Ibid*, 202.
[167] *Ibid*.
[168] *Ibid*.
[169] P.M.C. Minutes, 20th Session, at 205-210.
[170] *Ibid*, at 153.
[171] *Ibid*, 156.

contribute … to the maintenance of world peace'.[172] Merlin added that the principle was necessary precisely to protect the mandated territory from a situation where the ex-mandatory power would take advantage of its position and dominate the new state economically or to set a 'price for its emancipation'.[173] The principle of the 'open door' was, therefore, according to this argument, protection from the potential of future exploitation of the ex-mandatory power. It was, eventually, agreed that economic equality was to be extended through the 'most-favoured-nation-treatment' to members of the League, which should be granted on condition of 'reciprocity' for a transitional period.[174] In other words, it was not considered an obligation, but rather a right that would be voluntarily given by the new state as a 'price for its emancipation'. It was assumed that the abstract principle of 'reciprocity' in international law was enough on its own to protect the new state from the economic domination of the ex-mandatory, which was far from reality in Iraq, where Britain dominated nearly every aspect of its economy.

On September 4, 1931, the Council refered the question regarding Iraq's case to the PMC to advise whether it had been fulfilled based on the general principles previously laid down. The PMC ultimately, but reluctantly came to the conclusion that Iraq satisfied the general conditions above. In assessing the 'de facto conditions' in Iraq, the PMC examined *The Special Report … on the Progress of Iraq, 1920-1931*, which was submitted by the British representative, and painted an auspicious picture of the progress of the Iraqi state and its institutions. The lengthy report provided an overview of the history of Mandatory rule in Iraq from its inception in 1920, and described the transformations that occurred in the context of the social, political and economic reforms undertaken in the country for the past decade. The report emphasised that the 'British never regarded the attainment of an ideal standard of administrative efficiency and stability as a necessary condition either of the termination of the Mandatory regime or of the admission of Iraq to membership of the League of Nations'. Nevertheless, it claimed that Iraq had, 'all the working machinery of a civilised government,' as it should not be compared to 'the most highly developed and civilised nations of the modern world'.[175] The Report went on to describe a detailed narrative of a linear history of improvement in a backwards environment inherited by the Ottomans. Lazy and incompetent Iraqi natives were blamed for any setbacks, not to mention the 'dangerous' and 'subversive' social and tribal strata of those who opposed British mandatory rule. The report covered diverse topics of mandatory administration, such as education, infrastructure, agriculture, public debt, the judicial system, and the protection of minorities. In all of these areas, the British insisted that there were

[172] *Ibid.*
[173] *Ibid.*
[174] *Ibid*, 185.
[175] Colonial Office. *Special Report*, 11.

considerable improvements as a result of their responsible mandatory rule. The report concluded that the British government had appropriately fulfilled its obligations and that Iraq was ready for self-governance and independence.

By April 1932, the PMC skeptical throughout most of its deliberations, where it noted that certain provisions of the treaty were 'somewhat unusual', nonetheless, ultimately unanimously concluded that Iraq had met the general conditions for the termination of the Mandate after a declaration confirming Britain's continuing 'moral responsibility' to the implications of Iraq's independence was made.[176] On October 3 1932, Iraq became the first mandated state to gain formal independence through the Mandate System, and it remains the only state to have done so entirely under the League's formal procedures. The PMC's deliberations above reveal an attempt to construct within international law a specific form of non-European semi-peripheral sovereignty that would ensure the great powers' geopolitical and economic dominance of Iraq, and of the Middle East as a whole. One notices that although questions pertaining to economics were considered as paramount concerns, they were purposely set aside as either too political or technical in nature for the PMC to analyse in detail in pragmatic terms. Yet it is my argument that if one was to focus on the underlying economic aspects of these deliberations, the main purpose of the mandate system in the context of the 'A' mandates in the Middle East would be clear. As one commentator observed, although the 'A' Mandates were made to be transitory, they were likely to leave behind 'a permanent economic monument in the shape of a new overland route across the desert from Europe to India to Persia'.[177] The Mandate system as it relates to the semi-periphery was, hence, approached in a specifically geopolitical and spatial manner that was (ironically) somewhat similar to the economic framework that defined the Sykes-Picot agreement.

An examination of the oil concessions and pipeline agreements will further illuminate the specificity of the form of non-European sovereignty that emerged in Iraq. The 'A' mandate system linked the three mandated areas economically by an oil pipeline from the Mosul oilfields to the ports of Haifa in Palestine and Tripoli in Syria. Moreover, the British government surveyed the route for a railway from Haifa to Baghdad, 'that would pass by what is today British mandated territory, and thus bring the peoples of Iraq and Palestine into one trade orbit'.[178] Norman Bentwich considered these vital economic links to be the defining characteristics of the 'A' Mandates, which he believed would eventually bring forth the political integration of these Arab states.[179] Before moving forward to this analysis, the economic principles of the Mandate system must be identified and described.

[176] PMC, Minutes, 20th session, 134; and 21st session, June 1932.

[177] AJ Toynbee, *Survey of International Affairs*, (Royal Institute of International Affairs, 1930), 174.

[178] N Bentwich, "The Termination of the A Mandates', (Max-Planck Institut für ausländisches öffentliches Recht und Völkerrecht, 1933), http://www.zaoerv.de/03_1933/3_1933_1_a_176_191.pdf, 191.

[179] *Ibid.*

## VIII. THE PRINCIPLE OF 'ECONOMIC EQUALITY' OR THE 'OPEN DOOR': THE FREEDOM OF CAPITALIST ACCUMULATION UNDER INTERNATIONAL LAW

The principle of 'economic equality,' also known as the principle of the 'open door', was one of the most important economic principles of the Mandate system.[180] Its origins lie in innovations in US foreign policy, in particular the 'Open Door Notes' issued by Secretary of State John Hay in 1899, which aimed at opening Chinese markets to American businesses after the Opium Wars. It was later expanded as a global principle that furthered, 'the access of overseas markets for trade and investment and promote a stable international system of commerce'.[181] In a way, it was the US version of informal empire that expanded to Latin America, Europe, Asia and later, the Middle East. During the interwar period, it became an essential element in the US approach to international affairs, going hand in hand with Wilsonian self-determination.[182] It was referred to by diplomatic historian, William Appleman Williams as a distinctive form of US idealist 'imperial anticolonialism'.[183] Williams considered the open door policy as 'a brilliant strategic stroke, which led to the gradual extension of American economic and political power throughout the world'.[184] It would ultimately develop from a geopolitical principle of diplomacy into a principle of international law, although it certainly maintained the assumptions of civilisational and racial superiority of the nineteenth century.[185] In a word, the idea behind this principle was that equality of economic opportunity provided an alternative to the use of force and conquest, or the establishment of exclusive alliances or zones of exclusion and influence. Consequently, economic equality was said to be necessary for the maintenance of peace in the world.

During the interwar period, the open door principle was crystalised into a legal principle through the League of Nations, as Wilson made sure to inject clauses in the draft Covenant that emphasised 'equal treatment for the commerce of all Members'.[186] It was adapted into the documents and the structures of the Mandate System, specifically in relation to the 'A' Mandates and

[180] See EC Jenkins. 'Economic Equality and the Mandates Commission' *Journal of Political Economy*, Vol. 37, No. 5 (Oct, 1929), 604–616.

[181] MP Cullinane and A Goodall. *The Open Door Era: United States Foreign Policy in the Twentieth Century* (Edinburgh University Press, 2017), 1.

[182] Wilson's Fourteen Points drew heavily from Hay's insistence on access to the world's markets. His third point called for the removal of 'all economic barriers and the establishment of equality of trade conditions among all nations consenting to peace'. Wilson also called for free navigation of the seas and for 'open covenants of peace' as opposed to secret diplomacy. *Ibid*, 70.

[183] WA Williams, *The Tragedy of America Diplomacy* (W.W. Norton, 2009).

[184] *Ibid*, 45.

[185] Cullinane and Goodall, *supra*.

[186] See Articles 8, 22, 23, Covenant of the League of Nations.

the 'B' Mandates.[187] It was explicitly referred to in Paragraph 5 of Article 22 in the context of 'B' Mandates, which stated that the Mandatory shall 'secure equal opportunities for the trade and commerce of other members of the League'.[188] In this context, the open door ensured that these mandated territories were (legally) open to world markets, essentially allowing natural resources to be exploited by *all* members of the League. It was this principle, along with rapprochement,[189] and rationalisation[190] that made up the economic principles underlying the League.[191] The aim was that 'the Mandatory must be discouraged from deriving exclusive economic and other advantages from the performance of its task'.[192] This supposedly removed 'international friction' (in theory), which would naturally arise from the 'monopolisation of commerce and resources' by any one power, and which, in turn, was the main cause of war.[193] The international lawyer, Hersch Lauterpacht considered that based on the *travaux preparatoire* preceding the drafting of the Covenant of the League of Nations, the principle of economic equality was, 'admittedly modeled after the pattern of the Berlin Treaty of 1885 relating to the Congo and the treaty of St Germain of 1919 which revised it'.[194] However, the difference between this principle and its antecedent at the end of the nineteenth century was that it prohibited any 'position of unilateral advantage' for any great power, because,

> permanent inequality of the Mandated Territory in the field of international trade must ... be rejected as ... contrary to the intention of the framers of the Mandate .... The regime of the Mandate, [Lauterpacht continued] was not conceived as a system of economic exploitation of the Mandated Territories by all the Members of the League as distinguished from exploitation by the Mandatory only.[195]

The principle of economic equality or the open door was, therefore, interpreted under international law as *not* amounting to exploitation in any way, but the

[187] Wilson's third draft of the Covenant included the following provision: 'The Mandatory State or agency shall in all cases be bound and required to maintain the policy of the Open Door, or equal opportunity for all signatories to this Covenant, in respect to the use and development of the economic resources of such people or territory.' See, Gerig, *supra*, 101-102.

[188] It was not explicitly included under the 'A' Mandates, although it was referred to in Article XI of the 1922 Anglo-Iraq Treaty and the San Remo Agreement. The open door did not apply to 'C' Mandates, which were considered as de facto annexed territory. Moreover, British Dominions also abandoned the open door policy as the British Empire resisted having this policy applied to their territories. See Gerig, *supra*, 89.

[189] The principle that political and economic cooperation was necessary for the maintenance of peace.

[190] The principle that it was necessary to control economic conditions of production, distribution and consumption.

[191] M Fakhri, *Sugar and the Making of International Law* (Cambridge university Press, 2014), 74.

[192] H Lauterpacht, *International Law: Being the Collected Papers of Hersch Lauterpacht, Volume 3, The Law of Peace*, (Cambridge University Press, 1977), 89-90.

[193] *Ibid.*

[194] *Ibid.*

[195] Lauterpacht, *supra*, 90.

reality, as the case of Iraq exemplifies, was that economic exploitation continued unabated. The only difference was that it was now justified under the principles of the new international legal order, operated under the mantle of development, and cloaked by a new form of non-European sovereignty.

The 'open door' emphasised that the preservation of free trade and foreign investment was a necessary prerequisite for the non-European sovereignty that would emerge after a mandate had run its course. Even the 'maintenance of peace,' which as we saw was referred to throughout the PMC deliberations, actually meant the maintenance of peace *for the very purpose of free trade* and commercial activity between members states of the League.[196] Hence, in theory, the open door's purpose was to avoid the possibility of war by permitting all great powers a share in the spoils of war and to have access to the natural resources of the newly acquired mandated territories in opposition to the old nineteenth approach of 'economic fortification' around one's territories – a policy known as the 'sphere of influence'.[197] In addition, the open door was generally justified on the basis that the free market through competition would ultimately be beneficial for the development of the native society (driving up wages) and its economy. The open door was, therefore, maintained to be favourable for *all* those involved, including the local population.

Research on the economic functions of the League generally lacks analyses that *link* the political and juridical aspects of the Mandate system with its underlying economic features, and how it furthered capitalism and imperialism.[198] The fact was that a specific form of political order and a corresponding legal ideology/doctrine was essential for the principle of the open door to work in the semi-periphery. It was certainly for this reason that the US government was satisfied with Britain's ultimate control over Iraq, for as long as the semi-peripheral sovereignty that emerged would ensure, 'the kind of political order receptive to capitalism and [US] foreign investment,' preserving 'the proper climate for business activity,' the US government would not oppose British designs over Iraq or the region.[199]

Semi-peripheral sovereignty, therefore, could not be understood without an examination of the economic principles that were meant to be reconciled with it, and effectively maintained in the region. Benjamin Gerig, an American member of the League Secretariat and a proponent of the open door, wrote one of the most important studies on the principle of 'open door' in 1930 in which he highlighted the significance of this link when he concluded that 'the Mandate system is undoubtedly the most effective instrument yet devised to make the

[196] Fakhri, *supra*, 74.

[197] See S Hast, *Spheres of Influence in International Relations* (Ashgate, 2014).

[198] See P Clavin, *Securing the World Economy: The Reinvention of the League of Nations, 1920-1946* (Cambridge University Press, 2015).

[199] Stivers, *supra*, 74. The PMC held that property and contract rights were to be maintained beyond the mandate. The Council followed suit by ruling that successor states must honour economic agreements made by their previous imperial overlords. Pederson, *supra*, 235.

Open Door effective'.[200] It is exactly this *link* between the (economic) principle of the open door to semi-peripheral sovereignty that emerged in the case of Iraq that should be studied, as the subordination of the mandated territory of the semi-periphery to the world economy was meant to remain intact and sustained in another form after the termination of the mandate.

## IX. THE INDEPENDENCE OF OIL PIPELINES: THE CONSTITUTIVE LINK BETWEEN IRAQI SEMI-PERIPHERAL SOVEREIGNTY AND THE IPC OIL CONCESSION

To understand this link further, the final part of the chapter will explore the discussions regarding the IPC oil concessions in Iraq and the 1931 pipeline agreements with Palestine and Syria, to analyse how they overlapped with Iraq's newly acquired sovereignty. This analysis will illuminate the unique characteristics of semi-peripheral sovereignty. It will also reveal its effects on the changing spatial configuration of the region, and in turn, on the oil workers of IPC, which will be dealt with in Chapter 4.

Oil was always at the backdrop of Iraq's modern history, although it has at times been strategically downplayed. One notices this in the PMC deliberations – oil concessions in this case were merely discussed in the context of economic equality, and even then, they were only dealt with in detail in relation to the mandated territories that were affected by the construction of pipelines that were intended to allow access of Iraqi oil to the Mediterranean.[201] Although the 'semi-peripheral sovereignty,' discussed above, was intended to make the open door policy function on the ground, the question of oil was ultimately distinguished from it by certain legal reasoning. Instead, the open door policy that was meant to (in theory) protect the interests of the Iraqi government by allowing competitive tenders from various prospects on the market, and prevent monopolisation, was in reality evaded through the use of the innovative instrument of the oil consortium. This instrument allowed the (legal) principle of open door to be satisfied (at least as far as the PMC were concerned) partially, and only in theory, while effectively circumventing it in practice. Hence, in the end, the open door policy was differentiated by the PMC in every legal question that arose on the 'A' Mandates, whether in Iraq or the wider region. My intention in this part of my argument is to emphasise that only by bringing this oil narrative closer to the question of 'semi-peripheral sovereignty' can one grasp its unique features.

The 'A' Mandates were not confirmed nor allocated (as the 'B' and 'C' mandates) until Anglo-French negotiations over Mesopotamian oil (mostly

[200] B Gerig, *The Open Door and the Mandate System: A Study of Economic Equality before and since the establishment of the Mandates System*, (George Allen & Unwin, 1930), 199.

[201] PMC Minutes, 20th session, 144-9,168-77.

concentrated in the province of Mosul and described by a German technician as 'a veritable lake of petroleum of almost inexhaustible supply'[202]) were resolved and formalised in the San Remo Conference in April 1920. The complementary oil agreement secured a 25 per cent share of the oil output for the French government, but made it clear that 'the petroleum company shall be under permanent British control'.[203] In return, the French agreed to allow for oil pipelines to pass through their mandatory territories and to 'the construction of two separate pipelines and railways necessary for their construction and maintenance and for the transport of oil from Mesopotamia and Persia'.[204] The British justified taking control of the oil fields in Mosul by reference to the London-based Turkish Petroleum Company's (TPC) unratified prewar concession agreement with the Ottoman government of 1914, which secured the British APOC (later renamed BP) 50 per cent of the share of the concession, while promising the 'native government' up to a 20 per cent share.[205] The terms of the San Remo Agreement 'fed fires of mistrust and reinforced the American view that the British intended to exclude Americans from the exploration for oil in the old Ottoman Empire'.[206] The US protested their exclusion on political and legal grounds, alleging a violation of the open door principle, while the British denied that they were attempting to devise a monopoly.[207] The Americans used the open door principle to argue that the British should not discriminate against US citizens in Palestine and Iraq.[208] They also maintained that it had materially contributed to the Allied victory, and were, therefore, entitled to the fruits of this victory. The TPC concession, they argued, had no legal validity, and US citizens 'must … be given an equal opportunity to exploit Mesopotamian oil fields'.[209] Although

[202] See EM Earle, *Turkey, the Great Powers, and the Baghdad Railway: a Study in Imperialism*, (Macmillan, 1923), 15; as quoted in T Mitchell. *Carbon Democracy: Political Power in the Age of Oil*, (Verso, 2011), 48.

[203] See the full text of the agreement in JC Hurewitz, *Diplomacy in the Near and Middle East*, (Van Nostrad, 1958) 75-77. Anglo-Persian Oil was to hold half of the share in the ownership of the company, while Shell controlled the other half. See Mitchell, *supra*, 95.

[204] Quoted in B Shwadran, *The Middle East, Oil and the Great Powers* (Praeger, 1955), 203. Article 5 of the San Remo Agreement stated: 'It was agreed that the building of pipe-lines over French mandates territory was to entitle France to special consideration for procuring a portion of the oil from the Anglo-Persian Company's supplies. In turn, oil so conveyed and exported was to be free from export and transit duties, and all materials necessary to the construction of refineries, railways, pipe-lines, and other equipment was to be free from import duties and wayleaves.'

[205] See M Kent, *Oil and Empire: British Policy and Mesopotamian Oil, 1900-1920*, (Macmillan, 1976).

[206] JA DeNovo, *American Interests and Policies in the Middle East 1900-1939* (The University of Minnesota Press, 1963), 177. It was not until the signing of the Anglo-American-Iraqi Convention on January 9, 1930 that the US officially recognised the government of Iraq and the British mandate. After Iraq joined the League, the US signed a new treaty of alliance with Iraq in 1934. *Ibid*, 349, 350.

[207] See the Colby-Curzon correspondence: *Parlimentary Papers*, Cd. 1226 (1921).

[208] The Americans formulated a coherent policy towards the Middle East during the interwar period through the open door policy. See AT Samuel, 'The Open Door and U.S. Policy in Iraq between the World Wars' *Diplomatic History*, Vol. 38, No. 5 (2014).

[209] Shwadran, *supra*, 207.

unenthusiastic about the open door principle, the British decided to avoid any serious clash with the US government and granted a part of the concession to American companies, revising the agreement in 1923. The US-owned Standard Oil Company (with a consortium of US companies) was consequently promised a 25 per cent share of its monopoly concession in the exploitation of oil in Iraq.[210]

Following this understanding, the Turkish Petroleum Company (which was renamed, the Iraq Petroleum Company in 1929) began direct negotiations with the Iraqi government. Although the Iraqi government with the help of the British negotiated certain terms that would prevent the TPC from intentionally delaying production for the purpose of inflating oil prices on the market (such as a timeline for the construction of a pipeline and a minimum level of production), the most important demand, which would have ensured the implementation of these terms – an actual share of ownership – did not materialise. The oil companies refused to budge on this issue, and the Iraqi government finally capitulated, signing the concession in March 1925. The oil companies were, therefore, successful in establishing an exclusive TPC concession, which included exclusive rights of exploration in all of Iraq (with the exception of the province of Basra), while fully removing Iraqi part-ownership.

These negotiations occurred while the question of Mosul was still looming.[211] The territorial dispute over Mosul, the province where the bulk of these oil fields were located, was yet to be determined. The League of Nations Commission of Inquiry that was appointed and sent to investigate the validity of Turkish claims over the province eventually recommended that Mosul *vilayet* remained attached to the state of Iraq.[212] Although the Commission chose not to mention the recent extensive and exclusive concession in their report, there was a clear correlation between the two affairs, especially if one were to consider that the British inferred to the Iraqi government that resolving the oil negotiations swiftly would safeguard Mosul, Iraq's territorial integrity, and would, in turn, open the door for British support for Iraqi membership to the League of Nations.[213] Moreover, the Commission made an argument that Mosul must remain a part of Iraq from 'the purely economic' point of view, as it cannot be separated from 'its natural hinterland'.[214] The Commissioner's interpretation of 'purely economic

[210] *Ibid*, 212; Gerig, *supra*,137-144. The TPC shares were eventually distributed in the following way: the Anglo-Persian Oil Company (23.75%), Royal Dutch Shell (23.75%), Compagnie Francaise des Petroles (23.75%), and a US-based consortium made up of Standard Oil of New Jersey and Mobil (23.75% each) and C. Gulbenkian (5%). British shares were predominant in this arrangement.

[211] See S Shields, 'Mosul Questions: Economy, Identity and Annexation,' in R Simon and E Tejirian, (eds), *The Creation of Iraq, 1914-1921*, (Columbia University of Press, 2004); Q Wright, 'The Mosul Dispute,' American Journal of International Law 20:3, July 1926: 453-64.

[212] See League of Nations, *Question of the Frontier between Turkey and Iraq*, 1925 (Wirsen Commission Report).

[213] Mitchell, *supra*, 97.

[214] *Question* of the *Frontier between Turkey* and *Iraq*. *Report submitted* to the *Council* by the *Commission instituted* by the Council Resolution of September 30, *1924*. Geneva: League of

point of view' was in fact the view of the multinational corporations and foreign investors, especially the oil companies, who ensured access to the most valuable natural resource of the province.[215] The British subsequently (as per the Mosul determination) amended the Anglo-Iraq Treaty to extend the mandate to a further twenty-five years, while including a provision that immediately terminated the mandate once Iraq advanced to the stage of political development that qualified it for membership at the League. The oil concession could, therefore, not be understood in isolation from the semi-peripheral sovereignty that emerged in Iraq and vice versa.

The arrangement between the oil companies and the Western powers that was made to ensure that economic equality (at least in theory) was to be satisfied was in reality a 'slowly opening door' rather than an actual open door.[216] It has also been argued that the open door principle was effectively 'diluted' in this particular case, because of the fact that in reality American companies were not permitted to bid freely for concessionary rights; instead one exclusive American group was absorbed by a monopoly.[217] This explains why some members of the PMC made the observation that the Iraq government appeared to have agreed to a policy of monopolisation after all.[218] In that sense, what emerged was a special arrangement in the form of a consortium, which Gerig called 'a new experiment in international co-operation'.[219] This novel experiment was without precedent and was meant to become part of 'a specific code of international mandatory law', which would allow for the development of the natural resources of the Third World for the benefit of the global economy and the West.[220] It was for this reason that the Chairman of the PMC, Marquis Theodoli made the following observation: 'The [application of the] principle of economic equality … might contribute to the solution of the two greatest problems which lay at the basis of all international disputes, namely, the demographic problem and the distribution of raw materials'.[221] The open door policy and its mechanisms, therefore, should be analysed in relation to 'semi-peripheral sovereignty,' as it was a part of the overall legal arrangement that was intended to be a model for the manner in which the natural resources of the 'A' Mandates (in particular Iraqi oil) were to be exploited within the ambits of

Nations, 1925 (Document C.400. M.147, vii), as referred to in, M Taha, *Nation and Class Subjectivity in International Law and its Institutions in the Middle East, 1919-1939* (SJD Dissertation, University of Toronto, 2015), 127.

[215] *Ibid.*

[216] Gerig, *supra*, 149.

[217] W Stivers, "International Politics and Iraqi Oil, 1918-1928: A Study in Anglo-American Diplomacy", *Business History Review*, Winter, 1981, Volume 55, Number 4, 517–532; 533.

[218] 16 *PMCM*, 41-44.

[219] Gerig, *supra*, 184.

[220] M Van Rees, PMC, Minutes, V, 8.

[221] PMC Minutes, 12th Session, X, 168.

the new international legal order.[222] The usefulness of this mechanism in legal reasoning would re-emerge in PMC deliberations in Geneva.

The complex arrangement described above remained controversial, and Geneva was turned into an international 'arena for publicly contesting' the strategic interests of the great powers, especially oil claims.[223] These disputes generally occurred within the confines of the open door principle, and the PMC was called upon to consider petitions that alleged that this sacred principle was violated.[224] It was clear that the principle of the open door needed to be addressed and eventually reconciled with this new reality through legal reasoning by the PMC. In 1927, Kastl who was assigned by the PMC to write a report on whether the 1925 IPC concession was compatible with the principle of open door (already enshrined in Article 11 of the 1922 Anglo-Iraq Treaty) concluded that there was no violation. However, he made sure to voice his apprehension to the fact that Iraq's interests would have been better served if there was open competition, stating that 'there is no doubt that the extension of the Concession implies a very great advantage for the Company'.[225]

The interesting legal reasoning for our purposes was first put forward by Van Rees, who pointed out that the Anglo-Iraq Treaty was silent on the point of 'industrial concessions' and it could, therefore, be inferred that the Iraq government was 'free to act on its own discretion' with regards to the extension of the concession by thirty-five years.[226] The point was that there was no violation of the open door because oil concessions were an *exception*. Orts responded with a hint of irony that the Iraqi '... people would learn with surprise that the clause [in the Treaty] referring to economic equality did not apply to Iraq's principle industry'.[227] It was this sort of legal reasoning that distinguished oil concessions, which would reappear in later PMC deliberations, in particular in those regarding the pipeline agreements with the mandatory administrations of the other 'A' Mandates – Palestine and Syria.

After the IPC began drilling, the company discovered a vast oilfield stretching to the North of Kirkuk and decided to use this as an excuse to delay production for further reconnaissance. It was a longstanding strategy of oil companies to delay and sabotage production for the purpose of increasing global oil prices, and this was tactfully used against the Iraqi government, who were demanding the immediate construction of a pipeline to begin production as per the agreement. The Iraqi government, however, was crippled with a high deficit, and so had no alternative after prolonged and intense negotiations but to agree to sign a revised concession in 1925 in exchange for a modest cash advance in 1931.

[222] Gerig, *supra*, 152.
[223] Pederson, *The Guardians*, *supra*, 272.
[224] *Ibid.*
[225] PMC Minutes, 14th session, 1928, 214; *See* 247-249 for the full report.
[226] *Ibid*, 38.
[227] *Ibid.*

The agreement was later described by the US State Department's oil expert as 'one of the worst oil deals that has ever been signed'.[228] The revised concession eliminated all taxation of the company's profits, removed the minimum production obligation, and the company's relinquishment of undeveloped plots. It also extensively expanded the area of the concession from 192 square miles to 32,000 square miles.[229] The subjugating structures of this concession would extend to the entire region through the conventions signed by the other 'A' Mandate states (Palestine and Syria).

The construction of a pair of (bifurcated) oil pipelines was planned to transport Iraqi oil to the Mediterranean – one branching south to Haifa (Palestine) and the other north to Tripoli (Lebanon/mandate Syria). These were not only the biggest pipelines in the world at the time, but they were to increase global oil production fourfold (from 20,000 to 80,000 barrels a day) despite only representing a fraction of Iraq's oil production capacity.[230] To make this a reality, two identical pipeline agreements (or conventions) were signed between the IPC and the Palestine and Syrian mandatory administrations.

The PMC never actually discussed the revised 1931 IPC concession in Iraq, nor was the issue of whether this concession violated any of the Mandatory provisions of the Anglo-Iraq Treaty ever raised. There was no need to raise any issue as long as the initial 1925 concession was established not to have violated the open door principle. Besides, Iraq was close to attaining 'independence', and it was ironically this non-European 'sovereignty' that was to ensure that these crucial issues were resolved in international law. It is for this reason that one would need to follow the PMC deliberations elsewhere to get some clues as to the nature of the semi-peripheral sovereignty that was attained by Iraq. It is within the discussions regarding the pipeline agreements between the IPC and the two other mandated territories in the region (Palestine and Syria) that one would find some indicators as to the role of Iraqi semi-peripheral sovereignty on the entire region.

During the Twentieth Session, the PMC had lengthy discussions on the pipeline agreements between the IPC and the mandate administrations of Palestine and Syria. Although the PMC eventually decided not to denounce the British and the IPC, it was clear that several members were highly critical of these agreements. The two 'closely related' but 'quite distinct' issues in these discussions were whether the question of economic equality was violated by the (pipeline) concessions, and whether the interests of the territories in question suffered by the concessions in violation of the mandates.[231] The agreements appeared to provide the company with considerable benefits at the expense of the native populations of the mandatory territories: the company paid no import tax on

[228] Mitchell, *supra*, 47, 102.
[229] *Ibid.*
[230] *Ibid.*
[231] *See* PMC, 20th Session, 168-176; 168.

oil used for its own works or on construction material used for its operations, the oil in transit was not subject to export tax, the lands required for the pipe-line were rent-free, and the company was not liable to taxation by the mandatory administration.[232]

The questions that arose could be understood in the context of certain provisions in the Palestine Mandate. Article 18 of the Mandate, which reproduced the principle of economic equality, prohibited any discrimination in matters concerning taxation in favour of the nationals of any state members of the League (or its companies). Advantages that were precisely those granted to the IPC. Article 18 also made it clear that the mandatory administration, 'may impose such taxes and custom duties as it may consider necessary, and take such steps as it may think best to promote the development of the natural resources of the country and to safeguard the interests of the population'.[233] The question for the PMC was whether the pipeline agreement (the Convention of 1931) violated Article 18 of the Palestine Mandate.

The arguments that arose were interesting. The members, who believed that the concession did not violate the provision in the mandate, generally emphasised how the pipeline concessions would greatly benefit from the development of the mandated territories in question. The British member, Lugard argued vigorously to advocate for this position. He claimed that the privileges and exemptions were 'small in comparison with the benefits' that arose from the concession, such as the influx of capital, employment of labour, and the increase of shipping in its ports.[234] Merlin similarly claimed that the concession would in fact directly lead to 'changing completely the economic aspect of Iraq, Palestine and Syria … [especially through] the establishment of oil ports,' where 'many vessels would put in at those ports, and as a result, money would be spent there, and a commercial port would certainly develop ….' and these were very important factors from the standpoint of the development of these territories.[235] Besides, Lugard stated, the committee already questioned the representatives of the mandatory powers of Palestine and Syria earlier, who were clear that the agreements would greatly benefit the territories.[236]

Van Rees agreed that the concession should be exempted from both the application of the provision of the mandate and the principle of economic equality. However, he made the surprising argument that the concession had a 'special character', which covered a vast program of works that should be recognised as 'being of public utility'.[237] In other words, although the IPC was a private company that bore the expense of these works, the nature of the works remained

[232] *Ibid*, 169.
[233] *Ibid*, 144-45.
[234] *Ibid*, 169.
[235] *Ibid*, 172.
[236] *Ibid*.
[237] *Ibid*, 145.

of public utility. Van Rees actually went so far as to make the claim that the IPC 'was not engaging in commerce, but was dealing with Governmental affairs'.[238] The principle of economic equality therefore, did not apply in this case as it was a case of 'essential public works', and the concession did not infringe on the Mandate.[239]

These arguments were rejected by the other members of the PMC, who were openly critical of the pipeline agreements (in particular Orts, Ruppel, Rappard and De Penha Garcia). Orts responded to Van Rees that admitting an exception such as the one proposed would eventually lead to 'a class of privileged concessionaires exempt from ordinary law', opening up further disregard of the principles of the mandate.[240] Moreover, it appeared that the territory was actually paying the whole cost of the scheme in the form of exemptions from taxation and custom duties, and that this was 'the unpleasant feature of the scheme'.[241] Ruppel rejected Van Rees' reasoning, emphasising that the concession was in reality 'exclusively private in character' and it was not intended for public use as the use of the pipeline was reserved for the company.[242] Rappard was the member who was the most critical, appearing to almost denounce the mandatory power and the company when he said:

> Here was a British company exploiting for its own advantage the natural resources of Iraq. The company had found it advantageous to bring its pipeline through Palestine. But ... the concession given it by the mandatory Power ... granted it exemption from all the rules of common law ... therefore it seemed that ... [the mandatory Power] had subordinated the interests of the country under its mandate to the interests of a company of its own nationality.[243]

Although Rappard stressed that the company actually had a 'British legal personality,' Lugard insisted that the company was a consortium composed of four nations, and that Britain had no advantage in this arrangement.[244] Here, one notices how the legal mechanism of the consortium was referred to for the very purpose of avoiding any allegation that the open door principle was being violated.

The PMC's deliberations regarding these pipeline conventions concluded with the members unable to reach an agreement on the issues, and it was decided that it was not necessary to formulate *observations* to the Council, which would require a vote. The PMC's deep division could not possibly allow for an unprecedented denunciation of a mandatory power, although one could

[238] *Ibid*, 146.
[239] *Ibid*.
[240] *Ibid*.
[241] *Ibid*, 147.
[242] *Ibid*.
[243] *Ibid*, 147, emphasis added.
[244] *Ibid*, 148, 171.

easily interpret this calculated move as a partial denunciation by implication.[245] The statement submitted to the Council affirmed that the provisions of the mandate 'did not constitute an obstacle' to the granting of the advantages conferred by the concessions for the construction of a pipeline in Palestine and Syria/Lebanon, but the PMC made sure to mention the disagreements on the issue by stating that, 'during its discussion … doubts were expressed by certain of its members as to whether some of the clauses of the agreements in question kept the necessary balance between the advantages and privileges granted to the concessionary company and the advantages that would accrue to the two territories'.[246]

The fact that the pipeline agreements were a 'natural corollary' to the IPC concession illustrate that the subjugating structures within this concession extended to the entire region. The Commission's legal reasoning made a distinction between the principle of economic equality and the oil concessions in that the mandatory powers and oil companies were allowed to violate the principle of open door – they were turned into exceptions to the 'A' mandates in question. This is why these deliberations are revealing as they illustrate quite clearly the actual function of Iraqi semi-peripheral sovereignty in its intersection with the oil concessions. Lugard admitted, '[t]he oil came from Iraq. Surely that country was entitled to obtain access to the sea by the shortest route'. He went on to refer to 'the principle underlying the Navigation Act of Vienna of 1815 and the Berlin Act of 1885'.[247] As Bonné, emphasised, 'the antecedents of the Pipe-line Concession are inseparable from the actual [Iraqi] concession for the exploitation of oil … [as] … without the assurance of unhindered transport, the possession of oil wells is useless …'[248] It is apparent that the legal reasoning and the interpretation of the principles of international law in these discussions were advanced to ensure that the flow of Iraq's oil gained access to the shortest route to the sea. Here my argument comes full circle: just as the pipeline agreements cannot be understood without reference to the IPC concession, so the concession cannot be understood without Iraqi semi-peripheral sovereignty. As the Soviet international lawyer, Evgeny Korovin argued, 'an "independent" Iraq served as a bridge to the Mosul oil fields'.[249] Korovin revealed the continuities between nineteenth century international law and the Mandate System when he argued,

> whereas in the nineteenth century England would simply have acquired the [Mosul] oil fields by annexation, in the twentieth, control over Iraqi oil required … four

[245] As Fritz Grobba of the German Foreign Ministry mentioned if the two divided sides voted, the PMC would have narrowly condemned the British Government. *See* Pederson, *supra*, 274.

[246] PMC, 20th Session, *supra*, 230.

[247] *Ibid*, 170.

[248] A Bonné, "The Concession for the Mosul-Haifa Pipe Line," *The Annals of the American Academy of Political and Social Science*, Vol. 164, Nov. 1932, 116–126; 116.

[249] As quoted in BN Mamlyuk, 'Decolonization as Cold War Imperative: Bandung and the Soviets' in L Eslava; M Fakhri; V Nesiah (eds.), *Bandung, Global History and International Law: Critical Pasts and Pending Futures* (CUP, 2017), 203.

> additional legal steps: (1) participation in the creation of an Iraqi government; (2) acquisition of a mandate over it; (3) transformation of Iraq into a so-called 'independent' state friendly to England; and (4) active support for Iraq in its dispute with Turkey over Mosul.[250]

The doctrine of semi-peripheral sovereignty, therefore, turned out to be anything but the granting of complete independence to Iraq; rather, it amounted to a legal doctrine for the legitimised exploitation, and, in turn, for the geopolitical control of the region as a whole through the access, extraction, and transportation of Iraqi oil to the West. The importance of oil to the global economy was so vital that it was allotted exceptional status within the principles of international law at the time so that even the sacred open door principle of the Mandate System was contradictorily circumvented by the PMC in their deliberations through complex legal mechanisms (i.e. the consortium), and sophisticated legal reasoning.

## X. CONCLUSION

The main aim of this chapter was to illustrate the role of international law in the juridical formation of an 'independent' Iraqi state in the context of the Mandate system. I argued that the 'A' mandates were designated in the semi-peripheral Middle East with imperial considerations, primarily the control of natural resources, in mind that were exclusive to the semi-periphery (such as geopolitics and access to oil). The purpose of the juridical construction of semi-peripheral sovereignty must consequently be directly linked to the economic principles of the Mandate system, in particular the open door policy, which is analysed in detail. I revealed how the oil concessions that were negotiated in Iraq were intrinsically connected to the question of Iraqi independence and the semi-peripheral sovereignty that emerged. It was only after the question of oil was settled that Britain sought Iraq's independence in the League of Nations. The PMC in Geneva, who as jurists were knowingly making international law in their sessions, eventually confirmed the viability of this semi-peripheral sovereignty and welded its doctrines in the context of the international legal order. My argument was therefore not only that Iraqi semi-peripheral sovereignty was required for the Great Powers to gain access to Iraqi oil, but further to (economically) control the region as a whole. By analysing the contentious discussions relating to the pipeline agreements between the IPC and the other 'A' Mandate states, the role of semi-peripheral sovereignty in the entire region becomes clear.

The tracing of these legal mechanisms and instruments reveal that international law was continually present in the history of the Mandate system in the

[250] *Ibid.*

Middle East, and one could not ignore its significance. The shifting international legal order necessitated the juridical manufacturing of a semi-peripheral sovereignty to be granted to Iraq. This was the only way that Iraqi oil was to be *legally* controlled, extracted and transported to the Mediterranean ports, and, in turn, to the world. An entire legal edifice (of mechanisms, technologies, and structures) followed this narrative, especially instruments such as treaties and consortiums. It is ironic how Iraqi sovereignty, especially through the IPC oil concession and the 1930 Anglo-Iraq Treaty, actually further subjugated the other mandated territories in the region, notwithstanding the fact that these governments looked to Iraq's independence as a hopeful development. Iraq would be governed by the shackles of the semi-peripheral sovereignty that it gained in 1932, and its corresponding unequal treaty with Britain for another two and a half decades until revolution broke.

# 3

# *Civilising Labour Relations in Baghdad: The ILO and the Making of the Iraqi Working Class*

## I. INTRODUCTION

THE FORMATIVE YEARS of the urban Iraqi working class and its early movement can be traced to the local politics of Baghdad in the early twentieth century. The main task of this chapter is to contextualise this history and to analyse its relation to the Labour Law of 1936 showing how the drafting of this law was linked to the making of the Iraqi state – a state that was meant to have all the 'hallmarks' of a 'civilised' (liberal) and capitalist state, including upholding *minimum* international labour protections and standards. The International Labour Organization (ILO) along with the Permanent Mandates Commission (PMC) played a significant role in structuring Iraqi labour and social legislation as well as labour relations in this manner to ensure that the Iraqi state would transition through the Mandate process as a 'civilised' and 'independent' (capitalist) state and join the League of Nations. The Labour Law was also partly passed as a concession to the working class as a result of their persistent pressures through the initiation of strike actions. This chapter will examine how the provisions of the Labour Law were simultaneously a product of the mechanisms of international organisations, especially the ILO in its technical guidance of the government, as well as the result of strike actions and pressure from below. Although this piece of labour legislation (in combination with other legislation) was used to pacify and control the labour movement and was drafted in such a manner that heavily constricted workers' collective action, its provisions would eventually be appropriated and reinterpreted by the labour movement as a reference point for social reform, and later national liberation as it was integrated into workers' demands consistently until the end of the monarchy in 1958.

The 1936 Labour Law would eventually be used as a rhetorical tool by the working class' counter-hegemonic movement to legitimise their demands. It had a specific ideological function in that regard that was 'educative,' as it contributed to the expansion of workers' class-consciousness. In other words, the ideology of the Labour Law was appropriated to do exactly the opposite of what it was intended to do in that, rather than pacify the working class, it expanded and broadened their class-consciousness. Although the early labour movement believed that legal reform was possible and looked to the incipient Iraqi state to provide the necessary reforms to address their concerns, there was a radical shift in the 1940s and 1950s towards a more revolutionary approach, which put emphasis on structural change rather than mere reform. The suppression of the early labour movement would ultimately make communist ideas popular among the majority of the working class in the coming decades.

## II. THE 'GREAT RURAL-URBAN MIGRATION' AND THE FORMATION OF THE SLUMS OF BAGHDAD

Before turning to the history of the early labour movement in Baghdad, I must return to where my narrative ended in the Chapter 1 to describe the manner in which the rural farmers and cultivators, especially from the southeastern regions of the country, after being dispossessed from their lands, were ultimately forced to flee their miserable serf-like conditions in the landed estates and to migrate to the cities in search of employment. These migrants would eventually become the bulk of the 'labouring poor' masses[1] around the urban centres of Baghdad and Basra. They settled in the margins of large cities in 'empty lots' and wastelands belonging to the state, building *sarifas* (or mud huts).[2] In time, these collections of *saryif* (pl.) would turn into complex *sarifa* settlements[3] or shantytowns, transforming into enclaves separated from, and yet in close proximity to, the urban centres where the middle-class and wealthy resided. One economist, Doreen Phillips, described the largest slum of ʿAsima[4] in Baghdad, (which had a population of approximately 40,000), as being 'a world in itself', that was 'tied to the city through the labour market'.[5] The successive waves of migration continued for decades from the 1940s to the 1970s,[6] creating many problems for the Iraqi government relating to sanitation, urbanisation and

[1] I borrow this broad concept of the working class, which is 'inclusive' to the 'non-wage' and non-proletarian 'informal sectors,' from S Bhattacharya in his 'Introduction' to, Behal and Van der Linden (eds.) *Coolies, Capital and Colonialism: Studies in Indian Labour History* (CUP, 2006), 11.

[2] For a recent study of the *Sarifa* as 'an architectural mode of production,' see H Gupta, "Migrant *Sarifa* Settlements and State-building in Iraq" (PhD Dissertation, MIT, 2020).

[3] The *sarifa* is a hut made of mud or reeds supported by a ridgepole and wooden frame. This primitive architecture can be traced to the *hasir* or 'reed mat architecture' of the marsh dwellers of the southern basin of the Tigris and Euphrates. See SM Salim, *Marsh Dwellers of the Euphrates Delta* (Berg, 2004).

[4] *al-ʿAsima* means 'the capital'. The name was derived from *ʿArasat al-ʿAsima* (public land belonging to the state) and also possibly because it was the first large settlement of the early migrants to the city. See O Dewachi, *Ungovernable Life: Mandatory Medicine and Statecraft in Iraq* (Stanford University Press, 2017), 116-119.

[5] DG Phillips, "Rural-to-Urban Migration in Iraq," *Economic Development and Cultural Change*, Jul, 1959, Vol. No. 4, 405–421; 412.

[6] According to Basil Naim Najar, there were three major waves of rural-urban migration, the first began in 1918 and ended in 1939, the second from 1940 to 1950, and the third started in 1950 and continued to the late 1970s. See BN Najar, "The Dynamics of Rural-Urban Migration and Assimilation in Iraq" (Phd Dissertation, Wayne State University, 1976), 65.

development as the *sarifa* settlements were unregulated and considered as breeding grounds of disease and cholera. Michael Critchley, a Professor of Public Health and Social Medicine at Baghdad's medical college, described the ʿAsima slum in vivid detail in one of his reports:

> This area [he wrote] was the waste land to the East of the bund which surrounds Baghdad, and it was a desert site studded with pits of varying sizes, which have been produced by the excavation of mud and clay for building purposes. The area was also used by the Municipality as well as private individuals as a dumping ground for human and animal excreta, and rubbish. In addition the few surface water drains in the East of the city are pumped over the bund into this area, just after receiving the washings from the city abattoirs. The polluted and foul smelling liquids, which formed a sizable stream, wound its way through the conglomeration of mud buildings ... There were no sanitary arrangements in the houses or in the district, hence the inhabitants simply defecated indiscriminately, adding their small contributions to the already grossly polluted ground.[7]

The harsh living environment described above contrasted with the more urban parts of the city but was still considered by the tribal migrant as being better than the oppression he or she experienced under the landed shaikhs as a *fellah* in the farms of the rural villages. Nevertheless, the inhabitants of these shantytowns were strongly resented by the Baghdadi urban population, which considered them 'an inferior cast of *shroug* and *miʿdan*',[8] for they saw their tribal 'backward' ways as evidence of the 'incommensurability of rural and urban societies' in Iraq.[9] The migrant workers who inhabited the *sarifa* settlements found creative ways to sell their labour for a wage in any way they can to make ends meet. As 'unskilled workers' they would undertake informal casual work, whether as guards, porters, servants or using what skills they had in manufacturing, weaving, shoemaking, metal work, or as gardeners and taxi-drivers.[10] Many found their way in the employ of factories, workshops, as well as state or semi-public enterprises such as the railways, the oil fields and the railways. Others were recruited by the police force. Of course, the *sarifa* slums were also the habitat of 'criminal elements' or what could be called the *lumpenproletariat*. However, it was mostly in the urban sites of production, in particular in the factories, railway workshops, oil fields and the port, that in less than a decade, as we shall see, some of these migrant workers would become 'proletarised' with a unique working class consciousness, as they increasingly came into contact with the radical and socialist ideas of the labour movement and the organising tactics of the ICP.

The British mandatory authorities and their Iraqi counterparts saw the waves of rural-urban migrations as being an increasingly persistent problem

[7] Quoted in Phillips, *ibid*, 412.
[8] Dewachi, *supra*, 117.
[9] *Ibid*.
[10] Phillips, *supra*, 414.

that needed to be dealt with one way or the other lest it destabilises the developmental and modernisation process. The problem of the 'sarifa-dweller' was eventually turned into a persistent problem of governance as it was considered a potentially 'dangerous security situation in the towns'.[11] As Wilfred Thesiger describes in his report on the mass movement of tribesmen from ʿAmara to Baghdad and Basra in 1955, the sarifa slums were made up of 'large numbers of unsophisticated tribesmen, newly arrived in Baghdad and Basra, living together in tribal blocks, restless, defiant of authority as they have known it in the past, and blithely expecting to live an easy life and get masses of money, will offer them just the sort of material which they need to make trouble'.[12] British officials who read his report insisted that mass rural-urban migration had some positive effects as it disrupted the feudal 'slave-labour' relationship between the Shaikh and the *fellah* putting it into 'a better and more modern basis'.[13] In this way, the British mandatory approach, including the League of Nations institutions such as the ILO, approached the question of development in Iraq as being interconnected to questions of unemployment, labour relations and its management in an underdeveloped and non-industrial country. That is, they saw it as necessary to integrate the 'roaming' tribal *sarifa-dweller* into the industrial global economic order as 'wage-earner' by imposing structures of modern capitalist relations and 'civilised' notions (not merely of property law), but also of labour legal relations on Iraqi 'native society'. This was partly done with the passing of certain pieces of legislation based on international conventions and standards. I will return to this argument and the role of the ILO in this overall process after detailing the early history of the labour movement in Baghdad.

## III. THE JAS AND THE FORMATIVE YEARS OF IRAQI TRADE UNIONISM

The emergence of the labour movement in Iraq began with the establishment of the first organisation that advocated for workers – *Jamʿīyat Aṣ-ḥāb al-Sināʿa* (JAS), roughly translated as 'The Association of Craftsmen'. The JAS was officially formed on July 26, 1929, around a month after the *Law of Associations* (1929) was passed, legalising the formation of associations.[14] It was one of the first organisations that represented and tirelessly advocated for workers' rights, and in the short period of its existence became one of the most respected labour

[11] W Thesiger, "The Mass Movement of Tribesmen from Amara Liwa to Baghdad and Basra," enclosed with Letter from British Embassy Baghdad to Levant Department, August 5, 1955 FO371/91648 in AL Rush, J Preistland (eds.), *Records of Iraq, Volume II: 1953-1956*, (Archive Editions, 2001), 144.

[12] Ibid, 148.

[13] Ibid, 144.

[14] KM Ahmed, *al-Ṭabaqa al-ʿumāliya al-ʿIraqiyya: al-takkawwn wa bidāyāt al- ḥaraka* [The Iraqi Working Class: Its formation and the beginnings of its movement], (Dar al-Rashid, 1981), 123.

organisations in the country. At this point in Iraqi history, trade unions in the common meaning of the term did not exist. The JAS was more of a hybrid between a trade union and a craft guild.[15] There was certainly a more radical element of workers within its ranks, represented by the majority of its membership, the railway workers, which was what gave it certain characteristics of a trade union.[16] This also differentiated it from its counterparts, the Shopkeepers' Association and the Barbers' Association, which were akin to craft guilds. Still, as Iraq was largely an agricultural country and industrialisation was slow at the time, one could not really say that there was a fully industrialised or 'proletariatised' working class as of yet. The workers did not differentiate their interests from the artisans and small business owners. The JAS was, therefore, an alliance between the petty bourgeoisie (artisans, small business owners) and the industrialised workers (railway and oil workers, and factory workers, such as the tobacco workers).

The Ministry of Interior was reluctant to accept the JAS's application for a licence but it eventually acquiesced, and the union was formed. Elections were subsequently held and the founder of the JAS, Mohammad Sālih al-Qazzāz was elected as its first president.[17] Qazzāz, a mechanic and a descendent of a silk tradesman, is regarded as Iraq's first labour leader.[18] He came from a comfortable middle-class background, which allowed him to gain a broad education and eventually worked several government jobs. He joined the Artisans' Office in 1917, and for several years took night classes at the School of Commerce in Baghdad.[19] Qazzāz was considered fairly well educated for someone of his generation – fluent in several languages, including English, Turkish and Urdu. Despite his background, he identified as a 'worker.'[20] Politically, he was a liberal and a nationalist.[21] He took the plight of workers as his own and fought for them like no other leader in Iraq at the time. For this reason, Iraqi workers respected him and considered him their representative in the political and international arena.

The official goals of the JAS were detailed in its internal documents, which explicitly avoided any indication of political aims and used language that implied the cultivation of workers' education and legal reform.[22] The main

[15] The leadership was composed of artisans (petty bourgeoisie), while the majority of its members were workers. *See* A Sbāhī. *'Uqūd min Tārīkh al-Ḥizb al-Shīyū'ī al-'Irāqī, al-Juz' al-Awwal* [Decades from the History of the Communist Party of Iraq, volume 1], (Manshourāt al-Thaqāfa al-Jadīda, 2002), 76.

[16] Ahmed, *supra*, 144.

[17] *Ibid*, 140.

[18] Batatu, *The Old Social Classes, supra*, 296; M Farouk-Sluglett and P Sluglett, 'Labor and National Liberation, the Trade Union Movement in Iraq, 1920-1958', *Arab Studies Quarterly*, 5, 2, 1983, 147.

[19] Ahmed, *supra*, 133.

[20] *Ibid*.

[21] *Ibid*, 134.

[22] *The Internal Rules of Jam'īyat Aṣḥāb al- Sinā'a. See* Appendix 1, Ahmed, *ibid*, 241.

reason for this vague language was its attentiveness to the necessities of getting certified by the authorities, which, as mentioned earlier, were reluctant to give out licences due to fears that any form of politicisation and dissent, especially within an organisation with such a wide base, could be a threat to the state. In any case, the JAS was indeed reform-oriented, as it merely sought economic and legislative reforms from the state.[23] Qazzāz insisted on this narrow goal stating that the JAS was founded to 'defend the rights of workers and *kafihīn* ('toilers') who were unable to voice their demands, and to fulfil their interests', within the confines of the law.[24] There was, therefore, no attempt at this point to connect the problem of labour to the overall capitalist and semi-colonial structures of the Iraqi state, and the workers consciously avoided turning their labour struggle into a broader political nationalist anti-colonial one. This reformist orientation, as will be shown later, was starkly different from the later revolutionary (communist-led) years in which the workers regarded their struggle as principally a political one of national liberation. It was assumed by the JAS that once the state gained its independence from the Mandate it would be able to advance legislative reforms that would solve the problems faced by the working class.

Nevertheless, the influence of the early Marxists and communists was still present, as they were naturally allied with the JAS at the time. In fact, Marxist-influenced intellectuals, such as Mahmoud Ahmed al-Sayed, Hussein al-Rahāl and Abdullah Jadou, had a strong impact on workers at the time, and enthusiastically supported Qazzāz and his organisation.[25] Most of these intellectuals gave weekly public lectures on workers' rights, and other pertinent topics. They also edited and wrote for the working class press.[26] Despite its financial difficulties, the JAS organised massive social and literacy programs, developing an entire system of support for the labouring poor.[27] Physicians opened a free medical clinic, and lawyers took workers as their clients *pro bono*.[28] The emergent Iraqi state was unable to provide these basic services for the majority of labouring classes, who were in a desperate condition. As a result, the JAS grew rapidly and within a year of its founding it boasted a membership of 3,000 workers.[29] Its branches surfaced all over the country – from Basra to Nasiriya and Hila.[30]

The role of the early working-class press was an important space for the development of Iraqi workers' class-consciousness.[31] While the government

[23] Ahmed, *supra*, 142.
[24] *Ibid.*
[25] Sbāhi, *supra*, 119.
[26] Ahmed, *supra*, 145.
[27] *Ibid.*
[28] *Ibid.*
[29] *See al-ʿAlim al-ʿArabi* July 5, 1930, as referred to in Ahmed, *ibid*, 136.
[30] Ahmed, *supra*, 145.
[31] These were newspapers written for and by workers, such as *al-ʿAmil* ('The Worker').

press constantly attacked the working class and its leaders, the working-class press allowed workers a space to communicate amongst themselves, as well as to articulate their grievances, and to express their plight. Moreover, it was within their pages that novel and modern ideas were disseminated. The inaugural issue of *al-ʿĀmil* ('the Worker') newspaper, published in 1930, addressed workers in the following manner:

> O Iraqi Worker: This is your newspaper that carries your honourable name in its breast. And it is your literary weapon, which you have the right to treasure in your sustained struggle to claim your trampled rights and defend your cause, which is a part of the workers' cause in the Arab World. It is your crying voice that will be heard throughout the world, so that they know that you are alive and conscious of your injustices; conscious of the loss of your rights; conscious of the responsibility towards yourself and towards your brothers [...] Propose what you think would be useful for the worker, from your opinions and ideas – and say with it – always and forever: this is our motto ...
>
> WORKERS OF THE WORLD UNITE![32]

It was the first time that the phrase, 'workers of the world unite' appeared in print in Iraq, but soon it recurred elsewhere.[33] This was a clear turning point for the working class as it showed that a movement was emerging that was ready to organise its class to better its conditions.[34] The leftist novelist and intellectual, Mohammed Ahmed al-Sayyed wrote an article for the same issue of *al-ʿAmil*, in which he ends by asserting that only if all labour associations and unions united under one umbrella 'to strive for the introduction of special legislation for the protection of their rights', would Iraqi workers win their rights.[35] The working class press, therefore, cultivated and spread these ideas of unity and organisation to pressure the Iraqi state for the passing of labour and social legislation.

## IV. THE 1930 RAILWAY WORKERS' STRIKE AS A 'SCHOOL OF STRUGGLE'

It was the massive general strike of 1931 against the *Municipal Fees Law* that had increased taxes by threefold, which may be regarded as the moment that the question of labour was irrevocably forced into the political sphere. This general strike attracted around 8,000 workers and artisans, and 3,000 oil workers.[36]

[32] *Ibid*, 160. *See al-ʿAmil*, Baghdad, Issue 1, July 8, 1930.

[33] See NS al-Kadhimī. *Musāhama fi Kitabat Tarīkh al-Haraka al-ʿAmālīya fi al-ʿIraq hata 1958* ('An attempt at writing the history of the workers' movement in Iraq until 1958'), (Centre for the Research of Socialist Studies in the Arab World, 1991), 65.

[34] *Ibid*, 66.

[35] *Ibid*.

[36] P Marr, *The Modern History of Iraq* (Westview Press, 1985), 53.

However, the seeds of urban working-class discontent were actually sown several months earlier in the railway strike of 1930. The Iraqi State Railways (ISR), which was still under British 'executive control',[37] laid off a vast number of workers under the pretext of restructuring.[38] This was followed by the significant lowering of workers' hours, which, in turn, meant the lowering of wages.[39] The JAS began organising against these measures and used the working-class press to publicise their grievances.[40] One major issue was the unequal manner in which the Railway Directorate (RD) treated British workers compared with their Iraqi counterparts – a British worker's salary, for instance, was significantly higher than that of an Iraqi worker.[41] This dire situation led the JAS to call a strike, which commenced on December 30, 1930. Around a thousand railway workers assembled in the courtyard of the station in west Baghdad.[42] British-controlled management consequently made promises to meet the workers' demands, and so the workers returned to work.[43] This event was one of the first strikes of its kind – in terms of size, organisation and results.[44] It soon became clear that the promises made were empty ones. Management was not genuine about meeting any of the workers' demands and continued to lower their hours. A second strike was called, which attracted even more workers and gained the sympathy of the Baghdadi public.[45] The opposition and nationalist newspapers strongly supported the strike, and this broadened their solidarity with the public, a pattern that would remerge in future labour strikes.[46] The Iraqi government was clearly threatened by the widening support of the strike, and so requested the RD to look into the workers' demands.[47] This compelled management into accepting and signing an agreement with the workers, which ensured that the layoff of all 'non-expert' Iraqi workers was reversed, and that the payment of all workers' wages was made 'without exception'.[48] The working class and nationalist press presented this resolution as a victory for the workers[49] as it further strengthened the JAS's reputation and attracted more workers into its ranks.[50]

[37] Batatu, *supra*, 269.
[38] Ahmed, *supra*,184.
[39] SA al-Humeid, *al-Thawra al-Sāmita: Idrāb Baghdad 1931* (The Silent Revolution: The Baghdad Strike of 1931), (Baghdad, n.p.); 30.
[40] *Ibid*.
[41] Ahmed, *supra*, 183.
[42] *Ibid*, 185.
[43] *Ibid*.
[44] *See* Sassoon, *supra*, 185.
[45] Ahmed, *supra*, 189.
[46] *Ibid*, 192.
[47] *Ibid*, 193.
[48] INA, Files of the Monarchy, File Number: D/14, as referred to in Ahmed, *ibid*, 194.
[49] The headline of *Al-Istiqlāl*, April 6, 1931 read: "The workers return to work after they succeed in their demands".
[50] Ahmed, *supra*, 195.

The workers grew more confident in their ability to collectively organise and bring about changes to their labour conditions and their lives. Despite the fact that management eventually breached the agreement with the complicity of the government barely two weeks after it was signed, it would still be inaccurate to treat this strike as being 'ineffective'.[51] The reality was that Iraqi workers learned important lessons from these experiences, in particular in the collective power of their organised action and the economic 'weapon' of the strike. It was no coincidence, therefore, that less than a month after the strike, a petition signed by over a thousand workers was submitted to the government that asked for 'the rapid provision of a labour law to protect the rights of workers.'[52] The Iraqi communist historian, Azīz Sbāhī described these successive railway strikes as being analogous to *madrasa nidhālīya* ['a school of struggle'] that had a significant impact on the development of Iraqi working-class consciousness.[53] Strikes have a very significant impact on the development of class-consciousness, as it is through collective action that workers grasp the power of their own agency and their ability to bring about change to their conditions. Workers broaden their consciousness and recognise the role of the state and the law in maintaining their oppression. They experience their empowerment through collectively organising to bring about change into their lives and they begin to identify with their fellow workers as a class based on their shared experiences. V.I. Lenin described the transformational character of strikes as one that:

> ... opens the eyes of the workers to the nature, not only of the capitalists, but of the government and the laws as well ... The workers begin to understand that laws are made in the interests of the rich alone; that government officials protect those interests; that the working people are gagged and not allowed to make known their needs; that the working class must win for itself the right to strike, the right to publish workers' newspapers, the right to participate in a national assembly that enacts laws and supervises their fulfilment.[54]

The Railway Workers' Strike of 1930, therefore, was the beginning of a prolonged process in which the workers' awareness of the causes of their miserable conditions was amplified, especially discerning the role of the state and the law in sustaining these conditions. It also proved the workers' ability to organise collectively to bring about pressure on the state for change. It was the first time that the Iraqi working class acted in a unified and organised way even though it was still in its early stages. Although it was surely this illuminating experience that led the urban Baghdadi workers to actively demand the government to pass a labour law to protect their rights, it was in fact the massive 1931 General Strike

[51] Marr, *supra*, 52.
[52] *Al-'Iraq*, January 21, 1931 as referred to in Ahmed, *ibid*, 187.
[53] Sbāhi, *'Uqūd, supra* 118.
[54] VI Lenin, "On Strikes," in *Collected Works*, Volume 5 (Progressive Publishers, 1960 [1899]), 310–19.

that further kindled their capacity to connect their immediate labour conditions to the Iraqi state and its laws, broadening their solidarity with the 'poor labouring' masses, such as the *sarifa-dwellers*, on a national level.

## V. THE 1931 GENERAL STRIKE AND THE ENTRY OF THE IRAQI WORKING CLASS INTO THE POLITICAL ARENA

The intensity of the Railway Workers' Strike had a significant impact on the next episode of the early history of the Iraqi working-class movement: the 1931 General Strike against the *Municipal Fees Law*. This event transformed the apparent setbacks of the railway strike into more concrete results, cementing them further into the broader context of the early labour and nationalist struggle. The general strike lasted for 14 days and brought Baghdad to a complete halt. It was described by British officials as 'a frenzy' and 'a fanfare of riffraff',[55] while the Iraqi historian Abdul Razzāq al-Hasanī captured the feelings of the plebian when he called it 'the silent revolution of the people'.[56] What sparked the strike was the government's hastily passed law in June 1931, which increased municipal taxes by 200 per cent. Debate in Parliament was dominated by PM Nuri al-Saīd, and the law was ultimately passed after its third reading.[57] The law itself bordered on the absurd as it affected every aspect of the lives of the poor labouring masses. Not one craft, industry or profession was spared. A revised scale of around 119 different taxes was levied on all aspects of everyday life.[58] All workers had to pay a percentage from their income. The taxes were so high that it was impossible to expect workers to have enough for their daily needs after paying their share.[59]

The JAS immediately began to organise against this law and, after a petition led nowhere, a general strike was called on June 30 1931.[60] The Baghdadi public responded enthusiastically to this call. All coffee shops, artisan workshops, and pharmacies shut. Public transportation came to a complete halt. There was a deafening silence in the ordinarily busy streets of Baghdad.[61] The government baffled by this unprecedented course of events responded with violent threats under the pretence of the protection of 'individual liberty' from the 'bullying of shopkeepers'[62] into supporting the strike, while it cautioned that it would not allow anyone to 'threaten the freedoms of others' with their disruptive strike

[55] al-Humaid, *supra*, 14.
[56] AR al-Hasanī, *Tarikh al-Wizarat al-Iraqiya* [The History of Iraqi Cabinets], Vol. 3, 152.
[57] Ahmed, *supra*, 204.
[58] *Ibid*, 203.
[59] *Ibid*.
[60] *Ibid*, 205.
[61] al-Humaid, *supra*, 47.
[62] TNA, "Report by ... the UK ... to the Council of the League of Nations on the Administration of Iraq for the Year 1931" in *Iraq Administrative Reports*, Vol. 10 (Archive Editions, 1992), 344.

actions.[63] The government deployed police (some on horseback) to the streets to intimidate people into getting back to work.[64] Even any mention of strike action was punishable; plain-clothes policemen were ordered to arrest anyone overheard discussing the general strike in public.[65] The strikers demanded not only the annulment of the law, but also lower taxes, measures to address unemployment, and the release of those detained for striking.[66]

The strike leaders, including the JAS president, Qazzāz, the leader of the Barbers' Association, Mohammed Makī al-Ashtārī, and the leader of the Printers' Union, Abdullah al-Badrī, were all arrested for incitement under the *Baghdadi Penal Code*. Yet the authorities began negotiations with them in prison, where Qazāzz insisted that the annulment of the law was a precondition for ending the strike.[67] The government, consequently, promised that it would revoke parts of the law, which the strike leadership ultimately endorsed. Nevertheless, the strikers, weary of empty promises, refused to immediately end the strike and it rapidly spread to other cities, including Basra and Nasiriya.[68] It was at that moment that the strike was transformed into a much broader 'national movement,' that called for the fall of the government and the end of social injustice.[69] The British High Commissioner described the anger on the street in a memo to London, recalling that, 'Republican cries have been openly raised in the streets … [and that] there has been no sign of loyalty to King or support for the Government.'[70] The government turned to repressive legal tactics to quell dissent and violence ensued, especially in Basra.[71] A Royal Decree amended Article 83 of the *Baghdadi Penal Code* making it a criminal offence for a gathering of five or more people in public.[72] Police armed with machine guns guarded 'sensitive' areas in the city, and the military was put on high alert.[73]

As King Faisal and Prime Minister al-Saīd were both vacationing abroad in Europe during the strike, the viceroy warned that if they did not return immediately, the general strike would most likely turn into 'a great revolution.'[74] Heeding his advice, the PM travelled back to Baghdad, released the strike leaders

[63] The statement could be found in *Sadā al-'Ahd*, July 6, 1931, referred to in Ahmed, *supra*, 207.
[64] Humaid, *supra*, 49.
[65] WH Crook, *Communism and the General Strike* (Shoe String Press, 1960), 365.
[66] See *al-'Alim al-'Arabī*, July 9, 1931 as referred to in Humaid, *supra*, 67.
[67] Ahmed, *supra*, 208.
[68] *Ibid*, 209.
[69] Hasanī, *supra*, 143.
[70] TNA, Acting High Commissioner, Baghdad, to Secretary of State for Colonies, London, July 11, 1931. Delhi, National Archives of India, Baghdad High Commission File 7/4/22, Part II, as quoted in M Farouk-Sluglett and P Sluglett, *supra*, 148.
[71] For nearly two days, strikers were in control of Basra. The British, under the guise of protecting British lives and property, decided to send their forces to retake control of the city. This led to shots being fired into the crowd and the deaths of many Iraqis. *See Muhadir Majlis al-Nuwab*, (1931), 253.
[72] Ahmed, *ibid*, 210.
[73] *Ibid*.
[74] Hasanī, *supra*, 146-147.

from prison, and began to negotiate with them directly. He ultimately agreed to rescind taxes on nineteen different groups of workers, but refused to resign.[75] Moreover, a statement was made in a government newspaper that directly addressed the workers, claiming that the government planed to '[m]onitor the conditions of labour … for the fullfillment of the workers' well-being, and … the implementation of the provisions of laws relating to the organisation of work.'[76] The reality, however, was that the government blamed the strike on a 'handful' of ringleaders and 'secret associations', an obvious reference to the JAS and other trade unions.[77] This was the first attempt by the Iraqi working class to directly confront the state using the revolutionary weapon of the general strike[78] to attempt to reform state policies and to shape the law. The workers brought their specific labour concerns into the national and political arena. This explains why the parliamentary opposition felt that they had no choice but to rally behind them if they were to maintain any legitimacy.

The narrative above refutes the analysis in the historiography that disregards the role of workers in the strike, preferring the explanation that it was the parliamentary opposition parties that sustained the strike. Workers were generally presented as being led, influenced or organised by opposition parties and interests. There has been no attempt to focus on the workers' own independent role in organising against the state. A good example is Peter Sluglett's claim that the opposition joined the strike because it was the only way that the cabinet could be ousted at the time as there were no 'legal' mechanisms to do so in Parliament.[79] Sluglett seems to suggest that it was opposition party leaders who ultimately 'took charge' of and organised the strike, coordinating its spread into other cities, rather than the workers themselves. Even Batatu inexplicably remarks that the opposition party, *al-Ikha' al-Watanī* 'led' the 14-day General Strike.[80] This type of analysis reduces workers' struggle to political manoeuvring between opposition parties and the cabinet, neglecting Iraqi workers' agency. The reality, however, was that it was the workers and their leaders who planned, organised, executed and ended the strike. It was the workers and their leaders who were put on trial and imprisoned – not the leaders of the opposition. Although some MPs resigned after the strike broke, they did so for strategic purposes. Politicians took advantage of the situation. This was evident from the manner by which they politicised the strike by advocating for the necessity of overthrowing the Cabinet rather than by dealing with the specific issues that concerned the workers.

[75] Ahmed, *supra*, 211.
[76] See the opening of *al-Iraq*, July 27, 1931, referred to in Ahmed, *ibid*, 212.
[77] *Muhadhir Majlis al-Nuwab* (1931), 47.
[78] Only a few years earlier, the 1926 General Strike nearly brought the British metropolis to the brink of a revolution. See P Renshaw, *Nine Days That Shook Britain: The 1926 General Strike* (Anchor, 1976).
[79] Sluglett, *Britain in Iraq, supra*, 149.
[80] Batatu, *supra*, 200.

In that sense, even if the workers and the opposition were coordinating at times, the opposition parties did not lead, but rather merely guided certain aspects of the strike. In fact, the opposition made an attempt after the strike to co-opt the labour movement. This occurred when the leaders of the *Ikha'* party approached Qazzāz with the suggestion that he re-open a permanent association under its auspices. Qazzāz refused the offer realising that such an association 'would have put the labour movement under the control of the opposition leaders'.[81] This was one reason why the general strike did not transform into a revolutionary moment, for the nationalist movement at the time remained under the control of the (bourgeois) oppositional parties.[82] In addition, the JAS did not have a comprehensive political program, nor did it see itself as a political organisation per se, but merely as a labour union with a narrow economic and social reformist agenda.[83] The General Strike, therefore, started as a narrow economic strike and accelerated into a political one that sought to challenge the state and pressure it to change its policies. Nevertheless, it did not transform into a 'revolutionary general strike' or what Rosa Luxemburg referred to as the 'mass strike'[84] – one that aimed to overthrow the existing order.[85] Such revolutionary transformations had to wait for another decade.

The slow demise of the JAS began when the government instigated a campaign to shut it down soon after the strike ended by bribing some of its members, who in turn accused Qazzāz of rigging the union elections of its administrative committee.[86] Based on this fabricated accusation, the government ordered the JAS to shut down.[87] Qazzāz was arrested on allegations of rigging its elections.[88] At this point, there was another attempt to co-opt the labour movement by manufacturing a complicit leadership and an alternative organisation – *Jam'īyat 'Ummal al-Mīkanīk* (Mechanic Workers' Association). However, this tactic eventually failed as most workers refused to join it and instead called for the release of their leader and the reopening of the JAS.[89] After Qazzāz was released from prison, he succeeded in reclaiming this union from its government-sponsored leadership by overwhelmingly winning its elections in 1932; after which he decided to merge it with the (illegal) JAS, forming the *Itihād al-'Ummal fi al-'Iraq* (the Iraq Labour Union).[90] This new trade union

[81] Marr, *supra*, 53.

[82] See Editors, 'Mūsāhama fī Kitabat Tarīkh al-Haraka al-Niqābīya fī al-'Iraq' [An Attempt at writing the history of the labour movement in Iraq], in *Thaqāfa al-Jadīda*, Issue 39, August 1972, 17.

[83] *Ibid*.

[84] See R Luxemburg, 'The Mass Strike, The Political Party, and the Trade Unions' in Helen Scott (ed.), *The Essential Rosa Luxemburg* (Haymarket Press, 2008), 111-181.

[85] For one of the most influential articulations of the general strike, see G Sorrel, *Reflections on Violence* (CUP, 1999).

[86] Ahmed, *supra*, 214.

[87] *Muhadhir Majlis al-Nuwāb* of 1931, 44.

[88] Marr, *supra*, 53; Ahmed, *supra*, 215.

[89] Ahmed, *ibid*, 221.

[90] Sassoon, *supra*, 256.

continued the same work of the JAS, in particular lobbying for the passing and enforcement of labour and social legislation for the protection of workers' rights,[91] until it was permanently shut down by the government in 1935. The labour movement remained underground, disorganised and fragmented for years before its revitalisation by the communists in the 1940s and the 1950s.

## VI. THE ILO, THE 1936 LABOUR LAW AND THE EXPANSION OF 'CIVILISED' LABOUR RELATIONS

Less than two months after the end of the general strike in September 1931, the Iraqi government appointed former Prime Minister Jafar al-ʿAskarī and HI Lloyd, the British advisor to the Ministry of Labour, to consult with the ILO in Geneva on 'the question of the extent to which ILO Conventions should be applied to Iraq.'[92] During this first official visit to the ILO, the Iraqi delegation promised that once Iraq gained its independence and joined the League of Nations (becoming a member of the ILO), it would accede to all the major ILO Conventions, such as the *Forced Labour Convention*.[93] It was also after this meeting that al-ʿAskarī proposed to the government a draft law 'embedding all detailed [recommendations and] suggestions' of ILO experts to eventually pass the first labour law in Iraq.[94] CWH Weaver, the ILO representative on the PMC, made a list of recommendations for provisions of basic labour legislation in Iraq, including legislation to limit hours of work and to regulate certain aspects of labour relations, such as the employment of women and children; the health and safety of workers; workmen's compensation for industrial accidents; the contract of employment, and the registration of trade unions.[95] All of the above would eventually be incorporated into the first piece of labour legislation in Iraq – *Labour Law No.72* of 1936, which would only be passed in Parliament several years after independence by the al-Hāshimī Cabinet.[96]

The Labour Law of 1936 was, therefore, 'inspired by' and was drafted in full adherence to ILO Conventions and under the guidance of ILO experts.[97] Its purpose was certainly to structure labour relations in a future 'independent' Iraqi state that would be fully integrated into the capitalist system. It was

[91] Sbāhī, *supra*, 121.

[92] ILOA. Letter from JI Phillips to ILO Director, 18 September 1931, in ILO-BIT/ACD 2-85, 'Application of Conventions and Recommendations: Action taken with regard to ratification of ILO Conventions, Iraq' (01/1930-12/1949).

[93] ILOA. Letter from Jafar al-Askari to Albert Thomas, October 1931, ILO-BIT/ACD 2-85, *Ibid*.

[94] *Ibid*.

[95] ILOA, Letter from Weaver to ILO Director (7 Oct 1931), ILO-BIT/ACD 2-85, *Ibid*.

[96] Labour Law No. 72, Iraq Government Gazette, No. 20, May 17,1936, 278.

[97] For a brief overview of the 1936 Labour Law and its revisions in 1942, 1954 and 1956, *See*, ILOA. Rapport de la Commission de la Conference, 1957 in 'Application of Conventions and Recommendations: Art. 22 Annual Reports on Employment Services, ILO Convention 1948, Iraq'. ILO-BIT/ACD/ 8-2-85-88.

simultaneously no doubt the product of working-class pressure from below, as the labour movement would also appropriate this law as a 'rhetorical weapon' in its long class struggle. As we shall see, the Iraqi government assured the ILO that it would immediately accede to and ratify all major ILO Conventions once it joined the League in an attempt to convince the PMC of its 'enlightened' and 'civilised' labour policies, as well as, to illustrate that the 'native labour question' in Iraq would be properly dealt with in accordance with 'liberal' principles of the capitalist (welfare) state, demonstrating its readiness for independence and its willingness to join the 'civilised family of nations'. This understanding was conveyed in a letter from Albert Thomas, the Director-General of the ILO, wherein he congratulated al-Said for his government's engagement with the labour question and the ILO: 'I welcome,' he wrote, 'this decision as further evidence of the lively interest your government takes in the welfare of the people of Iraq and of its eagerness to cooperate fully with other nations of the world in the sphere of social progress'.[98]

To understand how the ILO structured a specific understanding of labour relations that safeguarded capitalism in Iraq and the colonies in general, we must return to the centrality of the so-called 'question of labour' to the emergent international legal order during the interwar period. The Treaty of Versailles was drafted to include a provision in Part XIII that emphasised that the maintenance of world peace, 'could be established only if it is based upon social justice', and that as long as 'conditions of labour exist involving such injustice, hardship, and privation [...] the peace and harmony of the world [was] imperilled'.[99] In addition, the Preamble to the ILO Constitution (which was consequently attached to the peace treaties) contained similar language with the statement that, 'universal and lasting peace can be established only if it is based on social justice,' including the improvement of global labour conditions, lest 'the peace and harmony of the world are imperilled'.[100] It was, in other words, recognised that international action in relation to labour was necessary for the maintenance of peace in the international order, especially in the wake of the 1917 Bolshevik Revolution.

The ILO consequently came into existence as an institution that, in the words of JT Shotwell, author of the provisions establishing the organisation, was explicitly 'an alternative to violent revolution'[101] – 'a non-revolutionary institution,'[102] that relied on a conciliatory tripartite framework that advocated a reformist agenda of a 'just equilibrium'[103] or 'class harmony' against

[98] ILOA, Letter from Albert Thomas to Nuri al-Said (11 December, 1931), ILO-BIT/ACD 2-85 *supra*.

[99] Part XIII, Section 1, *Treaty of Versailles* (1919).

[100] International Labour Organization (ILO) Constitution (1 April 1919).

[101] JT Shotwell, "The International Labour Organization as an Alternative to Violent Revolution," *The Annals of the American Academy of Political and Social Science* 166 (1933), 18–25.

[102] JT Shotwell, "ILO and the Tripartite System," *International Conciliation* 32 (1959), [iii]-448; 2.

[103] ILOA, Report of Governing Body Committee on Freedom of Association (1956) *Official Bulletin of the International Labour Office*, vol. XXXIX, no. 1, 478.

the Marxist notion of 'class struggle' and that prioritised cooperation between (reformist/non-militant) workers, (socially-oriented) states, and ('enlightened') employers.[104] It certainly embodied 'international law's aspiration to reform the world', which, as Guy Sinclair has shown, was indistinguishable from the 'civilising mission' and the imperial impulse to intervene in the making and disciplining of Third World states.[105] The ILO also based its agenda on the principle of universality, (in theory) allowing every government to join its organisation, apply its international standards and receive technical assistance. These two principles of tripartism and universality, however, as Mai Taha has argued, were in fact merely meant to regulate an illusory non-antagonistic notion of class society, ensuring it was sustainable under the capitalist system, in effect cementing the de-politicisation of the working class, and bringing about 'a durable and reformed class society under capitalism.'[106] In this way, the ILO was aimed at preserving the overarching capitalist status quo. It was no coincidence that the ILO itself was dependent on the existence of classes, but even an idealist 'harmonious' class society is an anachronism, as classes by definition historically contain contradictory tensions and social dynamics that cannot be eliminated merely through legislative reforms.

During the interwar period, the ILO was focused on standard setting, but it was the European (industrial/capitalist) labour standard, one which reflected the 'standard of civilisation' that all non-European countries were measured on.[107] As CW Jenks wrote, 'the international labour conventions that made up 'the International Labour Code has become for labour lawyers throughout the world what the *Corpus Juris Civilis* is for civilians or the works of authority of the common law for common lawyers' – 'a constitutional framework for social justice'... '[p]romoting greater uniformity in labour legislation over a large part of the world'.[108] Nevertheless, at the time, the ILO used a colonial framework to distinguish between industrial 'metropolitan or European labour' and non-industrial 'native labour' in the so-called 'non-metropolitan' world.[109] Despite this contradiction and the fact that the ILO would later move towards a more inclusive framework of technical assistance,[110] its origins were founded on this colonial framework, which is not only revealing of its constitutive structures

[104] *Ibid.*

[105] GF Sinclair, *To Reform the World: International Organizations and the Making of the Modern World* (OUP, 2019), 5.

[106] M Taha, "Law, Class Struggle and Nervous Breakdowns," in K Greenman, A Orford, A Saunders, N Tzouvala (eds.), *Revolutions in International Law: The Legacies of 1917* (OUP, 2021), 112–133; 133.

[107] L Rodriguez-Pinero, *Indigenous Peoples, Postcolonialism, and International Law: The ILO Regime (1919-1989)*, (OUP, 2005), 17-53; 76.

[108] CW Jenks, *Social Justice in the Law of Nations: The ILO Impact After Fifty Years* (OUP, 1970), 80, 82, 87.

[109] Rodriguez-Pinero, *supra.*

[110] See D Maul, *Human Rights, Development and Decolonization: The International Labour Organization, 1940-70* (Palgrave Macmillan, 2012).

whose remnants are still visible in the structures of inequality in the international legal order, but also underlies the importance of the interwar period in understanding development in the Third World.[111]

The ILO's Constitution contained a 'Colonial Clause' that allowed metropolitan powers to exclude their overseas colonial territories from the ratification of ILO standards. 'Native labour' was deemed a 'special' form of labour that did not require labour standards to be applied consistently. Consequently, 'universal' labour standards were applied unevenly in the colonies as this flexibility was seen as being necessary for imperial powers to govern these diverse territories and maintain capitalism – which was intrinsically connected to colonialism – by adapting to the distinctive 'local conditions' and the 'special circumstances' of the 'non-metropolitan' Third World. This 'colonial' framework, reflected in the Native Labour Code, ironically resulted to further legitimise colonial practices and racialised violence rather than to strengthen international labour standards and social protections. As with other technical missions in the region, especially in Egypt, the ILO experimented with what could be referred to as the 'technicalisation of [labour] crises' by developing technical mechanisms that resulted in the de-politicisation of labour relations in the context of subduing and governing the semi-colony.[112]

The ILO undertook the task of developing this 'native labour' policy through the work of the Permanent Committee of Experts on Native Labour, which essentially aimed to ensure that the 'lazy native'[113] began to 'work for his own civilisation,' and transform his primitive society into 'a producer and consumer society' – that is, a capitalist society.[114] The PMC relied on this committee's work to ensure that 'native societies [in the Mandate territories] were transformed in such a manner as to integrate themselves into the overarching system of the market economy'.[115] As one ILO pamphlet illustrates, it was imperative to integrate the 'idle' native 'dweller' into the 'world [capitalist] industrial system' and since 'the native is everywhere being called upon to aid in the task of world [capitalist] production [of raw materials] [...] it needs no demonstration to prove the necessity of action to provide that the conditions of this work should be just and reasonable'.[116] To achieve this it was necessary that labour legislation, international conventions and industrial norms were not only applied around the world, but also to valourise the ideology of 'free wage labour' against slave and forced labour. However, as I have argued elsewhere, these international efforts

[111] V Plata-Stenger, *Social Reform, Modernization and Technical Diplomacy: The ILO Contribution to Development (1930-1946)*, (De Gruyter Oldenbourg, 2021), 94.

[112] See M Taha, "Reading 'Class' in International Law: The Labor Question in Interwar Egypt" (2016) *Social & Legal Studies*, Vol. 25(5), 567–589.

[113] For a critique of the ideology of the 'lazy native,' see SH Alatas, *The Myth of the Lazy Native* (Routledge, 2006).

[114] A Alcock, *History of the International Labour Organisation* (Macmillan, 1971), 34, 83.

[115] Anghie, *Imperialism*, *supra*, 165, 168.

[116] ILO, 'Native and Colonial Labor in 1926' BRB7392 (Geneva, 1927).

to suppress slavery and to regulate forced labour to structure a supposedly more humane form of 'free labour' relations in the Third World did not in any way eliminate racialised violence or coercion but rather merely kept it out of view, illustrating how racial capitalism remained embedded within the structures of the international legal order.[117] This explains the manner in which violent methods of policing significantly increased in correlation with imperialist and ILO interventions in the management of labour unrest in the colonies, for the stability of both the imperial and international order against any form of revolution, not to mention the 'communist threat' was of paramount concern for many of these colonial officials.[118] As we shall see, the Iraqi working-class made use not only of the provisions of the new labour law, but also the international mechanisms of the ILO to express their grievances on the world stage.

## VII. THE DIALECTICS OF LEGALITY AND COUNTER-HEGEMONIC STRUGGLE

Despite the fact that it was barely enforced, the 1936 Labour Law was considered as a partial victory by the working class, as it was certainly also the product of the culmination of their strikes that pressured the Iraqi state to make concessions. Although its main purpose was clearly to slow down the momentum of the movement, in the long-term, it had the opposite ideological effect as the law ended up enhancing the workers' understanding of their rights, educating them to appropriate the language of legality into their struggle. As will be shown throughout this book, it was in fact this persistent appropriation, creative interpretation and reinvention of anti-hegemonic legality, which was what made the law, in particular the labour law, quite significant in the development of Iraqi working-class consciousness.

The 1936 Labour Law was quite basic in its provisions and contents (it consisted of 6 parts and 39 sections) and it was not only a close reflection of what the workers had been calling for in the past, but also as mentioned earlier, it incorporated many of the basic international labour standards.[119] It stipulated that 'in every industrial undertaking, such special precautions as are reasonable to secure the safety of the worker shall be taken'.[120] It made a provision for medical treatment for injured workers and for 'a rest period of at least 24 consecutive hours after each six days of work'. There was a provision for 'ordinary leave'

[117] See A Hammoudi, "International Order and Racial Capitalism: The Standardization of 'Free Labour' Exploitation in International Law" *Leiden Journal of International Law* (July, 2022), Volume 35, issue 4, 779–799.

[118] M Thomas, *Violence and the Colonial Order: Police, Workers and Protest in the European Colonial Empires 1918-1940* (CUP, 2012), 23.

[119] ST Mansūr, *Al-Wajīz fī Qānūn al-ʿAmal: Dirāsa Muqārana, al-Juzu' al-Awal* [A brief comparative study of the labour law, volume one] (Baghdad: Sharika al-Tibʿa wa al-Nashir al-Ahlīya, 1965), 30.

[120] *Labour Law No. 72, supra*, Chapter 2; Article 2.

with full pay of ten days a year, as well as sick leave with pay for 15 days for each year. It also explicitly forbade child labour.[121] Moreover, it empowered the Ministry of Interior to set up a conciliation/arbitration body for the purpose of settling disputes between employers and workers. Finally, Article 23 (the core provision of the law) provided that workers had a right to form trade unions, 'in order to care for their special interests, to spread the spirit of co-operation … between them, to effect improvements by educational, cultural, social and moral means to develop the industries in Iraq.' Articles 24, 25 and 26 presented the procedures required to form and certify a trade union, and the holding of elections of the administrative committee of a trade union.[122]

Although it represented a turning point in Iraq's labour history, the increasingly authoritarian Hashimī government did not implement any of the Labour Law's provisions, especially Article 23 concerning the recognition of the right to form trade unions.[123] The social democratic National Democratic Party, which temporarily came to power in the fall of 1936 were adamant on its application and also passed some amendments to improve it, the most important of which was limiting daily working hours to eight.[124] Unfortunately, however, with the failure of their reform program and their violent removal from power, the Labour Law would remain in the books without being consistently applied for years to come. Nevertheless, even if the government decided to apply these provisions, the reality was that combined with other legislation regulating strikes, it would have been nearly impossible for all of the Labour Law's provisions to be adequately enforced. The Iraqi state learned its lesson after the general strike and swiftly introduced legislation the next year that made it practically impossible to undertake collective strike action legally.[125] If a strike was seen in any way as not being directly connected to a (narrow) economic labour dispute or if it was deemed politically motivated, it was considered illegal. Moreover, the Minister of Interior had to be given notice of any strike; in other words, unauthorised strikes or spontaneous wild strike action was illegal. Picketing or spreading information that encouraged other workers to initiate sympathy strikes was also criminalised.[126]

[121] TNA, CO 730/168/1. (1931) 'Outline of a Law Limiting Hours of Work and Regulating the Employment of Women and Children'. This regulation was the first to be passed before the consideration of drafting a comprehensive labour law.

[122] *Ibid*, Chapter 4, Articles 23-31.

[123] Sassoon, *supra*, 257.

[124] TNA, Clark to FO, 23 Mar. 1937. FO 371/20795. A further amendment that year stipulated that workers were entitled to annual leave and sick leave with full pay. *See* Scott to FO, 26 Oct. 1937. FO 371/27096.

[125] Article 4 of the 'Law Relating to Maintaining Security during Strikes Number 70 of 1932' published in the *Iraqi Gazette* #115, June 30, 1932. This law was annulled in 1959 after the revolution. See SM al-Saīd. *Munāzaʿāt al-ʿAmal al-Jamāʿya wa Hismaha* [Collective Labour Conflicts and Resolution], (Baghdad: Mutabaʿa al-Maʿarif, 1961), 28.

[126] *Ibid*. The penalties for breaching this law were either six months' imprisonment or the payment of a fine of 20 liras.

As one British official admitted, trade unions, referred to in the law, would be 'subject to very close official supervision, and [so] it is unlikely that they will be allowed to attain any great political importance' and that 'most of the … provisions are merely permissive … [as] [t]he decision whether or not these provisions are to be put into force will rest with the Minister of Interior'.[127] Therefore, while the law technically granted workers the right to organise, it also gave the Minister of Interior wide powers to arbitrarily cancel the licences of unions. It was, in other words, the executive and not the judiciary that was the final arbiter on the interpretation of the law, and especially of workers' grievances against the cancellation of their union licences. In that sense, there was very little room to manoeuvre within the labour law as it was stripped of any teeth. It was no wonder that Joseph Sassoon described the law as not having 'any significant effect on the development of trade unionism'.[128] My argument, however, is that a closer and deeper socio-historical analysis of this law suggests that despite its unenforceability, it did in fact have a unique ideological significance for the labour movement and the counter-hegemonic struggle in general.

As mentioned earlier, from the perspective of the Iraqi government and its British overlords, the labour law was primarily drafted at the time in adherence to international labour conventions so as to be presented as evidence of its 'enlightened' labour policy with the purpose of including its plan as further evidence to the PMC that Iraq was ready for independence.[129] An ILO representative was tasked to advise the Iraqi government and the newly formed parliamentary labour committee[130] on the specific ratification process and adherence to certain international conventions, especially relating to the employment of women and children in factories.[131] Moreover, the Council of Ministers informed the High Commissioner, Francis Humphrys and the PMC that the ILO recommendations were 'accepted in principle' and would be applied to the new labour legislation once the Mandate came to an end.[132] The ILO's 'civilisational' approach towards labour issues was common elsewhere as it spread its conception of 'industrial life' and 'social justice' to other parts of the Third World. In that sense, the drafting history of the labour law certainly played an important role in the juridical construction and justification of the doctrine of 'semi-peripheral sovereignty', which was discussed in the previous chapter.

[127] TNA, FO 624/7/623 (1936): Labour Law 407/IT36. Sgd C.H. Bateman, British Embassy, Bagdad, to A. Eden, Foreign Office, London; April 25, 1936.

[128] Sassoon, *supra*, 257.

[129] TNA, A Thomas, ILO, Geneva to N As Saīd, PM of Iraq, Baghdad. 14th July, 1931 CO 730/168/1. Iraq: Labour Conditions (1931). *See* 'Abdul Qadir Rashid, Secretary to the Council of Ministers to The Legal Secretary to H.E. the High Commissioner for Iraq, Baghdad, 3rd November, 1931.

[130] This committee included a British lawyer, H.I. Lloyd, who was recommended due to his international legal experience in the Mosul Frontier Dispute; *ibid*.

[131] *Ibid*, *See* Sassoon, *supra*, 257.

[132] *Ibid*.

Yet, there was another ideological effect to this law. The labour movement would put emphasis on its core principles using the law as a rhetorical tool in every one of its lists of demands. If one considered that the labour law was itself a product of direct pressure exerted by the workers (from below) on the state, it would make sense not only why they decided to appropriate its language, but also why they interpreted it as *their* law or at least one that spoke to their aspirations. The workers were quite consistent throughout their strikes in their demands for a piece of legislation that adequately protected their rights. Furthermore, a few months before the general strike in March 1931, Qazzaz submitted a proposal for a draft labour bill to the government. There were clear parallels in this draft and the 1936 Labour Law that was eventually passed.[133] Consequently, it is not far fetched to make a direct connection between what the workers and their unions called for and the piece of legislation that was passed a few years later after a persistent struggle on the ground.

A year after Iraq gained its independence in 1933, the ILO sent a delegation led by American labour expert, John B. Weaver to Baghdad and other neighbouring cities in Persia, Turkey and India, to welcome these new members to the organisation, and to gain first hand impressions of the labour conditions there. Weaver spent no more than four days in Iraq, concluding that 'the fragmentary impressions of conditions of labour in Iraq that I was able to gather ... were sufficient to show the need for a small labour department and for simple labour legislation even in a country at an early stage of industrial development.'[134] Here one notices the colonial framework of the ILO at play as labour standards needed to be 'adapted to local conditions,' and that a 'simple' piece of legislation 'should be confined to provisions that could be effectively enforced,' was recommended – in other words, capitalist processes should never be disrupted. Furthermore, it was peculiar that Weaver was, in his words, 'unable' to meet with anyone from the labour movement, although he was aware of the existence of the JAS, which he admitted 'would appear to have definite organisation and a programme'.[135] The ILO did not at the time actively seek out the *independent* labour unions in these non-industrialised countries. However, the fact was that Qazzāz was directly communicating with the ILO that same year, not to mention several international labour organisations, such as the International Labour Syndicates in Berlin.[136] He forwarded the Constitution of the JAS and

[133] 'A draft project of an Iraqi labour law submitted by MS al-Qazzāz, the president of *Jami'yat Ashāb al-Sanā'* to the Prime Minister and the ministers of Interior, Justice, and Economy and Public Works, dated 31/3/1931,' *See* Ahmed, *supra*, Appendix 3, 268 for the full text.

[134] CWH Weaver. "Impressions of a Visit to India, Iraq, Persia, and Turkey", *International Labour Review*, Vol.XXVIII, No.4, October 1933.

[135] *Ibid*, 485.

[136] TNA. FO 622/1/155. Labour Organizations in Iraq (1933); Extract from *Sawt al Iraq*, 7th Feb 1933.

other internal documents to gain input from these organisations on whether they complied with international conventions.[137]

Another major concern for the working class was getting its own representatives to the International Labour Conference (ILC) in Geneva. Qazzāz was prevented from getting the official certification needed from the government to represent Iraqi workers despite the fact that he was elected as their representative for the seventeenth session of the ILC (1933).[138] He wrote a letter of protest to the ILO against the government's selection of an Iraqi official and a British lawyer as representative delegates of the working class. In one petition to the President of the Council of Ministers, which was attached to the ILO letter, Qazzāz conveyed

> the indignation of the workers against the step taken by the [Iraqi] government in the appointment of the official deputies to represent them in the session and [that] the workers can in no way recognise the deputies in question who represent the government's point of views. They further express their profound indignation with regard to the government's attitude towards [...] the working classes [which are regarded] as slaves [while] appointing men of "special classes" to represent them [...] who have not the least familiarity with [...] labour affairs and [...] lack the sympathy towards [their] fellow workers.[139]

He urged the ILO to pressure the Iraqi government to allow for the working class to choose their own representatives to the ILC. The ILO responded that it was not unusual in non-industrialised countries, where there was no 'well-organised genuine trade unions united in a central association,' to send government delegates to represent workers, and in any case that the decision was with the government.[140] Qazzāz clearly had confidence in the principles of international law and the workings of its institutions and believed that the ILO would pressure the Iraq government to change its labour policy. He did not consider how these international institutions in fact structurally contributed to the making and legitimisation of the semi-colonial Iraqi state, and in turn to the very conditions that Iraqi workers were suffering from. This was something that its successor communist-led labour movement would understand well.

The passing of the 1936 Labour Law should, therefore, be understood as a victory (albeit a partial one) for the Iraqi working class, even if workers would spend the next twenty years fighting for its enforcement and application. It certainly affirmed the success of working-class action in Iraq whether in the form of general strikes or boycotts. The workers continued to assert their own interpretation of the law (beginning with the call for its revision and enforcement)

[137] TNA. 'Local Press Extracts,' 6th February, 1933, 'The International Labour Office, Geneva, makes Enquiries about Labour in Iraq', *Sawt al 'Iraq*. FO 622/1/155.

[138] ILOA. International Labour Conference Sessions 17-25 (1933-41): Nomination of delegates for Iraq. D-600-C-200-85.

[139] *Ibid.*

[140] ILOA. Letter from the Chief of the Workers' Organizations Service (ILO) to al-Qazzaz, 12 July, 1933 D. 617/200/83. *Ibid.*

every time they went out on strike. It was arguably through these *illegal* strikes and acts of civil disobedience that they ended up slowly bringing changes to the law and its application.[141] The Labour Law's gradual development was shaped by the workers' pressure throughout the years as was evident by the passing of Law No. 36 of 1942, which permitted workers to organise legally, and later, Regulation (No. 63) of 1954, which developed a detailed arbitration scheme to settle worker-management disputes.[142]

To understand how the labour law was useful to the counter-hegemonic struggle in Iraq, it is instructive to refer to Antonio Gramsci's understanding of law in the context of his well-known concept of hegemony.[143] Gramsci claimed that the ruling class does not solely use violence to assert its control, but mostly uses ideology to develop a hegemonic culture that is propagated until it becomes 'common sense' to all classes in society.[144] Hegemony is how the working class identifies their own interests with those of the ruling class. The law then is one instrument that the ruling-class uses to materialise its hegemony and to secure its own coherence and unity.

The law, for Gramsci, works coercively and consensually within the state apparatus – what he referred to as the 'double face of the law.'[145] On the one hand, the law secures the economic interests of the ruling class by force. On the other hand, it has an ideological function whereby it disciplines the subaltern classes in every level of social and private life solidifying their conformity. Gramsci approaches law by referring to it as the 'juridical problem,' which is, 'the problem of assimilating the entire grouping to its most advanced fraction; it is a problem of education of the masses, of their 'adaptation' in accordance with the requirements of the goal to be achieved … through [the] 'law' the State renders the ruling group 'homogeneous' and tends to create a social conformism which is useful to the ruling group's line of development.'[146] The main function of law in the state and society for Gramsci is, therefore, its 'educative'[147] function– the law disciplines and persuades all classes in society into believing that the current governing establishment has a cohesive unity that renders it effective and efficient.[148] Furthermore, this educative function of law operates when the subaltern classes are constantly being told what is legal and what is illegal. This, in turn, establishes the ruling class' values in society, crystallising

[141] See Chapters 4, 5 and 7.

[142] Law No. 36 of 1942 (Amendment to Labour Law No. 72 of 1936), *Al-Waqā'i' al-Iraqiyya* (Official Gazette), No. 2028, 31 May 1942; Regulation (No. 63) of 1954 on Conciliation and Arbitration for the Settlement of Disputes between Employers and Workers.

[143] *See* M Cain. "Gramsci, The State and the Place of the Law" in D Sugarman (ed.) *Legality, Ideology and the State* (Academic Press, 1983), pp.95–117.

[144] A Gramsci. *Selections from the Prison Notebooks*, Q Hoare (ed.), (International Publishers, 1971), 325.

[145] M Benney, "Gramsci on law, morality, and power," *International Journal of Sociology of Law*, 1983, 11(2), 205.

[146] Gramsci, *supra*, 195.

[147] *Ibid*, 247.

[148] *Ibid*.

them as 'common sense.' As Duncan Kennedy explains, '[t]he idea of the legal and the illegal is something which, if you can manipulate it skilfully, you can use to exercise great power over people who believe it.'[149] This hegemonic power, then, generates among the subaltern classes a particular conception of the right way to live, authorising 'a particular form of life.'[150] The hegemonic function of the law, hence, allows for the naturalisation, rationalisation and universalisation of the dominant ideology of the ruling class.[151]

One could extend Gramsci's analysis of law to what has been detailed above in the context of the labour law's appropriation by the Iraqi counter-hegemonic movement. The 'educative' function of the law could go both ways and the labour movement was aware of this as its organic intellectuals (a lot of whom were lawyers themselves) would use the labour law as a way to educate the workers on their rights, but even more broadly construct a counter-hegemonic culture that includes new visions of a just social order. As will be shown, the law was used in such a fashion throughout the monarchical period even by the more radical communist-led labour movement, who did not cease to take the law seriously despite knowing that the real struggle lay outside the confines of the law. In this way, although the law was always contested, this did not mean that it was a neutral arena of class struggle, for it was merely *one front* wherein the workers exerted their vision of the future. As Issa Shivji emphasised in his own study of the Tanzanian working class:

> It is undoubtedly true that state and law ultimately serve the interests of the ruling dominating class. But this comes about in the process of complex social struggles. As a result of these struggles, undeniably the law comes to embody certain partial successes and concessions won from the dominated classes. But this should not be taken to mean that the law has no class character or that it is a neutral arena of class struggle. Neither law nor legality *per se* is in the interests of the oppressed classes. Rather, *it is the social struggles of the oppressed classes themselves which lend content to law and legality*.[152]

Hence, despite the fact that law was an 'instrument of the ruling class,' more so in a colonial or semi-colonial context, it remained one (limited) locus of working-class struggle. This indicates that the law was malleable enough to be imagined by the workers in their visions of a just alternative order that they were struggling for – uniting them to move towards some form of 'proletarian hegemony'. As Alan Hunt has similarly emphasised, '[t]he law and legal system form part of the context within which the class struggle takes place, and it is itself an

[149] D Kennedy, "Antonio Gramsci and the Legal System," *American Legal Studies Forum*, (1982), 6(1), 36.

[150] S Buckel, A Fischer-Lescano. "Gramsci Reconsidered: Hegemony in Global Law," *Leiden Journal of International Law*, 22, (2009), 447.

[151] D Litowitz, 'Gramsci, Hegemony, and the Law,' *Brigham Young University Law Review*, 2000, No. 2, 515–551, 522.

[152] IG Shivji, *Law, State, and the Working Class in Tanzania*, (Heinemann, 1986), 241, emphasis added.

arena in which the struggle occurs. [However,] to recognise that the class struggle occurs within the legal system is not to suggest that the legal system is some neutral territory over which the class struggle wrestles for control. As a major component of the state, law is necessarily part of the process through which the ruling class seeks to preserve its domination'.[153] Gramsci understood that there was a (class) 'struggle for the control of law,' which involves the need for 'subordinate classes to become "legislators" by achieving authoritative, norm-creating capacity'.[154] The organising actions of the Iraqi working class and their interactions with legality amounted to a form of 'norm creating' that would finally materialise during the 1958 revolution which overthrew the social order that was structured by international processes, such as the ILO. Consequently the appropriation and interpretation of legislation, such as the 1936 Labour Law 'from below' by the labour movement certainly had a significant impact on the development of working-class consciousness and the forging of the labour struggle ahead.

Before the demise of the JAS, a 1933 police intelligence report made note of the arrival to Baghdad of a young blacksmith and 'suspected communist,' Yūsuf Salmān Yūsuf (Known to his comrades by his *nom-de-guerre*, Comrade Fahad) from Nasiriya to attend a meeting with Qazzāz. Yūsuf, who would become the famed Secretary-General of the Iraqi Communist Party (ICP), was negotiating his appointment as Secretary to the Nasiriya JAS branch. The report warned that this indicated 'a possible attempt to introduce more direct communist influence into the Trade Union movement in Iraq'.[155] It certainly foreshadowed the coming influence of the communists on the labour movement in Iraq in the next decade, who continued to ingeniously appropriate legality, referring to the 1936 Labour Law (and certain principles enshrined in the Iraqi Constitution) to advance their rights and the counter-hegemonic struggle, as they were quite cognisant of the value of law in educating the masses.

In 1944, Yusūf penned an essay that illustrates this tactic of using legal rhetoric in the counter-hegemonic struggle, entitled 'The Trade Union is the Motto of the Worker Today', published in the communist paper, *al-Qā'ida* ('The Base'), in which he stresses the importance of extending the trade union movement to all sectors of the economy, so as to include all workers across sectoral lines.[156] Calling for the creation of a unified trade union representing all workers in Iraq, he refers to the law as a tool that should be appropriated by the workers in their struggle:

> it is necessary to include in the trade union movement all categories of workers, and for the word 'trade union' to be the slogan of the workers today … and [while

[153] A Hunt, "Law, State, and Class Struggle" in *Explorations in Law and Society: Toward a Constitutive Theory of Law* (Routledge, 1993), 32.

[154] A Hunt, "Rights and Social Movements Counterhegemonic Strategies", *ibid*, 236.

[155] TNA, FO 622/1/155. Labour Organizations in Iraq (1933).

[156] YS Yūsuf, *Al-Qā'ida*, Number 4 and 5, April 1944 in *Mu'alafāt al-Rafīq Fahad* ['The Works of Comrade Fahad'], (Baghdad: al-Thaqāfa al-Jadīda Press, n.d.), 291-297.

> carrying] *in their pockets the labour law* and the charter of one of the unions, so as to explain … [to their comrades] the benefits of the union and its necessity in workers' lives … it should not leave the worker's mind that their route is not furnished with flowers and basil, as their mission does not end when they submit their application nor when they are granted a license to establish a union, but they have to bring to their union the majority of the workers of their industry … to educate them … [on] … the union based on the Charter and [the 1936] Labour Law No. 72 …[157]

Yūsuf believed that the Labour Law of 1936 had a role to play in the working-class struggle despite (and especially considering) the fact that it was not being enforced by the state, and so he asked that workers keep the labour law 'in their pockets' to serve as a reminder of their rights.

Here, the workers' appropriation of the ideological force of the law in their struggle had its advantages, although it also had its limits, for, as we shall see, the Iraqi workers' struggle was not a legal one per se. It was largely waged outside the confines of the law, as it related to the structural question of conflicting visons of social orders, which in the end mere legal reform could not address. However, this did not mean that legality was not ideologically pertinent for the workers' assertions of their demands and their overall struggle. Although the continuous reference to the law and the use of legality was a powerful arsenal for workers' struggle, it also had its limits, especially in a semi-colonial context. The Iraqi state did not allow for too much elbowroom where law and legality became an arena of class struggle. This was quite different from the more developed Western liberal state, where legality was continuously used as 'a modality for shaping relations between labour and capital'.[158] The Western state eventually found it essential to use the law to institutionalise conflict between employers and workers, while attempting to avoid violent repression as much as is possible. The colonial and semi-colonial state, on the other hand, did not find it necessary to do so, and was hence more prone to use violence to suppress workers' demands. The workers' struggle in Iraq was, therefore, mostly waged outside the law out of necessity.

## VIII. CONCLUSION

This chapter detailed the history of the formative years of the Iraqi working class in Baghdad, while contextualising the first labour law passed in the country in 1936. I argued that despite the fact that this law was not enforced by the state, it was in reality a concession given to the workers, because of their unrelenting strike actions, in particular of 1930 and 1931. I then make the contention that the principles embedded in this law were later appropriated by the labour movement as it was denoted in nearly every list of demands, even so by the

[157] *Ibid*, 294.
[158] See E Tucker and J Fudge, *Labor Before the Law* (OUP, 2000).

later communist-led movement in the next decade. This fact illustrates that the law and its ideology was a useful tool for counter-hegemonic movements in the semi-colonial context as it had an educative function, expanding workers' class-consciousness by allowing them to understand their conditions in the overall semi-colonial capitalist system. In a sense, therefore, this chapter has shown that the ideology of the law provides those who are struggling against the entire social order with a language to articulate their demands, as well as the imaginations for alternative futures.

The fall of the JAS in 1935 and the failure of its reformist social-democratic vision permitted more radical and revolutionary ideas, which were in the margins previously, to emerge to the forefront of Iraqi working-class politics. Communism was to eventually become so widespread in Iraqi society that it organically evolved into a powerful grassroots anti-colonial movement while entrenching itself into working-class culture and political imagination. Although this is not the place to delve into a detailed history of the ICP and its sophisticated organisational and political underground structures, as will become clear later, the party was not only a genuine 'Iraqi' party that represented all sectors of the population, but its popularity would soar as the struggle for national independence intensified. It is enough to say that once communism arrived in Iraq, it was difficult for it not to spread the way that it did, especially considering that the social and economic dynamics described in Chapter 1 were gradually constituting extreme inequality in Iraqi society. Moreover, it was the manner in which the communists explained, in everyday layman's language, the important connections between the economic and political character of the working-class struggle, and how the Iraqi state operated within an international imperialist order, that made their approach persuasive and effective. As the next chapters on the oil, railway and port workers will illustrate, the communists maintained that British imperialism *and* the social, economic and political conditions of the working class were intertwined, and that therefore they must be dealt with together.

# 4

# *Disrupting the Circuits of Capitalism: The IPC Workers' Struggle against the Legal Infrastructures of the Oil Frontier in the Middle East*

## I. INTRODUCTION

We have already revealed the manner in which the Iraq Petroleum Company (IPC) oil concession and the pipeline agreements were intrinsically linked to the manufacturing of the doctrine of semi-peripheral sovereignty, and the making of 'independence' in Iraq. The purpose of this chapter is to analyse the implications and effects of the oil concession and the doctrine of semi-peripheral sovereignty on the socio-economic conditions of the working class, in particular by examining the micro-history of the oil fields in the provincial city of Kirkuk in the Mosul *vilayet*. To do this, we will begin by broadly situating the IPC oil fields in Kirkuk within the vast petroleum infrastructure and networks of the region, in particular illustrating the geopolitics of oil pipelines in the Middle East. The legal arrangements described in Chapter 2 simultaneously created an oppressive concessionary spatial configuration in the region that furthered capitalist accumulation and exploitation. My main argument is that the manner by which the oil workers organised their militant strike actions affected this legal spatiality of imperialism, and, in turn, brought alternative notions of legal and social order to the fore. After exploring how the rural-urban migration transformed the city of Kirkuk and its surrounding areas, I will turn to examine the everyday conditions of the oil workers and will illustrate the effects of the IPC on the urban landscape of the city. This will lead to an analysis of why and how the oil workers organised against the legal structures and spatialities of oil imperialism that were imposed upon them, and how their organised strike actions at specific points in space and time forced the IPC, the British and the Iraqi government to reassess their labour arrangements.

Turning to describe and analyse the Gāwūrbāghī strike of 1946, the chapter reveals how it was violently suppressed with the complicity of the IPC, the British Embassy and the Iraqi state. After critiquing the 'official' company narrative of the strike by reading British and IPC archives against the grain, it will be clear that the IPC's ultimate response to the strike was to shift its ideological approach from extreme paternal exploitation to that of urban social development, including attempts to impose an alternative labour ideology of trade unionism. Finally, it will be shown how law played a vital role in the production of the spaces of the Iraqi oil frontier with an examination of the legendary K3 pumping-station strike of 1948 in Haditha, which successfully disrupted the flow of oil. What this unique narrative tells us about the significance of strategic spatial resistance in the context of international law and the circuits of capitalism will consequently be explored.

The main task of this chapter is to examine what Joseph Sassoon referred to as the 'triangular relationship' between the Iraqi government, the IPC and the British Embassy.[1] I will illustrate how the oil workers exposed this 'triangular' relationship through their organised strike actions. The economic and political influence of the IPC on the city of Kirkuk occurred as a result of the legal structures imposed by the oil concession in conjuncture with the 1930 Anglo-Iraqi Treaty, which allowed it to wield broad governing powers on the local economy of the city, and indirectly on Iraq as a whole. The doctrine of semi-peripheral sovereignty described in Chapter 2 brought about an ambiguous jurisdictional space that allowed for such (fragmentary) hegemonic control to emerge, while contriving at least the appearance of an arm's length relationship between the three actors. So, despite the fact that the IPC and the British Embassy kept in regular contact, and coordinated and exchanged intelligence, British officials emphasised that the IPC was 'quite separate from His Majesty's Government'.[2] The fact was that their relationship was more harmonious, as the IPC was willing to assist the British Embassy in their political and imperial aims in the country and vice versa.[3] The ability to claim that there was a *separation* between the interests of the British and the IPC was partly made possible because of the juridical instruments at the intersection of the oil concession and the 1930 Treaty; the legal aspects of this history must therefore be taken more seriously in the current scholarship.

## II. THE INFRASTRUCTURE OF THE MIDDLE EAST PETROLUEMSCAPE: CONCEPTS OF THE COMPANY TOWN, THE ENCLAVE AND LEGAL SPATIALITIES

To grasp the significance of the IPC oil fields in Kirkuk, one must first locate it within the vast infrastructure of petroleum extraction in the Middle East. Considering that the international legal arrangements described earlier were essentially attempts to control, access and exploit certain territories, it only makes

[1] Sassoon, *supra*, 252.

[2] TNA, Comments by Beckett (Treasury), 29 May 1942. T 160/1157/17859, as referred to by Sassoon, *supra*, 251.

[3] One British official in London made it clear that there should be closer coordination between the British government and the oil companies in the region: 'His Majesty's Government and the oil companies are all in it together and … the more mutually helpful they can be to each other the better.' TNA, Minute by E.A. Berthoud, 18th May 1948, FO/371/68479.

sense to understand the ways that the petroleum infrastructures, or what I term the 'legal spatialities of the oil industry', are interrelated. Carola Hein conjures these interconnected networks in her concept of the *global palimpsestic petroleumscape*, which she defines as 'a layered physical and social landscape that reinforces itself over time through human action and connects urban and rural spaces, culture and nature, materials and intangible practices'.[4] This concept is helpful for understanding how various infrastructures, whether oil fields, refineries, company headquarters, pipelines, company towns, etc., which are all dispersed in uneven ways, although each serves distinct functions across borders and jurisdictions, and may appear disconnected, they are in fact part of *one* interconnected 'spatial system' of petroleum extraction, production and transportation.[5] The rural and urban landscapes of many underdeveloped territories were completely transformed by these interconnections, as these networks ensured that the circuits of capitalist accumulation operated smoothly, and by the contradictions of capitalist modernity and the global economy. The concept of *petroleumscape* is also useful to reveal how '[o]il extraction, production and resale are all spatially anchored through extraction, transformation, transportation, storage, and consumption', and how petroleum interests resulted in tense geopolitical conflicts, including wars that upended the structures of nation-states.[6] In that sense, it becomes clear that petroleum was 'an agent of spatial transformation'.[7] The argument of this chapter is that parallel to and constitutive of these spatial transformations was the production of *legal* regimes and spatialities. In other words, these oil spaces were also products of the international legal architecture that legitimised capitalist extractivism and labour exploitation in international and transnational law. They were, as we shall see, also products of the dialectical struggles between the oil company, and the locals and labourers who inhabited these contested spaces on the ground. I will return to this analysis in more detail in due course.

The focus of this chapter is the company town[8] and enclave of Kirkuk in the context of the infrastructure of the petroluemscape of the Middle East. The Arab oil company town has experienced considerable social disruption, development and urban transformations since the discovery of oil in the twentieth century.[9] Despite the unevenness and diversity of these urban transformations, company towns constituted one part of the vast petroleum infrastructure of extractivism and exploitation in the Middle East. As Nelida Fuccaro has demonstrated, the

[4] C Hein, 'Space, Time, and Oil: The Global Petroleumscape' in C Hein (ed.), *Oil Spaces: Exploring the Global Petroleumscape* (Routledge, 2022), 3–18.

[5] *Ibid*, 3.

[6] *Ibid*, 4.

[7] *Ibid*.

[8] The concept of the company town was first coined in the late nineteenth century and applied to mining camps in the US. *See* J Garner (ed.), *The Company Town: Architecture and Society in the Early Industrial Age* (OUP, 1992).

[9] For a study of oil company towns in the region, see IJ Seccombe and RI Lawless, *Work Camps and Company Towns: Settlement Patterns and the Gulf Oil Industry* (University of Durham: Centre for Middle Eastern and Islamic Studies, 1987).

'oil company town [in the Middle East] was ... the center stage of petroleum's industrial urbanism, and the headquarters of the powerful consortia of foreign companies that set up and controlled the industry throughout the Arab world until the 1970s'.[10] These foreign oil companies were legally and economically linked to the colonial and imperial powers, especially Britain, France and the US Empire. Serving as 'key nodes' of oil extraction and management, oil company towns 'underpinned the new geographies of petroleum refinement and transport that shaped local, regional, and global geopolitics'.[11] In that sense, these towns can only be properly analysed in the context of the *totality* of the structures underpinning capitalist extraction, as well as labour exploitation.

After the discovery of oil in southeastern Persia (modern-day Iran), the British-owned Anglo-Iranian Oil Company (AIOC) built the first oil company town of its kind in Abadan, which was completed in 1913.[12] By the 1950s it lauded the largest oil refinery and oil company town in the region. The location of the AIOC oil fields in Abadan was in close proximity to Iraq and the Persian Gulf, which explains why the Middle East region was considered so vital for British imperial interests. In a way, Britain's decision to dominate Iraq and control the Mosul oil fields after the war was certainly related to its proximity to this most valuable petroleum node of the AIOC. Following Abadan, British and American oil companies set up company camps in other parts of the region where oil was discovered: Awali in Bahrain (1937), Kirkuk-Arrappha in Iraq (1946), Ahmadi in Kuwait (1946), Dhahran, Ras Tannura, and Abqaiq in Saudi Arabia (post-1938), and Umm Sa'id in Qatar (1949).[13] Most of these towns were subsequently transformed from pre-industrial provincial villages into modern industrial cities, as petroleum was the most important industrial enterprise in the region. Considering the centrality of these nodes of petroleum infrastructure, oil towns intersected with multiple regimes of technology and expertise, as well as with urban life and labour regimes. Oil companies were also integrated into administrative zones, which served the operational needs of the oil fields, such as the transportation and communication networks, including roads, electricity grids, railways and ports. All these structures were highly integrated into the system of petroleum extraction. The British government, for instance, through the vast undertakings of the AIOC to connect the major nodes that were widely geographically separated, constructed production networks,

[10] N Fuccaro, 'Arab Towns As Petro-Histories' in *Oil Spaces: Exploring the Global Petroleumscape* (Routledge, 2022), 129–144; 130.

[11] Ibid.

[12] See K Ehasani, 'Social Engineering and the Contradictions of Modernization in Khuzestan's Company Towns: A Look at Abadan and Masjed-Soleyman' *International Review of Social History* Vol. 48, No. 3 (December 2003), 361-399. For an early history of the AIOC leading up to the Anglo-Iranian dispute, see LP Elwell-Sutton, *Persian Oil: A Study in Power Politics* (Lawrence & Wishart, 1955).

[13] Fuccaro, 'Arab Towns ...' *supra*, 131. For a documentary history of oil concessions in the region, see WJ Kennedy (ed.), *Secret History of the Oil Companies in the Middle East* (Documentary Publications, 1979).

transport links and pipeline infrastructure with the aim 'to build the company into one of the world's most effectively integrated oil organisations'.[14]

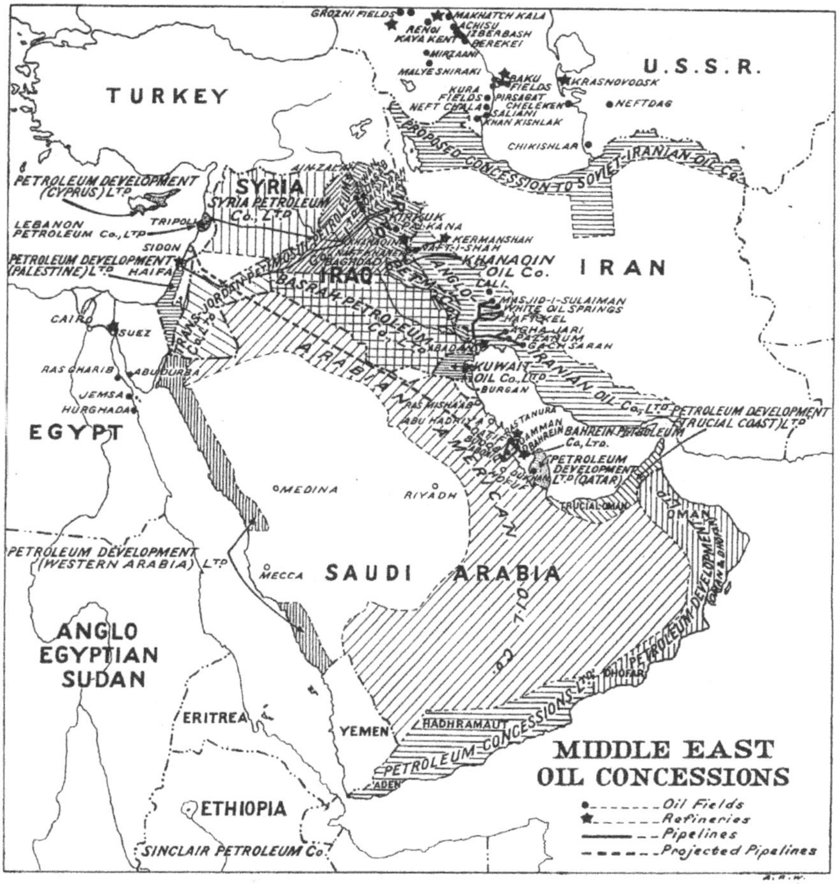


**Figure 4** 'Middle East Oil Concessions'; *Handbook of the territories which form the theatre of operations of the Iraq Petroleum Company and its associated companies* (Iraq Petroleum Company, London, 1948); ARC32260. Reproduced from the BP Archive.

Company towns, especially those in remote locations, required investment and planning including housing and services for workers, to ensure the efficiency of production. These experiments in semi-colonial and imperial governance were often infused with notions of civilisational paternalism, while following a capitalist logic hinged on capitalist accumulation and labour exploitation. In addition, company towns presented an idealist image of harmony between

[14] LM Fanning, *Foreign Oil and the Free World* (McGraw-Hill Book Co., 1954), 48.

workers and management – an ideology that represented company towns as model 'spaces of cooperation instead of conflict', the aim of which was to transcend the 'labour-capital confrontation', and its natural dialectical tension.[15] Although these experiments in social engineering seldom worked, they certainly had lasting effects on the local landscape.

Another important concept is the *enclave*, which was first used to analyse a model of export production by foreign capital in Latin American states, such as the banana plantations of the United Fruit Company in Guatemala, the sugar plantations of Cuba, and the copper mines of Chile.[16] This concept is useful in that it illustrates how industrial production of a commodity, rather than being fully integrated into the national or local economy, is exported to the metropole, usually in the form of raw materials. The enclave also emphasises its de facto autonomy, which is what allows it to function at times like 'a state within a state', operating with a certain independence from the municipal government, while using its foreign capital to wield its political power over its concessionary space and the local population. As Marecelo J. Borges and Susana B. Torres argue, the company camp[/enclave] reflects 'the double role' of the company as an employer and 'de facto local government and enforcer of community rules' – the company's control over production and labour gives it a governing capacity, and this was certainly the result of its power over space, and as we shall see, it was the law and its articulation that gave the oil company that power over space.[17] Keeping these concepts of the company town and the enclave in mind, we can now move to explore the changing patterns of the city of Kirkuk and the manner in which the IPC transformed its landscape, and affected its local population and the conditions of the working class.

## III. URBAN MIGRATION AND THE QUESTION OF LABOUR TRANSITION IN POST-WAR IRAQ

Although Iraq's population was mostly rural, by the end of the 1940s the urban populations of the cities were growing at a rapid pace, increasing from only 25 per cent in 1930 to 37 per cent in 1947.[18] I have already described one of the main reasons for this mass exodus in Chapter 1 – the intolerable conditions of

[15] MJ Borges and SB Tores, 'Company towns: Concepts, Historiography, and Approaches' in MJ Borges and SB Tores (eds.), *Company Towns: Labor, Space, and Power Relations across Time and Continents* (Palgrave Macmillan, 2012); 3.

[16] *Ibid*, 8. The concept was first coined by Fernando Cardoso. *See* FH Cardoso and E Faletto, *Dependencia y desarrollo en America Latina* (Mexico City: Siglo XXI, 1979). It was applied later to other contexts: see D Glanday, 'Le Domaine Colonial: Class Formation in a Natural Resource Enclave,' *The Canadian Journal of Sociology* 9,2 (Spring 1984): 159–77; TM Kublock, *Contested Communities: Class, Gender, and Politics in Chile's El Teniente Copper Mines*, 1904-1951 (Duke University Press, 1998); G McGillivary, *Blazing Cane: Sugar Communities, Class, and State Formation in Cuba, 1868-1959* (Duke University Press, 2009); SS Gillick, *Life and Labor in a Banana Enclave: Bananeros, the United Fruit Company, and the Limits of Trade Unionism in Guatemala, 1906 to 1931* (PhD, Tulane University, 1994).

[17] Borges and Tores, *supra*, 11.

[18] Sassoon, *supra*, 3.

the agricultural worker (*fellāh*), who took every opportunity to flee from his serf-like conditions, seeking a better life in the cities. No longer tied to the land, the *fellāh* became a wage earner. However, as we saw, when he reached the city, he found that conditions were not so much better. Most rural migrant workers became the bulk of the unskilled workforce, taking on precarious work, inhabiting the *sarifas* and squatting at the outskirts of the cities. One significant factor that contributed to the fast-changing labour conditions of underemployment in the 1940s, similar to other parts of the world, was directly caused by the winding up of the war effort that employed a bulk of the Iraqi working class. The Middle East Supply Centre (MESC)[19] commissioned a British academic (Dr. Robert Peers) to write a report to study the question of labour and provide advice on solutions regarding the anticipated mass layoff of local workers that were to be discharged from the service of the British Army by the end of the war.[20] Peers made several proposals that entailed that 'surplus labour' could be reabsorbed into certain sectors, in particular the 'modal points of movements, [communications] and trade' (i.e. the railways, the port of Basra and road transportation).[21] Other than the apparent development of irrigation and agriculture schemes, the expansion of public works allowed for the re-employment of those discharged, although Peers admitted that certain unskilled workers (what he referred to as 'black-coated laborers') were difficult to absorb into the peacetime economy.[22] The increased output of oil, a valuable 'exportable commodity' was regarded as a promising outlet that would help in this regard.[23] Despite having a somewhat positive outlook on the prospects of labour in post-war Iraq, Peers was cognisant of some of the difficulties that would arise. 'It is wrong to assume,' he wrote 'that the entire body of unskilled laborers recruited for the war effort will easily and automatically return to their villages, to be reabsorbed into agricultural pursuits …'.[24] It was clear that there was now 'an uprooted class' emerging that would not return to agricultural pursuits, especially considering that there was absolutely no security for the small cultivator and the *fellāh*. Peers' final report was submitted to labour committees, which were formed during the war and were composed of representatives from the Royal Air Force (RAF), The Royal Observer Corps (ROC), the IPC and the Iraqi government, aimed at framing the labour policy of the country, and were tasked with post-war labour transition.[25]

[19] The Middle East Supply Centre (MESC) was an agency set up in Cairo in 1941 during World War II as a clearinghouse for all matters of civilian supply and transport in the region. Its goal was to regulate and control shipping and commerce among the countries in the region to aid the war effort. See MW Wilmington, *The Middle East Supply Centre* (SUNY, 1971).

[20] TNA. FO 921/302. 'Labour, Middle East: Report on Iraq by Professor Peers' (1944).

[21] *Ibid*, 11.

[22] *Ibid.*

[23] *Ibid*, 17.

[24] *Ibid.*

[25] See TNA. FO 921/300. Director of Pioneers and Labour to Peers, 829/PL. 26 May, 1944; FO 371/45304. 22 June, 1945. 'Disposal of Civilian Labour discharged in Iraq by British forces'.

## IV. EVERYDAY LIFE IN THE IPC ENCLAVE OF KIRKUK & THE MISERABLE CONDITIONS OF THE IRAQI OIL WORKER

The economic power wielded by the IPC with the support of the British Embassy arguably made it function politically akin to a *de facto* 'state within a state' as it operated with its own governing capacity, particularly in its relation to its workers and the local Kirkuki population. Consequently, its labour policies made a considerable impact on the city, which affected the wider labour policy of the country as a whole. As described in Chapter 2, the 1931 Concession was favourable to the IPC. It eliminated the Iraqi government's power to tax the company's profits and removed the minimum-drilling obligation. By expanding the concessionary area from 50,000 hectares to 8 million hectares, the IPC would eventually gain a monopoly over the entire topographical area of the oil fields, and, in turn, oil production in Iraq (initially excluding Basra).

Although oil profits were not yet considerable for the development of the country, which only started after 1950 with the renegotiation of the oil agreement and the increase of royalties and the formation of the Development Board, it nevertheless significantly contributed to the finances of the government and its budget.[26] The Iraqi government regularly turned to the IPC for direct loans, which were never given unconditionally.[27] Furthermore, the central government in Baghdad seldom interfered with the IPC's operations in the city of Kirkuk, and the weak municipal government in many ways preferred to protect the IPC's private interests (even violently if need be) as opposed to that of its constituents. One company report described the IPC's power in freely wielding its political influence, stating that 'in Iraq … we are fortunate in having more freedom of action, with our operations not subject to the dictates of restrictive [state] legislation …'.[28] From the moment that oil volcanically erupted out of the drill at Baba Gurgur in June 1927, becoming the coronary artery of the Kirkuk oil fields and the Kirkuk-Haifa-Tripoli pipeline, Iraq was transformed from a potential prize to 'one of the most valuable [oil] concessionary areas in the world' with an estimated 5 billion barrels.[29] Considering the significance of oil for British geostrategic, economic and military interests, it was no surprise that the British government would choose to eagerly put their administrative and diplomatic resources at the service of the IPC, especially when it came to controlling labour unrest, which certainly took its inspiration from broader concerns of anti-imperialism, communism and nationalism.[30] The IPC, therefore, had the characteristics of both an imperial governing power and a private corporation, while it operated (after 1932) inside de jure 'sovereign' territory that belonged to Iraq. In other words, the IPC gained a

[26] For details on these negotiations and the agreement, see Penrose & Penrose, *Iraq: International Relations and National Development*, (Ernest Benn, 1978).

[27] Sassoon, *supra*, 249.

[28] BPA, 'Comments on: Report on Employees Housing Programme,' 23 June 1952. BP 135818.

[29] JH Bamberg, *The History of the British Petroleum Company: Volume 2, The Anglo-Iranian Years, 1928-1954*, (CUP, 1994), 157.

[30] TNA. FO 371/61673. 'Strategic Importance of Kirkuk oilfields' (9 April, 1947).

particular kind of corporate sovereignty granted by the oil concession. As such, it imposed its own capitalist social order onto the city – one that took into account the broader geopolitics of the Middle East petroluemscape, while the local population and especially the IPC workers found ways to subvert these structures through their counter-hegemonic struggles. This situation elucidates what James Ferguson revealed as the emergence of 'new forms of disorder and order' that accompanied the oil company's 'selectively territorialised' mineral-extraction enclaves, which allowed capital to flow and 'hop' freely in-between wide geographic spaces.[31] For this reason, as Fuccaro argues, an oil city with a turbulent history such as Kirkuk was located, 'at the *intersection* of the complex corporate, imperial, national and international politics that marked the development of oil production in the Middle East after the First World War'.[32] It was at this spatial intersection that contradictory tensions emerged and where urban violence and industrial unrest manifested, and it was also where legal spatialities that had been shaped by international and transnational law materialised into the everyday lives of the working class and the inhabitants of the Kirkuk enclave.

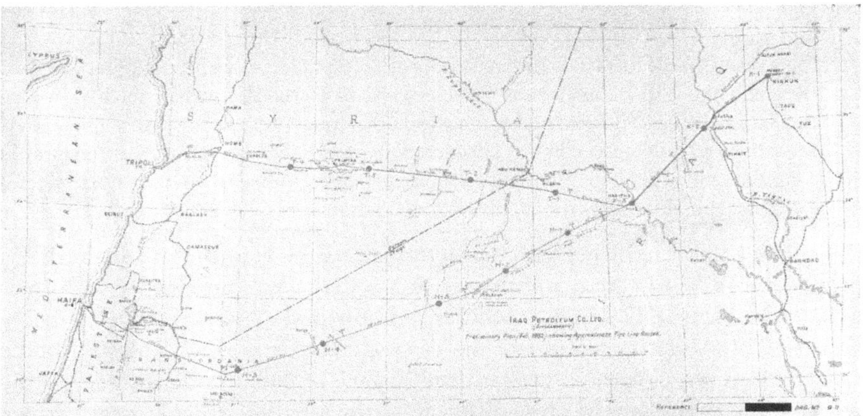


**Figure 5** 'Haifa-Tripoli-Kirkuk Pipelines' CO 732/70/2 (1). Iraq Petroleum Co (1932)

The IPC's arrival in Kirkuk considerably altered its urban landscape and demography as it attracted diverse labour migration of those seeking work from rural areas and surrounding cities.[33] These rapid changes would result

[31] J Ferguson, "Seeing Like an Oil Company: Space, Security, and Global Capital in Neoliberal Africa," (2005) *American Anthropologist*, Vol 7, Issue, 377–382.

[32] N Fuccaro, "Reading Oil as Urban Violence: Kirkuk and its Oil Conurbation, 1927-58," in Freitag, Fuccaro, Ghrawi & Lafi, (Eds.), *Urban Violence in the Middle East: Changing Cityscapes in the Transition from Empire into Nation State* (Berghahn, 2015), 222–242; 223.

[33] For a detailed discussion of the effects of the IPC on Kirkuk's urban landscape see, A Bet-Shlimon, *City of Black Gold: Oil, Ethnicity and the Making of Modern Kirkuk* (Stanford University Press, 2019), 79-106.

in an increase of Kirkuk's urban population from around 25,000 in the 1920s to 68,000 in 1947, nearly half of which were to be employed by the IPC.[34] Within the next two decades, Kirkuk would quickly be transformed not only into a modern 'oil city' but also into a focal pipeline town and terminus where Iraq's so-called 'Third River' emanates from.[35] The IPC went on to build a complex network of oil pipelines from Kirkuk across vast tracts of desert to reach the ports of the Eastern Mediterranean in Palestine and Lebanon. Twelve mini-company towns were erected along a parallel network of 12-inch and 16-inch oil pipelines that functioned as pumping-stations with a combined capacity of 84,000 barrels/day (4,000,000 tons per year).[36] Seven of these oil stations were in Iraq, (while three were in Syria and two in Transjordan): K1 was the first station built adjacently to the Kirkuk fields; K2 was 25 miles away; K3 was located in the small town of Haditha in the Upper Euphrates, and was the point of bifurcation (i.e. where the pipeline diverged into two directions, one going to Tripoli and the other to Haifa), and finally T1 was located not far from the Lebanese border (part of Syria at the time).[37] Three more pumping stations (H1, H2 and H3) crossed southwestward to the port of Haifa. One British exploration geologist described the complex IPC infrastructure that complemented this network of oil pipelines:

> There was a whole infrastructure to support the [pipe] lines: twelve pumping stations; 100 wells and 320 kilometres of water pipelines in the desert, serviced by twelve smaller pumping stations to provide drinkable water; terminals with eight underwater lines to moving berths 1.5 kilometers from the shore; a network of telegraph, telephone and wireless connections to support operations; an air transport system; four main rail heals workshops, offices and a labour force ....[38]

These interconnected towns of the petroluemscape were central to the IPC's propaganda effort in Iraq, and the region, as they were presented – with their modern residential buildings, facilities, schools and supermarkets – as being a part of the larger endeavour in the development of a 'new' modern Middle East.[39] However, concealed beneath the surface of this façade, reality for the working class could not be more different, as the majority of daily wage earners

[34] *Ibid*,161.

[35] Fuccaro, *supra*, 225. The propaganda film entitled 'the Third River' presented the IPC as producing the river of wealth that would flow into the world transforming everything it touches. Accessed at BPA, July 2016.

[36] S Longrigg, *Oil in the Middle East: Its Discovery and Development*, (OUP, 1969), 179.

[37] Fuccaro, *supra*, 225. *See* Iraq Petroleum Co. *An Account of the Construction in the years 1932 to 1934 of the Pipe-line of the Iraq Petroleum Company, limited, from its oilfield in the vicinity of Kirkuk, Iraq to the Mediterranean ports of Haifa (Palestine) and Tripoli (Lebanon)*, (St. Clements Press, 1934).

[38] MQ Morton. *In the Heart of the Desert: The Story of an Exploration Geologist and the Search for Oil in the Middle East* (Green Mountain Press, 2007), 11.

[39] Henry Longhurst describes the private company jets (named the IPC's 'Doves') as 'flying like clockwork between headquarters, the oilfields and the pumping stations'. H Longhurst, *Adventure in Oil: The Story of British Petroleum* (Sidgwick and Jackson, 1959), 204.

were subject to intense semi-colonial exploitation and racialisation. Desmond Stewart and John Haylock, two British school teachers living in the enclave at the time, described the K3 pumping station as an 'oil cage', denoted by 'a military abbreviation' that was more 'a nightmare settlement from science fiction', as it was based on a system of extreme racial-class exploitation:

> Nearly three thousand people live on [sic] the [pumping] station, and they are rigidly segregated into castes. British employees and a few Iraqis compromise the first class; school teachers are included with the clerks in the second; labourers are, of course, in the third ... The cool, thickening [British] officials give the Iraqis the impression that they regard themselves as superior beings, angels of technology with messages and orders, to be delivered in office hours ... In K3 [they conclude] even in politeness the class system prevails. The "first class" do not salute the "third class," the "second class" can only go into the first-class club by invitation.[40]

This 'caste-like system' of exploitation was a regular feature of colonial relations throughout the territories of the British Empire. These social relations clearly remained intact even after Iraq's independence, openly visible and unbroken within the IPC enclave.

Although the IPC controlled the supply of labour in its oil fields, a bulk of local workers were daily wage earners hired directly from Bedouin contractors.[41] An exploitative system of tribal 'racketeering' was in place, and it expanded due to the lack of trade unions at the time. It often put the worker in debt, forcing him to borrow money from local moneylenders and loansharks to pay the high employment fees.[42] The IPC did not contest this system of labour recruitment and was rather complicit in its perpetuation by regularly using it to hire many of its daily wage earners, at least until the early 1950s. It was this system of labour recruitment that was heavily relied on in the construction of the oil pipelines and its infrastructure described above, and it continued to exist thereafter.[43] Tribal sheikhs sold their tribesmen's labour on a daily basis to avoid the provisions of the labour law, which did not protect daily workers. Yet, the IPC was always careful to assert that their workers were paid a higher wage than any other industrial establishment in the country.[44]

IPC workers were hired on the basis of a hierarchal grade system – there were at least five grades of workers with different wage scales. For instance, the company hired 'coolies' and 'unskilled labour' as daily wage earners, as opposed to skilled laborers, who would have to receive a higher monthly wage. A labour sub-committee report indicated that the lowest daily wage paid in October 1946 was 310 fils[45] (or 260 fils without rent allowance), and the minimum living cost

[40] D Stewart and J Haylock, *New Babylon: A Portrait of Iraq* (Collins, 1956), 181-190.

[41] TNA. LAB 13/674. 'Notes on Labour Expert's visit to K3 & K2,' on 11th to 15th Jan, 1952, by Labour Advisor of Iraqi Government.

[42] *Ibid.*

[43] See Iraq Petroleum Co. *An Account of the Construction, supra.*

[44] TNA. FO 371/68482. 'Report on visit to Iraq from 8th June to 10th July by M.T. Audsley' (1 November, 1948).

[45] The Iraqi dinar was on par with the British pound.

index for a small family (or the 'labourer's basket') in June 1946 was 379 fils.[46] As the labour advisor of the British Middle East Office (BMEO) in Cairo, M.T. Audsley reported two months after the 1946 Kirkuk strike, despite the fact that the IPC paid higher wages compared to other large employers, because of growing inflation, no wage was able to keep pace with the rising cost of living index.[47] Hence, he argued that any increase in wages would only lead to an increase in rents and foodstuffs, and this would not have a favourable impact on the community. He, therefore, recommended an increase to the amenities provided rather than to cash wages as a more appropriate response.[48] By comparison, the average wage of semi-skilled labour in other large establishments (such as the ISR) was 230 fils. Audsley admitted that these wages meant that 'vast numbers of workers are very nearly half starved'.[49] This was only a couple of years before the massive *Wathba* uprising, when the cost of living had increased by sixfold as a result of inflation.

The labour conditions in the oil fields were ominously harsher than IPC and British officials would admit. It was not solely a question of the differences in wages between the 'grades' of workers, and the visibly large gap between the wages of officials and skilled workers (mostly British and Europeans), and non-skilled or semi-skilled workers (mostly Iraqi), but there were other broader concerns, which would in time transform the Kirkuk oil fields into the center of labour strike action and anti-imperial struggle. As already mentioned, the IPC operated in a socially segregated manner, not merely in the remoteness of the workers' quarters from the fortified company camp, where higher paid British IPC officials and their families resided, but in everyday company life.[50] One British Embassy councilor noted, 'I found that there was almost completely no intercourse between the IPC and the local inhabitants … and [not even] Iraqi officials ever seemed to be invited to the [company] camp'.[51] Warning of the repercussions, he advised the company to collaborate with the British Institute (a cultural organisation) to invite Iraqis to such things as cinema screenings, even if they 'do not understand a word of the film' as it would at least foster a good relationship.[52] A perceptive British Embassy official wrote an astoundingly candid account of what he encountered when touring the IPC pipeline stations for the first time, which is worth quoting in detail:

> Sometime ago a British businessman … said to me, "Iraq is just like a British Dominion". I was reminded of this remark during the tour which I just made of the

[46] TNA. FO 371/52456. Sir H. Stonehewer-Bird (Bagdad) to FO, 29/10/1946. 'Labour Conditions in Iraq'. See 'Labourer's Basket – man, wife and 2 children as revised by Central Labour Sub-committee ref. Minutes of Meeting of Dec. 22, 1942, Part 1(b)'.

[47] TNA. FO 371/68482. 'Report on visit to Iraq from 8th June to 10th July by M.T. Audsley' (1 November, 1948).

[48] TNA. Stonehewer to FO, 25 Oct 1946, 'Labour Conditions in Iraq', E10773/3860/93.

[49] *Ibid.*

[50] This was the case with other oil fields. R Vitalis brilliantly exposed how ARAMCO established a Jim Crow system – imported from the Southern US – in the Dhahran oil camps in the 1930s. *See* R Vitalis, *America's Kingdom: Mythmaking on the Saudi Frontier*, (Verso, 2009).

[51] TNA. FO 624/105. 'Oil: IPC Labour Welfare', 25 October, 1946.

[52] *Ibid.*

> IPC Pipe line stations … These foreign concessionary installations are directed by a handful of Europeans, mostly British, and the distinction between management and labour rather shocked me … It is difficult to make precise criticisms of the workers' conditions … they are well fed and are for the most part housed in Nissan huts, which are certainly far superior to the mud hovels of their villages … But the relation between management and labour is outwardly that of "sahibs" and "niggers" and this aspect is accentuated by the luxury in which the management and British staff live, and their remoteness. There is no unofficial social contact between British and Iraqis; in fact I gathered that such contact is discouraged … In brief, my impression was what our Russian friends would call capitalism at its worst, and foreign capitalism at that. It is rather a shock to anyone who sees it for the first time ….[53]

Here, one could see how the 'higher wage rate' that the company often referred to served more as a propaganda tool to deflect criticisms as the calculation of a wage could not in itself explain the shockingly humiliating conditions and the racial segregation of the Iraqi workers in these camps or the indignity they felt. The IPC treated the oil company town and the entire city of Kirkuk as its own enclave, for it was already de facto and de jure governed separately from the Iraqi state. IPC officials were generally oblivious to the conditions of the Iraqi workers before the eruption of the strike in 1946.[54] The extraordinary social tensions of semi-colonialism and racial capitalism described above were reflected in the manner in which workers were being discharged, usually without notice. One company response to press criticisms that workers were being unjustly discharged was scribbled on the side of a British report in the following way: 'the statement that "anybody who dares to disobey is discharged immediately" is of course … correct. You could hardly expect to run any undertaking … on any other basis, could you?'[55] Despite the fact that Iraq became an 'independent' state nearly two decades before Wells' report was written, racial colonial relations remained fully intact, especially within the IPC enclaves of oil production. This was certainly an effect of the juridical intersection between the IPC concession and Iraqi semi-peripheral sovereignty. As we shall see, these racial colonial relations, and the indignity that they evoked amongst the Iraqi workers would guarantee the detonation of a massive strike in no time.

## V. THE GĀWŪRBĀGHĪ STRIKE AND THE EFFECTS OF THE LEGAL SPATIALITIES OF THE IPC ENCLAVE

Communist parties around the world were generally given some freedom to operate during the Second World War due to the Soviet Union being an ally in the fight against fascism. The Iraqi Communist Party (ICP) took advantage of this respite by organising workers into trade unions. This had an effect of opening up some freedoms in Iraqi society, and it was around that time in 1942 that an amendment

[53] TNA. FO 624/130, Minutes by F. Wells, 7 April 1948.
[54] A Bet-Shlimon, "The Politics and Ideology of Urban Development in Iraq's Oil City: Kirkuk, 1946-58," *Comparative Studies of South Asia, Africa and the Middle East*, Vol.33, No.1, 2013; 29.
[55] TNA. FO/624/176. 'Oil: IPC Labour', 10 Aug 1949.

to the labour law was passed, which made further improvements in compensation, overtime pay and vacation terms.[56] It was also around that time that the Hamid al-Pachachi government legalised several trade unions – between 1944 and 1945, sixteen trade unions were licensed. Of these sixteen, communists led twelve, while the others were led by those affiliated with the left, such as the social democrats.[57] One of the first unions that was licensed in 1944 was the Railway Workers' Union (RWU). It was this union that would organise one of the most significant industrial strikes in the country – the 15-day *Schālchīyyah* strike of 1945, which became the precursor to the Kirkuk oil strike of 1946.[58] The RWU produced a cadre of labour organisers that would later lead the IPC workers in the Kirkuk oil fields. One of these leaders was a young communist by the name of Hannā Ilyās Kohārī (Abū Til'at),[59] an ex-member of the Supervisory Committee of the suppressed RWU; discharged from the ISR, he eventually found his way into the employ of the IPC.[60]

The ICP was a vast complex organic network organised by branch, district and local committees. The smallest unit in the network was the cell (*al-khaliyyah*) that was made up of two to five members who worked in a common location. The cell was the centre of organising action – the main point of contact with the masses.[61] Workers, peasants, and students were organised in local factory, rural and school committees. It was this type of organisational structure that made the party effective. The main characteristic of communist organising amongst the working class at the time was the strategy of *penetration* – the intention of which was to organically make communism a part of the 'flesh and blood' of the labouring masses.[62] The ICP planned to target the 'colossal enterprises' fully or partially managed and/or owned by the British – the Railways, the Port of Basra and the IPC oil fields. Although, the aim was to convert these monopolistic hubs of imperialism into 'Communist fortresses', it was rather the ability of a handful of communists to guide and influence workers to articulate their demands that eventually made their strikes effective.[63]

Learning of the successes of their fellow Palestinian workers' strike in the IPC terminus in Haifa,[64] the oil workers of Kirkuk (especially the daily workers) distributed a series of petitions. One pamphlet, which was circulated among IPC workers in January 1946, described their miserable conditions in detail, declaring that 'our standard of living … have [sic] become so low that it cannot be

[56] Law No.36 of 1942.

[57] Sbāhī, *supra*, 255.

[58] The *Schālchīyyah* railway strike will be detailed in Chapter 5.

[59] See H Kohārī, "Tahiya Ijlal wa Kībār li shūhadā' al-Tabaqa al-'āmīla" [A homage to the great martyrs of the working-class], in *al-Hīwār al-Mutamadin*, 5/3/2006 (http://m.ahewar.org/s.asp?aid=63746&r=0). After the Kirkuk strike, Hanna Kohārī, a Christian Chaldean, spent his days in prison until the 1958 July Revolution, but was later imprisoned again, tortured and killed by the Ba'athists during the bloody month known as 'Black February' of 1963.

[60] Batatu, *supra*, 622.

[61] J Franzen, *Red Star Over Iraq: Iraqi Communism before Saddam* (Hust & Co), 40.

[62] Batatu, *supra*, 605.

[63] *Ibid*.

[64] See Z Lockman, *Comrades and Enemies: Arab and Jewish Workers in Palestine, 1906-1948* (University of California Press, 1996), 232-34, 327-32.

considered fit for any free and civilised man in the age of the Atomic Bomb'.[65] It goes on to claim that,

> [t]his Concessionaire ... [and the] imperialistic foreigners seek nothing but to augment their own profits, and we, the human-beings, are left ... as a cheap commodity, subjected to those imperialists who cannot sympathise with us, simply because they have come to rob us of everything – our wealth ... independence ... [and] freedom.[66]

The workers went on to criticise their extremely low wages, lack of food, uninhabitable shelter, lack of transportation, and their severe working conditions; ending their appeal with a call for collective organised action: 'organise yourselves rank and file,' they wrote, through the formation of an independent trade union – the Iraqi Oil Workers' Union (IOWU).[67] The moment that the IPC received this petition, the Fields' Manager, H.H. Wheatley, contacted the head of the Kirkuk police, giving him permission to set up a base of operations from inside the oil fields and company camp.[68]

The IPC flatly rejected the oil workers' demands. Instead, they permitted the formation of a toothless 'workmen committee' after expelling several so-called 'agitators' and 'trouble-makers'.[69] Even though Abū Tilʿat was still elected to this committee, he considered it 'an imperialist device aimed at crippling the struggle of the workers and their basic rights'.[70] The workers then decided to meet at a local coffeehouse on June 13, where they agreed on the following list of demands rather than participate in the IPC workmen committee: the recognition of their legal right to form an independent trade union; the increase of their cost of living allowance from 80 to 250 fils; an end to arbitrary dismissal of workers; the arrangement of transportation to and from work; the granting of a war bonus (equivalent to that of the IPC workers in Haifa); and the introduction of sickness, disability and old-age insurance.[71] The *mutasarif* (governor), who acted as a mediator between the company and the workers, subsequently made a statement ensuring his sympathy with them and promising that he would convince the IPC to fulfil their reasonable demands within the provisions of the labour law.[72]

The oil workers then decided to give the authorities a two-week deadline until July 3 to fulfil their demands before calling a strike. On July 1, the company agreed to a mere 50 to 100 fils increase of the high-cost-of-living allowance, and

[65] BPA, 'The Miserable State of the Iraq Petroleum Company's Workmen at Kirkuk,' translated in English and enclosed in 'Iraq During the Year 1946,' File 162461.

[66] *Ibid.*

[67] *Ibid.*

[68] INA, 'Report by the Administrative Investigator Saīd al-Qazāz' in 'Workers' strike of the IPC' 17/Kirkuk/6; refereed to in JA Ḥumaidī. *al-Tatwurāt al-Syasīsya fī al- ʿIraq, 1941-1953* ['The political developments in Iraq, 1941-1953'] (Matbʿa al-Ni ʿman, 1976), 431.

[69] TNA. FO 371/52456. 'Strike of Iraq Petroleum Company at Kirkuk', 1 August 1946.

[70] *Ibid.*

[71] TNA. FO 371/52456. Telegram from Baghdad to Foreign Office, London, 19 July 1946, I.P.C. workers' strike at Kirkuk. Batatu, 623.

[72] INA. 'Statement of Mutasarrif of Kirkuk to IPC workers, No.4810, dated June 19, 1946,' referred to in Humaidī, *supra*, 422.

rejected all other demands.[73] The IPC point of view, according to Wheatley, was that the members of the workmen committee 'seemed satisfied' with this offer and only changed their attitude because of the intimidation tactics of 'political agitators' who 'harangued their colleagues', into believing that they had been 'swindled'.[74] This account was maintained throughout, and the IPC continued to insist that they had always been 'the best employers of labour in Iraq'.[75] The next day a Higher Strikers' Committee was formed, which constituted four worker-communists (including Hanna Ilyās), a Committee-in-Reserve of five, and five subordinate strikers' committees of four to six members each, representing a variety of workers, including, the workshop, motor and mechanical workers.[76]

When the two-week deadline ended, a strike was called on July 3. The response was instantaneous. Around 5,000 oil workers came out, ultimately turning into a massive demonstration in the streets of Kirkuk the following day, in which workers marched with their banners that bore their demands, chanting: 'Long live the working class; long live the oil workers' union';[77] 'we demand the right to organise our trade union,' and 'we demand the improvement of our labour conditions'.[78] Picket lines were formed around the entrances of the oil fields.[79] The strikers assembled daily in what became the focal point of the strike in Gāwūrbāghī, a large garden in the western outskirts of Kirkuk, not far from the company camp. There they held meetings, listened to speeches and poetry delivered in all local languages, representing the diversity of Kirkuk.[80] In one speech, a strike leader explained to the workers the semi-colonial character of the IPC and its role in the domination of Iraq:

> [W]e are all confronting *one* enemy. It is not only the oil workers by themselves who are the victims of the company, for the octopus spreads its tentacles into every aspect of our affairs; they stand behind the *iqtāʿīn* [feudalists] who exploit the *fellahīn* ... and the *mutasarrif* threatens the workers in defense of the interests of the company and the government persecutes the people ... so that the company may continue to exploit our oil ... and so that the boots of [British] soldiers remain defiling our land ... You say you hate colonialism, but what is colonialism? It *is* the monopolistic oil company precisely.[81]

[73] TNA. FO 371/52456. Telegram from Baghdad, to Foreign Office, London, 19 July 1946, I.P.C. workers' strike at Kirkuk.

[74] TNA. FO 371/52456. Wheatley, Kirkuk to Stock, London, dated July 30, 1946 in 'Strike of Iraq Petroleum Company at Kirkuk', 1 August 1946.

[75] *Ibid.*

[76] Batatu, *supra*, 623.

[77] CPGBA. CP/CENT/INT/17/01, 'Workers of the Iraq Petroleum Co. go on strike,' Baghdad, 5 Jul. 1946.

[78] M al-Ṭalibāni. 'Gāwūrbāghī Malḥama Buṭūlīya', ["Gawurbaghi: a heroic epic of the working class"] *al-Thaqāfa al-Jadīda*, Issue 26, July 1971.

[79] TNA. FO 371/52456. 'Strike of Iraq Petroleum Company at Kirkuk', 1 August 1946; Handwritten notes on Baxter's meeting with Wheatley.

[80] The speeches were delivered in Arabic, Kurdish, Assyrian, Armenian and Turkish. See R Hussein, 'Idrāb Gāwūrbāghī: Mūthīra Nidhālīya Kabīra' ['The Gawurbaghi Strike: a great glorious struggle'], *Tarīk al-Shaʿab*, Issue 230, July 12 2015.

[81] *Itiḥād al-Shaʿab*, 15 July, 1959, as quoted in S Khayrī. *Min Tārīkh al-Ḥaraka al-Watanīya*, [From the history of the Nationalist Movement], (Baghdad, 1975), 151.

There was no doubt that the IPC workers were at that moment united in class solidarity like they never were before. In the words of the novelist Fadhil al-Azzawi, 'the strike was a thrilling song fest'.[82] The entire city was attracted to this festive atmosphere in the gardens, while local people opened their doors to workers, and coffeehouses refused payment from any striker.[83]

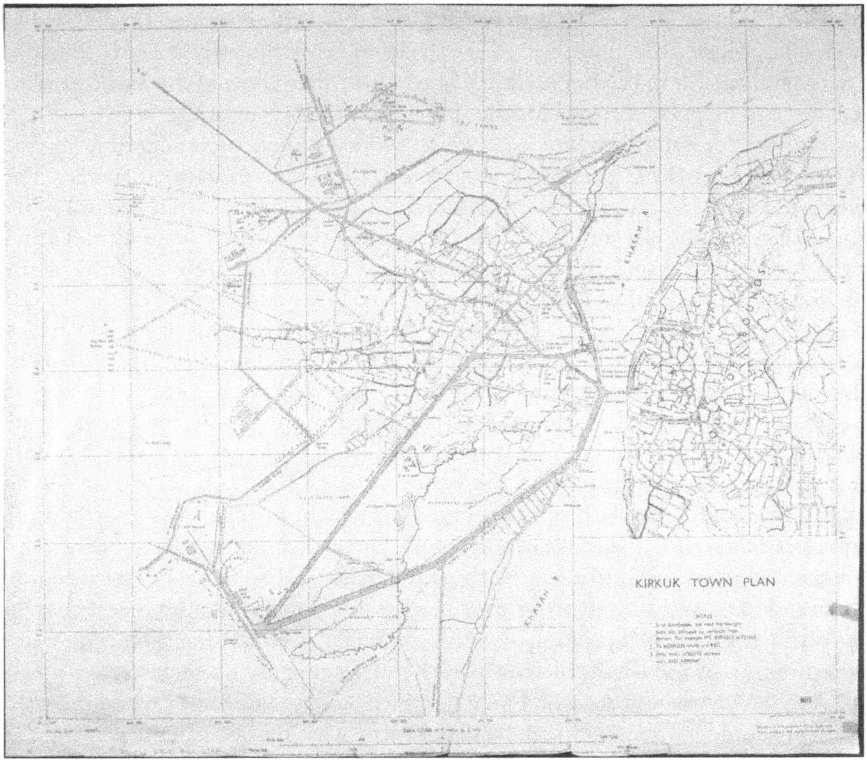


**Figure 6** 'Kirkuk town plan dated 1944'. F60131-94. Maps MOD IDR Misc. 6790. [Geographical Section, General Staff, India]. From the British Library Digital Collection.

On July 8, a new *mutassarif*, Hassan Fahmī, was appointed, undoubtedly due to his predecessor's sympathetic approach towards the strikers. On July 10, the British Embassy councilor, Sir Douglas L. Busk, urged the Prime Minister on the importance of 'strengthening the hand of the mutassarif' so that he could more effectively deal with the strike, and was told by the Foreign Minister that 'new regulations' were being drawn up to provide *mutassarifs* with wide executive powers 'to arrest agitators without legal formalities'.[84] Busk would later receive

[82] F al-Azzawi, *The Last of the Angels*, (tr. William M. Hutchins), (Free Press, 2007), 52. This is an autobiographical novel in which the Gāwūrbāghī strike and its aftermath are vividly described.

[83] Khayrī, *supra*, 150.

[84] TNA. FO 371/52456. 'Strike at Kirkuk'. Busk to FO, No. 637. 10 Aug, 1946.

personal assurances from the PM that 'any threat to the IPC' would be dealt with 'firmly'.[85] Meanwhile, the new *mutassarrif* released a statement, in which he was dismissive of the workers' demands, maintaining that the current labour law already provided them with protection, and that the IPC had already made 'concessions' that would only be released once the workers returned to work immediately.[86] The workers refused to end their strike until all their demands were unconditionally met. It was at this point that Fahmī decided that he would no longer tolerate the 'illegality' of the strike. He consequently dusted off an old Ottoman law still in the books (No.131 of 1910) that allowed the authorities to use force to disperse a crowd for the 'protection of the public'.[87]

On the evening of July 12, while workers were congregating in the Gāwūrbāghī gardens, the police commander ordered them to disperse. The workers began chanting for the fulfillment of their demands. The commander then whistled, and the police rapidly surrounded the gardens from all sides and began forcefully dispersing the crowd.[88] Shots were ultimately fired. As many as 18 workers were killed and 27 were wounded.[89] As news spread of the massacre, there was public outrage throughout the land. In the words of Suʿad Khayrī, it became clear that 'the Iraqi government was prepared to kill Iraqi workers to defend the interests of a colonial company'.[90] The ICP argued that there was 'a high-combination of government and company,' emphasising the imperialistic character of the IPC and the Iraqi state's collusion with it.[91] This was certainly not a far-fetched conspiracy as the records show. The Iraqi state was clearly acting on the advice of the British Embassy, which, in turn, was guarding the interests of the IPC. The workers were no longer dealing with a sophisticated abstract analysis given to them by the intelligentsia. The bullets that rained on them that day were all the proof they needed to grasp the semi-colonial character of the Iraqi state, its complicity with the IPC in maintaining their oppressive conditions, and the effects of semi-peripheral sovereignty on their lives.

As a massive demonstration broke out the next day, the crowd carried the dead on their shoulders, demanding the resignation of what they called 'the government of bullets', and for those responsible to be brought to justice.[92] In a dispatch, the British government in London confirmed their satisfaction with the actions of the local authorities, who acted 'wisely in defense of public security,' and praised the 'satisfactory attitude' of the IPC throughout the strike.[93] One of the workers in the demonstration rose up and said, 'these dead are the victims of foreign influence and imperialistic interference'.[94] The oil workers were now clearly conscious

[85] *Ibid.*
[86] TNA. FO 371/52456; 'Strike at Kirkuk' July 15, 1946; Humaidi, *supra*, 435-436.
[87] Humaidi, *supra*, 437.
[88] CPGBA. CP/CENT/INT/17/01.'The Slaughter of Kawer Baghi', 31 Oct, 1946.
[89] Humaidi, *supra*, 438. Batatu, *supra*, 624.
[90] Khayrī. *Min Tarīkh*, *supra*, 150-152.
[91] Batatu, *supra*, 624.
[92] Talibānī, *supra*, 7.
[93] TNA. FO 371/52456. 'Strike at Kirkuk of IPC', July 19, 1946.
[94] CPGBA. CP/CENT/INT/17/01.'The Slaughter of Kawer Baghi', 31 October 1946.

of how imperialism, and its legal manifestations, created a violent space that allowed for such slaughter to occur with impunity. The British government, on the other hand, accepted the IPC narrative that the strike was 'principally the work of political agitators,' and 'not the spontaneous result of discontent' among the workers, with little to no scrutiny.[95] Shortly thereafter, responding to a question in the House of Commons on the effects of the 'stoppages of work' at the IPC oil fields, the Secretary of State for Foreign Affairs, Phillip Noel-Baker, without any mention of its violent suppression, affirmed that the strike has come to an end and assured his colleague that the 'output of oil was not reduced'.[96] Meanwhile, at a press conference in Baghdad, the PM insisted that it was only due to the efforts of the government, who successfully negotiated with the IPC, that certain 'concessions' were granted to the workers, and that strike action itself did not amount to anything.[97] The Gāwūrbāghī massacre eventually led to the fall of the ʿUmarī cabinet, while the IPC decided to increase the minimum basic day wage from 80 to 140 fils and the total minimum basic day wage from 200 to 310 fils, but refused to reopen the IOWU. IPC officials immediately embarked on a long-term urban development plan (beginning with a housing scheme for IPC workers) with an attempt to shift its policy towards what it refered to as a more positive 'sociological' approach towards its workers and the city as a whole for ideological and propaganda purposes.[98]

The battle rapidly moved from the Gāwūrbāghī gardens to the streets of the large cities, and finally to the courts, which were transformed into 'theatres of struggle for the defense of the rights of the people'.[99] Over a hundred lawyers attended trial in solidarity with the two-dozen workers who had been detained, and who were all, eventually, released by order of the Kirkuk Penal Court.[100] The new government swiftly ordered an investigation of the massacre and a report was later released that found that the police were unprovoked, the workers unarmed, and all vicitms shot in the back. The report also acknowledged that there were no security risks to the public as had been alleged by the police, since the gardens were far from the city-centre.[101] The Minister of Interior, convinced of these conclusions, requested the resignation of the police commander of Kirkuk. However, the PM refused, and the commander was only suspended.[102] Workers representing 14 trade unions subsequently submitted a petition to the PM demanding that the IPC, and its administration, be held

[95] *Ibid.*
[96] TNA FO 371/52456. 'Strike of Iraq Petroleum Company at Kirkuk', 1 August 1946.
[97] *al-Zamān*, July 19 1946.
[98] TNA. FO 371/61673. 'Development of the Kirkuk Oil Fields' 28 August, 1947.
[99] al-Talibanī, *supra*, 6.
[100] R Hussein, *supra*.
[101] Hasanī, *supra*, 121. *See* Humaidī, *supra*, 442 for the detailed report of the investigation.
[102] After the fall of the monarchy, al-Qassab claimed that it was in fact at the insistence of the British Embassy that the police commander and *mutasarif* were not dismissed. See NK Oughlo, *Safahāt Min Tarīkh Kirkuk minthū Fajir al-Tarīkh ila 1958* [Pages from the History of Kirkuk from the Dawn of History until 1958], (Dar al-Hikma, 2015), 454.

to account.[103] This did not happen. The Iraqi justice system was unable to penetrate the semi-colonial legal structures maintained by the Treaty that shielded the IPC enclave. I will return to this analysis after examining certain aspects of the IPC narrative on the origins of the strike and the company's development of its own ideology of trade unionism.

## VI. THE COMPANY NARRATIVE OF THE GĀWŪRBĀGHĪ STRIKE AND ITS IDEOLOGY OF TRADE UNIONISM

The company's narrative of the strike, which was accepted by both the British Embassy in Baghdad and the Foreign Office in London, was that it was contrived by outside political agitators. However, as my counter-narrative above suggests, the causes of the strike were evidently based on the genuine grievances of the workers against economic exploitation by the company in an extreme environment of semi-colonial subservience. The strike could not have been singlehandedly instigated by external political agitators; it was a strike that was initiated by the workers themselves.

A close reading of British records reveals the contradictions inherent in the IPC narrative. The IPC official, H.H. Wheatley, refused to consider that the company was at fault, preferring the explanation that the arrival of a handful of communist outsiders and 'political agitators' from Baghdad, supposedly singlehandedly and in a mere couple of days, got the workers to strike.[104] This, he argued, happened due to their use of 'a weapon, which was not customary in England, namely, intimidation'.[105] Spontaneity was, therefore, rationalised as actual evidence of political agitation and violence rather than as illustrating the workers' own organisational efforts. For this reason, Wheatley was convinced that 'practically the whole of our local staff and labour did not wish to strike'.[106] In addition, he went so far as to claim that the 'undoubted support' of the Russian delegation in Baghdad was at play.[107] More interestingly, he rationalised that the solidarity between the workers that emerged during the strike was a result of 'Arab resentment' over Palestine. The 'question of Palestine,' he said, 'was a very serious matter for the company,' as it was the one issue that united all workers (Arabs, Kurds and Assyrians) and the agitators used it to manipulate the workers to strike.[108]

The complete dissection of the workers' economic grievances from the political aspects of the strike was a reoccurring feature of dispatches to and from

[103] See F al-Būtī, *Mawsu'a al-Sahafīya al-'Iraqīa* [The Encyclopedia of Iraqi Journalism], (al-Mada, 2010), 270-271 for a copy of the petition.
[104] TNA. HH Wheatley to K Stock, 30 July 1946. FO 371/52456.
[105] *Ibid.*
[106] *Ibid.*
[107] *Ibid.*
[108] *Ibid.*

London. Company statements were recycled uncritically throughout: the IPC workers were described as being the best-paid workers in the country, and the company was referred to as the most 'enlightened' employer in Iraq. These claims, and, in particular, that of definite political agitation, were so overstated in the dispatches that some British officials in London could not help but question this narrative. Even the Secretary of State, Ernest Bevin, for instance, a former and experienced trade unionist, was shocked to learn that the strike was not analysed as an industrial dispute in any way. Asking for more information on whether the workers were in fact treated fairly by the company, he emphasised that 'men do not strike for political reasons unless they have also real [economic] grievances'.[109] The responses to these criticisms tended to be that even if economic grievances existed, they were surely exploited by political agitators.

The other line of reasoning in the IPC narrative that was generally accepted by London was that political agitation was clear because the workers were given a 'substantial increase in their cost of living allowances'[110] only two days before the strike was initiated.[111] The workers' rejection of this offer was seen as being completely irrational. As is evident from our counter-narrative above, the IPC workers did not merely strike for a wage increase or for quantifiable benefits, but were insistently concerned with regaining their dignity, which was a matter of principle.[112] This was clear from their most significant demand, which was their continuous assertion that the IPC adhere to the law, in particular the 1936 Labour Law. This, for them, could only materialise if they were allowed to form their own *independent* trade union. Finally, the ending of the common practice of discharging workers at will (in a manner that circumvented the labour law) was another significant demand. This practice, which occurred in the context of a marked racist environment, was a very sensitive issue for the workers indeed.

Wheatley's conception of Iraqi workers was not merely one that was dehumanising in that it took away from the workers' agency, but it was also based on orientalist and racist ideas that Iraqi workers were unable to think for themselves as to what was good for them, and that they were easily manipulated en masse by a few political saboteurs. There tended to be two explanations given for such an analysis throughout the British and IPC records. First, the Iraqi was often described as being governed by a certain irrational and emotional temper that made him prone to external agitation. This is best reflected by one British official's statement that 'the Iraqi is like a gypsy dancing girl who when she hears the voice of the drum must dance. In other words, Iraq is a fertile field

[109] TNA. Minutes by Howe, 22 July 1946. FO 371/52456. 'Strike at Kirkuk of IPC', July 19, 1946.
[110] Around two shillings or one dinar.
[111] TNA. Minutes by Howe, 22 July 1946. FO 371/52456. 'Strike at Kirkuk of IPC', July 19, 1946.
[112] E Davis, "History for the Many or History for the Few? The Historiography of the Iraqi Working Class," in Z Lockman (ed.), *Workers and Working Classes in the Middle East*, (SUNY Press, 1994), 292.

for agitation'.[113] Any sober organisational and strategic planning on the part of Iraqi workers was, therefore, completely discounted as an explanation for effective strike action. Even the 'leftist' and communist pamphlets that were in circulation at the time were seen as impossible to have been 'drawn up by an Iraqi mind'.[114]

Second, this denial of Iraqi agency was generally conveyed in parallel to references to a vague subversive (external) invisible hand that continuously overshadowed Iraqi agency. There was no way that Iraqi workers were acting on their own, and for their own specific interests. This could not possibly have been a sound explanation for analysing the Middle East, the land of endless mystery and subversive intrigue. This denial of agency reverberates in what Priya Satia has argued in her description of the underpinnings of British thought in Arabia: '[a]ll Middle Eastern avowals of nationalism [or anti-imperialism] were degraded and delegitimised by absorption into a grand conspiracy of indeterminate authorship'.[115] This conspiracy theory was indeterminate as there could not be 'a single mastermind' behind them, because 'Orientals did not posses individual minds as such,' but rather 'a collective existence, made possible by the magic information network' of spies and subterfuge.[116] By way of contrast, as one veteran Iraqi organiser pointed out, what made this strike unique was precisely the workers' participation in the administration of their own strike action.[117] It was only natural that the communists would guide the workers in matters of strategy and tactics, but it was the workers' own agency of organisation that steered the strike and theirs alone.

The IPC learned some vital lessons from the events of the Gāwūrbāghī strike and, as mentioned earlier, the company immediately began to undertake a shift in its policy; one that would put more emphasis on social and urban development, in particular housing schemes and educational projects for their workers. Just as significant was the appointment by the British Embassy in Baghdad of a labour attaché, and by the Iraqi government of a full-time labour advisor.[118] The escalation of labour troubles and strikes in the coming years would lead the IPC to eventually appoint a Chief Labour Officer,[119] as well as Information Officers a few years later, with the task of keeping in contact with the Baghdadi press, and directly responding to criticisms of the IPC in

[113] TNA. CSJ Berkeley, Office of the Political Adviser, Nasiriyah to British Embassy, Baghdad. FO/624/72. Communism: 323/5/45. (14 Sep, 1945).

[114] TNA. Minutes by Walker, British Embassy Baghdad, 8 Jan 1947. FO/624/116.

[115] P Satia, *Spies in Arabia: The Great War and the Cultural Foundations of Britain's Covert Empire in the Middle East*, (OUP, 2008), 226.

[116] *Ibid*, 223-224.

[117] S al-Nū ʿmān, *Al-Hizb Al-Shīyu ʿi al- ʿIraqi bi-qayādat Fahad* ['The Iraqi Communist Party under the Leadership of Fahad'], (al-Mada, 2007),194.

[118] TNA. Busk (Baghdad) to Baxter (London), 17 August 1946. FO 371/52456.

[119] TNA. A.M. Morgan to M.T. Audsley, 11 May 1948. LAB 13/674.

the press.[120] These defensive measures had some significant ideological motivations, including countering the influence of communism, but especially urgent was the demonstration that Britain (with its commercial and industrial enterprise) was 'the world's pioneer in the promotion of social justice'.[121]

The IPC's 'sociological' effort was aimed at bringing about some changes to workers' conditions, providing them with transportation, hospitals, maternity and infant welfare centres, cinemas and above all housing.[122] The housing scheme in particular was meant be a 'tangible manifestation' of the IPC's 'goodwill'.[123] By 1950, according to a British report, 246 'bungalows' were built on the new Arrapha Estate for Iraqi staff, and within five years that figure rose to over 450 houses.[124] The IPC would commence a home-ownership scheme for the very purpose of furthering this ideology so as to appear to be contributing to Kirkuk's economy and its development.[125] The hope was that such an approach would prevent more labour strikes from happening, allowing the IPC to appear favorably to the public. The supply of electricity to the municipality, for instance, led one pro-British Iraqi newspaper to praise Kirkuk, describing it as the 'the city of black-gold' where 'the company supplies electricity from which all is benefiting'.[126]

The IPC later referred to this tailored approach in a confidential and exhaustive report, commissioned and released in 1955 as the 'integration approach', which was aimed at integrating the company (including its subsidiaries the B.P.C. and the M.P.C.) into the Iraqi economy, on the one hand, and making the company 'more acceptable to the Iraqi way of life' and community on the other.[127] The overall goal of the approach was to 'secure the position' of the IPC, 'beyond disturbance *in any event*' and to prevent nationalisation at all costs.[128] In terms of the non-economic aspect of the approach, the aim was to break out of the 'physical and mental compounds, the *imperium in imperio* which they [i.e. company officials] tended in the past to inhabit'.[129] This approach was, therefore, a pre-emptive measure that came out of the experience of the Gāwūrbāghī strike. I will not get into all the details of this important report,

[120] TNA. FO/624/176. Oil: IPC Labour.

[121] TNA. D Busk, Baghdad to E Bevin, 13, August 1946. LAB 13/193.

[122] TNA. FO/624/105. 'Oil: Iraq Petroleum Company Labour Welfare,' Nov 20, 1946.

[123] TNA. FO 371/52456. 'Iraq Petroleum Company's Housing Scheme', Dec 10, 1946.

[124] TNA. WJ Hull, 'Visit to IPC, Kirkuk Fields, 15-18 August 1950,' August 1950, LAB 13/672; 'Guide to Kirkuk,' c. 1955, File 119015, BP. H.S. Gibson to Hoard Page, London, 10 July 1952. BP 135818.

[125] BPA. 'Notes on IPC Group Meeting on 9th November 1950,' File 60550, BP.

[126] BPA. *Al-Sha'b*, 3 August 1950 enclosed and translated in HH. Wheatley to Sir John Cunningham, 29 August 1950, File 135819, BP.

[127] BPA. J Murray, *Policy and Practice of the Iraq Petroleum Company, Limited and Associated Companies in their Economic and Other Relations*, London, 31/12/1955, File 4656 BP, i. This report was commissioned after industrial strikes continued to escalate between 1948 and 1954. The aim was to develop an approach that would 'prevent nationalisation and expropriation of the IPC' by eliminating 'the climate of opinion which is favorable to nationalisation'.

[128] *Ibid*, 3, emphasis in original.

[129] *Ibid*, ii.

but rather will focus on the section that deals with the company's treatment of workers,[130] in particular on the question of trade unions. Despite taking a similar view with regards to the role of communist political agitation, as mentioned above, this time with regards to the Basra Strike of 1953, the author stressed that 'a foreign company … cannot afford to treat its Iraqi personnel worse than its foreign ones'.[131] Consequently, the company, he emphasised, must treat its workers 'so obviously good' that people 'merely laugh' at any 'propaganda' that claims otherwise.[132] One of the primary efforts focused on was the development of 'joint consultation' committees as a substitute for independent trade unions and its relation to the law.

After the suppression of the Gāwūrbāghī strike and of the trade union that organised it, the IPC reintroduced the 'joint consultation' worker committees, which were considered adequate substitutes for independent trade unions. Despite the fact that the British Embassy encouraged the formation of what it referred to as 'genuine trade unions' amongst the oil workers of Kirkuk, this really meant unions (and committees), which were pro-British and anti-communist.[133] This was, therefore, a part of a broad top-down ideology of trade unionism that targeted the Iraqi labour movement. In fact, the British government was constantly concerned with establishing new devices to co-opt the leadership of the labour movement. 'We should endeavor,' a Foreign Office official wrote, 'to put into control of labour unions in Kirkuk … labour leaders who are known to have anti-communist views'.[134] Another official reiterated this position by arguing that 'medical rather than surgical measures' must be used to treat communism, and this could only be done by 'jockeying' a 'non-communist labour leader' into control of the labour unions in Kirkuk.[135] Similarly, the 1955 IPC report suggested that government unions should be encouraged, as they would form at once, 'a safety valve and a point of contact'.[136] Referring to the assessment of the IPC's Personnel Adviser, the author illustrates the manner in which government-sponsored rather than independent trade unions would function:

> It is possible that they [i.e. government unions] may not be effective for some time; but, in the words of the Personnel Advisor, "it is the Communist-inspired ad hoc 'union' that is to be feared at this stage and not a Government-organized union. The latter frequently provides a harmless outlet for the aspirations of potential trouble-makers who become so preoccupied by the internal organization and politics of the union that they forget the purpose for which it was formed". This is a useful, if slightly Machiavellian, point.[137]

[130] *Ibid*.
[131] *Ibid*. Chapter XII, 4.
[132] *Ibid*.
[133] TNA. Bagdad to FO, 12 July 1946, FO 371/52459.
[134] *Ibid*.
[135] TNA. Minutes by RMA Honkey. FO 371/52459. 'Communism in Iraq', 4 July 1946.
[136] BPA. John Murray, *supra*, 11.
[137] *Ibid*.

The government-sponsored unions would, therefore, function in the same way as the company's joint consultative committees – to insulate and depoliticise the workers, and ultimately to pacify any form of genuine struggle against the IPC. A Machiavellian technique if ever there was one. The IPC established an administrative machinery to deal with disputes in the form of joint consultative committees (as well as general welfare committees) as a way for workers and management to communicate on issues of mutual interest. These committees were ultimately unsuccessful as all the 'best workmen' considered them as having been discredited by the recent strike, especially seeing as those who had led the former committees were opposed to the strike.[138] It did not help that dialogue in these committees was heavily restricted by management, who did not allow any discussion on matters covered by the labour law or that concerned wage rates.[139] This was the same criticism made by the author of the 1955 IPC report, who argued that these committees were supposed to address questions of production, but this was rarely done.[140] Instead, the committees merely acted in an 'advisory' capacity and were turned into a forum wherein workers could make suggestions on efficiency, welfare and educational issues.[141] The IPC acted like a 'benevolent paternalist' in the settlement of disputes.[142] There was, therefore, more than a general lack of interest in joining these committees, for most workers did not want to be seen as 'stooges' of the company.[143]

In any case, the development of a pro-management and pro-British ideology of trade unionism after the strike was clearly advanced to undermine the workers' ability to run their own unions. It was, therefore, not out of genuine concern for the workers that they were put into place, but rather to control and 'keep tabs' on them.[144] Furthermore, the new IPC fields' manager, Mainland, who was hired after the strike, was described by a British Embassy counselor, as 'a nervous individual' who was 'preoccupied by the dangers of subversive elements' and was determined to cleanse the company of political agitators.[145] After visiting the oil fields, the counselor explained the ideological basis of this new developmental policy, referring to it as 'Calpurnian', that is, one that would ensure that the company was 'above suspicion'.[146] This, he wrote, could only be done if they endeavored to achieve 'occidental [labour] standards' in Iraq.[147] In other words, if the IPC at least appeared to be treating its workers on the basis of ('civilised') 'western standards' they would be beyond reproach, and no one could criticise

[138] TNA. FO 624/105, *supra*.
[139] A Badre and S Siksek, *Manpower and Oil in the Arab World*, (Hyperion Press, 1960), 183.
[140] BPA. Murray, *supra*, Chapter XII, 13.
[141] See TNA. LAB 13/1634. Hull, 'Iraq Labour Memorandum No. 4' August, 1950; for details on the workings of these committees, see Badre and Siksek, *supra*,184.
[142] Badre and Siksek, *ibid*.
[143] *Ibid*, 187.
[144] TNA. FO 624/105. 'Oil: IPC Labour Welfare', 25 October 1946.
[145] *Ibid*.
[146] *Ibid*.
[147] *Ibid*.

them for not following the labour law of the state. Even in the midst of the strike, the British Ambassador, Hugh Stonehewer-Bird, suggested that the company did not have to 'stick strictly' to the Iraqi Labour Law as long as it treated its workers by what it regarded as Western or British standards.[148] Here, it is clear that this new policy – as it was applied to trade unionism – was meant to reinforce the IPC by putting it in an 'invulnerable' position,[149] as it allowed it to once more avoid the labour law whenever it pleased by reference to its 'enlightened' and 'occidental' standards. These colonial double-standards were precisely what the workers were opposed to when they decided to strike. In many ways, this strategy was effective as the newly appointed labour attaché, A.T. Audsley, visiting the IPC a couple of years later would come to the conclusion (once again) that the company provided 'more favorable conditions than the labour law'.[150] I shall now turn to analyse how and why it was that Iraqi state law was ultimately unable to penetrate the concessionary space of the IPC enclave to hold it accountable for what transpired in Gāwūrbāghī.

## VII. LAW AND SPACE IN THE MOSUL OIL FRONTIER: THE INFRASTRUCTURE OF LAW IN A DESERT SPACE

Returning to the overarching argument of the book, the semi-peripheral sovereignty granted to Iraq under international law in tandem with the 1931 IPC Concession, contributed to the spatial specificity of the material social and labour conditions in the Kirkuk enclave. In fact, one of the main functions of the doctrine of semi-peripheral sovereignty was to allow the IPC to operate with a certain amount of freedom. Consequently, the wide powers that the IPC acquired from the concessionary agreement were further bolstered by the weak sovereignty of the Iraqi state. This surely had a hegemonic influence over the social and economic dynamics of Kirkuk, as well as of the Iraqi state as a whole. Vast social transformations occurred in the city, which in turn had an impact on the labouring classes as described above. Furthermore, it was precisely because the IPC was shielded by an assemblage of legal structures that it was able to completely evade any liability for the massacre of oil workers at Gāwūrbāghī. Here, the law played a significant role in the social production of the oil space of Kirkuk and its network – a space, which, being a part of the Iraqi oil frontier and its international dimensions, could not have functioned without the legal infrastructure that was put in place and the streamlining of all its parts in tandem.

Here, I am not only following from scholars who have highlighted the constitutive connection between law and space,[151] but also recent legal scholarship

[148] TNA. FO 371/52456. Stonehewer-Bird to Sargent, 9 July 1946.

[149] TNA. FO 624/105, *supra*.

[150] TNA. FO 371/68458. M.T. Audsely, Report on Visit to Iraq from June 8th to 10th, 1948.

[151] See N Blomley, *Law, Space and the Geographies of Power* (Guilford Press, 1994); T Mahmud, "Law of Geography and the Geography of Law: A Post-Colonial Mapping" *Jurisprudence Review*,

that highlights the significance of infrastructure in understanding law and legal transformation.[152] In his classic work, *The Production of Space*, Henri Lefebvre argues that space is not only 'a means of production' but also 'a means of control, and hence of domination, of power'.[153] In addition, he emphasises how space 'lays down the law because it implies a certain order'.[154] Therefore, since space needs to be produced before it is lived, Lefebvre implies that space is made up of a certain legal configuration that allows it to materialise a specific order. Furthermore, adding the notion of 'infrastructuring law' to this analysis allows one to see how law interacts and contributes to the making and operation of infrastructure and its capitalist logic, and similarly, as we shall see, how infrastructure could be used 'against the grain' as it were to subvert its operations, spaces and legal structures.[155] The 'infrastructures of law' and/or 'law as infrastructure' reveal why the tensions described earlier manifested in such a way in the IPC enclave of Kirkuk, culminating in violence. It explains how this spatiality of law shielded the IPC enclave, contributing to the company's power and impunity over its violent actions. The legal arrangements described earlier, therefore, allowed for the IPC infrastructure to operate in a particular way, and to produce the spatial configuration required for the operations of the oil enclave to materialise. Finally, my argument also emphasises the significance of the local and its spaces in the making certain aspects of international law – this has been referred to elsewhere as the 'imperial location' – which is the geographical location where the local, international and transnational converge, thereby transforming the local into an interconnected imperial space in which local actors could indirectly transform international legal structures.[156] It is from this (critical) 'imperial location' that the K3 oil workers organised their actions.

The law of concession, especially as it relates to oil, is itself a perfect illustration of how law completely alters geography and produces the space that is its subject. A 'concession' is generally defined as a grant or a licence that is granted by a state to a private individual or a corporation ('the concessionaire') to undertake works of public character extending to a considerable period of time and involving the investment of substantial capital and expertise.[157] An oil

Vol. 3.064, (2010), pp.64–106; A Philippopoulos-Milhalopoulos. "Law's Spatial Turn: Geography, Justice and a Certain Fear of Space" *Law, Culture and the Humanities* (2010), XX(X) 1–16.

[152] See B Kingsbury, 'Introduction to the Symposium on the Infrastructuring of International Law' 117 *AJIL Unboud* (2023); D Cowen, 'Law as Infrastructure of Colonial Space: Sketches from Turtle Island' 117 *AJIL Unbound* (2023); M Valverde, *Infrastructure: New Trajectories in Law* (Routledge, 2022).

[153] H Lefebvre, *The Production of Space* (Willey, 1991), 26-27.

[154] Ibid, 143.

[155] Valverde, *supra*, 5.

[156] See L Nuzzo, 'The Birth of an Imperial Location: Comparative Perspectives on Western Colonialism in China" *Leiden Journal of International Law* (2018), 31, 569–596.

[157] S Siksek, *The Legal Framework for Oil Concessions in the Arab World* (The Middle East Research and Publishing Centre, 1960), 4-5.

concession is one that is generally granted as an exclusive right to 'search for, obtain, exploit, develop, render suitable for trade, carry away export and sell petroleum'.[158] Despite having an international character, a concession contract is recognised as being governed by the municipal law of the local jurisdiction it applies to, and not by international law.[159] However, in the case at hand in which a foreign oil company was granted wide powers by a concessionary agreement with a weak (mandatory) state, the law of the state cannot effectively be enforced on the company. This was due to the fact that concessionary agreements had a very specific function at the time, as they were de facto colonial and imperial instruments initially used by the oil industry to essentially generate 'transfers of sovereign powers over vast tracts of land' to foreign companies for long periods of time, and guarantees of payment of fixed royalties calculated by the quantity of oil produced.[160] As M.N. Sornarajah illustrates, only an arsenal 'web of power' wielded by the home state and its concessionaire alongside 'a concentrated dominance exerted within the international system by the dominant powers' could ultimately maintain these concessionary agreements.[161] The concession, therefore, contributed rather violently to the production of the oil enclaves of Iraq and the Middle East. It is within this context that the IPC caused social and economic tensions within its spaces: unregulated by the state, it was ruled by what could only be referred to as the 'international law of primitive accumulation'.[162]

Kirkuk being a part of the Iraqi oil frontier where oil extraction occurred at a 'specific, focal point of its location' constituted a *unique*ly situated space in the international machinery of oil production in the region and the global capitalist economy at large.[163] It was this specificity that made it both the centre of imperialist and capitalist exploitation, as well as the very beating heart of anti-imperialist struggle in Iraq. The oil frontier is, as Michael J. Watts has shown, already a unique space in that it operates not only on its 'own temporalities and spatialities' of global capitalism,[164] but also within 'an astonishing spatial patchwork, a quilt of multiple, overlapping, and intersecting spaces of territorial concessions, blocs, pipelines, risers, rigs, flow stations, export terminals … [It is, in other words] a cartographer's dream-space: a landscape

[158] H Cattan, *The Evolution of Oil Concessions in the Middle East and North Africa*, (Oceana Press, 1976), 2.

[159] This was firmly established in the ICJ decision *Anglo-Iranian Oil Co. (Jurisdiction) Case* (1952).

[160] M Sornarajah, *The International Law of Foreign Investment* (Cambridge University Press, 2004), 40.

[161] *Ibid.*

[162] M Neocleous, "International Law as Primitive Accumulation; Or, the Secret of Systemic Colonization" *European Journal of International Law*, (2012) Vol. 23, no. 4, 941–962.

[163] T Dunning and L Wirpsa, "Oil and the Political Economy of Conflict in Colombia and Beyond: A Linkage Approach" *Geopolitics*, Vol. 9, No. 1 (Spring 2004), 81–108; 82.

[164] MJ Watts, "Securing Oil: Frontiers, Risk, and Spaces of Accumulated Insecurity," in H Appel, A Mason & M Watts (eds.), *Subterranean Estates: Life Worlds of Oil and Gas*, (Cornell University Press, 2015), 211–236; 221.

of lines, axes, hubs, spokes, nodes, points, blocks and flows'.[165] The IPC operated on similar lines in Kirkuk. Its space was dynamic, multilayered and was connected across an infrastructural network of pipelines and pumping stations to the ports and cities of the Mediterranean. As Iraq's gateway to the world, this oil frontier was also where order and disorder manifested, where the tensions of capitalist modernity were reproduced and where violence ultimately broke out.

In parallel to and constitutive of this spatial specificity was a legal specificity, which made all this a reality, for before pipelines could be erected, one needed to construct the legal infrastructure for this space to be a reality in the first place – the 'primordial straight line' drawn on the map if you will. The law and its structures played an essential role in bringing all of this about. The semi-peripheral sovereignty in conjuncture with the IPC concessionary agreement played a role in this process as it allowed for the triangular relationship between the IPC, the British and the Iraqi government to *appear* to be functioning at a certain arms-length, when in fact this was not the case as we have seen in the preceding narrative, for these processes were much closer in proximity and at times entirely interconnected – what happened during the Gāwūrbāghī strike and the massacre of workers was a perfect illustration of this. The British government frequently evoked Iraqi (semi-peripheral) sovereignty to put the blame on the Iraqi government for all its shortcomings in its dealing with the labour question, diverting from their own responsibilities. Iraq was an 'independent' and 'sovereign' state after all, notwithstanding the influence the British had through its advisors.

Only a couple of years after the Gāwūrbāghī strike and the *Wathba* uprising of 1948, the labour attaché to the British Embassy, M.T. Audsley, released a report in which he used the same inconsistent and contradictory line of reasoning in that, on the one hand, he severely criticised the 'feudal reactionary character' of the Iraqi government in its dealings with the working class, while, on the other hand, he recommended the following 'security' measures when responding to any labour troubles in the IPC:

> If the Government is unwilling or unable to put its house in order … we must always have a strong and pro-British Mutasarrif, Commandment of Police, and G.O.C. 2nd Division who have instruction to make it clear at all times that the IPC is a vital Iraqi interest, and that *incitement of our labour ranks is a crime against the state*. At the same time, care should be taken in the appointment of judges to Kirkuk, and the Ministry of Justice should instruct the President of the Courts that *no lenient treatment is to be given to cases of incitement of labour to strike*.[166]

This is a remarkably candid recommendation and in many ways illustrates exactly how the complicity of the triangular relationship between the IPC,

[165] *Ibid*.
[166] TNA. FO 371/68482. 'Report on visit to Iraq from 8th June to 10th July by M.T. Audsley' (1 November, 1948); Appendix D, 'The Security Situation in Iraq as it Affects the Company,' 3. Emphasis added.

British Embassy and Iraqi state functioned during the Gawūrbāghī strike in 1946. The labour attaché (who acted more like a labour strike 'fixer') was merely conjuring up an already tried and tested method of labour suppression.

## VIII. PRESSURE POINTS IN THE CIRCUITS OF CAPITALISM: HOW TO USE INFRASTRUCTURE TO SUBVERT LAW

The concluding angle to the narrative in this chapter conjures an important episode in the labour history of Iraq that advances my argument about the spatiality of law, and how infrastructures of capitalist accumulation were inventively used by workers to subversively assert alternative visions of legal order, namely the massive K3 pumping station strike in the isolated desert town of Hadītha, which took place during the revolutionary period of the *Wathba* uprising in April of 1948.[167] We have already described the IPC network of pipelines. The K3 pumping station was the most important IPC pipeline station from which oil flowed across the desert to the Eastern Mediterranean ports, and, in turn, to the world – it was the critical point of bifurcation where the trunk lines of the Kirkuk (K1) pipeline separated to form the arms of a Y, diverting into two lines, one going southward to the terminal of Haifa and the other northward to Tripoli. The pipeline network that transported oil from the Middle East to the world was one of the most vital engineering feats of Western imperialism of the time, and certainly had significant geopolitical and geographical implications on the region.[168] As American writer Charles Morrow Wilson elucidated in 1946, 'our world today has several political states that have been founded and boundaried [sic] deliberately as right-of-ways for oil pipelines. These include the Levant States … of Syria, [and] the hinterlands of Tripoli [in Lebanon], which is France's vital Mediterranean terminal for the desert pipelines that lead to the crucial oil pools of Kirkuk, some 700 miles inland in Iraq …' while the pipeline to the port of Haifa 'carries oil from Kikruk to the fuel tanks of Britain's merchant ships,' and its Navy. These power-driven high-pressure pipelines, he concludes, were the 'heart arteries of the British [imperial] lifeline …'[169] In addition to this pipeline network, a refinery was constructed at the Haifa terminal by the AIOC to process their share of the IPC output from Kirkuk.[170] In 1945, plans were made for the construction of another 16-inch diameter pipeline from Kirkuk to Haifa, but the *Nakba* in Palestine disrupted its completion for

[167] The *Wathba* is covered in Chapter 7.

[168] For a contemporary geopolitical analysis of oil pipelines *See* G Dietl, *The Global Game of Oil Pipelines* (Routledge, 2022).

[169] CM Wilson, *Oil Across the World: The American Saga of Pipelines* (Longmans, Green and Co, 1946), 4,5.

[170] WE Pratt and D Good (eds.), *World Geography of Petroleum* (Princeton University Press, 1950), 163.

an indefinite period.[171] By 1952, a single 30-32-inch pipeline was constructed from Kirkuk to the Syrian terminal of Banias, 55 miles north of Tripoli, which included four pumping stations and increased output by 14 million tonnes/year.[172] The other important transdesert pipeline project, which made up part of the petroluemscape of the region, was the US built Trans-Arabian Pipeline (Tapline), completed in 1950 that connected ARAMCO's fields in Saudi Arabia to a Mediterranean terminal in Sidon in Lebanon.[173]

The role of oil pipelines and energy transit in general has had an important impact on the development of international law akin to that of the governance of international rivers and waterways in the nineteenth century.[174] The significance of these global infrastructures is that they tend to convolute the traditional understanding of sovereignty and the territoriality of nation-states, since 'transit is a type of transportation involving the physical *passage through* the territory of a state'.[175] From this transnational perspective, states had to be divided into three categories: 'states of origin,' 'transit states' and 'destination states'.[176] This definitional division, however, must be seen as being part of the overarching global capitalist system of extractivism in the region that certainly does not generally take national borders into consideration. In that sense, we get a better grasp of the global reach of capitalism, its influence on Arab states and the manner in which these states relate to each other economically, geopolitically, and in particular through the lens of the imperial interests of Western states on the region. These trans-desert pipelines, which linked states of the Middle East to the circuits of capitalist accumulation, required all of their interconnected parts, including of course its labour force, to maintain its operations and to work together in the process of oil extraction. Any obstruction to one of these parts of the infrastructure could possibly affect the operations of the entire system. The K3 workers took advantage of this fact in their strike actions against their conditions, and as a consequence asserted an alternative legal order. The narrative will now move to emphasise how anti-hegemonic actions waged using the infrastructures of capitalism and its circuits on the ground ultimately had a long-term impact on international law, especially as it relates to oil decolonisation, the just distribution of royalties and transit fees, and the principle of sovereignty over natural resources.

The idea of a strike in the K3 station of Haditha originated with the ICP, but it was only after organising a mass meeting of 3,000 oil workers that a resolution was democratically passed to undertake wildcat strike action. Led

[171] Longrigg, *Oil in the Middle East*, 180.
[172] *Ibid*, 181.
[173] See D Little, 'Pipeline Politics: America, TAPLINE, and the Arabs,' *Business History Review* (Vol. 64, Issue 2, 1990).
[174] This is especially the case in international treaty law and state responsibility; see D Azaria, *Treaties on Transit of Energy via Pipelines and Countermeasures* (OUP, 2015).
[175] *Ibid*, 4.
[176] *Ibid*.

by a charismatic labour organiser, Shanwar Oūda,[177] the strike began the following day on April 23. Almost immediately, a series of ad hoc committees emerged: a strike committee, which was kept out of view was considered the 'living brain of the strike'; a negotiating committee, which although a façade of the strike committee was also its 'chief lever'; an organisers' committee that was tasked to select orators and poets; and strike's prefects led by the chief of the guard.[178] The prefects were tasked to oversee meetings and gatherings by preserving order and discipline. Station patrollers took shifts to enforce the strike. A picket guard controlled those who entered or exited the station, ensuring that, except with the written permission of the strike committee, 'not even a pint of gasoline' would leave the station. The entire K3 pumping station, which at that point was under the workers' control, came to a complete standstill.[179]

The main demands of the workers encompassed the following: a wage increase of 25 per cent for workers of grades (0-1), and 50 per cent for those of grades (3-5); the enforcement of the labour law; providing K3 workers the same amenities as those given to the Kirkuk (K1) workers; adequate housing and transportation; making Saturday a half-day; ending the overseeing of workers by security guards; and ending the practice of dismissals-at-will, fines, and retaliatory dismissals for strike actions.[180] The company's response was not only to regard the strike a 'breach of the law'; it also made the typical accusation that the strike was not a genuine industrial dispute, but rather 'a subversive movement' concocted by the communist party.[181] The British Vice-Consul in Baghdad seemed rather astonished when he admitted that, 'the strike was from the outset organised with remarkable efficiency. The strikers took over the whole plant and picketed the ferry across the river Euphrates near Hadītha and all roads leading to the camp'.[182] The exceptional organisational capacity of the strikers was attributed to being actual evidence of outside political influence rather than stemming from the direct actions of the workers themselves.

Although the IPC eventually conceded to some minor demands, it rejected the key demand of a wage increase. The strike committee refused to back down, and the workers' spirits remained high. By May 5, a squadron of nearly 30 armoured police cars arrived on the scene, circling the station and workers'

[177] Oūda was a former schoolteacher who was dismissed by the authorities for spreading communist propaganda in 1946. He found his way into the employ of the IPC as a mechanic to make ends meet. He was later imprisoned, tortured and killed by the Baʿathists during the 1963 coup. *See* F Haīdar, "Meḥdi (Shanwar) Oūda: Qa'id ʿUmālī Salib wa Masīra Yathkurūḥa al-Tārīkh" ["Mehdi (Shanwar) Ouda: A steadfast labour leader and a march remembered by history"], *al-Hiwār al-Mutamadin*, 2009/6/5, (http://www.ahewar.org/debat/show.art.asp?aid=174173).

[178] Batatu, *supra*, 625.

[179] TNA. FO 371/68479. Telegram No. 478 from Mack, Bagdad to FO, 4 May, 1948. 'Strike on the Iraq Petroleum Company's Pipeline' 5 May 1948.

[180] Humeidī, *supra*, 563-564.

[181] TNA. FO 371/68479. F Wells Minute, 14 May, 1948. 'Strike on Iraqi Petroleum Co Pipeline', 21 May 1948.

[182] *Ibid*.

quarters with machine guns. Shortly thereafter, the celebrated national poet, Mohammed Mahdī al-Jawāhirī, furiously protested in an op-ed in a Baghdad newspaper, '[d]o they [he wrote] want to repeat the Gawūrbāghī massacre?!'[183] The strike committee, which at first unsuccessfully tried to 'enlist the sympathy of the [police] rank and file', then ordered the workers to stay away from the police and to avoid confrontation at all costs.[184] The British Vice-Consul, who considered Oūda a communist 'fanatic', wrote of his organisational methods that he maintained firm discipline, 'repeatedly impressing upon the strikers the necessity for avoiding violence whilst at the same time showing that they were effectively under control'.[185] A couple of days later, police cut off food rations, water and electricity from the station. Realising that they could not rely on the local bread offered by the neighboring villagers for long, and insisting on avoiding what would certainly turn into a violent confrontation with police, the workers held a meeting in which they decided to embark on a long march to Baghdad, 250 kilometres away, to present the government with a petition comprising of their demands. The next morning on May 12, the K3 workers began their long journey to Baghdad. At the head of their column they carried a banner that read: 'We the Oil Workers Have Come to Claim Our Violated Rights'.[186]

By the time the workers crossed 24 kilometres to the Hurān valley, they were exhausted from the scorching heat. Taking shelter in the closest village of al-Baghdadi, many of them lost consciousness. As news spread, eight trucks carrying food and water arrived from the people of Hīt in solidarity with their cause. Their brethren then drove them back to Hīt where they took repose. The next morning on May 13, the K3 workers left Hīt on foot. They endured their journey, only to be knocked down once again by the desert sun at noon, at which point they were offered hospitality from the tribe of al-Muhamadī, who fired rifles and chanted tribal songs in their honour. When the sun set, they returned to the sandy road, sightlessly trailing in the dead of night. In the morning, they realised that they arrived in a place called al-Warrār, one kilometre north of al-Ramadī, and 126 kilometres west of Baghdad. Mounting on small handmade boats, the workers began traversing the Euphrates to get to al-Ramadī. When they reached the other side of the river, still raising their large banner, they continued to march until they approached a bridge that led to Fallūjah. There, the police were waiting for them. It was a trap. The K3 workers were apprehended approximately 60 kilometres from their final destination in Baghdad. Although some were forced to return to Hadītha, Oūda and the strike leaders were all arrested and charged under martial law.[187]

[183] *Jarīda al-ʿAsūr*, Issue 14, 9 May 1948, as quoted in al-Humeidī, *supra*, 571.

[184] TNA. F. Wells Minute, 14 May 1948. FO 371/68479. 'Strike on Iraqi Petroleum Co Pipeline', 21 May 1948.

[185] *Ibid.*

[186] Batatu, 625.

[187] This narrative of al-Masīra is based on Batatu, *ibid*, 625-627.

This heroic episode of labour struggle, which would be known as 'al-Masīra al-Kubrā' (The Great March), was to assume legendary significance in the annals of Iraqi labour historiography. I have recounted the entire narrative so as to make several points to illuminate my argument on legal spatiality and infrastructural resistance. It was only after the K3 workers decided *where* in the vast imperial infrastructural map of the petroluemscape they were located did they decide to undertake strike action, and it was only then that they were able to effectively disrupt the operations of oil production and, in turn, target Western imperialism, while they asserted their normative demands, which they regarded as their violated *natural* and *legal rights*. The workers used spatiality as a strategy of counter-hegemony and to overcome the legal spatiality of imperialism. It was how they grasped the map of the oil frontier – the network of oil pipelines and the manner in which they were all interconnected to the infrastructure of oil extraction of the region – that allowed them to sabotage its circuits and to assert their own interpretation of the law. Indeed, they were directly challenging the legal structures that were imposed on them; the semi-peripheral sovereignty that was maintained by the Anglo-Iraq Treaty and that, only months earlier, had been challenged in the streets of Baghdad during the *Wathba*, was the same legal configuration that was challenged by the workers during their strike in an isolated town in the middle of the desert.

The narrative of the IPC workers' control of the K3 pumping-station above is a great illustration not only of the spatiality of law – or how legal structures were spread out in unique spatial configurations, which corresponded to the operations of global capitalist system of extractivism – but also how counter-hegemonic uses of infrastructural configurations could have an effect on the transformation of law (even if in the long-term). Despite not having reached their destination, the K3 strike was not a failure, for it was a culmination of various workers' struggles and their corresponding anti-imperialist demands that envisioned an alternative legal order whereby Iraq gained its complete independence, and that would eventually materialise with the coming 1958 Revolution. Timothy Mitchell implicitly emphasised this link between spatiality, protest and law in the context of the oil frontier of the region when he wrote:

> in building the infrastructure of oil, the petroleum companies were also laying out the infrastructure of political protest. The points of vulnerability, where movements could organise and apply pressure, now included a series of oil wells, pipelines, refineries, railways, docks and shipping lanes across the Middle East. These were the interconnected sites at which a series of claims for political freedoms and more egalitarian forms of life would be fought.[188]

Mitchell suggests that organised action on specific 'vulnerable' points of a spatial infrastructural arrangement disrupted the everyday operations of the

[188] Mitchell, *supra*, 103.

global capitalist machinery by blocking the circulation and velocity of capitalist processes. However, he should have added that this 'infrastructure of political protest' was only conceivable because of the existence of a corresponding legal infrastructure that was part and parcel of the spatial configuration in question, and so by applying pressure on these vulnerable sites, workers ultimately had an effect on the law that maintained it. The K3 workers with their comrades in Gāwūrbāghī before them, were not only rejecting their role in the operations of an exploitative system of capitalist accumulation, but also were simultaneously asserting their own alternative legal order given that they considered Iraq's oil as 'the property of the people'. The strike was, in other words, more than an isolated labour grievance – it was, rather, a direct anti-colonial challenge to the British presence, and the basis of its exploitative legal order in Iraq. It was the rejection of Iraq's semi-peripheral sovereignty that was gained through the mandatory process. It was also the repudiation of the hated 1930 Anglo-Iraq Treaty, which the workers regarded as the source of their miserable conditions. The K3 workers were consciously inserting praxis into their hopes to create what the philosopher Ernest Bloch called the 'not-yet' and to bring forth a *concrete* utopia through their agency – *an alternative, imaginative and emancipatory legal order*. This explains why one worker believed that the 'dictatorship of the proletariat'[189] was temporarily established at K3 that day, while his comrades repeatedly referred to K3 as 'the *State* of Shanwār Oūda'.[190]

Throughout the 'key nodes of industrial [oil] conurbations' of the region, workers organised similar strikes to their counterparts in K3 and Gāwūrbāghī, as the oil petroluemscape of the Middle East was transformed into multiple spaces of anti-imperial struggle, turning workers into 'vanguards of nationalist and left-wing politics, [and] trade unionism'.[191] From the oil towns of Abadan in southwestern Iran to the oil pipeline terminus in Haifa in Palestine, and the segregated ARAMCO oil camps of Dhahran in the Eastern Province of Saudi Arabia, militant strike actions erupted, disrupting the circuits of capitalist accumulation and extractivism.[192] This put pressure on many oil companies and their government sponsors to rethink their strategies and to consider reform. These labour struggles from below, which were the working people's insistence on the sovereignty over their petroleum resources, materialised with the attempts to nationalise oil in the region, beginning with Iran in 1952.[193] Their struggles also contributed (in the long-term) to the ultimate

[189] Batatu, *supra*, 625.

[190] A Khājādwr, "Maʿan al-ʿUmālīya Tuhāwir Ara' Khājādwr" [Maʿan converses with Ara' Khājādor], *al-Hīwār al-Mutamadin*, 6/8/2008, http://www.ahewar.org.

[191] Fuccaro, 'Arab Oil Towns,' supra, 136.

[192] See T Atabaki, 'Chronicles of a Calamitous Strike Foretold: Abadan, July 1946' in KH Roth (ed.), *On the Road to Global Labour: A Festschrift for Marcel van der Linden* (Brill, 2017), 93-128.

[193] See M Elm, *Oil, Power and Principle: Iran's Oil Natinalization and its Aftermath* (Syracuse University Press, 1992). For a history of the nationalisation of the IPC in Iraq, see B Wolfe-Hunnicutt, *The Paranoid Style in American Diplomacy: Oil and Arab Nationalization in Iraq* (Stanford University Press, 2021). See A Orakhelashvilli, 'Anglo-Iranian Oil Company', *Max Planck Encyclopedia of*

decolonisation of the oil concessionary system in international law after the emergence of the newly independent states in the Third World, and with the formation of OPEC,[194] the revision of what was considered unequal 'colonial' oil concessionary agreements, and the subsequent assertion and affirmation of 'the principle of sovereignty over natural resources' in the GA Resolution 1803 in 1962.

The beehive-like organising capacity of the K3 workers in controlling the strategic pumping station in Haditha is a remarkable illustration of how precise and organised action – that took into account its unique petro-spatial configuration – affected and eventually transformed semi-colonial law and its governing structures. More so, the workers' very determination to assert their rights after being forced out of their station was itself replete with meaning. For, unlike the oil pipelines that they operated under the desert sun that pumped a lifeless commodity into the machinery of the global capitalist economy, Iraqi workers were determined to materially impress to the world that their violated natural rights and living demands would traverse the vast desert all the way to the seat of state power in Baghdad, and explode into a revolutionary mode that would shake up the despotic order that oppressed them. This did not happen. Not yet. Their unwavering movement was temporarily blocked. Although the strike failed in that none of the workers' demands were fulfilled, these tactics in worker organisation and agency would reemerge in a radical way with the coming of the July Revolution of 1958.

## IX. CONCLUSION

This chapter detailed the social and economic conditions of the oil workers of the Kirkuk IPC enclave, examining its micro-history. It showed that the doctrine of semi-peripheral sovereignty had considerable impact on the lives of the working class in the oil frontier of Iraq. In particular, it exposed how the legal arrangements of the Anglo-Iraq Treaty and the oil concession described in Chapter 2, had material effects on the workers on the ground that were transformative by structuring capitalist relations of labour exploitation and oil extraction in Kirkuk. The concessionary agreement and the doctrine of semi-peripheral sovereignty produced a unique space that gave the IPC wide discretionary powers to operate, which, in turn, reproduced colonial capitalist relations in the company town and beyond. The chapter then went on to

*Public International Law* (October 2007); S Pahuja and C Storr, "Rethinking Iran and International Law: The Anglo-Iranian Oil Company Case Revisited' in K Crawford, Mahmoudi and Pellet (eds.), *The International Legal Order: Current Needs and Possible Responses, Essays in Honour of Djamchid Momtaz* (Brill, 2017), 53–74.

[194] For the role of OPEC and oil on decolonisation, see C Dietrich, *Oil Revolution: Anticolonial Elites, Sovereign Rights and the Economic Culture of Decolonization* (OUP, 2017).

uncover how the juridically constructed triangular relationship between the IPC, the British Embassy and the Iraqi government allowed for the violent suppression of the 1946 Gawūrbāghī oil strike that was initiated by IPC workers to resist the imperial structural constraints imposed on their lives. The 1946 strike demonstrates how the imperial and capitalist spaces that emerged from the workings of international and transnational law insulated the reach of Iraqi law and prevented the Iraqi people from pursuing justice in the courts by seeking accountability against the IPC for the murder of dozens of Iraqi workers. The chapter consequently critiqued the IPC narrative of the workers' strike, and its responses to it, revealing its conception of a particular reactionary ideology of trade unionism as a form of co-option. It concludes by revisiting the famous K3 pumping station strike to illustrate how oil workers used the spatiality of the petroleumscape of the region against the IPC as a strategy to assert their own alternative proletarian legal order and to eventually bring about transformation of the oppressive legal structures of oil imperialism.

# 5

# *Forging Independent Labour Unions: The Railway and Port Workers' Struggles against the Arteries of Imperial Communications and Trade*

## I. INTRODUCTION

I SHALL NOW turn to explore the remaining advanced sectors of the Iraqi working class of the time, namely the railway and port workers. The previous chapter dealt with the oil workers and showed the ways by which they organised against the 'triangular' relationship and complicity between the IPC, the Iraqi state and the British Embassy. This chapter will expand this analysis, moving from the provincial city of Kirkuk and its surrounding area to two other sites of geostrategic capitalist accumulation and anti-imperial labour struggle: the Iraq State Railways (ISR), concentrated in the railway workshops in the western Baghdad neighborhood of Schālchīyyāh, and the Port of Basra, governed by the Port of Basra Directorate (PBD) in the South. Both the Railways and the Port were arranged as semi-autonomous extraterritorialised entities – administratively and functionally separated from the Iraqi state. This was the direct effect of the 1930 Anglo-Iraqi Treaty and Iraqi semi-peripheral sovereignty. After detailing the legal structures that governed the railway system and the Port of Basra, I will explore the social conditions of the railway and port workers to analyse their various organisational efforts to improve their plight, while simultaneously challenging the oppressive semi-colonial legal structures that were imposed on them through collective strike action. I will end with an analysis of the ideological underpinnings of British labour expertise – especially the labour attaché to the British Embassy and the labour advisor to the Ministry of Social Affairs and Labour – and their influence on the institutions of the Iraqi state. I will show how the British labour expert's approach conceived of Iraqi trade unionism, and how even the existence of an urban working class in Iraq, was denied. The argument of this chapter is that while the railway and port workers were structurally challenging the semi-colonial institutions of the Iraqi state, British experts were devising top-down social and labour reforms to ensure the maintenance of this order and their hegemony. I will conclude by critically examining the limitations of British expert analyses to explain their failure in preventing the advent of revolution.

## II. THE ROLE OF RAILWAY INFRASTRUCTURE IN INFORMAL EMPIRE AND IMPERIAL GEOPOLITICS

The emergence of railroads and steam power in the nineteenth century prompted the coming of modernity with vast industrialisation in Europe and the United States. Karl Marx illustrated its centrality to modernity and its transformative function when he famously used it as an analogy for revolutions, which he called the 'locomotives of history'. Marx has emphasised that railways were the modern means of communications that allowed for the conquering of 'the entire earth' to transform it into a gigantic market.[1] In this way, one could not understand the role of railways in the Third World without grasping its purpose of 'opening up' territories for conquest and exploitation of raw materials to further European capitalism.[2] Whether it was in Africa or the Middle East, the aim of railway infrastructure was the construction of transcontinental arteries as instruments of 'informal empire-building' and of European expansion.[3] Ronald Robinson has demonstrated how railways were 'the principal generator of informal empire' as they constituted 'the locomotive ... [that] had a unique propensity for integrating and annexing territory, for monopolising its resources, and for preempting the future of great stretches of country'.[4] Walter Rodney, writing in the context of Africa, has likewise shown how the construction of 'roads and railways [with the use of forced native labour] were built to move troops and make conquest and oppression easier ... [for] [a]ll roads and railways led down to the sea. They were built to extract gold or manganese or coffee or cotton', rather than for the interests of African peoples.[5] The railways of India were also seen as being part and parcel of the 'civilising mission,' while they maintained connectivity of all its regions, assisting in communications, and in turn maintaining British colonial control.[6]

In the Middle East, British railway infrastructure was similarly developed to solidify 'arteries of imperial communications' for the purposes of commerce, and for the geostrategic military defence of the 'overland route' and to shorten this journey through the overland 'highway' to India.[7] In combination with the sea-routes, the railways formed one part of the 'great lines of imperial communication', which were the means of intercommunication and transportation, and

[1] See E Traverso. *Revolution: An Intellectual History* (Verso, 2021), 44.

[2] For studies on 'railway colonialism', see M Karuka, *Empire's Tracks: Indigenous Nations, Chinese Workers and the Transcontinental Railroad* (University of California Press, 2019); JP Daughton, *In the Forest of No Joy: The Congo-Ocean Railway and the Tragedy of French Colonialism* (W.W. Norton, 2021); W Biermann, *Tanganyika Railways – Carrier of Colonialism* (LIT Verlag, 1995).

[3] RE Robinson, 'Introduction' in CB Davis and KE Wilburn, Jr with RE Robinson (eds.), *Railway Imperialism* (Greenwood Press, 1991), 2.

[4] Ibid, 3.

[5] W Rodney, *How Europe Underdeveloped Africa* (Verso, 2018).

[6] RA Butlin, *Geographies of Empire: European Empires and Colonies c. 1880-1960* (CUP, 2009), 476.

[7] MB Statton, 'British Railways and Motor Roads in the Middle East – 1918-1930', *Economic Geography*, Apr. 1944, Vol. 20, No. 2 (Apr., 1944), 116-129; H Hoskins, *British Routes to India* (Longmans, Green & Co, 1928).

which amounted to 'the life-blood of the [British] Empire'.[8] This infrastructure was therefore vital for the defence of the British Empire east of the Suez, and it was intimately linked to the construction of these strategic railways as underscored by the reports of the Committee of Imperial Defence created in 1903.[9] Inter-imperial rivalry between the great powers over the control of these strategic railway lines in the Middle East could be traced to the tense geopolitical conflicts over the 'Berlin-Baghdad Railway,' which was initially obtained as a concession by the German-controlled Anatolian Railway in 1902, and was arguably one contributing factor that ultimately sparked the war.[10] With the expulsion of German influence from the Arab territories of the Ottoman Empire, the British proposed the construction of the Haifa-Baghdad railway with the geostrategic aims of linking 'the Mediterranean coast to the Persian Gulf under exclusive British control.'[11] The objectives of the railway lines in the region were specifically bound up with the protection and defence of the network of oil pipelines that transported Iraqi oil from the Mosul to the West.[12]

## III. THE IRAQI STATE RAILWAYS AS IMPERIAL ARTERIES OF COMMUNICATIONS IN THE MIDDLE EAST

The Iraqi railway system was initially constructed for a military purpose, but it was always at the centre of British geostrategic and imperial thinking. Only a few years after the British occupied Iraq, a 74-mile section of standard-gauge railway between Baghdad and Samārra was under construction.[13] Although it was as a result of the war that the British Army decided to build the railway system in Iraq, with the end of the war effort, it was maintained as a geostrategic node.[14] As the Director-General of the ISR wrote in one of his reports in 1947, 'the railway [system] is virtually a product of two wars'.[15] The British, who always regarded the railways as essential for their strategic network of imperial communications in the region, ensured the safeguarding of their interests in what Longrigg and Stoakes considered to be the 'arteries of Iraq's [imperial] communications'[16] after

[8] See AVT Wakely, *Some Aspects of Imperial Communications* (Sifton Praed & Co, 1924), 2.

[9] K Neilson, 'The Baghdad to Haifa railway: The culmination of railway planning for Imperial defence east of Suez,' in T.G. Otte and Keith Neilson (eds.), *Railways and International Politics: Paths of Empire, 1848-1945* (Routledge, 2006), 156-172; 157.

[10] The literature on the Baghdad-Berlin Railway is vast. See EM Earle, *Turkey, The Great Powers, and The Bagdad Railway: A Study of Imperialism* (Russell & Russell, 1966). For a more recent study see, M Ozyuksel, *Berlin-Baghdad Railway and the Ottoman Empire: Industrialization, Imperial Germany and the Middle East*, (I.B. Taurus, 2016).

[11] MB Stratton, *British Communications in the Middle East 1885-1939*, (PhD Dissertation, University of Pennsylvania, 1943) 120.

[12] Ibid, 9.

[13] Naval Intelligence Division. *Iraq and the Persian Gulf* (B.R. 524, Geographical Handbook Series, September 1944), 579.

[14] *Ibid*, 580-581.

[15] Iraqi State Railways, *Report on the Administration of the Railways*, 1945-46, (Baghdad: September 1st, 1947).

[16] S Longrigg and F Stoakes, *Iraq* (Ernest Benn, 1958), 133.

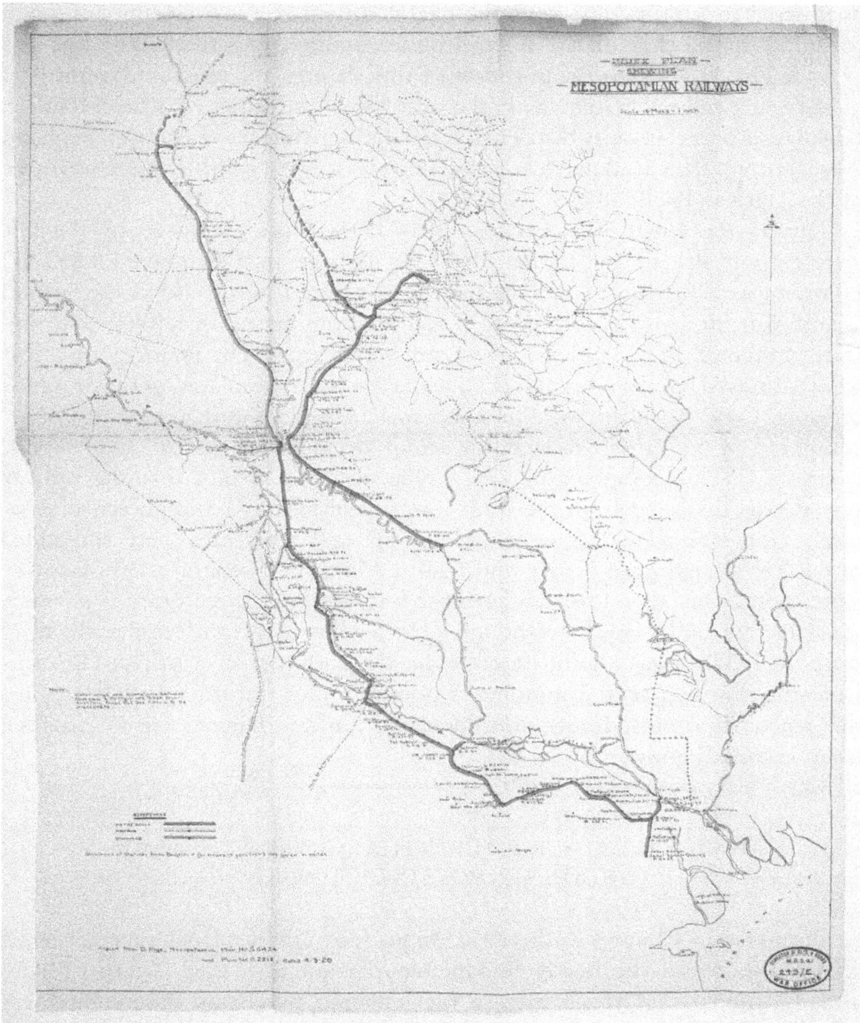


**Figure 7** 'Index Plan Shewing [sic] Mesopotamian Railways' [133r] (2/4), British Library: India Office Records and Private Papers, IOR/L/MIL/5/790, f 133, in *Qatar Digital Library* <https://www.qdl.qa/archive/81055/vdc_100094403025.0x000043> [accessed 20 February 2025].

independence. It is for this reason that the railways were explicitly referred to in the 1930 Anglo-Iraq Treaty, which fundamentally influenced the institutions of the emerging Iraqi state. The main lines of the railway system were divided into two sections: standard gauge north of Baghdad to Baijī along the Tigris; and metre gauge from Baghdad to Basra, along the Euphrates, and from Baghdad to Jalūla on the Diyāla, where it branched eastwards to Khanaqīn, and northward to Kirkūk.[17] In 1939, the Baghdad-Baiji line was extended through Mosul to Tell Kochek on the Syrian frontier, and by 1945, the Kirkūk line was extended to Arbīl.[18] For the purposes of this chapter, the most important part of the entire railway system lay in the workshops and stores of Schālchīyyāh in Baghdad (a working-class district situated 4 kilometres north-west of Baghdad West station). The headquarters of the ISR was located nearby, on the west side of the Tigris in Baghdad.[19]

During the Great War, between 1914-1918, those employed by the ISR were entirely British and Indian. By 1940, its total staff numbered 8,863 (32 of whom were British, 31 Indian, and the rest were Iraqis).[20] After the Second World War, in 1946, according to a railway administrative report, the total staff numbered 14,522 (14,461 of whom were Iraqis). The majority of Iraqis were employed as labourers (11,211), while the others were low-grade or junior officials. Only 43 Iraqis were in some sort of middle and 'senior positions' compared to 59 British officials in senior or higher technical and 'expert' positions.[21] This composition was a reflection of the fact that the railway system was dissected from the Iraqi state – administered and governed separately from the state. These semi-colonial legal structures were embedded in the 1930 Anglo-Iraq Treaty and finalised later in a separate 1936 Railway Agreement. This, therefore, rendered the Iraqi Railway Directorate as having a special status under law, for although its ownership was transferred to the Iraqi state (in 1936) it was administered under the authority of a British Director-General, who had semi-autonomous powers under statutory law. It was for this reason that most Iraqis considered the Railway Directorate as 'an alien [semi-colonial] body'.[22]

## IV. THE LEGAL STRUCTURES THAT GOVERN THE IRAQI STATE RAILWAYS DIRECTORATE

As discussed in Chapter 2, the 1930 Anglo-Iraq Treaty of Alliance governed relations between the newly 'independent' Iraqi state and Britain. I have already argued that this treaty in fact ensured that Iraqi sovereignty was constricted as it gave Britain significant room to influence the vital functions of the Iraqi state through its advisory system amongst other things.

17 Naval Intelligence Division, *supra*, 581; Longrigg and Stoakes, *ibid*, 133.

18 *Ibid*, 133. For a detailed description of the railway lines see, H Hughes, *Middle East Railways* (The Continental Railway Circle, 1981), 89-90.

19 Naval Intelligence Division, *supra*, 585.

20 *Ibid*.

21 Iraqi State Railways. *Report on the Administration of the Railways*, 1945-46, (September 1st, 1947), 36.

22 Batatu, *The Old Social Classes*, *supra*, 617.

Furthermore, it gave way for the development of a novel form of sovereignty – semi-peripheral sovereignty – under international law, as the PMC in Geneva considered it adequate for the termination of the Mandate. In the annex to the treaty, it was stipulated that a 'close' alliance between the two states would be maintained, especially relating to the military, as two bases were to be established rent-free inside Iraq, while British troops had a (virtually unlimited) right to move troops over Iraqi soil. Article 7 of the annexure stated that Iraq would,

> … afford, when requested to do so by His Britannic Majesty (HBM), all possible facilities for the movement of British forces of HBM of all arms in transit across 'Iraq and for the transport and storage of all supplies and equipment that may be required by these forces during their passage across 'Iraq. These facilities shall cover the use of roads, railways, waterways, ports and aerodromes of 'Iraq and HBM's ships shall have general permission to visit the Shatt-al-Arab.[23]

A separate financial annexure, which was attached to the treaty, dealt with the railways. It was stipulated that the ownership of the railway system would be transferred by the British administration to the Iraqi government and that it would be registered under its name, while full beneficial ownership would be vested by lease at a nominal rent in a special body or corporation having a separate legal personality to be constituted by special Statute of the Iraq Legislature.[24] This corporation was wholly responsible for the administration and management of the railway system, subject to limitations imposed by the statute.[25] The Board of the corporation consisted of five members, two of whom would be appointed by the British government and two by the government of Iraq; the fifth, who was the Chairman, would be appointed by both governments in agreement.[26]

It took a longer time than anticipated to negotiate and finalise the agreement by which the railway was to be transferred to the Iraqi state. The disagreements mostly regarded the amount to be paid for purchase, and the composition of the Board mentioned in the treaty and its statutory powers. E.G. Hogg, the British Advisor to the Ministry of Finance, explained the difficulties surrounding the negotiations in a Note, in which he wrote,

> in the case of the Railways … [the] Iraqi [government] feel that operations are conducted inside a wall which they cannot see through and can only to a very limited extent look over. They are told that the existence of the Board will make all the difference, since they will have their representation on the Board, which will be composed

[23] *The Anglo- 'Iraq Treaty of 1930*, (Baghdad, June 30, 1930), Art. 7 of the Annexure to the Treaty of Alliance.

[24] *Ibid*, *Notes Exchanged with the Iraq Prime Minister Embodying the Separate Agreement on Financial Questions Referred to in the second Exchange of Notes Appended to the Anglo-Iraq Treaty of 30th June, 1930*; Art. 4(a).

[25] *Ibid*, Art. 4(b).

[26] *Ibid*, Art. 4(d).

> of reasonable men ... [who] will listen to their views. On this they are skeptical [...] [considering that they would become] [...] 'a permanent minority' on the Board.[27]

Eventually, the Railway Agreement was concluded in March of 1936. A law was passed to create a corporation that would govern the railways.[28] It was agreed that the Iraqi state would take over ownership of the railways (including its material assets and Reserve fund) for a nominal sum of £494,000.[29] The Iraqi Government accepted all liabilities relating to the railways. Furthermore, it was agreed that for 20 years from the date of the transfer, the management of the railways would be entrusted to a five-member Board of Management appointed by the Iraqi Government, only one of whom would be a British subject. However, the Agreement made it clear that British subjects would hold all key positions of administration, such as General Manager, Inspector-General of Traffic and Chief Engineer. In this way, the 1936 Railway Agreement and the 1930 Anglo-Iraq Treaty ensured that the railway system was to remain under British administrative control, although it was legally the property of the Iraqi state. This was one of the legal instruments that were innovatively constructed to dismember the strategic parts of the country, turning them into semi-colonial enclaves, with the purpose of safeguarding British geostrategic interests. As I will show later, a similar approach was used with the governing institutions of the Port of Basra. It was no wonder that these enclaves would eventually turn into important sites of anti-colonial and anti-imperial struggle.

## V. THE FIRST 'EXPERIMENT' IN STRIKE ACTION AT THE SCHĀLCHĪYYĀH RAILWAY WORKSHOPS

In Chapter 3, I recounted the role of the railway workers in the formative years of the history of the labour movement in the mid-1930s. It should be kept in mind that the railway workers had a considerably longer history of labour organising activities, and it was therefore not surprising that the communists decided to begin their involvement with labour in the railways, leading to the 15-day 1945 Schālchīyyāh strike that had a significant impact on the overall history of the trade union movement in Iraq. The communists' strategic approach was to gradually organise cells in different railway stations throughout the country (such as Ma'qīl, Sāmāwah, Diwanīyyah, Baghdad West, Baghdad North, Baghdad East, and Kirkūk).[30] They focused their energies on the Schālchīyyāh workshops as

[27] TNA. CO 730/172/4. Note by CMG Hogg, Advisor to the Ministry of Finance, (Baghdad, 7th August, 1932).

[28] *Ibid*, 'Railway Corporation Law' (1932).

[29] The text of the Railway Agreement is in TNA, Kerr to FO, 1 April, 1936, FO 371/19998.

[30] Batatu, *supra*, 617.

they were considered as the 'most fundamental point in the entire system,' where they would be able to affect the most damage if a strike was called.[31] The workers of the Schālchīyyāh workshops numbered 1,265 in May 1945 (comprising about 12 per cent of all railway workers in Iraq).[32]

Most of the railway workers were uneducated, had rural origins, and remained attached to their tribal roots.[33] It was therefore a difficult task for the urban communist intelligentsia to shake their consciousness as their peasant-outlook and tribal affiliations made them less susceptible to notions of class solidarity, and appeared to fragment their ability to unite across class or even nationalist lines.[34] Yet, despite these misgivings, the railway workers were successful in forming certain levels of labour solidarity at pivotal moments, under the notions of class and anti-colonial nationalist struggle. It helped that the communists were sensitive to recruit the workers' most respected leaders into their ranks (in particular Alī Shūkūr and ʿAbd-Tamr), and this eventually made the party quite attractive. In time, the communists succeeded in becoming an intrinsic part of the lives of railway workers, providing them with the powerful analytic language and conceptual tools that they needed to understand the world around them.[35]

The Iraqi Railway Union (IRU) received its licence from the Ministry of Social Affairs in September 1944.[36] Its first congress was held in Baghdad on November 7, 1944.[37] Hāshim Jawād, the well-respected Iraqi member of the International Labour Organization chaired the elections, which gave it a kind of legitimacy.[38] Sixty-four delegates representing 17.6 per cent of all railway workers attended.[39] The Assembly elected a Supervisory Council of twelve (ten of which were members of the ICP), and an Administrate Bureau of seven members (four of which were members of the ICP). Alī Shūkūr, a charismatic and well-respected communist-worker, was elected as the president of the IRU, and Abbūd Hamza as secretary.[40] The union charter stated that it would seek improvements in wages and working conditions strictly by 'legal' means, discouraging any confrontation with the state.[41] It called for workers' education (to teach them how to read and write), to improve their technical skills, and 'to cultivate brotherly ties amongst themselves in the interest of the working class, their Iraqi homeland, and 'international

[31] *Ibid.*
[32] *Ibid.*
[33] Nūʿamān, *supra*, 122.
[34] *Ibid.*
[35] Batatu, *supra*, 620.
[36] TNA. Thompson (Bagdad) to FO (London). 15 Sep, 1944 'Formation of Trade Association in Iraq' FO 371/40096.
[37] TNA. Thompson (Bagdad) to FO (London). 18 Aug, 1944 'Formation of trade associations in Iraq' FO 371/40096. It happened to be the 27th anniversary of the Bolshevik Revolution.
[38] TNA. Mr. Thompson to Mr. Bevin, 8 Oct, 1945. FO 371/45281.
[39] Batatu, *supra*, 618.
[40] TNA. Mr. Thompson to Mr. Bevin, 8 Oct, 1945. FO 371/45281.
[41] Batatu, *supra*, 618.

democracy'.[42] Within a month of its establishment, a third of the railways workers (around 11,000 workers) joined the IRU.[43] In fact, the licensing of this union was such an important event that its headquarters was transformed into an epicentre of far-reaching labour organising and solidarity across sectoral lines, bolstering the Iraqi labour movement as a whole.[44]

At the Congress, the new president of the union, Alī Shūkūr made a speech in which he emphasised that the union's main role was to advocate for the rights of the railway workers and to resolve all their problems.[45] He then turned to identify some of the main problems facing the workers, in particular their drastically low wages, which were inadequate to live on. He recommended that wages should be fixed on a yearly rather than daily basis.[46] He also addressed the question of hours of work, stating that most workers worked overtime to the detriment of their health. One of the main issues that he tackled related to dismissals-at-will and the manner in which management abused their powers, often fining workers in a highly punitive manner.[47] Shūkūr insisted that this needed to be regulated and clearly defined within the law so that it was not abused. Finally, although he agreed that open communication channels and full cooperation between management and the union was a necessity – even suggesting the formation of a special committee to look into workers grievances and to educate them on their rights under the labour law – he made it clear that an *independent* trade union *must* be recognised by the administration as the sole bargaining agent for all of the railway workers.[48]

From the very beginning, the attitude of the British Director-General of the Railways, Major General H.C. Smith, was hostile towards the formation and licensing of the union. Rather than recognising its elections as a legitimate and democratic process, he saw it as being instigated by communist agitators who were 'political opportunists'.[49] Smith kept a close eye on these developments, privately encouraging workers to 'squeeze out' those undesirable (elected) leaders from their ranks.[50] Even the British Embassy councillor, who agreed that the new union was for the most part promoted by 'political busybodies', would go on to criticise Smith's uncompromising approach, writing in a dispatch to London: '"political opportunists" or not, leaders with some education and independence will be necessary if workers in this country are to improve upon their miserable status. They are unlikely in my view to make such progress if merely organised

[42] *Constitution of the Iraqi Railway Workers' Union* (Baghdad, 1944), Articles 2-7, *Ibid.*
[43] *Ibid.*
[44] Sbāhī, *supra*, 255.
[45] *Ṣawt al-'Ahālī*, 10 Nov, 1944.
[46] *Ibid.*
[47] *Ṣawt al-'Ahālī*, 10 Nov, 1944.
[48] *Ibid.*
[49] TNA. Thompson to Bevin, 8 Oct, 1945. FO 371/45281.
[50] *Ibid.*

into "company unions" which is evidently what Smith would like to see'.[51] As one would expect from a semi-colonial enterprise, the British Embassy believed that the numerous allegations regarding the working conditions of the railway workers were exaggerated. At one point, it was claimed that the conditions of railway workers were much higher than in other industries. Moreover, the contravention of the Iraqi labour law by the railway administration, which was one of the main allegations made by the workers, was astoundingly admitted, but cunningly it was claimed that this contravention was done 'to the advantage of the workers'.[52]

On April 11, the IRU submitted a petition to the railway administration which listed the demands of the Schālchīyyāh workers, which were raises of 50 per cent, 40 per cent and 30 per cent on day wages of less than 200 fils, between 200-300 fils, and of more than 300 fils, respectively.[53] The question of higher wages was the most important concern for the workers, because if one were to calculate the wages of railway workers at the time and compare it to the cost of living index, it would be obvious that they were utterly inadequate. The lowest wage for day labourers was 150 fils,[54] while the 'labourer's basket' for one family to live on in December 1945 was calculated at approximately 405 fils.[55] In other words, wages were less than inadequate to live on, especially considering the continuing rise of the cost of living. In fact, even by 1948 when some increases in wages were applied while living costs rose to six times before the war, the labour attaché to the British Embassy wrote in his report that 'the purchasing value of these wages was much below the lowest subsistence level', and that, therefore, a wage of about 230 fils a day meant that workers were 'nearly half-starved'.[56]

The conditions of the railway workers could also be ascertained from the descriptions of their living quarters, which were tiny mud huts surrounding the workshops. One lawyer, Sālim al-Nūʿamān, described these huts, where the administrative bureau of the union would sometimes meet, in the following manner: 'the hut … was made up of one room [and] built from mud … its space was no more than thirty square feet; [and] a family of five lived in

[51] *Ibid.*

[52] TNA. Note by P Rex Marriot, 'Enclosure: Iraq Communist Party', 25 Sep, 1945. FO 371/45281.

[53] The petition and demands are included in JA Ḥumaidī. *Al-Taṭwurāt al-Syāsīsya fī al-ʿIraq, 1941-1953* ['the political developments in Iraq, 1941-1953'] (Matbʿa al-Niʿaman, 1976), 153.

[54] TNA. Iraqi State Railways, Establishment General Order No. 76: Schedule of Wages for Daily Paid Railway Workmen, 1st May, 1945; in 'Labour Conditions in Iraq' Stonehewer British Embassy, Bagdad to FO, Oct 29, 1946, FO 371/52456.

[55] TNA. 'Labourer's Basket: Man, Wife and 2 Children as revised by Central Labour Sub-Committee. Minutes of Meeting of Dec 22, 1942, Part 1 (b)'; in 'Labour Conditions in Iraq' Stonehewer British Embassy, Bagdad to FO, Oct 29, 1946, FO 371/52456.

[56] TNA. FO 371/68482. 'Report on visit to Iraq from 8th June to 10th July by M.T. Audsley' (1 November, 1948).

it ... [T]hese [he goes on,] were the conditions of the railway workers'.[57] Even the labour attaché, who was given a tour of these quarters in 1948, described them as 'nauseating'.[58] In another description, Azīz al-Hājj, one of the foremost communist intellectuals, who was assigned the task of coordinating union activities with the party, described how a railway worker portrayed his miserable conditions in a union meeting. The worker, he wrote, weeped as he described in detail, 'the unaffordable rents, dismissals-at-will, high costs and black housing, the police chase, the abuse of the British administration ... [It is clear, the worker cried, that] the [British railway] administrator Smith and his kind were the ones running these [Iraqi] governments.'[59] The Railway Directorate's response to the union's demands was an unqualified refusal, and Shūkūr consequently had no choice but to order a national strike four days later. The response was instantaneous. The Schālchīyyāh workshops came to a complete standstill for ten consecutive days. This naturally put a great strain on the entire railway system, as strike action spread to other stations in Basra and Mosul.[60] On the third day, Smith cut off water supplies to the workers' mud hut dwellings that surrounded the railway workshops.[61]

On April 17th, the *mutasarif* of Baghdad ordered the suppression of the IRU, and the arrest of the members of the Administrative Bureau. The justification for the revocation of the union's licence and its suppression could be found in a letter sent to Parliament from the Minister of Social Affairs, which claimed that Iraqi workers were too 'socially and intellectually immature' to form a union, as they were easily prone to manipulation by political agitators, in turn, threatening the 'peace of the Monarchy.'[62] The Minister urged that the union's licence be revoked, and Parliament agreed. During the strike, the railway administration formed a spineless 'Labour Committee' that called for an end of the strike before any demands were met. The workers were aware of this strategy, boycotted it, and mockingly referred to it as 'Smith's Committee'.[63] General Smith consequently warned the strikers to resume work by the morning of the 21st, or be considered, 'as having left the service of the railway without notice'.[64] The workers remained firm for the most part. At this point, Smith appealed to the workers: 'Your interests are our interests. Therefore, return to work and have confidence that your Administration ... will improve your condition as far as is possible'.[65] There was no response. On April 24th, he threatened to import Indian labour. Five days later, the strike subsided after a promise by the Ministry of Social Affairs to increase wages to a certain extent.[66] Consequently,

[57] al-Nūʿamān, *supra*, 299.
[58] TNA. FO 371/68482. 'Report on visit to Iraq from 8th June to 10th July by M.T. Audsley', *supra*.
[59] A al-Hājj. *Dāfatir al-Shakhis al-Ākhir*, [Notebooks of the Other Person] (Muʾasasa al-ʿArabīya lil-dirāsāt wa al-Nashir, 1985), 104.
[60] Humaīdī, *supra*, 154-55.
[61] Batatu, *supra*, 619.
[62] As quoted in Humaidī, *supra*, 155.
[63] Sbāhī, *supra*, 258-259.
[64] Batatu, *supra*, 620.
[65] *Ibid.*
[66] *Ibid.*

worker disintegration spread for fear of losing their jobs, and the strike eventually ended.[67] The IRU was permanently shut down and would not reemerge until after the fall of the Monarchy.

The significance of the 1945 Schālchīyyāh strike in the history of the labour movement can not be overstated, as it was, in the words of Sbāhī, the first 'experiment' in organisational strike action in post-war Iraq.[68] It was, in other words, the beginning of a pattern that would occur elsewhere, in which a union would be democratically formed by the workers then violently suppressed by the government, leading to the emergence of a (hidden) 'strike committee' that would undertake a more offensive militant strategy of wildcat strike action. This pattern continued sporadically until the advent of the revolution. As Batatu illustrates, the railway strike demonstrated that the communists did not actually have unlimited influence or control over the workers. That is true. However, Batatu did not fully or explicitly acknowledge the independence of the trade union and its administrative bureau from the ICP. In other words, his narrative assumes that the party was the prime mover of *every aspect* of the strike, including the union itself, which was not the case. The union was influenced by the ICP, and very closely coordinated with the party, and its president was a communist, but he took the workers' concerns to the party leadership rather than imposed party instructions on them.[69] The fact was that the leadership of the union was democratically elected for a reason and that was that they were trusted to further the workers' interests while keeping wider political questions in mind. Close coordination and guidance does not necessary mean full control (although it could surely at times imply strict discipline) and that was never really the policy of the party in the first place.

The ICP was successful in broadening workers' consciousness and facilitated its practice of an all-embracing solidarity. In short, the workers were given a lens to see the larger picture of their exploitation. Hence, the strike brought workers from different industries together to defend the very idea of trade unionism, which was being attacked by the government and the railway administration. Numerous sympathy strikes were initiated by mechanics, carpenters, electrical workers, cigarette workers and printer workers.[70] One petition submitted to the government made it clear that, 'this attack on the railway workers is considered as directed towards all the workers of Iraq'.[71] The other consequence of the railway strike was the gradual radicalisation of the working class as labour issues were now understood in the context of the nationalist movement and its political discourse. In other words, the role of the labour movement in the overall nationalist movement was further clarified, and workers were able to grasp how 'workers solidarity' came hand in hand with nationalist 'popular solidarity'.[72] This allowed for the escalation

[67] Batatu, *supra*.
[68] Sbāhī, *supra*, 257.
[69] al-Nūʿamān, supra, 298.
[70] Ḥumaidī, *supra*, 155.
[71] *Ibid*, 156.
[72] al-Nūʿamān, *supra*, 126.

in the popular 'hatred towards British colonialism [and imperialism]' within and beyond the Iraqi working class.[73] So, for example, the Iraqi Federation of Students organised sympathy strikes in support of the railway workers' struggle, referring to the Railway Directorate in their petition to the government as a 'colonial entity'.[74] The significance of the formation of this bond between the students and the workers would be one of the most effective relationships during the *Wathba*.

More importantly for our purposes, the communists exposed the manner in which Iraqi law was being undermined by the semi-colonial legal structures that governed the railways. The response of the British-run Railway Directorate with the violent suppression of the IRU and its replacement with what workers would later refer to as the 'colonial Smith Committees' demonstrated how the Anglo-Iraq Treaty and its legal structures had a direct effect on the workers. The ICP was central in contributing to broadening workers' consciousness in this regard, allowing them to learn from their past experiences. This was clear in a communist declaration written by *Fahad* and addressed to the railway workers in February of 1946, that called for the re-initiation of strike action, and directly critiqued the neo-colonial legal structures of the Directorate and its restrictive impact over Iraqi law:

> [...] Comrades! [...] We understand why you want your trade unions [rather than the 'workers committees'] [...] you want them because they represent you and because you struggle under their banner to implement the labour laws, and to improve your living [...] conditions, and to respond to the assault and injustices that you are exposed to by the Colonial Smith Administration. And we understand why Smith and the Iraqi government want to strip you and strip [all] the workers of Iraq from the trade unions and replace them with 'worker committee[s];' because they want the labour law to remain – like the Iraqi Constitution – a dead law, and because they want to exploit the Iraqi worker like an animal without any rights to raise his voice or respond against any injustice perpetrated against him [...].[75]

The struggle, therefore, moved from one generally concerned with a wage increase to one that specifically called for the *very existence of trade unionism* in Iraq, the *recognition* of an *independent* railway trade union and (quite explicitly) the *implementation of the labour law*. The workers were aware that through their own actions, they were injecting real content into the empty shell of the 1936 Labour Law, and this had an important effect on their nationalist struggle against the semi-colonial legal structures that governed the Iraqi state.

In that sense, the 1945 *Schālchīyyāh* strike would later resume under a new form of organised action with the 1946 strike (and later in massive successive strikes during the *Wathba*), which was now not only more political, but brought to further prominence the organisational institution of the 'higher

[73] *Ibid*.
[74] *Ibid*, 125.
[75] *Declaration of the Iraqi Communist Party to the Railway Workers*, Feb 28 1946 reproduced in full in *al-Thaqāfa al-Jadīda*, Issue 132, 1981, 77.

strike committee'. As the democratically elected trade unions were systematically suppressed by the Iraqi state and their British administrative overlords, the higher strike committee, which tended to operate underground, would therefore emerge as an important organisational structure for the labour movement; whereas the tactic that would eventually distinguish this change in strategy (as was already detailed with the actions of the K3 oil workers) would become *offensive wildcat strike action*. This happened hand-in-hand with the development of a cadre of worker-communists, who would gain and hone unique organisational experiences in the strategies and tactics of strike action, and who would move to coordinate their efforts into other industries, in particular the IPC oil fields and the Port of Basra.

## VI. THE PORT OF BASRA: THE LEGAL STRUCTURES OF THE PORT DIRECTORATE AND ITS EXTRATERRITORIALISED ENCLAVE

One of the most important sites of labour struggle in Iraq was the Port of Basra. As 'political and economic domain[s] where mobility over land connects to mobility over seas', ports have been conduits of European colonial and imperial expansion from the sixteenth century.[76] Kris Manjapra has described how colonial ports in various parts of the Global South, such as Bombay, Madras, Calcutta, Colombo, Singapore and Hong Kong, were all 'woven together by spindles of British, [Dutch] and French imperial oceanic trading'.[77] Basra was situated and embedded within the trading routes of the Arabian Peninsula, as its rivers and shores were vital nodes of the economic and social structures of the region. The Port of Basra has had a long historical role in the traditional trading routes of the Persian Gulf and the Indian Ocean, whereby traditional handmade *dhows* served its regional trade quite efficiently for centuries.[78] Founded in A.D. 636, the city of Basra would, by the nineteenth century, turn into an urban centre that one historian dubbed 'the Manchester of lower Mesopotamia'.[79] Its Port became an important commercial centre of the global trade routes between Europe and India, by way of the Persian Gulf and the Indian Ocean.[80] The history of Basra, which was commonly known as the 'Venice of the East' due to its narrow canals and waterways, could therefore not be understood without its major Port,[81] which served as the only 'sea-gate'

[76] K Manjapra, *Colonialism in Global Perspective* (CUP, 2020), 102.

[77] Ibid, 104.

[78] For a *long durée* history of trade in the region, see LT Fawaz and C.A. Bayly (eds.), *Modernity and Culture: From Mediterranean to the Indian Ocean* (Columbia University Press, 2002). For a more contemporary and brilliant study of ports and the shipping industry in the region, see Laleh Khalili, *Sinews of War and Trade: Shipping and Capitalism in the Arabian Peninsula* (Verso, 2020).

[79] GF Hourani, *Arab Seafaring in the Indian Ocean in Ancient and Early Medieval Times* (Princeton University Press, 1951), 69.

[80] G Alexandersson and G Norstrom, *World Shipping: An Economic Geography of Ports and Seaborne Trade* (John Woley & Sons, 1963), 401.

[81] See M Khudayyir, *Basrayatha: Portrait of a City,* William Hutchins (tr), (AUC Press, 2007), 5.

to 'the Land of Two Rivers'.[82] It remains a vital link for Iraq to the global economy.[83] The Basra Port and its gateway also provided a 'roundabout route for dominating trade with Europe,' naturally serving the main entry point for export and import trade into the country.[84] Basra, situated on the right bank of the Shatt al-Arab, 70 miles (112 km) by river above Fao, is in fact an agglomeration of three towns: Basra City; Ashar; the modern port of Maqil [where the main port of Basra is located]; and several large villages: Jubaila (on the river front); Manawi and Rubat Saghir.[85] The Maqil port is situated 2,500 km from the international navigational routes of the Indian Ocean, as well as, 100 km from the head of the Persian Gulf.

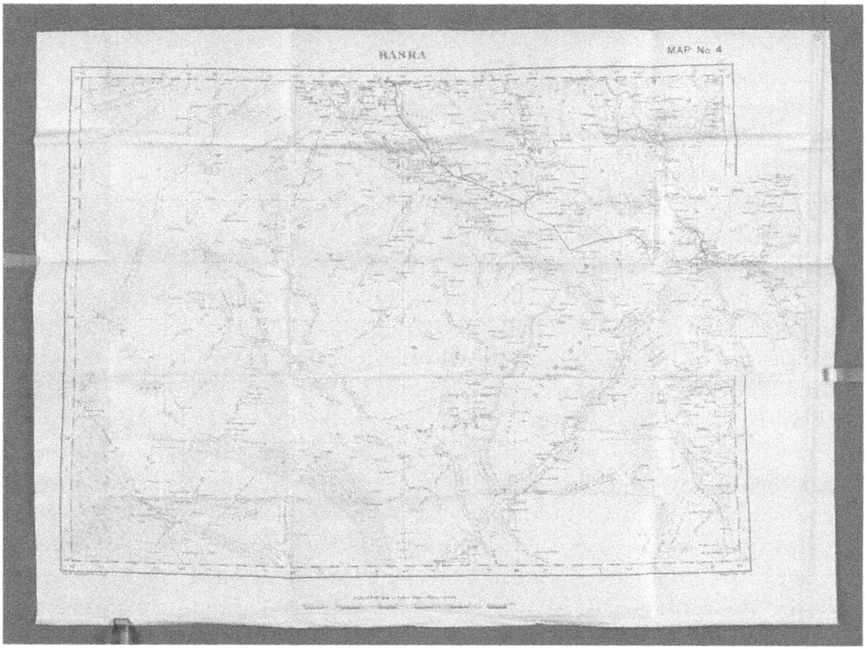


**Figure 8** 'Basra. Map No. 4' [35r] (1/2), British Library: India Office Records and Private Papers, IOR/L/PS/20/C204, f 35. From the British Library Collection.

[82] C Byford, *The Port of Basrah Iraq*, (Waterlow & Sons, 1935). For an overview of the history of Basra, see H al-Bazi, al-*Basrah fi Fatrah al-Muzlimah* [Basra in the Unjust Era] (Dar Manshourat al-Basrah, 1969); R Visser, *Basra, the Failed Gulf State* (LIT Verlag, 2005).

[83] For the role of Basra in the history of trade in the region and its relation to other ports, see H Fatah, *The Politics of Regional Trade, supra;* T Abdullah, *Merchants, Mamluks, and Murder: The Political Economy of Trade in Eighteenth-Century Basra,* (SUNY Press, 2001); FA Bishara, *A Sea of Debt: Law and Economic Life in the Western Indian Ocean 1780-1950* (CUP, 2017).

[84] The chief imports were sugar and steel products, while the main exports were dates and barley, accounting for 200,000 tons each. Iraq at the time furnished about three-quarters of the world trade in dates. *See* Alexandersson and Norstrom, *supra*.

[85] Naval Intelligence Division, *supra*, 505-506.

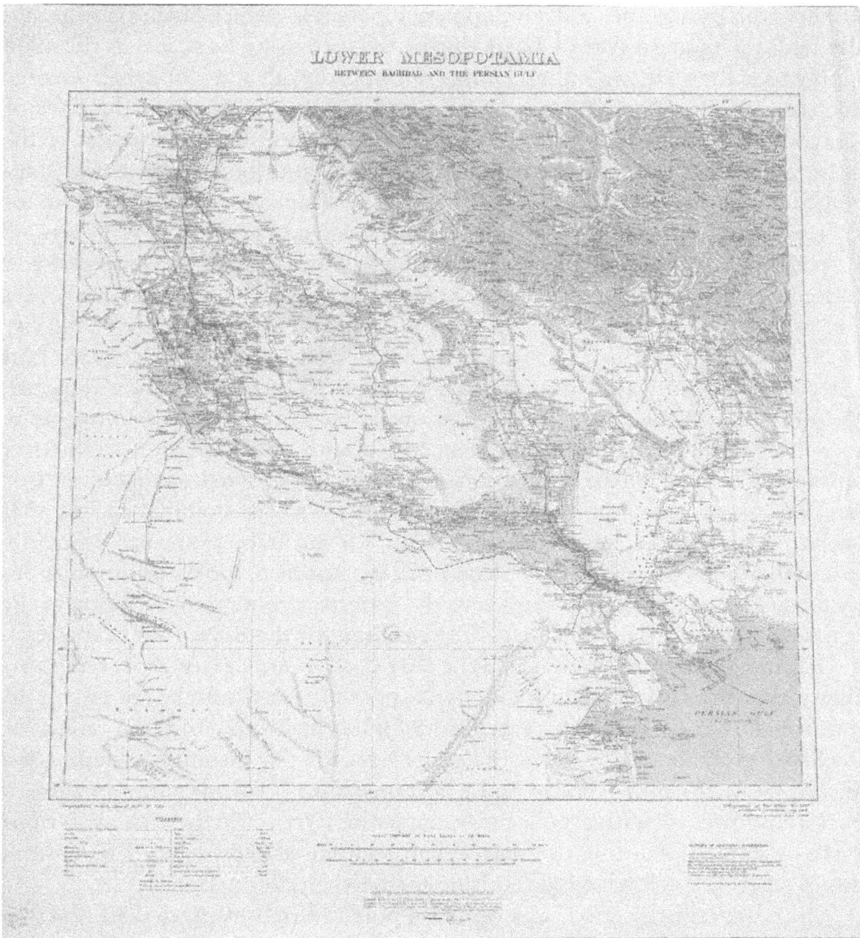


**Figure 9** 'Map of Lower Mesopotamia between Baghdad and the Persian Gulf' [Including Basra]; B20005-52. Maps MOD GSGS 2563; [London: GSGS, War Office], 1919.

The British first entered Basra in 1914, and occupied it thereafter, eventually constructing a modern port, and turning it into 'an appendage of British India'.[86] Even before this military expedition, by the late nineteenth century, trade in Ottoman Basra was already 'almost entirely in British hands,' especially after the opening of the Suez Canal, and in the context of the role of British-owned companies, such as the Euphrates and Tigris Steam Navigation

[86] P Rich (ed.), *A Voyage in the Gulf:* C.M. Cursetjee's *The Land of the Date* (1918) (Allborough, 1991), 157.

Company in local trade, and developmental policies.[87] The British Army gradually built the modern Port of Basra during the war, using its access as the main supply base for their two military bases in Habbānīyyāh and Shūʿaybāh. George Buchanan, a British civil engineer who had previously managed the port of Rangoon, was appointed in December 1915 to oversee the construction of the Basra port.[88] Buchanan oversaw the construction and the design of new shipping facilities, in particular the implementation of an administrative system for the regulation of the port and its traffic. The construction contract was awarded to a Chinese contractor, employing thousands of Ottoman prisoners-of-war and conscript labourers from India and China to build wharves, warehouses and other port infrastructure. The port was later linked by railway to the city of Hillah, which further encouraged its urban development.[89] The Basra Port Directorate (BPD) was centralised as a semi-autonomous institution responsible for administrative tasks, such as the mooring of vessels, river conservancy, as well as monitoring navigation from 'the mouth of the Shatt-el-Arab River upwards'.[90] On that basis, the Basra port was constructed (de facto and de jure) as 'an extra-territorial[ised] infrastructure' – a semi-colonial enclave that projected its hegemony not only internally on the Iraqi state, but especially externally on its surroundings.[91] The BPD, for instance, took over responsibility for guiding and securing ships into the waterway route to other ports in the region, such as to Abadan in Iran.[92] The passing of the *Basra Port Declaration* in October 1919 legally entrenched the Port Directorate's extraterritorial sovereignty over the critical nodes of imperial port infrastructure in the region, as it affirmed that its authority 'extended 90 miles upstream from the mouth of the Shatt al-'Arab and […] over the entire river for this distance, including the anchorage facilities of Abadan and Khorramshahr'.[93] This declaration allowed port authorities to station police over the entire river – whether the western or eastern (Iranian) sides of the river – and legitimised their levying of custom duties on all boats entering the Gulf no matter their destination.[94]

Once the military effort was over, the port reverted to its civilian function and officially reopened in April 1920 – its new commercial status was affirmed in the *Port of Basra Proclamation 1919 (Provisional)* – considered as 'the Port of

[87] AC Wratislaw, *A Consul in the East* (William Blackwood and Sons, 1924), 139.

[88] See G Buchanan, *The Tragedy of Mesopotamia* (William Blackwood, 1938).

[89] For an urban history of Basra including its port, *See* AA Al-Khattab, *Basra City: A Study in Urban Geography* (PhD Dissertation, SOAS, University of London, 1972), 84-85.

[90] See Buchanan, supra, 98.

[91] G Young, 'Infrastructures of Empire and Sovereignty: The Port of Basra in Interwar Iraq,' *Journal of Arabian Studies* 9.2 (December 2019), 123-144; 125.

[92] Al-Khattab, *supra*.

[93] RN Schofield, *Evolution of the Shatt Al-'Arab Boundary Dispute* (Middle East and North African Studies Press, 1986), 52.

[94] Young, *supra*, 133.

Basra Code',[95] which was eventually incorporated into the Iraqi Constitution or Organic Law in 1925.[96] The BPD remained under British ownership, although it was placed under the control of the new Iraq government and subsequently administered by the Ministry of Finance.[97] By the time the 1930 Anglo-Iraq Treaty was signed, the port was governed by very similar legal structures to the Iraq State Railways in a semi-autonomous manner. The financial annexure of the Treaty set up an autonomous Port Trust, whereby the property of the port would be (legally) transferred to the Iraqi government.[98] The Port Trust had its own 'legal personality,' and this legislation could not be amended without the agreement of the British, as long as Iraqi government owed debt with respect to the port.[99] The Iraqi government would consequently confer 'full beneficial ownership' upon the Port Trust, although it is unclear whether this arrangement was ever properly codified.[100]

The Iraqi government ultimately paid a nominal sum of £540,875[101] Hence, by the Second World War, the port would technically become the property of the Iraqi government, although it was in fact administered by an independent Port Authority headed by a British Port Director, and a Director General of Navigation (including British senior administrative staff).[102] Furthermore, the finances and budget (receipts and expenditures) of the port were fully separated from that the Iraqi state budget.[103] The Port Directorate remained under British control and oversight two decades after the end of Mandatory rule, as the first appointment of an Iraqi Director-General was not until 1953.[104] The Basra Port was, therefore, one of the geostrategic sites that were so vital for British imperial interests that it had to be dismembered from the institutions of the Iraqi state, and transformed into a separate semi-colonial enclave. Like the IPC in Kirkuk, the BPD had a significant hegemonic influence over the governance of the city of Basra. As one Iraqi who lived in Basra during this period observed, it was the Director of the BPD, who at the time was Colonel J.C. Ward, who was the de facto 'real ruler' (*al-hakim al-haqiqi*) of the city.[105] This was once again one of the material effects of semi-peripheral sovereignty, which, as discussed earlier, was characterised by a fragmented and proscribed sovereignty at its core with merely the formal appearance of a legally conferred (political) sovereignty.

[95] Byford, *supra*, 36.
[96] *Ibid.*
[97] Sassoon, *supra*, 51.
[98] *Anglo-Iraq Treaty, Annexure to the Treaty of Alliance.*
[99] *Ibid.*
[100] *Ibid.* See Byford, supra, 27.
[101] Naval Intelligence Division, *supra*, 508.
[102] *Ibid.*
[103] Byford, *supra*, 24.
[104] Sassoon, supra.
[105] M Shabandar. *Dhikrayāt Baghdādiyya: al-ʿIrāq bayna al-Iḥtilāl wa-l-Istiqlāl* [Baghdadi Memories: Iraq between Occupation and Independence] (Riad al-Rayyes, 1993), 255-256.

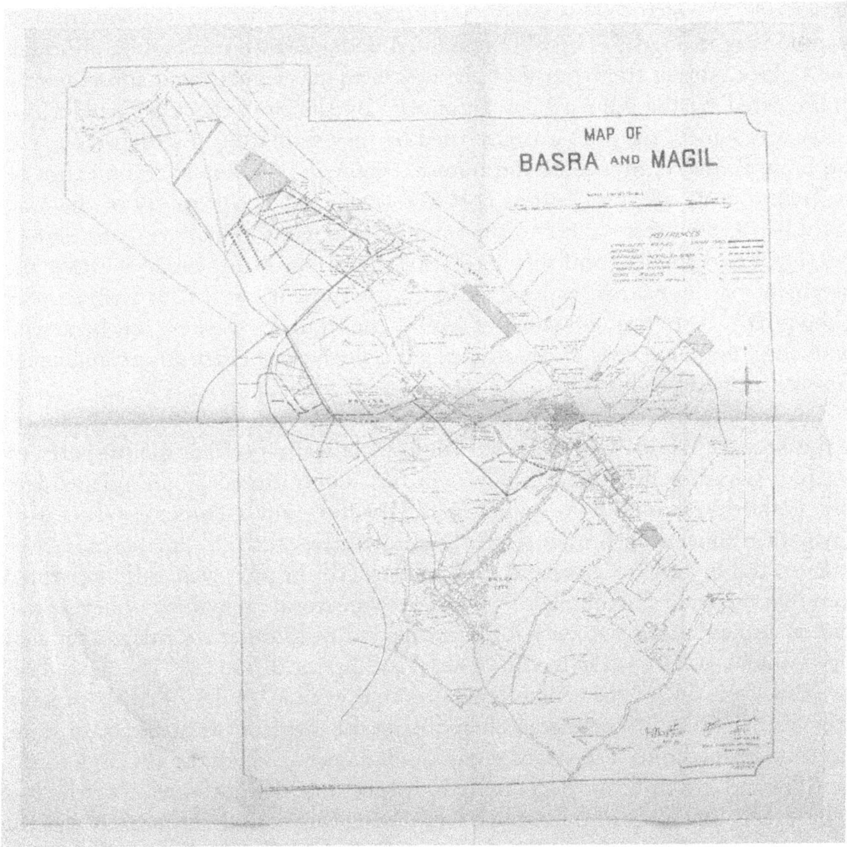


**Figure 10** 'Map of Basra and Magil' [Port] [52r] (1/2), British Library: India Office Records and Private Papers, IOR/L/PS/20/35, [1919] in *Qatar Digital Library* <https://www.qdl.qa/jump-to-archive-item>.

## VII. THE CONDITIONS OF THE BASRA PORT WORKERS AND THEIR COUNTER-HEGEMONIC LABOUR STRUGGLES

Port labour is unique in that it emerges within spaces that are interlinked through shipping routes, making it central for the smooth operations of global capitalism and trade. It is for this reason, as Frederick Cooper emphasises, that port labour is, 'absolutely crucial for capital to realise the fruits of its productive efforts'. Yet at the same time it is vulnerable to disruption, in particular at strategic chokepoints.[106] Many port workers experienced similar labour and social

[106] F Cooper, 'Dockworkers and labour history' in S Davies, CJ Davis, D de Vries, LH van Voss, L Hesselink and K Weinhauer (eds.), *Dock Workers: International Explorations in Comparative Labour History 1790-1970, Volume 1* (Ashgate, 1970), 526.

conditions, especially with the casualisation of their work. On the other hand, the interconnection of ports make these spaces dynamic, allowing for the free circulation of new revolutionary ideas on social organisation and for radical forms of political protest.[107] The port workers of the Middle East, and especially in the Arabian Peninsula, have had, against all odds, a long history of militant strike action and political protest, whether it was in the ports of Beirut, Aden, Doha, or Abu Dhabi, especially during the era of decolonisation in the 1950s and 1960s.[108]

The port and dockworkers of Basra suffered in similar ways to their counterparts in the colonised world. They were differentiated and casualised into numerous categories according to their functions in the port system – there were, for instance, not merely skilled, semiskilled and unskilled, but also marine ratings, monthly labourers, day labourers, labourers on contract and labourers on piecework.[109] Furthermore, according to Batatu, the bulk of these workers came from rival tribes –Nassār and Bahrakān – which made them even more difficult to unify under class or nationalist lines.[110] The communists and their allies, therefore, had a difficult road ahead in 'loosening the workers from their old tribal moorings and fastening them to new proletarian anchors'.[111] The national campaign for the establishment of a Port Workers' Union began in 1944. As will be shown, one of the main characteristics that distinguished the struggle of the port workers was the uncompromising attempt to *unify all the fragmented port workers*, and to guarantee that the Iraqi labour law was applied *universally* to *all* port workers rather than to only some workers.

In one revealing petition to the port authorities during the campaign, which was published in the working-class press, the manner in which the Port Directorate intentionally avoided the application of Iraqi law (namely the 1936 Labour Law) was described in colourful language, while the miserable conditions of the port workers were compared to the 'slave-workers of Pharaohs'. It is worth quoting below:

> Our [port] workers have lived under the shadow of the British Directorate that controls the Port, a life of misery and despair and slavery [...] representing the cruellest form of colonial exploitation, [...] a life that ... does not fit with [the principles of] human rights of our age today ... [The port administration] have taken away [...] our rights [...] Yes we have built the pyramids of the Pharaohs of the Port with our empty stomachs and our bodies half naked, but we will not lose our conscience, as honourable workers and as citizens, we rose like other workers [before us] of our dear Iraqi nation to demand for *our legal right to establish a trade*

107 A good history on the transnational militancy of port and seamen labour during the interwar period, see H Weiss, *A Global Radical Waterfront: The International Propaganda Committee of Transport Workers and the International of Seamen and Harbour Workers, 1921-1937* (Brill, 2021).

108 See Khalili, *supra*, 207-214; Khuri-Makdisi, *supra*, 142-143.

109 Batatu, *supra*, 621.

110 *Ibid.*

111 *Ibid.*

> *union, we seek to resurrect the labour law* [of 1936] *from under the layers of accumulated neglect throughout the years...* [we demand for the establishment of] ... [a] trade union that seeks to raise our standard of living and improve our conditions of work. However, the foreign directorate of the Port has ... attempted to intervene – to prevent us from acquiring our right to establish a trade union [...] The workers of the Port want to [...] enforce Iraqi laws [and] their rights. However, the masters of the Port see in the extension of the provisions of Iraqi laws into their independent directorate – which they consider as their own personal state – a danger that threatens their independent entity [...] and the loss of their control over this directorate ....[112]

The petition made it clear that one cannot understand the conditions of the port workers without grasping the reality of the port as a semi-colonial enclave and the legal structures that govern it in the first place. Moreover, the port workers, in a similar way to that of their comrades in the oil fields and railways managed to bring the labour law to life by consistently referring to it in their petitions, while connecting it to what they considered as their violated rights. The use of the law in such a way could be considered as the use of a strategic arsenal of resistance – the appropriation of legality and legal rhetoric to further their just cause. In many ways, what they were asking for was not radical, but rather moderate social reform. However, for a semi-colonial British administration and an Iraqi authoritarian government, this was too much to ask for.

The Port Workers' Union (PWU) was ultimately granted a licence from the Ministry of Social Affairs despite several setbacks on 15 August, 1945. The first Congress was held on 12 October in a local coffeehouse, leading to the election of a Council of 13 Supervisors (which included seven communists), and an Administrative Bureau of eight led by the worker-communist, ʿAbd al-Husān al-Jabbār, who was elected as president.[113] Around 3,125 workers (60 per cent of all port workers) subsequently joined the union by April 1946.[114] According to a prominent labour organiser and leader, Nāsir ʿAbbūd,[115] despite gaining a licence, the port administration rapidly waged its own repressive campaign against the union with the goal of disrupting its activities at every move, especially by increasing its outright dismissals of any worker suspected of organizing for the union.[116] A small strip of land in the Port was chosen as the official headquarters of the union and a mounted structure was erected, while workers were assigned to guard its entrances night and day, as union meetings and

[112] Quoted in Z Khayrī and S Khayrī, *Dirāsāt fī Tarīkh al-Hizb al-Shīūʿi al-ʿIraqī*, [Studies in the history of the Iraqi Communist Party, Vol. 1], (al-Yūbil al-Thahabī, 1984), 134.

[113] Batatu, *supra*, 621.

[114] *Ibid*.

[115] N ʿAbbūd, "Liqa' Mʿa al-Rafīq Nasir ʿAbbūd" ['An interview with Comrade Nasir Abbud'] in *al-Thaqāfa al-Jadīda* (Issue 152, 1984), 51.

[116] *Ibid*, 52.

heated debates were held, especially regarding the role of trade unionism and the importance of worker solidarity.[117]

The PWU decided to organise its first strike on 21 May 1947, and a higher strike committee was formed.[118] The Union's list of demands included the recognition of the PWU by the port administration, the application of the labour law to *all* port workers regardless of their grade, the reinstatement of those dismissed for their trade union activism, and the raising of wages.[119] This first experiment in strike action failed as police swiftly arrested the strike leaders and two-dozen workers.[120] According to ʿAbbūd, those arrested were ill-treated by police and then taken to appear in front of criminal courts, which took on a popular significance as their trials were 'transformed into a political demonstration against [police] terrorism and the defence of trade union rights and political freedoms' and especially 'the right to strike', which the workers had consistently fought for to be enshrined into the 1936 Labour Law.[121] Several lawyers appeared in court in defence of those arrested, in particular the prominent leftist lawyer, Mohammed Hussein Abū al-ʿaīs, who denounced the violent tactics used against the working class with his distinctive oratorical voice.[122]

Despite the fact that this first experiment in strike action by the port workers was technically a failure in that none of the workers' demands were fulfilled and at least 65 so-called 'agitator-workers' were expelled from the port,[123] 'Abbūd considered it as a key moment whereby the workers gained experience and discipline, while solidarity materialised between the port workers and the Basrawi masses as a whole.[124] The determination of the port workers did not falter as they returned to plan new strategies and tactics in strike action in their next confrontation soon afterward, during the *Wathba* uprising of 1948. I will return to the *Wathba* in Chapter 7, but for now what is important to note is that a wave of labour strikes, one of which was the K3 oil strike detailed earlier, intensified and spread throughout the country during the months of April and May of 1948, including in Basra and its port.[125]

An atmosphere of despair was prevalent in Basra as the common people struggled with extreme inflation that characterised the year of 1948 – the prices of necessities continued to rise, while there was a shortage of wheat and barley.[126] The situation was so unbearable that its stark effects became more

[117] *Ibid.*
[118] *Ibid*, 53.
[119] *Ṣawt al- ʾAhālī*, 28 May, 1947.
[120] ʿAbbūd, *supra*, 513.
[121] *Ibid.*
[122] *Ibid.*
[123] Batatu, *supra*, 621.
[124] ʿAbbūd, *supra*, 513.
[125] TNA. 'Basra Monthly Summary', 18 May, 1948; FO 371/68459.
[126] TNA. 'Basra Monthly Summary, Oct, 1948'; FO 371/68459.

visible when the Regent visited the city, and a British official wrote, 'the common people contrasted the magnificence of the HRH's reception with the terrible quality of bread they were forced to eat'.[127] It was later reported that bread was thrown at his car, while an elderly woman presented him with a piece of black bread, which she pointed out was 'a specimen of what the poor had to eat in Basra'.[128] The PWU once again drafted a signed petition listing their demands and sent it to both the Port administration and the Ministry of Social Affairs.[129] Their main demand was similar to what had been called for before: the application of the Labour Law to all port workers. They were explicitly opposed to the piecemeal system of employment (*nithām al-qitʿa*), in which workers were hired and paid extremely low wages for specific tasks, such as loading and unloading cargo.[130] These workers, who were called *ʿUmmāl al-Arṣīfa* ('the workers of the streets'), were colloquially referred to as *al-Masālīkh* (literally, 'the naked ones'), an indication of their miserable conditions. One of the union's main and most consistent demands, therefore, was to address the plight of those most vulnerable workers and to include them under the protections of the Labour Law, which was only applied to certain grades of workers, if at all.

The Port administration refused to negotiate with the workers or to even discuss their demands, while the Electrical Manager called the police to prevent the electrical port workers from entering the offices of the administrator.[131] The Head of the Dredging Port at Fao was consequently asked whether he had a response to the petition. He replied, 'there is no response and whoever does not want to work should leave immediately'.[132] It was this uncompromising attitude of the Directorate that forced the workers at Fao to come out to strike on April 4, followed by all port workers in Basra the next day.[133] Only a couple of days earlier, the dockworkers of the British shipping company Gray Mackenzie & Co went on strike as a result of their 'exceptionally low wages' and the company's evasion of the labour law with regards to sick and annual leave.[134] Therefore, for the first time in the history of the Port of Basra, *all* the port workers of every department were on a coordinated strike action which brought the entire port to a complete standstill. The port workers showed ingenuity in their organisational strategy when they used a new tactic, namely sabotage, as they cut electricity from the port generator, which supplied the entire city.[135] The city was consequently deprived of electricity and water for several hours, forcing the

[127] TNA. 'Basra Monthly Report, 1 March, 1948'; FO 371/68459.
[128] *Ibid.*
[129] *Ṣawt al- ʾAhālī*, 30 February, 1948.
[130] Batatu, *supra*, 443.
[131] *Ṣawt al- ʾAhālī*, 30 February, 1948.
[132] *Ibid.*
[133] TNA. 'Basra Monthly Summary for April 1948', (18 May, 1948); FO 371/68459.
[134] TNA. 'Reported Ill-Treatment of Workers by Gray, Mackenzie and Co. Ltd', 18 May 1948. FO 371/68482.
[135] TNA. 'Basra Monthly Summary for April 1948', (18 May, 1948), *supra*.

*mutasarrif* (in defiance of the Director-General of the Port) to end the strike on the same day with the 'complete capitulation to the workers' demands'.[136] The agreement that was reached included an all-round increase of 50 fils, and the reinstatement of 96 agitators, who were dismissed for their actions in the previous strike.[137]

The strike ended with a clear moral and tactical victory not only for the port workers, but the labour movement as a whole, and the BPD authorities were forced to negotiate with the PWU, implicitly recognising it as the sole bargaining agent for all port workers. This triumph, however, did not last for long, as martial law was declared in May, apparently due to the termination of the mandate in Palestine and the impending Arab-Israeli war.[138] The 'new weapon'[139] of emergency law, as one British official called it, and which will be analysed in the next chapter, was not only used by the Iraqi government to suppress all dissent, but also to arrest all labour organisers and union leaders.[140] By the 2nd May, the PWU was entirely suppressed, while the search for communists was intensified to the extent that it was described in one report as having 'taken on the characteristics of a medieval witch hunt'.[141] Nevertheless, the deep knowledge that the port workers had gained from these experiences was ingrained into their consciousness, and their innovative approaches in strike action would be further developed, tried and tested in the Port Strike of 1952, and later on in the massive Basra General Strike of 1953.

Before moving on, it is useful to summarise some insights from this narrative of the railway and port workers. It is clear that Iraqi workers were learning from their experiences. While the first strikes in the railways failed, those in the port were eventually successful. This illustrates the gradual but inevitable development of the labour movement as a whole. Furthermore, the manner in which the law was appropriated by these workers in their demands is a recurring theme, but here it happened in a much more cognisant way as semi-colonial legality, which was seen as a barrier to the proper application of Iraqi law as a whole (whether the Iraqi Constitution or the Labour Law) was specifically confronted.

The port and railway workers (arguably more than the oil workers, who targeted the transnational infrastructure of oil as well as imperialism in the region at large) were directly challenging the semi-colonial character of the Iraqi state and its structures. This is considering the fact that the semi-autonomous administrations of the railways and the port were de jure state-owned institutions that were not de facto controlled by the Iraqi state. Furthermore, the strategic

136 *Ibid.*
137 *Ibid.*
138 TNA. 'Basra Monthly Summary for May, 1948,' (14 June 1948), FO 371/68459.
139 *Ibid.*
140 TNA. M.G. Little, Basra Consulate-General to J.C. Richmond, British Embassy, Bagdad, I June 1948. No. 1021, FO/624/127 (1948).
141 TNA. 'Basra Monthly Summary for June 1948' (7 July, 1948), FO 371/68459.

uses of and references to the labour law by the workers as the main source of their natural rights, which they saw as having been violated by the semi-colonial legal structures of the Anglo-Iraq Treaty and its annexures, demonstrates that the workers were not only concerned with the interpretation of law, but also with the overthrow of the repressive semi-colonial British legal order itself, and the establishment of a just alternative legal order in Iraq.

## VIII. SEEING LIKE AN EXPERT: TRADE UNIONISM AS SUBVERSION & REFORM AS COUNTER-REVOLUTION

I will end this chapter with an analysis of the role of British labour experts within the institutions of the Iraqi state. Despite the claim that they did not have much control or influence, I will show that this was not the case and that the failure of the Iraqi government in dealing with the labour problems of the country was not merely due to their authoritarianism or incompetence, but rather to the very intervention of these so-called 'experts'. British experts refused to admit that it was their presence that was the problem, nor that the history of British intervention in any way instigated what they called the 'labour troubles' that they were appointed to examine. In fact, these British labour experts, who were assigned the tasks of addressing the major labour problems to make recommendations for the Iraqi government, were not genuinely concerned with the plight of the workers nor did they have a moderating effect on labour issues; rather, they were producing top-bottom social reforms to *prevent* any revolutionary or structural change to emerge from below. In other words, these experts were in fact concerned with the maintenance of the status quo of British influence over Iraq, and this was the reason that their symptomatic recommendations were ineffective, and instead caused further radicalisation of the working class and the eventual eruption of revolution.

It was after the election of the Labour Party in 1945 that a strategic shift occurred in British foreign policy concerning the colonies and semi-colonies in the Empire. This new ideological shift was influenced by the initiative of the Foreign Secretary, Ernest Bevin, whose aim was to focus on social and economic development with the intention of countering the influence of revolution and communism while maintaining British control in the region.[142] As Paul Kingston has shown, despite the fact that the social problems in Iraq were fundamentally structural, Britain was merely interested in 'promoting socio-economic development without structural reform'.[143] Although there was a long history of British technical assistance in Iraq before the war, more emphasis (at least in theory) was now put on serving the plight of the working class, the poor, and

[142] P Kingston, *Britain and the Politics of Modernization in the Middle East, 1945-1958* (Cambridge University Press, 1996).

[143] *Ibid*, 99.

the peasants. The point was to reframe the relationship between Britain and the region in a way that *appeared* to be reconciliatory to some nationalist demands, while ensuring that it would remain within 'the larger imperial design for the region'.[144]

It was, therefore, during this period of late British imperialism, which has been described as 'an imperialism of science and knowledge,' whereby academic and scientific experts rose to positions of 'unparalleled triumph and authority'.[145] It was in this context that British labour experts were appointed to deal with the 'labour questions' of Iraq; questions that the British Ambassador considered as 'the most vital that this country has to face and that on their solution will largely depend the future of this country'.[146] The main concern was regarding the effects of labour militancy and communist influence on trade unions.[147] It was accordingly no coincidence that soon after the violent suppression of the Gāwūrbāghī strike in the oil fields of Kirkūk in 1946 that a serious proposal was made for the need to have a British labour advisor in the Ministry of Social Affairs of the Iraqi state or, in the alternative, to have a permanent labour attaché to the British Embassy.[148] After some discussions on what would be more effective, it was ultimately settled that a labour attaché[149] would be appointed as a 'special agent en mission' rather than be permanently attached to the Embassy while the Iraqi government would eventually hire a labour advisor who would work from within the ministry.[150] It was noted that only 'long and sustained pressure' on the Iraqi government by an 'Advisor working inside and an Attaché working outside' that any results in implementing labour reforms would be achieved.[151] M.T. Audsley, an official of the Ministry of Labour and National Service, was appointed as labour attaché in the British Middle East Office in Cairo in 1945 and would later act as the labour attaché to the British Embassy in Baghdad, frequently travelling there to investigate and write several detailed reports on labour issues. It was, however, only by the end of 1948, after the *Wathba* and following the severe waves of strikes that a labour advisor (W.J. Hull) was retained by the Iraqi government's Ministry of Social Affairs – at the time, the ministry responsible for all labour issues in the country.[152]

[144] *Ibid*, 18.
[145] JM Hodge, *Triumph of the Expert: Agrarian Doctrines of Development and the Legacies of British Colonies*, (Ohio University Press, 2007), 11.
[146] TNA. 'Labour Conditions in Iraq' Stonehewer British Embassy, Bagdad to FO, Oct 29, 1946, FO 371/52456.
[147] TNA. Killearn to Bevin, 16 Jan 1946. FO 371/53327.
[148] TNA. Busk (Bagdad) to Baxter (London), 17 August 1946. FO 371/52456.
[149] On the Labour Attache service, see G Ince, *The Ministry of Labour and National Service*, (George Allen & Unwin Ltd, 1960), 57-58.
[150] The role of the labour advisor in the Ministry of Social Affairs was detailed by Audsley in his 1948 report. TNA. FO 371/68482. 'Report on visit to Iraq from 8th June to 10th July, 1948 by M.T. Audsley'.
[151] TNA. Audsley to Waterlow, 'Report on Iraq Labour problems' FO 371/68458.
[152] TNA. FO 371/68482. 'Report on visit to Iraq from 8th June to 10th July by M.T. Audsley'.

If one read the voluminous labour reports and dispatches written by these experts, it would be quite evident that the Iraqi worker was not only conceived in a certain orientalist manner, but that he was also essentially erased as an agent from history. That is, for the British expert, a socially conscious *Iraqi working class did not exist* – at least *not as an organised labour movement*, but instead it was merely a group of illiterate workers who were being manipulated by subversive foreign forces, and so was not genuinely representative of the working class. For that reason, it is quite ironic that the British expert would criticise the Iraqi government for being so irrationally repressive of labour in the country or quite incompetent in industrial relations, when he similarly saw the labour movement as a purely political subversive organisation. The British Ambassador, for example, considered Iraqi workers as 'illiterate workers' who were constantly being exploited by 'crooked lawyers and politicians', while he referred to the Iraqi government as 'a reactionary dictatorship to which the name of labour is anathema'.[153] Even if one did not take into account the fact that the Iraqi state was itself functioning through the constraining legal structures of the Anglo-Iraq treaty, the British response towards labour-organising activities in Iraq was quite contradictory in terms, and as I have shown earlier in the context of the railways, port and oil fields, was still repressive and violent.

In one labour report, Hull, the labour advisor to the Iraqi government, wrote, 'the few trade unions here are not representative of the wage earners',[154] and in another, that, 'there is no likelihood of any organised or effective labour movement developing in the near future in Iraq'.[155] These claims were made while he endlessly criticised the Iraqi government for not having proper (technical) understanding of the concept of trade unionism. As another British official illustrates, this incompetence of the Iraqi government that regarded 'the movement of labour as the movement of gangs of low paid workers from one place to another' without having any conception of the organisation of labour, and considered all trade unions as 'hotbeds of communism'.[156] The fact was, however, that British administrators in general, rejected the legitimacy of the indigenous (grassroots) labour movement in a similar manner. In other words, it appears that the expert was merely critical of the Iraqi government because its repression was not done through a certain orderly and bureaucratic system of labour organisation. What is interesting about this contradictory line of reasoning was that Hull as the British 'expert' analysed trade unionism in a similarly narrow manner. The only difference was that he claimed to be an 'expert' who had 'expert knowledge', which was supposedly unbiased, and he was developing

[153] TNA. Stonehewer to FO, 25 Oct 1946, 'Labour Conditions in Iraq', FO 371/52456.

[154] TNA. Hull to Guildhaume, 26 June 1951. FO 371/91704.

[155] TNA. 'Note on a meeting with Mr. Hull, Labour Advisor to the Iraq Government' FO 371/98783 (23 July, 1952).

[156] TNA. M.S. Rose, 'Iraq Labour Problems' 21 Feb. 1951. FO 371/98783.

a national scheme and labour policy with the main purpose of *maintaining* British hegemony over the country.

Hull also wrote that there was no freedom of association in Iraq, and that the executive of the Iraqi state would never relax its control over trade unionism and 'the right to combine for any purpose'. He then referred to a conversation he had with someone he called an 'astute' Iraqi banker, who explained to him that this was necessary because no political parties in Iraq had any real popular support and so 'a street riot or strike could unseat a government'.[157] He continued by arguing, approvingly of such analysis, that trade unionism in Iraq derives 'from a conviction of immense power that could be exercised by anyone with only a few thousand well-organised workers behind him.'[158] Hull seemed to be perpetuating the same analysis of trade unionism, of which he was criticising the Iraqi government's incompetence for using. His analysis maintained that all trade unionism in Iraq (whether it was anti-British or nationalist) had its basis on 'purely political' foundations and was therefore illegitimate and subversive. Furthermore, his conception of Iraqi workers was one that completely negated rational organised action, and in an orientalist manner reduced it to Arab emotional temper when he described 'the general state of the Iraqi worker as one of apathy', from which 'he could suddenly be stirred into outbursts of uncontrollable violence'.[159]

In this way, trade unionism in Iraq (and the region) was not considered as being akin to trade unionism elsewhere in the world (particularly in the West) and for this reason could not be analysed as such, but rather could only be understood through the lens of an 'expert' with unique 'expert knowledge' of the local conditions and 'the Arab mind', whatever this may be. This same line of reasoning was made by Audsley, the labour attaché, when he wrote, 'the present "industrial relations" bear no comparison with the pattern described in books. The Middle East is being shaken to its depth by the surge of political fanaticism, the fast growing "workers' demands" and the grinding never-ceasing wheels of communism'.[160] The quotation marks in this sentence alone reveal more than anything the manner in which the British expert viewed trade unionism and the working class in Iraq and the Middle East.

The claim that was always maintained was that British experts and advisors in the Iraqi government did not in fact have any significant influence over the 'independence' of the Iraqi state but were merely there on a limited advisory role for the benefit of providing technical 'expertise' and to advise ministers on the appropriate course of action. This arrangement was quite convenient in that the Iraqi government was always blamed if problems persisted. However,

[157] TNA. Hull to Guildhaume, 26 June 1951. FO 371/91704.
[158] *Ibid*.
[159] TNA. 'Note on a meeting with Mr. Hull, Labour Advisor to the Iraq Government' FO 371/98783 (23 July, 1952).
[160] TNA. Audsley (Cairo) to Morgan (Ministry of Labour, London), 18 May, 1948. LAB 13/674.

reading the records closely, it is clear that these experts actually had much more influence than was admitted. So, for example, Hull, the labour advisor to the Ministry of Social Affairs, demonstrated such deference towards his views in one episode, in which he urged the Minister not to interfere with the elections of the tobacco and carpenter workers, claiming that these unions were harmless.[161] The Minister responded with an Arab proverb – 'the man who has once been bitten by a snake will start [sic] in fear at the sight of a piece of rope'. To this Hull replied, 'there was here not even a piece of string'. The Minister then conceded that, Hull was the 'expert' and he knew better, so he would have to 'reverse his view'.[162] Reflecting on this episode, Hull wrote the following: 'I dislike being called an expert but the title is the very essence of the position of a British official here. It implies if I am not mistaken an authority whose views may be overridden by other authorities but until they are must be listened to with respect even if not too much is done about them. These people are impatient of "advisors" – one must never call oneself that.'[163] Hull's observation reveals the manner in which British experts preferred not only to do their work out of view, but also to insist that they did not have any discretionary powers whatsoever. That is, the expert denied and underplayed his influence and role within the ministry and the functions of the Iraqi state, although this was in fact exactly the main result of semi-colonialism and the Anglo-Iraq Treaty.

In the end, the recommendations and reforms of the labour advisor and attaché, and their attempts at developing an overall national labour policy in Iraq, was a complete failure. It was not primarily, as it was consistently claimed, because of the incompetence of the reactionary and 'feudal character' of the Iraqi government and state; it was rather due to the fact that these reforms were useless as long as the structures of semi-colonialism existed. That is, as long as the constraining legal structures of the Anglo-Iraq Treaty were maintained. The main aim of the overall workings of the advisor and attaché was to counter revolutionary change so as to maintain British hegemony. It was, in other words, devised as 'reform from above to forestall revolution from below'.[164] The recommendations for social reform, which included: the drafting of and application of labour legislation; the establishing of minimum wages to alleviate the high cost of living; planning agricultural developments; and the development of what was referred to as 'a constitutional Trade Union movement,' were therefore all means to ensure that British semi-colonial control was not faltered.[165] They were merely a safeguard against any changes in the legal structures of the treaty and the semi-colonial legal order. Audsley made this very clear when he wrote that Iraqi workers should not be encouraged as they have been by the

[161] TNA. Hull to Guildhaume, 18 July 1950. FO 371/98783 (3 Sep, 1950).
[162] *Ibid.*
[163] *Ibid.*
[164] See RA Alexander, 'Leadership in the National Movements of Egypt and Iraq 1945-1963', (PhD Dissertation, University of Exeter, 2007), 151.
[165] TNA. FO 371/68482. 'Report on visit to Iraq from 8th June to 10th July by M.T. Audsley'.

Russians, 'to rebel against their government', but rather to pursue their interests in a 'democratic manner':

> The Russians have no scruples in this respect, as elsewhere. They are anti-Government, anti-British, anti-evolution, anti-democratic; their methods of encouraging revolution are well-known ... [W]e are ... anti-Communist. We do not preach revolution; the Russians do ... We want to see orderly progressive social betterment of the people, the removal of injustice, better living conditions, freedom to create democratic workers' organizations – even if the pace is slow; the Russians do not. Somehow or other we must convince the Iraq Government ... that it is in their hands to pave the way towards bringing order out the present social chaos ... and that they must give encouragement to and secure the co-operation of, workers' leaders and others who are hostile to revolutionary methods.[166]

Here, Audsley did not mince words when he elucidated the real aim of these labour and social reforms, and the role of British experts in dealing with the question of labour in Iraq. Even Hull, the labour advisor, viewed his initiative of developing a new Directorate-General of Labour as not merely being as 'an essential service for a modern state', but specifically because it 'could do more than any other to prevent the growth of communism'.[167] In that sense, despite the fact that the British viewed themselves as having a 'moderating influence' on a 'reactionary' government, their actions in fact had the opposite effect in further radicalising the working class.[168] This is probably because Iraqi workers (especially in the oil fields, railways and port) rather than being illiterates with no agency were quite conscious of what was being done to them and to their movement.

Furthermore, legal reform in the context of semi-colonialism, could never bring about real structural change. This was due to the controlling influence of the legal structures of the Anglo-Iraq Treaty and the doctrine of semi-peripheral sovereignty, which retarded the effectiveness of Iraqi law. It was also due to the *political* question of semi-colonialism, which concerned the entire social order over Iraq, and was not merely a question of legality. It was this underlying fact that was completely ignored by British experts. As Fahad wrote on the expert's narrow analytic lens: some British experts would soon 'rise to the moon and some would sink into the depths of the earth' before admitting that 'the main cause of unemployment in this country is in front of their eyes: the foreign monopolistic companies that control the economy'.[169] Audsley and Hull likewise refused to admit what was in front of their eyes, which was British semi-colonial intervention, which they were a part of. It explains why Audsley did not interview a single trade union leader to include in his investigative reports, supposedly for fear that his motives would appear suspicious

[166] *Ibid.*
[167] TNA. Hull to Guildhaume, 18 July 1950. FO 371/98783 (3 Sep, 1950).
[168] Alexander, *supra*, 152.
[169] Yūsūf, *supra*, 186.

to the government.[170] Even when he was approached by a trade union leader, who conveyed to him the concerns of the majority of the working class, Audsley completely disregarded his statement referring to it as being too 'sweeping':

> I remember an Iraq Trade Union official saying to me … that the workers blamed us for everything that happened in their country; that the Treaty of Alliance which replaced the Mandate in 1932 had not lessened our interfering influence and that we had something to do with everything major event in Iraq since then; that if the country had remained backward, if its general standard of life was terribly low and if the social conditions were appalling the most accepted reason among large sections of the public was that British policy wanted it to be so … These were sweeping statements and I doubt whether the antagonism towards us is as general as they imply but they are certainly the ammunition used by the vocal extremists and political agitators to further their subversive and destructive ends.[171]

Audsley's refusal to admit that British intervention in Iraq was a major cause of the conditions of the Iraqi working class is more than disingenuous, for it was the arrival of British semi-colonialism and capitalism that permanently destabilised the rural areas and the socio-economic structures of Iraqi society, structuring underdevelopment, as I have shown in Chapter 1. Of course, Audsley's view was also informed by his conception of the Iraqi worker and the Arab as having a 'fanatical temperament', who was incapable of consciously and deliberately organising effective action against the semi-colonial conditions that oppressed him. My narrative of the railway and port workers above exposes the absurdity of such an analysis. It was the limitations of the British expert's view and his narrow lens (as well as its specific ideological purpose) that prevented any of the social and labour reforms (no matter how genuine they may have appeared to be) from being effective, and which ultimately failed to prevent the outburst of revolution from below.

## IX. CONCLUSION

This chapter detailed the struggles of the railway and port workers to improve their social conditions and to challenge the legal structures of semi-colonialism that governed their workplaces. The workers in these industries directly challenged the semi-colonial character of the Iraqi state and its semi-autonomous extraterritorialised enclaves of the railways and Basra port. This was somewhat different from their counterparts at the IPC oil fields, whose struggle had more of a transnational and even international dimension in resisting the imperialism of the petroluemscape of the region. I have shown how the railway and port workers gradually, but inventively, developed their organisational tactics and

[170] TNA. FO 371/68482. 'Report on visit to Iraq from 8th June to 10th July by M.T. Audsley', 19.
[171] *Ibid.*

strategies in strike action from their first attempt at the railway workshops to their pivotal victory at the port. The port and railway workers were attempting to bring structural and normative change into their lives through their actions from below and they often did this by strategically using and referring to the law as being (only) *one* of their arsenals of organised action, which went hand in hand with wild strike action and sabotage. This was in complete opposition to how British experts used the law in their development of labour and social reforms to supposedly remedy the ailments of the working class – theirs was an imposed top-bottom and bureaucratic development for the mere purpose of preventing any structural change. The British labour expert's approach was merely a strategy for the maintenance of British hegemony over Iraq, which the port and railway workers completely rejected as they considered British intervention as being the main cause of their miserable conditions.

# 6

# *Permanent Emergency and the Criminialisation of Dissent as Technologies of Semi-Colonial Governance*

## I. INTRODUCTION

THE IRAQI GOVERNMENT mimicked the hallmark techniques of colonial violence of the British Empire, which employed emergency legislation to violently crush rebellions, imprison dissidents, criminalise labour disputes, and torture the suspect native populations. Although this method was already common throughout the Empire in the nineteenth and early twentieth centuries, it would become systematised and eventually made permanent between 1948 and 1960 – so much so that this period has been referred to as the 'Age of Emergency'.[1] In this chapter, I will argue that the Iraqi government's use of the doctrine of emergency and criminal law amounted to technologies of semi-colonial governance that were borrowed from the British. By exploring the constitutive interconnections between law and violence, I will reveal the manner in which the Iraqi state used a combination of criminal law, martial law and the doctrine of emergency to suppress all forms of dissent and opposition to the social order with the aim of maintaining its hegemony. It will be clear through this analysis that the semi-colonial Iraqi state used tried-and-tested British colonial techniques of governance, in particular, by constitutionalising the Crown's ability to proclaim emergencies to quell any disorder that it considered as a threat to its rule. By delving into the historical origins of the doctrine of emergency, it will be shown how this was a technology of semi-colonial governance rather than a temporary response to isolated crises. Martial law was the standard mechanism used to protect British interests in the colonies, and

[1] See E Linstrum, *Age of Emergency: Living with Violence at the End of the British Empire* (OUP, 2023). Emergency laws were enacted in Jamaica, Cyprus, Malaya, Kenya and Palestine among others. Caroline Elkins traces this phenomenon throughout the British Empire, which she refers to as "legalized lawlessness,": the process '... of incrementally legalizing, bureaucratizing, and legitimating exceptional state-directed violence ...' to maintain law and order in the colonies. See C Elkins, *Legacy of Violence: A History of The British Empire* (Knopf, 2022), 15.

it was in turn repurposed and regularly used by the semi-colonial Iraqi state. This chapter will elucidate how these mechanisms were ingrained – with the legal advice of British experts – into the institutions of the Iraqi state and its Constitution, but more specifically into the doctrine of semi-peripheral sovereignty, which could not be maintained without permanent emergency rule. Iraq was certainly considered as being ungovernable (as an 'independent' 'parliamentary democracy') without these legal techniques, as revolutionary change was inevitable considering the inequality and the structural contradictions in its society. In fact, it was through the reliance on the doctrine of emergency that the Iraqi state was able to temporarily interrupt the advent of revolution until 1958.

Before turning to the debates surrounding emergency law, especially in the context of the *Intifāda* of 1952 (an attempt to renew the *Wathba*), in which the military was called into the streets for the first time in the history of the country to quell demonstrations, I will begin with a brief examination of how the criminal law was used to pacify all forms of dissent under the guise of 'fighting communism'.[2] These laws were, in turn, complementary to the effectiveness of a state of emergency. This is clear when analysing the amendment to the *Baghdad Penal Code* of 1938, and its application in the first trial of the Secretary-General of the ICP, Yūsuf Salmān Yūsuf (Comrade Fahad). The military courts relied on the 1938 amendment to imprison thousands of dissidents, while eventually sentencing ICP leaders to the death penalty.

## II. 'GROBBA'S LAW AGAINST BOLSHEVIK COMMUNISTS' AND THE CRIMINALISATION OF DISSENT IN IRAQ

Even before the institutionalisation of emergency with the controversial amendment of the Iraqi Constitution in 1943, the Iraqi government was consistently developing new ways of drafting legislation against what it saw as the spread of communism and leftist ideology in the country. This eventually led to the passing of an amendment to the *Baghdad Penal Code*, which was considered as the harshest piece of legislation against communism – defined in the broadest possible way – in the entire Middle East: the *Law Supplemental to the Baghdad Penal Code No. 51 of 1938*.[3] This draconian law made it a crime to espouse any 'doctrines of communism, anarchy and the like, which aim at the change of the system of government'. This was interpreted broadly enough to include anything that called for social reform, and the dissemination of these ideas. The Supplemental Law was, therefore, in essence more than the criminalisation of

[2] The detention of colonial subjects and dissidents was widespread in the British Empire. See M Lobban, *Imperial Incarceration: Detention Without Trial in the Making of British Colonial Africa* (CUP, 2021).

[3] *Iraq Government Gazette*, No. 30, Baghdad, 24th July, 1938, 475.

dissent, but in many ways amounted to the criminalisation of *thought*, and it would be consistently used by the Iraqi state to suppress all forms of dissent and the nationalist movement at large throughout the history of the monarchy.

In April 1936, the Iraqi government passed a law that amended the *Baghdad Penal Code* in a manner that made it more effective to prosecute those who possessed, printed or intended to publish, in the words of the amendment, 'communist propaganda [and] endeavor[ed] to create hostility to the established system of government'.[4] Although the definition of 'communist propaganda' was already broad, the Minister of Interior approached the British Ambassador, Archibald Clark Kerr for advice on the 'form and scope' of drafting 'special legislation' that would be even harsher, and would essentially 'make it a crime to be a Communist'.[5] Despite admitting that the Iraqi government was 'exaggerating the dangers of the spread of modern political ideas in this country' by seeking to draft such draconian legislation, Kerr contacted the Foreign Secretary to the Government of India, and asked him to send copies of laws passed in India, which he considered to have been effective.[6] By September 1937, *Ordinance No. 44 for the Prevention of Harmful Propaganda* was passed. This ordinance increased the powers of the government to deal with 'communism' further by enlarging the scope of the term 'harmful propaganda' to include the following:

> Any publication effected in bad faith … of a nature calculated to arouse: (a) Feelings of hatred or aversion for the state, or (b) Feelings of aversion or hostility among various classes of the inhabitants. (2) Any publication effected in bad faith … citing fabricated reports or misinterpreting any true report, with the object of disturbing public security or good foreign relations.[7]

The definition of 'harmful propaganda' included 'meetings' intended on 'exciting the public against the state or arousing feelings of aversion or hostility among the various classes of the inhabitants'.[8] In July 1938, *Law Supplemental to the Baghdad Penal Code No. 51* was passed and, made it a crime not only to disseminate 'communistic' ideas, but to 'express approval' of these ideas. Article 1 (1) read:

> Whoever expresses approval of or disseminates by any of the means of publication mentioned in Article 78 of this Law, any doctrines of communism, anarchy or the like, which aim at the change of the system of government and the fundamental

[4] TNA. FO 624/7. AC Kerr, Bagdad to FO, London, 29 April, 1936. A copy of the law [*Law Amending the Bagdad Penal Code No. 45 of 1936*] is enclosed.

[5] TNA. FO 624/9/516. AC Kerr, Minute Sheet, 19 November, 1937.

[6] TNA. FO 624/9/516. AC Kerr, British Embassy, Bagdad to Sir H Metcalfe, India; 23 Nov, 1937.

[7] TNA. FO 624/9/576, O Scott, British Embassy, Bagdad to FO. 18 December, 1937. Enclosed: *Ordinance for the Prevention of Harmful Propaganda No. 44 of 1937*. This law was eventually repealed.

[8] *Ibid*. It is interesting that the term 'class' is used, which is of course a reference to the poor workers and peasants.

> principles and status of human society that are guaranteed by the Organic Law, shall be punished with penal servitude or with imprisonment not exceeding seven years or with fine or both.[9]

Article 1(2) increased the sentence to penal servitude for life or imprisonment for fifteen years if the 'expression of approval or dissemination of the doctrines' was carried out with violence. Article 1(3) stated that if the latter occurred before more than one member of the military forces or police, the death penalty would be applied. Article 5(a) extended these penalties to anyone 'who becomes a member of an association the aim or object of which is to approve or to disseminate' these doctrines.[10]

*Law No. 51* was used to suppress not only communism but all forms of dissent. It was particularly useful for the military courts that were active when martial law was proclaimed. It is interesting to note that even the British advisor to the C.I.D. criticised the law for being drafted in a manner that would undoubtedly bring about hostile comments from the Soviets, who the advisor said would 'rightly protest that this law is a Nazi law'.[11] He pointed out that the *Baghdad Penal Code* was already sufficiently worded to deal with communism and that the 'institutions of prosecutions against alleged "communists" for their actions as such, and not as ordinary disturbances of public peace stirring up and propaganding [sic] in a manner intended to cause hatred and contempt against other sections of the people and against the Government charged under the appropriate sections of the Baghdad Penal Code, would undoubtedly call forth hostile comment, if not actual diplomatic protest ...'[12] The *Baghdad Penal Code*, he wrote, was 'strong enough – if applied properly and impartially'.[13] This advice was not taken seriously and instead *Law 51* – or what would later be dubbed in British reports as, 'Grobba's law Against Bolshevik Communists'[14] – would be used extensively, especially during the *Wathba* as a legal and violent measure to suppress the entire Iraqi nationalist movement.

In fact, by March 1948 (before the proclamation of martial law), Najīb al-Rāwī, the Minister of Justice, was described in a dispatch by the British Ambassador, Henry Mack, as 'refreshingly active and vigorous' in his pursuance of communists, who were being sentenced under this law in the courts. al-Rāwī directly consulted British Judge and Legal Advisor to the ministry, Sir John Prichard, to put together a list of suspected communists who should be arrested, while suppressing the opposition press, and ensuring that suspected

[9] *Ibid.*
[10] *Ibid.*
[11] TNA. FO 624/101. CID TO AH Ditchburn, Advisor to Ministry of Interior, 30 June 1946.
[12] *Ibid.*
[13] *Ibid.*
[14] *Ibid.* It was named after the former Nazi German Ambassador to Iraq, Fritz Grobba, who supported the Rashid Ali Coup of 1941 against the British-sponsored monarchy.

communists were removed from 'positions important to the security of the state'.[15] Furthermore, other countries in the region were coordinating in this regard. al-Rāwī was in close contact with the Minister of Justice in Egypt, who was looking to pass similar legislation against 'communism' there.[16] The head of the Criminal Investigation Department C.I.D. of Egypt visited Baghdad to discuss such 'security' measures with his counterpart to exchange lists of suspected communists. He ultimately took back with him copies of the Iraqi laws (specifically *Law 51*). al-Rāwī made similar arrangements with his counterparts in Syria and Lebanon, supplying them with Iraqi laws with the purpose of developing 'a common Arab League policy against communism'.[17] Mack expressed 'great pleasure' at this development.[18] The diffusion of these draconian laws suggests that they were of great benefit to the maintenance of semi-colonialism in the region.[19]

It was on the basis of *Law 51* or *Grobba's Law* that Yūsuf (Fahad), the Secretary-General of the ICP, along with his close comrade and Politburo member, Zakī Basīm, were prosecuted after their capture on January 18, 1947.[20] They were accused of reliance on 'foreign sources of income'; contacts with a 'foreign state' (i.e. the Soviet Union); incitement to armed insurrection; and the most serious offence: the propagation of communism among members of the armed forces.[21] All these accusations were flatly denied by Fahad, who eloquently addressed the judge on each of them, stating that the party was independent in its finances and organisation, was not intent on overthrowing the monarchy, but rather merely struggling for the people's natural rights and the democratic order as defined by the Iraqi Constitution.[22] It was quite revealing that he explicitly referred to the Constitution, especially to argue that *Law 51* was unconstitutional. He considered the ICP as being in a struggle to protect the provisions of the Iraqi Constitution against the regime's 'terroristic' policies and the 'imperialist' 1930 Anglo-Iraq Treaty, which undermined it.[23] This sort of reasoning would be reiterated in nationalist discourse (including by opposition

[15] TNA. FO/624/127. Minute by H Mack, 16 March 1948.

[16] *Ibid.*

[17] *Ibid.*

[18] *Ibid.*

[19] The reworking and redrafting of draconian legislation in such a manner did not end here. By 1954, a list of ordinances and amendments were passed that were even more severe. One was *Ordinance No. 17 of 1954 Supplemental to the Iraqi Nationality Law*, which basically stripped Iraqi citizens of their Iraqi citizenship if they were convicted under the 1938 law above. This rendered communists or anyone who opposed the regime as stateless. The legal advisor to the British Embassy found this law completely 'indefensible' and contrary to the 'general principals of international law'. This practice, which began during the *Wathba*, was later institutionalised in law. See Minutes in TNA. 'Communists in Iraq,' Oct 14, 1954, FO 371/110991.

[20] Batatu, *supra*, 537.

[21] *Ibid*, 539.

[22] *Ibid*, 540.

[23] A public memorandum written by the ICP and addressed to the international community with reference to the UNO Charter and international law made a similar point. TNA. FO/624/116 Translation of memorandum by ICP dated 5 June 1947.

MPs in Parliament) in the context of martial law and emergency legislation, as will be shown later. Fahad had already referred to *Law 51* in his writings, calling it a 'reactionary fascist law' that was a 'weapon in the hands of the Iraqi regime and its police' not merely to suppress the communist movement but also to suppress the labour movement and the nationalist movement in its entirety.[24] He repeated this point to his interrogator the day he was arrested. When asked whether he knew that propagation of communism is liable to punishment under the Penal Code, he responded: 'The relevant article 89a of the Code … is out of accord with the Iraqi Constitution, which has conceded the freedom of belief of every Iraqi citizen.'[25]

A public memorandum written by the ICP described the trial proceedings as 'nothing … [more] … than a comedy of which the acts were set by the C.I.D.'[26] This was not an exaggeration. The trial proceedings became increasingly farcical when resembling a Kafkaesque subplot, Kāmil Qazānchī (who would later lead the Coordination Committee of the *Wathba* movement) at the time, chief defence counsel, was arrested in the middle of the trial and charged under the very same law (*Law 51*) after he made an impassionate plea on behalf of his clients. This, of course, demonstrates how broadly drafted this piece legislation was and how it was used by the police and prosecutors. Qazānchī was accused of being a communist agent financed by the Soviet Legation.[27] This led the other nine attorneys to resign, and the defendants were left 'deprived of the sacred right of defence'.[28] Consequently, the police and prosecutors in 'an exposed manner, was itself conducting the court proceeding, in directing questions and in answering them sometimes, instead of the accused'.[29] The Higher Criminal Court ultimately found Fahad and Basīm guilty, sentencing them to the death penalty. The ICP memorandum argued that the verdict was decided in unison with the government without taking any of the evidence into consideration, abandoning both Iraqi law and the principles of international law. It was only due to an unexpected regional and international outcry that the sentences were

[24] Yūsuf. *Kitābāt*, *supra*, 434-435.

[25] As quoted in Batatu, *supra*, 538.

[26] TNA. Translation of memorandum by ICP dated 5 June 1947, enclosed in FO/624/116.

[27] British Embassy, Bagdad to FO, London; 4 June 1947, FO 371/61664. See *al-Zamān* newspaper, September 2, 9 and 10, 1947 for details of the court proceedings. Qazānchī's office was raided and papers were confiscated that were used to prosecute him. The chief evidence relied on were letters of correspondence with Labour MP, Denis Pritt, regarding the translation of his books into Arabic. The prosecutor considered Pritt a 'Communist [British] MP'. See, D. Pritt to McNeal, 18th July 1947, FO 371/61664. On appeal, the court eventually acquitted Qazānchī probably due to Pritt's pressure on the FO. The nationalist movement never forgot Pritt's contribution to their struggle. After the Revolution, Pritt was greeted at the airport by a large group of lawyers and half the Cabinet as he recounts in his memoirs: 'As I entered the [airport] building itself, I heard an Iraqi bystander say something which made people smile. I asked what he had said, and was told that it was: "What Englishman could there possibly be who deserves such a welcome here?" *The Autobiography of D.N. Pritt*, (Lawrence & Wishart, 1965), 135.

[28] TNA. Translation of memorandum by ICP dated 5 June 1947, enclosed in FO/624/116.

[29] *Ibid.*

eventually commuted to penal servitude for life and fifteen years respectively. One of these appeals came from the British socialist lawyer and MP Denis Pritt, who in an intense exchange in the House of Commons, questioned the Secretary of State for Foreign Affairs, Christopher Mayhew, on these political trials: 'Is the hon. Gentleman aware that …. [t]hese [Iraqi] gentlemen have, in fact, been sentenced to death for writing pamphlets, in support of trade unionism?[30] Will he, therefore, get our representatives in Iraq to have an unofficial word with that country? It is controlled by our Army [after all].' To which Mayhew's response was to evoke Iraqi (semi-peripheral) sovereignty to argue that there were no grounds for intervention, while completely denying that the British Army controlled Iraq through the Anglo-Iraq Treaty.[31]

It was only after martial law was declared during the *Wathba* that the regime had another chance to retry and ultimately execute the ICP leaders. I will return to this episode in the final chapter on the *Wathba*. The point for now is that an intricate web of draconian criminal legislation was developed to criminalise dissent and complement the Iraqi state's uses of the doctrine of emergency so as to maintain the regime's semi-colonial hegemony.

## III. THE 'MAGICAL WEAPON' OF EMERGENCY RULE AS A TECHNIQUE OF GOVERNANCE

The remaining part of this chapter will revolve around the doctrine of emergency. Why was it that up to the 1958 Revolution, Iraq was dominated by continuous states of emergency and proclamations of martial law? In fact, there were a total of sixteen proclamations of martial law in the 37 years of the existence of the Hashemite monarchy (between 25 October 1925 until the eve of the revolution on 13 July 1958).[32] From the seventeen years between the second occupation of Iraq in 1941 up to the fall of the monarchy in 1958, nine of these years were dominated by a state of emergency of one form or another.[33] The question, therefore, is whether this pattern reveals something of how a semi-colonial state that was considered 'independent' under international law still heavily relied on the doctrine of emergency borrowed from British colonial techniques to govern its population and maintain its rule over its people. This pattern suggests that it was partly due to such (legal) techniques that the Iraqi regime lasted a decade after the *Wathba* before it was finally overthrown. Furthermore, it was with the uses of martial law that the criminal legislation detailed above was used more effectively and systematically in the military courts. A good example

[30] Ibid.
[31] Ibid.
[32] H ʿAbdul Hādī, *Dirāsāt fī Qānūn al-Huqūq al-Insān* [Studies in Human Rights Law], Dār al-Hamad, 2009), 191.
[33] A al-Nāsirī. *Al-Jaīsh wa al-Sulta fī al-ʿIraq al-Malakī*, 1921-1958 [The Military and Government in Monarchial Iraq], (Dār al-Hassād li al-Nashir wa al-Tibāʿa wa al-Tawzīʿ, 2000) 154.

of the effects of martial law can be found in the monthly reports of the Basra Consulate-General, which, in an astounding tone, referred to martial law as a 'new magical weapon' of the Iraqi government. Referring to the declaration of martial law in May of 1948, the report stated that 'the situation cleared almost magically' and that 'power was now once more in the hands of government and there were few delusions as to how it would use its new weapon'.[34] It also suggested that 'British popularity [had] soared' right after the imposition of martial law.[35] How and why one might ask was this the effect of the declaration of martial law?

A detailed exploration of this 'magical [legal] weapon' of governance allows one to grasp just how it operated and how it affected the organising efforts of the national and labour movements. After briefly recounting the historical origins of the doctrine of emergency in Britain and its colonies, the chapter will detail how it was used in response to the *Intifāda* of 1952, which was an uprising that eventually brought the military into the streets of Baghdad to maintain order. The chapter will analyse the drafting history of the doctrine of emergency, focusing specifically on the constitutional amendment of 1943, which gave the Crown the authority to proclaim a state of emergency whenever it was threatened by a 'crisis'. After tracing how the doctrine was institutionalised in the governing and constitutional structures of the Iraqi state, I will end by exploring the heated debates inside and outside of parliament that revolved around this question, focusing on the work of the social democrat, opposition MP and lawyer, Hussein Jamīl.

## A. Tracing the History of the Doctrine of Emergency

As John Reynolds argued in his book, *Empire, Emergency and International Law*, if one were to trace the historical development of martial law from England to the colonies, it becomes clear how the doctrine of emergency was used specifically as a 'technique of governance and instrument of [imperial] control, rather than a purely reactive and temporary response to an isolated crisis'.[36] Martial law and the doctrine of emergency were, therefore, in fact 'technologies of colonial governance' that were applied in many parts of the Empire as strategic legal modalities to suppress anti-colonial movements.[37] In the region, emergency law was likewise developed and relied on to violently pacify the 1936 Arab Revolt in Palestine.[38] Moreover, it was not just in the colonies that the doctrine

[34] TNA. 'Basra Monthly Summary', Oct 1948, FO 371/68459.

[35] *Ibid*.

[36] J Reynolds, *Empire, Emergency and International Law*, (CUP, 2017), 70. *See* JM Collins. *Martial Law and English Laws, c. 1500-c.1700* (CUP, 2016).

[37] Reynolds, *supra*, 55.

[38] See M Hughes, *Britain's Pacification of Palestine: The British Army, the Colonial State, and the Arab Revolt, 1936-1939* (CUP, 2019).

of emergency was diffused, it was also distilled into the normative framework of international human rights law, with the inclusion of derogatory provisions.[39] In our case, the doctrine of emergency should be understood broadly in relation to semi-peripheral sovereignty granted to Iraq through international law and the mandate system – the latter could not be understood nor could it be maintained without the former.[40]

The origins of martial law in England can be traced to the medieval conception of 'military law', which was a system of regulations developed to maintain order and discipline of the armed forces. From the fourteenth century onwards, the 'justice of martial law' was to be applied not only to soldiers and sailors in wartime, but later extended to civilians, including rebels, traitors and rioters, among others.[41] There were competing theories as to the foundations and parameters of martial law amongst English legal scholars. One theory emphasised that martial law operated within the parameters of the rule of law. A.V. Dicey famously asserted that martial law was, 'unknown to the law of England', which illustrates, 'unmistakable proof of the permanent supremacy of the law under our constitution'.[42] Dicey meant that under English law, authority would never fully pass to the military and so martial law remained within the purview of the rule of law. It was, in this sense, derived from the common law 'right of the Crown and its servants to repel force by force in the case of invasion, insurrection, riot, or generally of any violent resistance of law'.[43] This had its basis in the common law defence of necessity. In other words, as long as the force used to suppress a riot was 'necessary' it was considered to be lawful.[44] An alternative theory suggested that martial law *did* suspend ordinary law for military rule, but it was only temporary and hence still operated within the constraints of the law. A third view stated that martial law was not law, but rather the 'will of the General who commands the army'.[45] Here, emergency law is considered as being outside the purview of the law, merely limited by the General's practical judgment on the field.

It was not until the mid-sixteenth century that martial law in Britain was extended from instances of war and rebellion to an offensive measure of governance used in peacetime. It was during this time that martial law was used as a weapon of class and political repression.[46] This use of martial law, which was first widely used in Ireland, continued in England in certain variations

[39] B Simpson, *Human Rights and the End of Empire: Britain and the Genesis of the European Convention, (OUP, 2001).*

[40] *Ibid*, 5. The ratification of the Anglo-Iraq Treaty in parliament was itself imposed through martial law. See Chapter 2.

[41] JV Capua, 'The Early History of Martial Law in England from the Fourteenth Century to the Petition of Right,' 36:1 Cambridge Law Journal (1977), 152, 153.

[42] AV Dicey, *Introduction to the Study of the Law of the Constitution*, (8th ed. 1915), 289.

[43] *Ibid*, 284.

[44] See M Head, *Emergency Powers: Theory and Practice* (Ashgate, 2016), 99.

[45] Hansard, cxv 880 (1 April 1851).

[46] Capua, *supra*, 164.

until it was outlawed by parliament after the passing of the Petition of Right in 1628.[47] Although the Petition of Right led to the disuse of martial law in Britain, this was not the case abroad where its colonial uses proliferated to become, 'an essential part of the security apparatus of many colonies in the empire'.[48] Martial law was turned into a mechanism of control in the colonial context with the aim of protecting British imperial interests and suppressing any form resistance from the native populace. The proclamation of martial law was, therefore, considered a common law right for the maintenance of 'the safety of the colony' as Robert Peel accentuated during the parliamentary debate on the uses of martial law in Ceylon in 1848.[49] Any threat against the established colonial order was deemed to necessitate the use of martial law to bring back public order and to ensure that 'uncivilised' natives remain obedient. The extremities of violence that would ensue during a period of martial law would always be justified, as passing this test of 'necessity' for violent punishment or reprisal was a *central technique* to the practice of martial law.[50]

The codification of martial law into emergency codes was a corresponding part of colonial governance in the Empire. This institutionalisation of martial law became more expansive as it was practically and widely applicable, for there was no need for the military to justify its actions under the common law test of strict necessity. As Brian Simpson has shown, it was in Ireland that Britain first decided to turn martial law into written law. Simpson considered the 1883 *Act for the More Effective Suppression of Local Disturbances and Dangerous Associations* in Ireland, as 'the ancestor of the modern code of emergency law'.[51] This Act gave the Lord-Lieutenant the power to declare a 'state of emergency' and to suppress meetings, impose curfews, and try offenders by court martial. Most significantly, 'nothing under the Act could be questioned by any court of law'.[52] The Act was naturally aimed at crushing the Irish peasantry's nationalist struggle. Ireland was, therefore, turned into a laboratory for experimentation on emergency law techniques that would later be exported to other parts of the Empire. By the First World War, the exclusive use of martial law in the colonies ended, and a 'sharp break from the centuries old tradition of martial law occurred' when the drafting of more comprehensive and draconian emergency codes institutionalised emergency powers in Britain.[53] Under a series of Defence of Realm Acts (DORA), the executive passed regulations,

[47] *Ibid*, 171-172.

[48] RW Kostal, *A Jurisprudence of Power: Victorian Empire and the Rule of Law*, (OUP, 2005), 10.

[49] Quoted in C Fairman, "The Law of Martial Rule and the National Emergency," *Harvard Law Review*, Vol. 55, (June, 1942), 1260.

[50] B Simpson, *supra*, 62-63.

[51] See the *Palestine (Defence) Orders of Council* of 1931 and 1937. 2 & 3 Government of Palestine Ordinances, Regulations, Rules, Orders and Notices 259 (19 April 1936 and 20 March 1937).

[52] Simpson, *supra*, 79.

[53] Simpson, *supra*, 80-81. *See* O Gross and FN Aolain. *Law in Times of Crises: Emergency Powers in Theory and Practice*, (Cambridge University Press, 2006), 182.

'for securing the public safety and the defence of the realm'.[54] This transformed 'the executive into the legislature', which gave it wide powers and allowed it to surpass parliament. The DORA technique was later exported to India, where 'emergency powers were [to become] a regular feature of the legal system'.[55] From there it was diffused into all corners of the Empire, including the Middle East, particularly Palestine and eventually Iraq.

## B. The Advent of Emergency Rule in Iraq

Martial law was already in use by the British administration in Iraq under the Mandate system. In fact, the subsidiary military agreement to the 1922 Anglo-Iraq Treaty gave the British the right to compel the King to declare martial law and to entrust its administration to a British officer.[56] In other words, the administration of martial law was exercised by the British military rather than by the Iraqi government. Moreover, as mentioned in Chapter 2, the 1922 Anglo-Iraq Treaty was itself only ratified by Parliament in 1924 when Percy Cox, the High Commissioner, used this right to proclaim martial law after the king fell ill. This is quite significant, for one must understand the 'independence' of Iraq and its ensuing semi-peripheral sovereignty (as governed by the 1930 Anglo-Iraq Treaty) in relation to the performative functions of martial law and the doctrine of emergency. In other words, *semi-peripheral sovereignty and the doctrine of emergency went hand in hand. The Iraqi state required martial law and emergency law to exercise its semi-colonial/semi-peripheral sovereignty*. A weak sovereignty could be (re) imposed over and over to be maintained and its hegemony held together, especially over its unsatisfied and distressed population.

Even before the controversial 1943 amendment, the 1925 Iraqi Constitution already contained a provision – Article 120 – that gave power to the King to proclaim martial law. It stated that, 'should disturbances occur, or should anything happen indicating the likelihood of the occurrence of events of such a character in any part whatsoever of Iraq, or should there be a menace of hostile attack upon any part whatsoever of Iraq, the King shall have power … to proclaim martial law …'[57] However, this power was subject to the Council of Ministers and martial law could only be proclaimed 'provisionally' in the districts of Iraq that were 'exposed to the danger of disturbances or attacks'.[58]

[54] *Ibid*.

[55] *Ibid*, 83. On emergency law in India, See J McQuade, *A Genealogy of Terrorism: Colonial Law and the Origins of an Idea* (CUP, 2021), 163–204.

[56] D Silverfarb, *Britain's Informal Empire in the Middle East: A Case Study of Iraq 1929-1941* (OUP, 1986), 9.

[57] *The Iraq Constitution (Organic Law)* – 21 March, 1925, passed 10 July, 1924, as amended 29 July, 1925 and 27October, 1943.

[58] *Ibid*.

The Article goes on to state that, 'the application of existing laws and regulations may be suspended by the proclamation declaring martial law in force' and Parliament may pass a law exempting those charged with the execution of the proclamation.[59] Finally, it states that 'the method of administration of the places in which martial law has been declared to be in force shall be prescribed by Royal *Irda'* or ordinance'.[60] Therefore, despite having the ability to proclaim martial law, the proclamation was explicitly provisional and limited to 'a menace of hostile attack' implying either an internal or external threat to the state. This was significantly altered by the 1943 amendment with the addition of a much wider and flexible power to declare a state of emergency.

By 1935, the *Ordinance for Martial Law Administration – No. 18* was passed, which detailed the manner in which martial law would be administrated.[61] The Military Court, for instance, was to be made up of a (military) president and four members (two military officers and two civilian judges). The procedures of the military court were detailed therein. The death penalty was the sentence to be applied to anyone who, 'uses arms against the government or its military and police forces'; 'participates in an armed rebellion against the government or armed forces'; disrupts the lines of communications; 'gives assistance to rebels'; 'spreads propaganda amongst members of the military or police forces'; or 'conducts espionage'. Penal servitude was the sentence for anyone, who 'gives [sensitive] news or information to rebels;' 'encourages the rebels to continue' their activities; or 'spreads false news'.[62] Under this Ordinance, the Officer Commanding the Military forces had wide powers, including the imposition of curfews; conducting searches of persons and houses at any time of day; suspending and seizing newspapers and periodicals; preventing or dispersing a public meeting; and making arrests.[63]

The Constitution was amended in 1943 to strengthen the prerogative powers of the King, one of which was the ability to dismiss the prime minister and dissolve parliament.[64] These major amendments were passed as a result of the 1941 anti-British coup of Rashid Ali, which threatened the existence of the monarchy and ultimately led to the second British occupation of Iraq that reinstalled the preceding order.[65] The amendments were, hence, meant to ensure that such a coup that threatened the monarchy would not reoccur. It did this by guaranteeing that the executive remained loyal to the monarchy, and accordingly

[59] *Ibid.*

[60] *Ibid.*

[61] 'Ordinance for Martial Law Administration – No. 18 of 1935'. *Iraq Gazette*, No. 1420, 14-5-1935.

[62] *Ibid.*

[63] M Kāmil. *Sharḥ al-Qānūn al-Idārī al-'Iraqi* [A commentary on the administrative law of Iraq], (Matb a al-Najah, 1949), 376.

[64] See al-Hasani, *Tārīkh al-Wizārāt*, Vol. 6, *supra*, 121-142.

[65] *The Iraq Constitution (Organic Law)* – March 21, 1925, passed 10 July, 1924, as amended 29 July, 1925 and 27 October, 1943.

weakened the powers of parliament. Furthermore, it gave the King the authority to issue royal prerogatives that were upheld as law, when parliament was not in session, surpassing parliamentary scrutiny. One of the most significant amendments was to Article 120, which incorporated the powers of the Crown to declare a state of emergency if he felt the monarchy was under threat.[66] The addition to the article read:

> upon the occurrence of danger or rebellion or anything which disturbs the peace, in any part of Iraq, the King may, with the consent of the Council of Ministers, notify a state of emergency in the whole of Iraq, or in any part thereof. The districts affected by the notification shall be administered in accordance with a special law, which shall provide for trial, by Special Courts, of those who commit specified offences, and prescribe the administrative measures to be taken by specified authorities.[67]

This amendment was inserted at the insistence of the British Legal Advisor to the Ministry of Justice, Edwin Drower, who was a member of the committee tasked with drafting the amendment.[68] Drower argued that the proclamation of martial law was not enough by itself for the government to function effectively, especially since the proclamation of martial law could only be done within the narrow condition of wartime – i.e. 'should there be a menace of [an external or internal] hostile attack'.[69] In other words, in peacetime when this external or internal threat was not present or was unclear, the government would not have a justification for the proclamation of martial law. What was required was a legal justification for the proclamation of an emergency, and so Drower insisted that this could only be done by inserting such a wide power into the Constitution itself, which basically constitutionalised the executive power to declare a state of emergency. A majority in the Drafting Committee were strongly opposed to this recommendation, but despite this, Nurī al-Saīd forcefully inserted this article into the list of amendments ensuring it would be passed.[70] As Kāmil al-Chādirjī argued in *Sadā al-Ahāli* newspaper, the vagueness of the phrase, 'danger or rebellion or anything which disturbs the peace' ensured that a state of emergency could be declared in peacetime, and did not have to be provisional as with the proclamation of martial law in the first part of the Article. In other words, it could now become a de facto *permanent* state of emergency,[71] which was in fact exactly what transpired, in particular after the 1952 *Intifāda*, and later the Basra General Strike of 1953.

[66] *Ibid.*

[67] *Ibid.*

[68] K Chādirji, 'Sin Qānūn al-Tawār' Yastabqī al-Mamlīka fī Hāla Ahkām 'Irfīya Dā'īma' ['The Emergency Law Ensures that the Monarchy will remain in a Permanent State of Emergency'], *Sadā al-Ahāli*, 3/1/1951; included in Rif'at Chādirjī. *fī Haq Mumārasa al-Sīyāsa wa al-Dīmuqrātīya: Iftitāhāt Jarīda al-Ahālī, 1944-1954* [The Right to Pursue Politics and Democracy: the Openings of *al-Ahali* Newspaper, 1944-1954], (al-Jamal, 2003), 436.

[69] *Ibid*, 437.

[70] *Ibid*, 438.

[71] *Ibid*, 440.

## C. The 1952 *Intifāda* and Permanent Emergency Rule as Governing Technique

I will now briefly shift the narrative to the streets by recounting the events of the *Intifāda*, which, once again, brought military rule back to the fore. Some major events at the time shook the entire region and certainly had a major impact on Iraqis; only a few months earlier the 1952 July Revolution instigated by the Free Officers overthrew the British-sponsored monarchy in Egypt, while a movement for the nationalisation of oil in Iran was underway. The *Intifāda* of November 1952 could be considered as the 'continuation' of the *Wathba*, which will be dealt with in the next chapter, as it was an attempt to revive the vitality of that emancipatory event. The nationalist movement, and especially opposition parties became aware that without a properly organised and unified flank, they would fail to bring any real change to an order that was increasingly intransigent.

It was this understanding that led the parliamentary opposition (the Independents, the National Democrats, the United Popular Front), and the communist-dominated Partisans of Peace[72] to negotiate an organised 'Contact Committee,' with the aim of 'facilitating the exchange of views and ensuring uniformity of action.'[73] On 28th October, the opposition sent petitions to the Regent that made the following demands: the amendment of the constitution 'to safeguard the sovereignty of the people' by abolishing the power of the Crown to dismiss cabinets; the granting of civil liberties; and the institution of a direct electoral system. The National Democrats and the Independents went further, calling for the abrogation of the 1930 Anglo-Iraq Treaty, the eviction of all British forces, and a limit to landownership.[74] Other significant demands included the end to all 'reactionary laws', (a clear reference to the Tribal Criminal and Civil Disputes Regulation and emergency law), the abolition of feudalism and the freedom to form trade unions.[75] The Regent's response was that reforms could only be enacted in a 'constitutional' manner through Parliament and 'the responsible government in office'.[76] The opposition consequently decided to boycott the elections, which led the British Ambassador, Sir John Troutbeck, to refer to them in his dispatch as a 'band of gangsters' that must be 'hit hard'.[77]

On the 22nd of November, demonstrations erupted in Baghdad as students, workers, and street vendors sprang to action under the guidance of the newly

[72] For more on the Partisans of Peace in the region, see M Kirasirova, 'The Partisans of Peace in Lebanon and Syria: How Anti-Nuclear Activism in the 1950s Revitalised the Arab Left' *International Journal of Middle East Studies* (2023), 55, 650-674.

[73] Batatu, *supra*, 667.

[74] For the full transcripts of the petitions See: TNA. Troutbeck to. Eden, 5 November, 1952, 'Recent Developments in the Political Situation in Iraq', FO 371/98735.

[75] *Ibid*.

[76] *Ibid*.

[77] TNA. Troutbeck to FO, London, 14 November 1952, FO 371/98735.

formed committee.[78] The shouts against the Regent were widespread, but more significant were the slogans: 'Anglo-American Imperialists Leave our Country!'[79]; and 'O Allah, O People! Renew the Wathba!'.[80] Crowds clashed with armed police, who fired shots, leading to the killing of one person, while fifty-two others, including thirty-eight policemen were injured.[81] On the 23rd of November, the demonstrations intensified its organisational capacity and quickly broadened, assuming 'a more distinct plebeian aspect'.[82] The ICP, who at that point dominated the rhythm of the streets, led the multitudes the next morning with the slogan, 'We Want Bread not Bullets!' and eventually stormed the Qambār Alī police station.[83] The anger intensified when, in the afternoon, the United States Information Service library was burned down, while another police station was occupied and set ablaze. The poet Badr Shākir al-Sayyāb would later describe the scene: 'they burned and looted and destroyed, as if they were destroying colonialism itself and not tape recorders and burning exploitation rather than cinema reels'.[84] The violence spiralled even further after police gunfire brought death to several demonstrators. In an act of vengeance, a policeman was dragged by a mob and set alight.

By sundown, the army was called into the streets of Baghdad for the first time in its modern history. Tanks rolled into the squares of the city. A special session was held in parliament where it was decided that martial law would be proclaimed in Baghdad Governante under Article 120 of the Constitution.[85] The application of ordinary laws ceased, and the civil courts shut down. General Nurī-ud-Dīn Mahmūd, a loyal Royalist officer of Kurdish origin, was given wide powers to form a new government and to rule under military administration. Referring to the provisions of 1935 *Ordinance for Martial Law Administration – No. 18*, General Mahmūd issued decrees that prohibited further demonstrations, dissolved all political parties, called for the arrest of their leaders, suppressed the press, and imposed curfew.[86] Despite these measures, demonstrations did not cease until they were violently crushed when military forces were ordered to shoot into the crowd.[87] Military rule lasted for 318 days until direct elections were called and a civilian government was formed, but the state of emergency remained in place.

The *Intifāda* was suppressed even more violently than the *Wathba* before it, and similarly with the use of the weapon of martial law. The process of

[78] Batatu, *supra*, 668.
[79] *Ibid.*
[80] BD Nurī, *Muthākarāt Baha' al-Dīn Nurī* [The Memoirs of Baha' al-Dīn Nurī], (Dār al-Hikmā, 2001), 164.
[81] Batatu, *supra*, 668.
[82] *Ibid.*
[83] Batatu, 669.
[84] BS al-Sayyāb, *Kuntū Shūʿīyan* [I Was a Communist], (Manshūrāt al-Jamal, 2007), 204-9.
[85] Hasanī, Vol. 8, 319.
[86] *Ibid*, 321-322.
[87] *Ibid*, 323.

normalising the state of emergency in law now started to materially take pace and to reveal itself in the everyday lives of Iraqis. The doctrine of emergency was a technique of governance that was an integral part of the structures of the semi-colonial Iraqi state. I will get to this argument in due course, but for now it is important to mention that if one read through the parliamentary records of this period, one would be astounded to find heated debates not only on the constitutionality of martial law, but also on the semi-colonial character of the Iraqi state.[88] The parliamentary opposition openly attacked the government and the British, referring to the Iraqi state as a dictatorship disguised as a parliamentary democracy. It considered the prolonging of martial law and the state of emergency as being unconstitutional. What is more, the opposition was in some way cognisant of the uses of the doctrine of emergency as a technique of governance. So, for instance, the foremost social democrat, Mohammed Hadīd claimed that the government could not govern or even survive without its uses of martial law.[89] Hadīd emphasised that martial law was merely used to 'protect the ruling classes,' turning Iraq into a 'police state'.[90] Hussein Jamīl, Hadīd's colleague, made a similar point when he wrote in *Sawt al-Ahālī* that the government used martial law 'to protect its back' whenever it needed to.[91] In one parliamentary session, Fāʾiq al-Sāmurāʾī of the nationalist Independents stated that, 'ever since Iraq became a member of the League of Nations until now, it has been ruled by martial law', and that Iraqis have forgotten what 'ordinary conditions' look like and have become 'accustomed to this type of rule'.[92] This was not an exaggeration as I have shown earlier. In fact, only six months earlier, Nurī al-Saīd endeavoured to pass another emergency law through parliament that would bring about the normalisation of emergency before elections took place. This law would be 'less restrictive than martial law' and would allow civil courts to 'continue to function' in a state of emergency.[93] This sort of normalisation was in fact what would emerge as the next elections went ahead when a state of emergency was still in place to the advantage of al-Saīd's Constitutional Union Party, and the ruling class.

## D. The Rule of Semi-Colonial Law: Hussein Jamīl and the 'Legal Aporia' of Emergency

I will now turn to the work of Hussein Jamīl, a social democrat and opposition MP, lawyer and a brilliant legal scholar, who was one of the foremost critics of

[88] For a history of the parliamentary system in the region during this period see M Rey, *When Parliaments Ruled the Middle East: Iraq and Syria, 1946-63* (AUC Press, 2022).

[89] *Muhāthir al-Nūwwāb*, (3-5-1949) [Iraqi Parliamentary Records], 481-482.

[90] *Ibid.*

[91] H Jamīl, "*al-Aḥkām al-ʿUrfiyya wa-Atharuhā fī Iḍṭirāb al-Ḥayāt al-ʿĀmma*" [Martial Law and its Effects on Public Life], *Sawt al-Ahālī*, 9-10-1949.

[92] *Muhāthir Majlis al-Nūwāb*, (19-12-1948) [Iraqi Parliamentary Records], 73.

[93] TNA. T.E. Bromisy to Eastern Department, FO; 27 March, 1952. FO/371/98734.

the uses of martial law in Iraq.[94] He wrote extensively on the topic and in 1953 published a pamphlet entitled *al-Aḥkām al-'Urfiyya: Baḥith Fiqḥī* [*Martial Law: A Doctrinal Analysis*].[95] His overall argument was that martial law (and the doctrine of emergency) did not suspend the law, but rather was governed by the Iraqi Constitution, and therefore, must be constrained by clearly identified parameters. In other words, he saw martial law as being rooted in law, and so consequently could not (legally) override the fundamental constitutional rights of the Iraqi people.[96] Martial law, he wrote, 'although provisional, is still not an absolute order, but rather is subject to the law ... [as] the constitution being its source ... it must be supervised by the judiciary'.[97] Jamīl considered the proclamation of a state of emergency under Article 120 as creating a 'political legal order that is based on constitutional rule, by reference to the constitution' and 'within the limits of the law'.[98] Not only was Jamīl an advocate of subjecting the military courts to appeals after the state of emergency ended, which would determine the constitutionality of its rulings, he also strongly criticised the composition of the military courts that were made up mostly of military rather than civilian judges as being in contravention of the constitution.[99]

Jamīl, was a social democrat of a liberal (Fabian) variety, and so had a strong affinity to the notion of the rule of law.[100] He made reference to the Magna Carta and *habeas corpus* in his writings to emphasise the principles inherent in the Iraqi Constitution that all citizens have a right to be heard by the ordinary (civil) courts of the land.[101] Furthermore, he argued that the ordinances issued by the military administrators during a state of emergency do not have the authority of law and cannot remain valid after a state of emergency ends, which was what often happened in Iraq.[102] In that sense, Jamīl believed that a clearly defined limitation to a proclamation of martial law and a state of emergency would prevent injustices from occurring.[103]

[94] Hussein Jamīl (1908-2002) was born in Karbala in 1908, where his father was a judge. He moved to Baghdad for secondary education, and eventually attended the Law College in Damascus, graduating in 1930. Jamīl was one of the founders of the reputable social democratic *al-Ahālī* newspaper, and he was a leader of the National Democratic Party, which was founded in 1946. He was elected to parliament in 1947, 1948 and 1954, and worked for the Ministry of Justice between 1949 and1950. He became the head of the Drafting Committee of the Iraqi Constitution after the July Revolution of 1958. A prominent member of the Iraqi Lawyers' Union between 1953 and 1957, he served as secretary-general of the Arab Lawyers Union between 1956 and 1958. He died in Baghdad on 6 January 2002.

[95] H Jamīl. *al-Aḥkām al-'Urfiyya: Baḥith Fiqḥī* [Martial Law: A Doctrinal Analysis], (Matba'a al-'Anī, 1953).

[96] *Ibid*, 3, 11.

[97] *See* AH al-Sha'abān. *Jithūr al-Tayyār al-Dimūqrātī fi al-'Iraq: Qira'a fī afkār Hussein Jamīl*, [The Roots of the Democratic Current in Iraq: A Reading in the Thought of Hussein Jamil], (Bīsān, 2007), 210.

[98] Jamīl, *supra*, 11.

[99] *Ibid*.

[100] See his book, *Huqūq al-Insān wa al-Qānūn al-Jinā'ī* [Human Rights and the Criminal Law], (Ma'ahad al-Bihūth wa al-Dirāsāt al-'Arabīya, 1972).

[101] Jamīl, *supra*, 10.

[102] *Ibid*, 33-34.

[103] *Ibid*.

Despite his sophisticated legal analysis, Jamīl was limited to a narrow doctrinal analysis, presenting a legal solution to a non-legal problem. In other words, he refused to grasp the doctrine of emergency beyond a narrow legal lens by studying it from a historical lens and grasping its function as a social and political technique of governance in a semi-colonial context. The question of martial law in Iraq was not a question of legal or constitutional interpretation. The semi-colonial state may be obsessed with its constitutionality, but that was merely a façade for its real intentions – the maintenance of its hegemony and the crushing of anything that would threaten its rule. Jamīl thought that the ideal of the rule of law would solve the problem of martial law in Iraq. However, he did not realise that martial law and the doctrine of emergency had a specific function in the colonies and semi-colonies. Jamīl underscores more than once in his pamphlet that, 'it is not the purpose of martial law to create a dictatorial order in a country which is a democracy'.[104] However, as I have shown, this was in fact exactly the (performative) function of martial law for the semi-colonial Iraqi state if one looked at its effects on the ground – the maintenance of the semi-colonial social order; whether it was referred to as dictatorial or democratic was not the issue.

If one approached martial law as actually being governed by the rule of law of a genuine parliamentary democracy, then Jamīl's analysis might arguably have some weight. In Iraq, however, martial law had a very specific function and Jamīl was merely describing what in his view *should be the law rather than what was the social reality*. An important example of how the doctrine of emergency was used as a technique of governance occurred during the massive Basra General Strike of 1953.[105] Propelled on the first anniversary of the *Intifāda*, it was organised under the guidance of a Strike Committee, which was led by the renowned Iraqi communist Salām Ādil.[106] The oil workers of the Basra Petroleum Company went on strike and eventually workers of the entire city joined the strike, including the port workers. The government at the insistence of the Minister of Interior, Saīd al-Qazzāz, decided that the proclamation of a state of emergency under the guise of 'combating communism' and reinstituting 'law and order' was necessary.[107] Police were ordered to violently shoot into a crowd of striking workers, while newspapers that spread the strikers'

[104] Jamīl, *supra*, 3.

[105] Su'ād Khayrī considered this strike as 'the Wathba of the workers' as it contributed to the 'economic liberation of oil resources from imperial hands'. Khayrī, *supra*, 204.

[106] Husain al-Rādī, aka Salām Ādil (b.1924, Najaf – d. 24 Feb 1963): Ādil was a schoolteacher and poet, who rose to become a member of the Central Committee of the ICP in 1953. He represented Iraq in the Second London Conference of the Communist Parties with the Sphere of British Imperialism the same year. He was heavily involved in the struggles of the labour movement in Basra and especially the oil workers. He died under torture by the Ba'athists during Black February in 1963. Batatu, *supra*, 712-717. For a biography *See* T Nājī Yūsuf and Nizār Khālid. *Salām Ādil: Sīra Münādil* [Salam Adil: The Story of a Resister] (Dār al-Madā, 2001).

[107] See AR al-Bayātī, *Saīd al-Qazzāz wa Dourihū fī Sīyāsa al- 'Iraq* [Said al-Qazzaz and his role in Iraqi politics], Beirūt: Mu'asasa al-'Arabīya lil-Dirāsa wa al-Nashir, 2001), 92-102.

declarations were suppressed and their journalists arrested.[108] A massive public outcry ensued in response to these violent measures and the use of emergency law against the working class. Only several months earlier one elder statesman, Mohammed Ridhā al-Shabībī made the argument in parliament that the government was using this technique to institute *hikūm tabaqī* ('class rule').[109] In a sense, this was true, for the use of the doctrine of emergency to deal with economic and labour relations was unprecedented in scale, and certainly revealed its specific uses by the ruling class as a tool of class repression to violently crush the stirring momentum of the working class movement. Iraqi workers organising for better conditions were viewed strictly from the perspective of 'national security'. In this manner, the semi-colonial Iraqi state mimicked the oppressive apparatus of the British colonial state. This certainly illustrates exactly how a semi-colonial state functions in its governing capacity. Ironically, Jamīl was not unaware of this, for he wrote an article in the *Saūt al-Ahālī* newspaper in which he condemned what transpired in Basra and stressed that this technique had become 'the normal response to the everyday affairs of the people'. Will an emergency be proclaimed, he continued, 'every time a strike occurs … and … every time workers demand their rights?'[110] The rule of law, therefore, that he claimed could (in theory) constrict a state of emergency in his pamphlet was rather useless in doing so in reality. The doctrine of emergency was more a Pandora's box that was impossible to constrain by law.

In any case, the fact was that the Iraqi Constitution, the legal structures of the Iraqi state, and its semi-peripheral sovereignty, were all the products of British semi-colonialism and imperialism. One could refer to the impassioned speech in parliament by opposition MP 'Abdul Razzāq al-Shaikhlī as a case in point. al-Shaikhlī infuriated the Speaker and others by arguing that it was in fact the Constitution itself that 'denied the rights of the people' as it was put into place by the British.[111] He pointed out that the government was democratic and nationalist only in appearance, while in reality it was akin to pieces of a 'wooden prop, which the … coloniser hides behind …', manipulating it out of view.[112] It was the 'coloniser', he continued, who manufactured Iraq's independence, which he compared to the idols of pre-Islamic *Jāhilīya* that were made of mud. Referring to the constitutional rights of the Iraqi people, he emphasised that they were given by the government 'with its right hand and taken with its left', as the permanent state of emergency illustrates that Iraq was in

[108] 'A Sbāhī. *'Uqūd min Tārīkh al-Ḥizb al-Shīyū'ī al-'Irāqī, al-Juzu' al-Thāni* [Decades from the History of the Communist Party of Iraq, volume 2], (Manshourāt al-Thaqāfa al-Jadīda, 2003), 125-127.

[109] *Muhāthir Majlis al-Nūwāb*, 23rd Session of the years 1952-53, (11-5-1953), 389. Reynolds emphasises the uses of emergency law as 'a mode of class repression' that went hand in hand with colonial expansion. Reynolds, *supra*, 96.

[110] *Ṣawt al-Ahālī*, 20-12-1953.

[111] *Muhāthir Majlis al-Nūwāb*, supra, 15-03-1953, 54.

[112] *Ibid.*

fact a 'dictatorship in its essence, even if they tell us we live in a democracy'.[113] al-Shaikhlī suggested the redrafting of the entire Constitution and the establishment of a nationalist government that truly serves the people rather than the British –i.e. *the end of semi-colonialism and its legal manifestations* – in a word, an end to imperialism in Iraq. This, he said, was the 'first step for the path to a truly democratic rule and towards liberation from the bonds of treaties and unjust agreements', and it was the only way to end this interminable conflict between the government and the people.[114]

Putting al-Shaikhlī and Jamīl into conversation, the limitations of the latter's analysis becomes clearer. Of course, Jamīl admits that the Constitution was the product of the British Mandate, but he claims to defend the actual *ideals* of the Constitution and the rule of law, *as it should be*.[115] This was how much he believed in the ideal of the rule of law. This, however, did not change the fact that he regarded that there was a way to resolving the 'legal aporia' of martial law. That is, that emergency could somehow be constrained even if the structures of semi-colonialism remained intact. However, my argument is that the violence of martial law could not be constrained by the rule of law per se, especially in a semi-colonial context. It was after all a manifestation of the semi-colonial Iraqi state, and consequently the mere reform of law in itself would not bring real democratic change in Iraq.

Stephen Morton has emphasised that one needs to distinguish between the violence of colonial sovereignty and martial law/emergency, as the 'legal aporia of emergency' is merely a 'colonial fiction' for the colonised, who experiences violence regardless in his or her everyday life.[116] In other words, the issue for the colonised is not that of martial law or emergency per se nor its legality or constitutionality, but rather the structures of (semi-)colonialism and political and economic sovereignty as a whole. The violence of emergency – and the 'state of exception' – is in this way already ingrained within (semi-)colonial sovereignty or rather (semi-)colonial sovereignty precedes the normalisation of the state of emergency. We could go further and argue that the legal structures of emergency became even more important as a technique of governance in the semi-colonial state. Instead of being a mere 'political strategy' or even a 'tool of political management', as was the case in the British response in its colonies, such as in Malaya, Kenya and Cyprus,[117] emergency powers were legally entrenched into the very structures of the semi-colonial state, which needed it to

[113] *Ibid*, 55.
[114] *Ibid*.
[115] Jamīl, *supra*, 10.
[116] S Morton, *States of Emergency: Colonialism, Literature and Law*, (Liverpool University Press, 2003), 9.
[117] F Furedi, "Creating a Breathing Space: The Political Management of Colonial Emergencies," in R Holland (ed.), *Emergencies and Disorder in the European Empires after 1945*, (Frank Cass, 1994), 94.

survive. The semi-colonial Iraqi state *relied on* martial law and the doctrine of emergency to preserve itself, while it remained obsessed with its own legitimacy and the constitutionality of its actions. As the late Nasser Hussein has revealed, 'martial law [in the colony] seeks to effect not just the restoration of order, but the restoration of the general authority of the state. In doing so, it takes advantage of the absence of normative constraints on power not just to punish more … but to punish out of a different logic.'[118] It is, in other words, he writes, 'what is needed to construct the state all over again … [i.e.] the condition for the possibility of law's existence'.[119] It was therefore these (pre-)conditions of the semi-colonial order in Iraq that were the target of the counter-hegemonic movements rather than the actual interpretation of law. The Iraqi state continuously used the (colonial) doctrine of emergency to fracture the possibilities of the emergence of an alternative counter-hegemonic space and legal order. Every time such a space sought to emerge, it was swiftly and violently suppressed.

Consequently, one could see the limitations of Jamīl's liberal idealism, which implied that the struggle between the people and the regime was more concerned with the law and its interpretation. As if the demonstrators evoked the rule of law (in their minds) every time they took to the streets, and that this was what produced these revolutionary spaces. This, however, was not the case. Firstly, what the masses were calling for with *their very actions* (whether during the *Wathba* or the *Intifāda*) was a *new social and legal order* – and therefore a novel conception of law *or* what Gramsci referred to as a new 'usage' of the law.[120] One that was free from semi-colonialism and imperialism. Secondly, the conditions for these counter-hegemonic spaces emerged because of several intersecting local, regional and international factors and not (solely) because of the pluralistic uses of law by the movement. This analysis will become clearer when I examine the emergence of the spaces in which these struggles converged – namely when I provide a 'conjunctural' analysis of the *Wathba* uprising. In this chapter, I have shown the (legal) violent techniques used by the Iraqi state to *fracture* the manifestations of any revolutionary spaces so as to re-impose its own hegemonic order. In the next chapter, I will examine the counter-hegemonic and revolutionary space that emerged during the *Wathba* and will analyse its consequences.

## IV. CONCLUSION

This chapter detailed the uses of criminal law and martial law by the Iraqi state before the July Revolution. The Iraqi ruling class used the law to violently

[118] N Hussein, *The Jurisprudence of Emergency: Colonialism and the Rule of Law*, (University of Michigan Press, 2003), 124.

[119] *Ibid.*

[120] Gramsci, *Selections from the Prison Notebooks*, *supra*, 195.

suppress dissent and to safeguard its hegemony. I began by detailing the manner in which the *Baghdad Penal Code* was amended in 1938, making it a crime to be a 'communist' or even a potentially progressive social democratic reformist. This was one of the harshest pieces of legislation in the region. Moreover, the military courts found it very useful to sentence and imprison thousands of Iraqis in military courts, including the leaders of the ICP. The fact was that martial law and criminal law came hand in hand as the latter was more effective in a state of emergency.

In the second part of this chapter. I traced the history of martial law and emergency doctrine to illustrate its uses in the colonies. It was argued that its uses in Iraq (especially after the *Intifāda*) had a specific performative function as it allowed the semi-colonial Iraqi state to reestablish itself and its hegemony over and over again. It was, therefore, a technique of governance that ensured that the fragmented and weak semi-peripheral sovereignty did not falter. This was clear in how it was used to deal with labour strikes, such as the Basra General Strike of 1953. A critical analysis of the liberal views of Hussein Jamīl revealed that the law could not constrain the 'magically' expansive powers of the doctrine of emergency as it was only by ending its root cause – the semi-colonial structural conditions in place – that the permanent state of emergency would finally come to an end. To paraphrase Walter Benjamin, it is only by seeing things from the perspective (or tradition) of the *colonial* 'oppressed' that one could grasp how permanent emergency emerges in the everyday materiality of life. One could add that this 'tradition' also teaches us that just because the 'emergency situation' becomes the 'rule' it does not entail that it could be constrained through its internal (legal) origins.

# 7

# *The Defeat of the Portsmouth Treaty: al-Wathba and its Contribution to the Conjuncture of Decolonisation in International Law*

## I. INTRODUCTION

DURING THE THIRD session of the United Nations General Assembly held in Paris in 1948, the delegate for the Philippines, Carlos Romulo, insisted on a broad interpretation of the ambiguous Chapter XI of the UN Charter,[1] stressing that 'the force of history which had brought about many changes in the British Empire was far stronger than legal or constitutional barriers'.[2] Romulo was directly referring to what he called the 'impetus of revolutionary forces' that was bringing about transformations on the ground in the Third World, to make a legal argument.[3] This 'non-juridical' approach, which was used extensively by the 'Afro-Asian bloc' in the UN, demonstrates that the anti-colonial and anti-imperial struggles unleashed by Third World peoples at the time could not be ignored and had direct implications on international law and its interpretation.

In this chapter, the revolutionary uprising known as *al-Wathba* will be analysed as an event in which all of the seemingly confined labour struggles recounted earlier culminated into an all-encompassing nationalist and anti-colonial struggle for decolonisation. This chapter is, therefore, concerned with the vital question of how revolutionary agency is articulated within international legal scholarship related to the Third World. I will address the limitations of the methodologies and analyses of Third World Approaches to International Law (TWAIL) scholarship by detailing this event of people's agency in Iraqi historiography, situating it broadly within the international conjuncture of decolonisation. The *Wathba* of 1948 was essentially a great popular uprising

[1] UN Charter, Chapter XI: Declaration Regarding Non-Self-Governing Territories (Articles 73-74).
[2] Quoted in YEl-Ayouty, *The United Nations and Decolonization: The Role of Afro-Asia*, (Martinus Nijhoff, 1971), 35.
[3] *Ibid*, 34.

of the Iraqi urban poor and working classes that successfully prevented the imposition of a revised unequal treaty by Britain on Iraq, which ultimately sparked a decade-long revolutionary process that would eventually overthrow the British-sponsored monarchy. The *Wathba* will be shown to be one historical manifestation of the wider conjuncture of the decolonisation of international law. I will argue that critical legal scholars and TWAIL scholars must begin to undertake the study of these historical conjunctures, which allowed certain social and labour movements ample room to wage counter-hegemonic struggles against the structures of imperialism and which had wide repercussions for international law. It is consequently only through such close examinations that the *present* conjuncture can be understood and the future transformed.

## II. THE LIMITS OF THE STUDY OF REVOLUTIONARY AGENCY IN TWAIL

TWAIL scholars have been at the forefront of exposing how colonialism and imperialism are constitutive of the history and discipline of international law.[4] They have done so by reverting to an examination of history to expose the legacy of imperialism in international law. In fact, it is this particular method of historical analysis that has been said to be 'the feature most fundamental' to TWAIL scholarship;[5] one which regards 'historical perspective' as the 'key technique' in understanding the current features of international law.[6] TWAIL encompasses a political commitment to counter traditional approaches that have disregarded the colonial past and considered it of trivial concern to international law. Instead, it illustrates that international law as a discipline was developed in the West and through its positivist predisposition tends to repress its colonial past, and in so doing reproduces and legitimises the version of the past that is better suited for its hegemonic discourse.[7] TWAIL analysis generally resists this process, and aims to expose the hidden colonial origins of international law, and most importantly, emphasises the *continuity* of colonial and imperial relations in the contemporary structures of international law.[8]

Despite this radical commitment, there still appears to be considerable limitations to TWAIL analysis, which is primarily due to the manner in which TWAIL scholars often approach the question of agency. As Owen Taylor has argued, TWAIL scholars tend to invoke notions of 'resistance' (the word most

[4] For a good overview of the literature, see Gathii, *supra*.

[5] K Mickelson, "Rhetoric and Rage: Third World Voices in International Legal Discourse," *Wisconsin International Law Journal*, 16, No. 2, (1998): 406.

[6] O Okafor. "Newness, Imperialism and International Legal Reform in our Time: a TWAIL perspective," *Osgoode Hall Law Journal*, 43, No.1&2, (2005): 178.

[7] A Anghie, "The Evolution of International Law: colonial and postcolonial realities," *Third World Quarterly*, Vol. 27, (2008): 739–753.

[8] *Ibid.*

often used to evoke agency) that are highly selective of the conceptual history of revolution.[9] In other words, when TWAIL scholarship turns from an analysis of the structures of imperialism within international law to address the issue of agency, it does so in a highly idealised manner that locates the agency of social movements within a narrative of 'resistance' as a 're-conceptualisation [of law] as an act of will,' while emphasising the necessity of 'radical legal pluralism' as fundamental to emancipation.[10] Balakrishnan Rajagopal, for example, takes such a position in situating the revolutionary potential of social movements in 'non-institutional, non-party, and cultural terms'.[11] Despite recognising the importance of 'the question of agency' in the development of a theory of resistance, B.S. Chimni goes on to argue that '*the ideal* [of an emancipatory democratic socialism for the Third World] *is to be realised through non-violent means and* ... [it is to be] *actualised by way of reform and not revolution* ...'[12] This narrow conception of agency suggests that as long as 'resistance' is 'sanitised' – namely, spontaneous, without central or party organization, and non-violent – then it would automatically bring about true political and democratic change *within* the liberal promise of international law, whatever the state of the current conjuncture or the structures of world order.[13]

The problem with this approach is that it assumes that law is abstract and can be easily re-conceptualised into an emancipatory plural form, rather than being *already* entrenched (and so constrained) within certain material social conditions and legal forms. What this also does is it ignores the entangled *connection* between agency and structure – what is referred to as the *conjuncture*, leading to a fanciful situation whereby 'any kind of agency' appears possible, while 'the structure becomes *entirely* contingent'.[14] The reality, however, is that different forms of action can be effective depending on the particular structural conditions at any given time.[15] This chapter will deal with this disconnect between notions of structure and agency that is prevalent in TWAIL scholarship. My analysis will illustrate why scholars should shift their focus to a study of what I refer to as '*conjunctural* agency,' rather than focus on (non-contingent) '*plural* resistance' that is waged against the structures of the international legal order and international law at any given time. To do this is to realise that it is the *conjuncture* that should be studied to grasp and to understand agency and its complexity.

[9] O Taylor, "Reclaiming Revolution" *Finnish Yearbook of International Law* (Vol. 22, 2011), 259-292. Taylor expands this analysis in his book, *International Law and Revolution* (Routledge, 2019).

[10] *Ibid*, 273.

[11] B Rajagopal, *International Law from* Below, *supra*, 293.

[12] Chimni, 'Third World Approaches to international Law: A Manifesto,' *supra*, 21. Emphasis in the original.

[13] Taylor, *supra*, 263.

[14] *Ibid*, 274.

[15] *Ibid*, 271.

## III. THE NECESSITY OF THE CONCEPT OF THE CONJUNCTURE IN PRAXIS

The concept of the *conjuncture* is generally derived from Marxist theory, in particular the formulations of V.I. Lenin and Antonio Gramsci. Louis Althusser defines the conjuncture as denoting, 'the exact balance of forces, state of overdetermination of the contradictions at any given moment to which political tactics must be applied'.[16] Referring to Lenin's approach in the 1917 Russian Revolution, Althusser demonstrates how 'the history of imperialism' was analysed by Lenin in its *current* conjuncture as opposed to the typical Marxist theoretician and historian who was merely concerned with historical knowledge: 'Lenin meets Imperialism in the modality of a *current* existence: in a concrete present. The theoretician of history or the historian meet it in another modality, the modality of non-currency and abstraction.'[17] He goes on to argue that Lenin's (conjunctural) approach to the 'current situation' was unique, as he was concerned with the 'typicality of the contradictions, with their displacements, their condensations and the "fusion" in revolutionary rupture that they produced … [in other words] what makes it possible to act on History from within the sole history present … not [merely] to demonstrate or explain the "inevitable" revolutions *post festum*, but to make them in our unique present …'[18] As Stuart Hall elucidates, the conjuncture is the product of 'many determinations', not of one.[19] Conjunctural thinking, therefore, involves 'clustering' or assembling elements into a particular formation with the aim of addressing the political problem at hand.[20] In this way, the concept of the conjuncture can be useful as an analytical tool to identify the present situation, which in turn allows for the articulation of the strategic sites of political action, and when used properly can open up possibilities for concrete transformation and revolutionary change.

TWAIL analyses have, for the most part, disregarded the significance of the determination of factors that create the conjunctures that allow for the possibilities of 'resistance' to emerge and their implications to international law. By shifting the focus from an idealist interpretation of agency to the conjuncture that opens up a space for political action to materialise, TWAIL scholars would become more attentive to the pressing question of *praxis*. TWAIL scholarship has often concerned itself with the question of the agency of Third World peoples, and there have been a number of works that have examined the

[16] L Althusser. *For Marx*, (Verso, 2005), 250.

[17] *Ibid*, 178.

[18] *Ibid*, 180.

[19] J Koivisto, M Lahtinen, 'Historical-Critical Dictionary of Marxism: Conjuncture, politico-historical' *Historical Materialism* 20.1 (2012) 267–277, 274.

[20] *Ibid*.

role of *social* movements in the development of international law.[21] However, it has generally failed to grasp the necessity of locating agency conjuncturally within the wider narrative of the history of international law. My intention in this chapter, therefore, is to extend certain aspects of the conjunctural analysis to TWAIL methodologies through this study of Iraqi history, so that one can more effectively grasp (and more importantly *apply* the lessons of) the history of revolutionary action and 'resistance' to international law's imperialism in the *present* conjuncture in the Middle East and indeed in the Third World at large.

## IV. THE BRITISH EMPIRE'S 'NEW CLOTHES OF TREATIES AND PACTS'

What follows is a detailed account of *al-Wathba*, a revolutionary event of 'conjunctural agency' and resistance in Iraq that was aimed against the extension of the unequal 1930 Anglo-Iraq Treaty 'under the guise' of its revision.[22] The *Wathba* eventually turned into the Iraqi people's complete rejection of the 'semi-peripheral sovereignty' that was granted to Iraq through the Mandate system in 1932, and became a call for complete independence and self-determination. I refer to 'conjunctural agency/resistance' as a kind of counterweight to TWAILian 'plural resistance' to illuminate the fact that it is the conjuncture that should inform one's understanding of agency rather than its 'plural' character. It will be clear from my analysis that agency and resistance could only be said to be constitutive of international law (if at all) *at certain conjunctures* and not *tout court*. I will use the *Wathba* to illustrate an example of *how* a 'conjunctural analysis' could be undertaken in relation to the history of Iraqi struggle against imperialism within international law. After detailing this narrative, I will return to the present analysis to tease out the unique conjunctural characteristics of this revolutionary event by assessing how working-class agency succeeded to subvert the imperialism of international law, eventually situating it more broadly within the conjuncture of decolonisation of the international legal order.

*al-Wathba* (which translates to 'the Leap') was a massive uprising initially sparked by news of negotiations and later the signing of a revised unequal treaty between Iraq and Britain in 1948. In Chapter 2, I traced the evolution of the unequal Anglo-Iraq Treaty and its role in the manufacturing of what I referred to as 'semi-peripheral sovereignty', a form of sovereignty that was particularly unique to the geopolitical specificities of the semi-peripheral Middle East. The *Wathba* should be understood within this context of the history of international

[21] See B Rajagopal, *supra*; P Parmar. *Indigeneity and Legal Pluralism in India: Claims, Histories, Meanings*, (CUP, 2015); V Nesiah, 'Resistance in the Age of Empire: occupied discourse pending investigation' *Third World Quarterly*, Vol. 27, No. 5, pp. 903–922, (2006); R Buchanan, "Writing Resistance Into Law" *International Community Law Review* 10 (2008), 445–454.

[22] Batatu, *supra*, 546.

law and the Mandate system so as to appreciate why the Iraqi masses decided to wage a struggle against it. As I have argued, semi-peripheral sovereignty was constructed to ensure Iraq's 'independence' would *legitimise* and *legalise* the control, extraction, production and transportation of Iraq's most valuable natural resource of oil across the region to the West – for the benefit not only of Britain, but the capitalist world economy at large.

The Iraqi state was unable to sustain its hegemony because the sovereignty it was granted constricted it from doing so as it fragmented its governing capacity. Fragmentation was present not only, as detailed in Chapter 1, in rural Iraq, where there were two separate legal systems, but also in the oil fields, which were imperial enclaves governed by the IPC concessionary agreement, as well as in the railways and the Port, which were de facto autonomous extraterritorialised enclaves. It was this type of fragmentation that made it very difficult for the Iraqi state to impose its hegemony without the use of the violent doctrine of emergency. As will be shown, it was during a decisive moment in Iraqi history where the British aimed to reassert imperialism once more under the guise of international law that all of the isolated localised struggles of the past converged, and where the counter-hegemonic nationalist movement found itself in a position to take the opportunity presented to it by history to wage an overall anti-colonial struggle against the social and semi-colonial legal order in Iraq.

## V. THE MAKING OF THE 1948 PORTSMOUTH TREATY AND ITS IMPLICATIONS

Once the British and their Iraqi counterparts agreed that they needed to revise the now visibly outdated and much hated 1930 Anglo-Iraq Treaty, secret negotiations commenced in 1946. The 1930 Treaty was drafted under the Mandate system and League institutions that the Iraqi government found to be no longer viable in a post-war world. The British government saw this as an opportunity to update the treaty under the guise of the UN Charter, which emphasised the notion of 'equality' between nations under international law. In that sense, rather than actually addressing the limitations of 'semi-peripheral sovereignty', the new Anglo-Iraq Treaty (named the Portsmouth Treaty) merely redefined it in a manner that appeared to be acceptable for Iraqis, but more specifically, to be consistent with the newly emerging post-war international legal order. It was for this reason that throughout the negotiations, Ernest Bevin was insistent that the treaty was being drafted 'under strict conformity with the UN Charter' while he emphasised that it was 'in spirit and in heart' drafted on the basis of 'perfect equality'[23]

[23] TNA. 'Minutes of a meeting with the Iraqi Delegation held at the Foreign Office on the afternoon of 7th January, 1948', FO 371/68442; 'Minutes of a meeting held at Foreign Office on January 9th to consider the Anglo-Iraqi Treaty at 2:30 p.m.', FO 371/68442.

and 'complete equality in all respects'. Bevin hoped that this new arrangement would be as much a breakthrough for Iraq and the Middle East, as the Empire's settlement with India.[24]

Examining the provisions of the 1948 Portsmouth Treaty closely, it is clear that although it promised the eventual withdrawal of British troops and the surrendering of military bases to Iraq, it gave the British a say in Iraq's military planning through the establishment of a Joint Defence Board (JDB), which continued the employment of British military 'experts'. The JDB, which was a joint high-ranking military body tasked with the coordination of defensive plans, had explicit advisory powers under the Treaty to make decisions on when the Iraqi government may 'invite' British troops back into the country.[25] In other words, the Treaty ensured that the Iraqi government would surrender their military bases to Britain in wartime, making it impossible for a stance of neutrality. Moreover, it made a provision for the continued access for 'operational forces' of the Royal Air Force to the Shuʿaybah and Habbaniyyah bases until withdrawal of the 'allied armies' from 'all-ex-enemy countries' (a far-fetched possibility from the Cold War reality).[26] The new treaty also safeguarded British influence fifteen years beyond the time limit of the old treaty.[27]

The Iraqi delegation, which had arrived in London to secretly negotiate and sign the new treaty, were so overtly concerned with the nitty-gritty legalese and specific wording of the document that they ignored the larger implications of the Treaty, which in fact entrenched Iraq further into imperialist control. In this way, the Portsmouth Treaty turned out to be no more than an extension of the 1930 Anglo-Iraq Treaty couched in 'new-fashioned terminology' that did not alter much of the old relationship.[28] The PM himself was aware that what was being done was merely cosmetic in nature when he bluntly stated during negotiations that despite the end of the Mandate in 1932, the Iraqi people considered 'the present position of their country was that of an occupied country' [...] 'it was [therefore] essential for the Iraqi government to *show* the people the effect of the treaty. The departure of British forces in Iraq would convince the people that their country had really gained full independence, *even if these* [military] *units were later invited to return*.'[29] One British official foreshadowed the troubles that would ensue when he cautioned that, 'we should be careful not to take the line that the above provisions of the treaty cement to our retention of our strategic hold on Iraq, i.e. that we have

[24] *Ibid*.

[25] Article 1(b), *Treaty of Alliance between His Majesty in respect of the United Kingdom of Great Britain and His Majesty the King of Iraq*, Portsmouth, 15th January, 1948, Cmd. 7309.

[26] Article 1(d).

[27] *Ibid*.

[28] Batatu, *supra*, 550.

[29] TNA. Minutes of a meeting with the Iraqi Delegation held at the Foreign Office on the afternoon of 7th January, 1948', FO 371/68442.

tricked the Iraqis into letting us continue our military occupation in practice at the expense of a few concessions'.[30] As we shall see, the Iraqi people were in fact quite aware that the treaty was not merely a sham, but a form of sophisticated legal trickery that aimed to prolong the military, semi-colonial *de facto* 'occupation' of their country. Consequently, while the revision of the 1930 Treaty was clearly meant to ensure the continuation of British intervention in Iraqi affairs, it was also explicitly meant to be a 'model' for the entire region, whereby all so-called 'bilateral' treaties[31] were to ultimately be brought together into a 'common defence system' for the Middle East.[32]

## VI. THE '*WATHBA* OF THE PEOPLE' TAKES FORM

Although Iraqis were continuously resisting the 1930 Treaty and its wide reach into every aspect of their lives, it was the event of the *Wathba* uprising that was the defining moment of revolutionary struggle against imperialism in Iraq. Despite its heterogeneous character, the working class was the *Wathba*'s quintessence. A robust alliance between workers and students led massive demonstrations on the streets of Baghdad. In the gripping words of Hanna Batatu,

> an atmosphere redolent of social revolution enveloped Baghdad during the *Wathba*, as it was 'the most formidable mass insurrection in the history of the monarchy … It was the social subsoil of Baghdad in revolt against hunger and unequal burdens. It was the students and the Schalchiyyah workers braving machine guns … and dying for their ideas … [I]t was the political representatives of the various layers of the middle class … resentful of constraints or plotting for political gains. It was the privileged stratum [of the ruling and landowning classes] … menaced in their political power and social interests. It was British overlordship shaken, the Anglo-Iraq Treaty of 1930 sapped, and the Portsmouth Agreement of 1948 abolished.[33]

The struggle against the Treaty started the day after the official announcement of negotiations on January 5, 1948. Mass demonstrations originated at the Law College of Baghdad. Law students left their classes to demonstrate against the Treaty, as well as the partition of Palestine.[34] The police, taking 'precautionary measures', attempted to disrupt their plans and prevented anyone from leaving the college building.[35] Stones and bottles were thrown at police.[36] Thirty-nine students were arrested.[37] The Iraqi government headed

[30] TNA. FO 371/68442. Signing of Iraq Treaty: Publicity. 3 Jan 1948.
[31] Such as the (failed) Anglo-Egyptian Treaty of 1946 and the treaty with Jordan.
[32] TNA. FO 371/68442. Signing of Iraq Treaty: Publicity. 3 Jan 1948.
[33] Batatu, *Supra*, 544, 551.
[34] Humaīdī, *al-Tatwūrāt*, *supra*, 519-525.
[35] TNA. British Embassy, Bagdad to FO, London, 7 Jan, 1948. FO 371/68442.
[36] *Ibid.*
[37] Ḥumaidī, *supra*.

by PM Sālih Jabr decided to shut down the Law College and launched a criminal investigation into the incident, which was in reality an excuse to purge the College of those involved in the protest.[38] The cabinet claimed that the protestors were 'anarchists' looking to spread discord on campus.[39] Several law professors were suspended, and the Dean was transferred to another city. The ensuing witch-hunt led to numerous sympathy protests in other colleges that called for the release of their fellow students. Those apprehended were eventually released a few days later, and the Law College reopened.[40] The movement at this point had a distinctive student character, and it would not be an overstatement to claim that the initial dynamo of organisational action originated at the level of the students' political party organisations.[41] In fact, one participant referred to student action as the 'seed' that led to the unification of the Iraqi nationalist movement.[42]

In no more than ten days, these seemingly circumscribed student demonstrations would erupt into an unprecedented fervour of discontent, composed of the majority of the underclasses of Iraq. Following the government clampdown at the law college, the opposition – in particular the outlawed but popular ICP – began organising all workers on the ground. The "Cooperation Committee", which united most leftist and nationalist parties under its leadership, was formed a few months earlier. Now an adjunct ICP-dominated "Student Cooperation Committee" was created and joined with it.[43] These two committees would lead the movement's demonstrations and strikes throughout the *Wathba*.

The illusive stillness of the next week was broken when the official announcement was made on the 16th of January that the Portsmouth Treaty had been signed in London the previous day. A three-day general student strike exploded instantaneously. The students called for the resignation of the cabinet and for the cancellation of the Portsmouth Treaty, eventually heading to the headquarters of the infamous Criminal Investigation Department (CID), calling for its downfall and referring to it as the 'Gestapo of Iraq'.[44] On January 20, the *Schālchīyyah* workers and the famished *sarīfa-dwellers* (squatters) joined the student protests for the first time, broadening the movement beyond the narrow confines of parliamentary politics. It was also the day that police shot into the crowd. The next day, as students carried the dead to their resting place, police

[38] *Ibid*, 521.

[39] *Ibid*.

[40] *Ibid*.

[41] Sbāhī, *supra*, 335.

[42] Editors, 'al-Majid lil-Wathba al-Amis, al-Thāfir l'intifāda al-Youm,' [An interview with participants of the *Wathba* on its 40th anniversary], *al-Thaqāfa al-Jadīda*, 193, Issue 3 (35), 1988, 13.

[43] For a detailed account of the role of students in the Wathba, see F Proto, "Min Thikrīyāt al-Haraka al-Talābīya fī Wathba Kānūn al-Thānī" [Memories from the student movement during the Wathba of January], *al-Thaqāfa al-Jadīda*, Issue, 293, Mar/Apr, 2000, 83.

[44] Ḥumaidī, *supra*, 523.

fired shots in their direction and chased them while they were still on hospital grounds. Two died and seventeen were wounded. Outrage spread throughout the city for what was considered the criminal actions of the police.[45] A student who was shot in the head was carried by his colleagues to the office of the dean of his school in protest, leading to the dean's resignation. The resignation of other deans and professors followed. The masses became bitter, but remained defiant.

The street became 'a symbol of national unity' as Muslims (Shia and Sunni), Jews and Christians, joined arms in solidarity.[46] The young Karīm Murūwwa, who would later become one the most prominent Lebanese communists, participated in the demonstrations, which had an immense influence on him and further radicalised his political trajectory.[47] He described the uniqueness of those days by revealing that there emerged 'a kind of democracy [and freedom] that had no constraint,' as illegal newspapers were distributed in the streets, while the leaders of outlawed political parties which were underground for years, emerged from hiding in full view.[48] Eventually, more Baghdadis from other walks of life joined the protests. The *Wathba* rapidly spread to other parts of the country.[49]

Overwhelmed, the Regent, against the advice of his British advisors, capitulated, renouncing the Treaty in a public statement, and guaranteed that it would not be ratified against the will of the people.[50] This led to a splintering of the opposition, as some of the right-wing nationalist bourgeois parties recoiled, calling for the end of demonstrations. The left, led by the communists, however, refused to retreat, as they considered the Regent's statement as a mere tactic. The ICP and its uncompromising position became the dominant force in the demonstrations, and the *Wathba* was transformed into an event with a categorically revolutionary character.[51] The protests were now calling for more than just the cancellation of the Treaty, but for the end of the British imperial connection *tout court* and for the formation of a truly national democratic government. Their calls were not merely concerned with 'political freedoms' but at the core of the protests were issues relating to economic and social injustice. This could be especially ascertained by their calls for 'bread'.[52] The *Wathba* quickly turned

[45] *Ibid*.

[46] O Bashkin, "A Patriotic Uprising: Baghdadi Jews and the *Wathba*," in N Fuccaro (ed.), *Violence and the City in the Modern Middle East*, (Stanford University Press: 2016), 151–167;163.

[47] K Murūwwa, *Karīm Murūwwa Yatathakar* [Karim Muruwwa Remembers], S Abu Fakhir (ed.) (al-Mada, 2002), 42–43.

[48] *Ibid*, 42-43.

[49] Batatu, *supra*, 551.

[50] *Ibid*.

[51] According to one participant, 'If we had followed the instructions of the national bourgeois parties [of easing the demonstrations], there would have been no *Wathba*." *al-Thaqāfa al-Jadīda*, 193, Issue 3 (35), *supra*, 14.

[52] *Ibid*, 15.

from a demand to replace the cabinet to a call for a profound transformation of the social and political order.[53]

The respected social democrat and lawyer, Kamil Qazānchī, who was the head of the movement's "Cooperation Committee," addressed the cheering crowd from the rooftop of the Wadī Coffeehouse, asserting that, 'You must declare a great people's revolution, and struggle to establish a people's government that represents these [laboring] classes.'[54] The crowds carried the renowned worker-poet, Mohammad Sālih Baḥr al-ʿŪlūm on their shoulders. Baḥr al-ʿŪlūm had been reciting his improvised thunderous poetry during the past few days, furiously condemning the government's complicity with imperialism, giving voice to the people and mesmerising the crowds. That day, he recited his most memorable poem, 'The People's Leap':

O *Wathba* of the People, rend apart
With your maledictions this stupid treaty
For the Portsmouth treaty is a chain
The fetters of unconditional occupation

O *Wathba* of the People, send away
The grief and sadness of sheer evil
That descends upon us, for Iraq
Is the death of every shuttering fool
The stronger logic lies in the struggle of the resisting people
So Bevin will be shut up just as the villain Churchill was muzzled![55]

Qazānchī's speech and Bahr al-ʿUlūm's poem emphasised that the cancelation of the Portsmouth Treaty (or what he referred to in another poem as 'the covenant of the slave')[56] was in fact more about the liberation of the country from imperial and semi-colonial rule than the negotiation of the contents of the treaty. The statement released by the social democratic National Democratic Party explains this well, plainly stating that 'the truth of the matter is that the British, since its occupation of Iraq, intended to make this country a strategic site in the Middle East, for its own interests … to exploit its resources, and control its markets'. It goes on to argue that the British were in fact merely 'dressing up colonial [imperial] control with the new clothes of treaties and pacts.' The Portsmouth Treaty was, therefore, merely 'a new colonial [and imperial] project … a blatant attack on Iraq's very being, its sovereignty and political future,' and for this reason it should be resisted by Iraqis with all their might.[57]

[53] Batatu, *Ibid*, 553.
[54] *Ibid.*
[55] MS Bahr al-ʿUlūm, *Diwan Bāḥr al-ʿŪlūm*, (Baghdad: Matbʿa Dar al-Tadāmūn, 1968), 132-134. For his role in the *Wathba*, see KM Jones, 'A horizon lit with blood: public poetry and mass politics in Iraq,' *Social History*, 2014, Vol. 39, No 4, 443–461. Translation of Jones.
[56] *Ibid.*
[57] For the full text, see al-Hasanī. *Tārīkh al-Wizārāt*, Vol. 3, *supra*, 249.

## VII. 'THE DAY OF THE BRIDGE' AND THE SUPPRESSION OF THE *WATHBA* MOVEMENT

The *Wathba* came to a bloody culmination in Baghdad on the 27th of January when intense street battles were waged between the unarmed multitudes (carrying only canes and rocks), and the police equipped with machine guns and armoured vehicles. A pendulum-like flowing movement between the two sides became a regular feature of the narrow streets of the city. Demonstrators took advantage of the urban geography of Baghdad, while the police were overwhelmed given that they had little experience in the tactics of riot suppression and crowd control.[58] Factories were turned into makeshift infirmaries, where injured demonstrators were stitched up.[59] A police car was burned and the headquarters of the British-owned newspaper, *Iraq Times* (which only weeks earlier described demonstrators as 'a mob of looters'[60]) was set alight. Baghdad, in the words of one writer, resembled a 'war zone'.[61] The PM Salah Jabr transmitted a radio broadcast calling for demonstrators to end their disturbance of 'the peace and order or [the] contravene[ing] of laws,' as this exposed people to 'danger and death'.[62]

Police then scrambled to maintain barricades, while others were stationed on roofs and minarets, and had express orders from their commander to break up demonstrations and to shoot to kill if necessary. Huge crowds gathered on both sides of the entrance of the Maʿmūn Bridge[63] with the intention of meeting at the centre of the bridge in defiance of the police. As the crowds courageously moved forward, police sprayed bullets in their direction. The shots only fell silent after a fifteen-year old girl (later coined 'the girl of the bridge') appeared out of the chaos and continued towards the centre of the old bridge.[64] The police pulled back and the two flanks of the masses ultimately converged. An estimated 300 to 400 died on the bridge that day.[65] Bodies hung from the bridge, and others floated in the Tigris River below.[66] This bloody event led to the resignations of over a dozen ministers, including the Speaker of the *Majlis*, who watched the entire incident from the balcony of the Parliament building.[67] The 'Day of the Bridge', as it came to be known endures in the annals of Iraqi history and folklore as the moment when ordinary unarmed Iraqis gave their lives to rid

[58] TNA. G.C. Pelham to FO, 21 Jan 1948. FO 371/68443.
[59] *Thaqāfa al-Jadīda*, 193, Issue 3 (35), 1988, *supra*, 15.
[60] TNA. Pelham to FO, Confidential, 25 Jan. 1948, FO 371/68446/E2217.
[61] *Ibid*.
[62] TNA. 'Broadcast Communiqué by Iraqi PM on 27th January, 1948', FO 371/6646/27.
[63] After that day the bridge was renamed to 'The Bridge of Martyrs'.
[64] Batatu, 557.
[65] *Ibid*.
[66] Sbāhī. *supra*, 340.
[67] AA al-Qassāb. *Muthakarat Abdul Azīz al-Qassāb* [The memoirs of Abdul Aziz al-Qassab], (al-Muʾasasa al-Arabīya lildirāsat wa al-Nashir, 2007), 286.

themselves from the chains of imperial and semi-colonial rule and expunge the ruling class' black ink with which the Portsmouth Treaty was signed, with their blood.

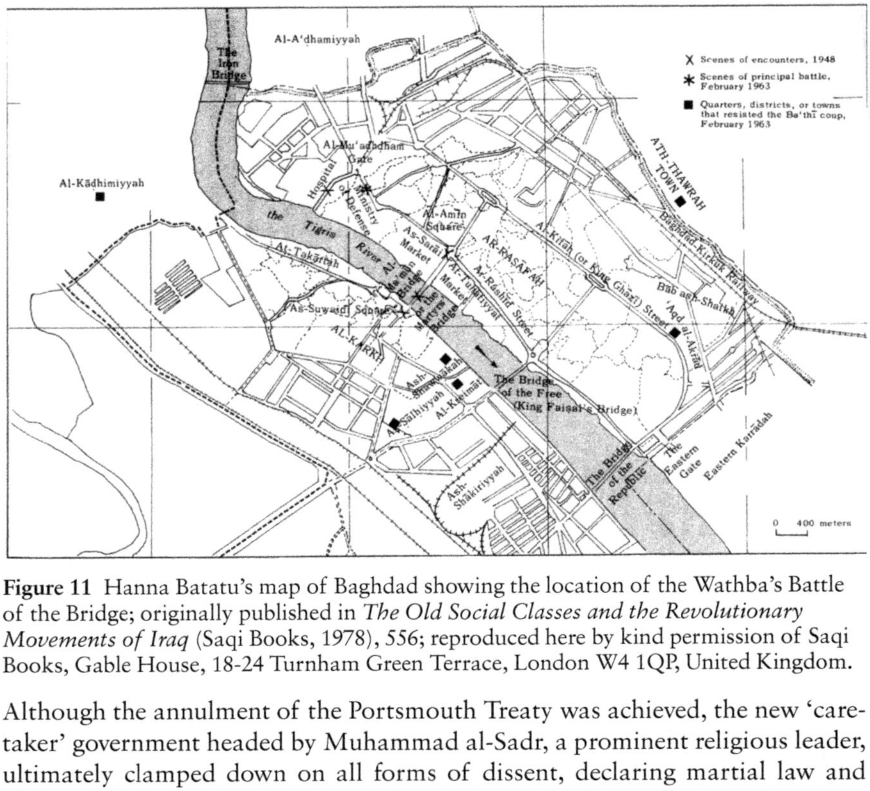


**Figure 11** Hanna Batatu's map of Baghdad showing the location of the Wathba's Battle of the Bridge; originally published in *The Old Social Classes and the Revolutionary Movements of Iraq* (Saqi Books, 1978), 556; reproduced here by kind permission of Saqi Books, Gable House, 18-24 Turnham Green Terrace, London W4 1QP, United Kingdom.

Although the annulment of the Portsmouth Treaty was achieved, the new 'caretaker' government headed by Muhammad al-Sadr, a prominent religious leader, ultimately clamped down on all forms of dissent, declaring martial law and shutting down newspapers and trade unions on the basis of national security. It was, moreover, on the basis of the proclamation of martial law on the 15th of May, 1948 during the *Wathba* that the Iraqi regime had another opportunity to re-try the leaders of the ICP. A wave of repression spread throughout Iraq, and the military courts took every opportunity to make use of the Penal Code's amendment described earlier – *Law 51* of 1938 – which was referred to in nearly every summary judgment made to sentence thousands of communists, leftists, nationalists and other Iraqis who participated in the *Wathba* demonstrations.[68]

[68] See *Mawsu'a Siriyya Khāssa bi'l hizb al-shuyu'ī al-'iraqī al-Sirī* (*A Secret Encyclopedia Concerning the Secret Iraqi Communist Party*); 1949 (Baghdad: Maktaba al-Nahda al-'Arabiya). This three-volume collection of 1,525 pages includes confessions, interrogations, police files and rulings of the military tribunals. The police published it in 1949 with the hope of exposing the ICP and discouraging people from joining the party. It turned out to have the opposite effect as it revealed the injustices of police tactics and the regime.

On 10 February 1949, the ICP leader, Fahad, and Politburo members, Zakī Basīm and Mohammed Husayn al-Shabībī, were convicted of having led protests from prison and were sentenced to death once more. This time, however, the sentences were swiftly carried out the next day at dawn. Executed in three different squares in Baghdad, their bodies were left hanging as a clear warning to anyone who dared to challenge the semi-colonial Iraqi order. One British official at the scene vividly described these violent displays of power in the following manner:

> … ordinary people on their way to work found still hanging these pathetic objects, each moving slightly as it hung from its temporary gallows, the rough prison clothes wrapped around the shrunken-looking body, the ghastly angle of the head behind the mask, the cheap notice describing the crime for which he suffered … Every man in Baghdad was nauseated by this display ….[69]

It was reported in the communist press that Fahad's last words were: 'we are bodies and thoughts; if you destroy our bodies, you will not destroy our thoughts';[70] while al-Shabībī kept repeating, 'it is an honour to be executed in the same square where the *Wathba* of the people was launched'.[71] Basīm cried, 'if I was to return to life for a second time, I would not take any other path but this one, which I have already taken'.[72] It is unclear whether these statements were actually made. What is certain was that these executions were meant as the regime's retribution for what transpired during the days of the revolutionary *Wathba*.

With these violent acts, however, the ruling class made a grave error. Not only was communism now, in Batatu's words, 'surrounded with a halo of martyrdom'[73] but also the people's attempts to renew the emancipatory spirit of the *Wathba* persevered rather than dissolved into thin air. Despite the slow strangulation of the movement, it was the *Wathba* that ignited the revolutionary process that would materialise in the July Revolution a decade later during the turbulent year of 1958.

## VIII. THE BRITISH VIEW OF THE *WATHBA* AND THE 'LOGIC OF THE RESISTING PEOPLE'

The British assessment of the *Wathba* and its causes was, as would be expected, considered as anything but a genuine nationalist movement. A detailed report by G.C. Pelham, the Acting Chargé d'Affaires at the time, surprisingly identified the causes of the 'troubles' as having 'little connection to Anglo-Iraq relations' but rather to the peoples' mistrust of corrupt government, which he described

[69] Caractacus, [pseudonym of Norman Daniel], *Revolution in Iraq: An Essay in Comparative Public Opinion* (Gollancz, 1959), 51.

[70] Batatu, *supra*, 569.

[71] As quoted by Sbāhī, *supra*, 408.

[72] *Ibid.*

[73] *Ibid.*

as an Ottoman legacy.[74] Refusing to admit that the demonstrations were anti-British, he saw them solely (and 'personally') aimed at Sālih Jabr and his cabinet. Mentioning the government's mishandling of the dire issue of economic situation that year, he especially focused on the public outrage against the partition of Palestine as an underlying cause.[75] It was, nonetheless, the speed with which the treaty was concluded that he argued intensified the suspicions of the people. 'Colour was lent to the accusation', he wrote, '… that the treaty was made in London and handed ready made to the Iraqi delegation for signature'.[76] The unavailability of an official Arabic translation of the treaty further fuelled such suspicion.[77] Pelham's reference to demonstrators as a 'mob' that was menacing 'law and order' and his warning that Iraq was threatened by 'mob rule' illustrates the British view that the *Wathba* was an irrational event.[78] Pelham went on to critique Iraqi 'student thought', which he saw as conditioned by the view that 'any foreign commitment takes away from full national sovereignty', stating that Iraqis suffer from 'an inferiority complex'.[79] Admitting that the belief that the government of Sālih Jabr must fall was 'all but universal,' he maintained that although such a situation would be 'hopeless in a Europe country,' 'in an Arab one there is perhaps a slender chance' that the British connection would remain unscathed, as it would merely fall back on the old treaty.[80] This admission was nothing less than the recognition of the imperial characteristics of the treaty itself.

Finally, one of the most recurrent analyses of the underlying causes of the demonstrations given by both the British and the Iraqi ruling class (including the PM himself)[81] was that common Iraqis were too illiterate to even understand the meaning of the Treaty. The British blamed the Iraqi government for not educating the public about the contents of the Treaty, going so far as claiming that the population was 'largely illiterate and … therefore incapable of reading the treaty itself'.[82] One official claimed that only 'an ill-intentioned person could have misunderstood the Treaty'.[83] Douglas Busk wrote, 'I had heard the vague slogans of the demonstrations in the streets, but I had not learned from them what were the [legal] points in the treaty to which they objected …'[84] Putting aside the racist connotations in this overall analysis and the fact that

[74] TNA. GC Pelham to FO, 21 Jan 1948. FO 371/68443.

[75] The 'Palestine argument', as we have seen in an earlier chapter, has been frequently used by British officials, even when assessing labour strikes. One official wrote, 'if it had not been for Palestine, we should have seen the treaty ratified'. Broadman to Bevin, 1 June 1948, FO 371/68386/E7801.

[76] TNA. GC Pelham to FO, *supra*.

[77] TNA. Telegram No. 45, FO to Baghdad, 14 Jan, 1948; 'Iraq Treaty: Publicity', FO 371/68442.

[78] TNA. GC Pelham to FO, *supra*.

[79] *Ibid.*

[80] *Ibid.*

[81] See N Fathī Sūfwā. *Sālih Jabr: Sīra Syāsīya*, (Dar al-Saqi, 2017).

[82] TNA. H Mack, British Embassy, Bagdad to M Wright, London, 9 Feb 1948. FO 371/68446.

[83] *Ibid.*

[84] TNA. D Busk, British Embassy, Bagdad to E Bevin, FO, London. 6 Feb 1948. FO 371/68446.

the organised committees detailed above made their demands quite clear, the very working actuality of the *Wathba* illustrates the exact opposite: *the emergent consciousness of the Iraqi masses of how imperialism functions, especially through the law*. One of Baḥr al-ʿŪlūm's poems, entitled 'The colonial (Portsmouth) treaty,' which he recited to cheering crowds during the early days of the *Wathba*, demonstrates how the masses grasped the meaning of the treaty in their minds (even if they had not read its every provision):

> A draft law sent to pave the path for the invader
> The propositions of this bill sanctioned invasion
> Employing the language of bullets to impose itself
> And compelling co-operation from the barking dogs
> While the people prepare for the tribulations of night
> A language for understanding the occupation of yesterday[85]

Busk's insistence, therefore, that the crowd give him a '(legal) argument' regarding their rejection of the Treaty misses the point that the very existence of a 'colonial' treaty that practically 'sanctioned occupation' and prolonged their domination by an imperial power, was the problem. The contents of the treaty mattered little if the intention of the contracting parties remained the same – the maintenance of the British imperial connection. As Marx once wrote about the Paris Commune, 'the great social measure of the Commune was its own working existence'. In other words, one should not measure a revolutionary event such as the *Wathba* solely based on its ideas, let alone its legal arguments, but rather it should be measured based on its 'working existence', i.e. its manifestations on the ground. Here, it is plain that the movement's organisation and committees – its organised actions – were an indication of the type of social order that was being sought: one that allowed for the democratic participation of the majority of the Iraqi people, and especially the working classes and the peasants. It is this that could be referred to as the 'logic of the people' in counterposition to the logic of the law.

## IX. THE *WATHBA* FROM THE LENS OF THE LABOUR MOVEMENT

The *Wathba* has been largely interpreted as a nationalist anti-colonial struggle for the assertion of the constitutional rights of the Iraqi people, which were infringed and weakened by the 1930 Anglo-Iraq Treaty.[86] However, it also contains a labour narrative underlying its history, which had a unique

[85] M Bahr al-ʿUlum, *Diwan*, *supra*, 129.
[86] K al-Chadirjī. *Mudhakkirat Kāmil al-Chadirjī wa Tārīkh al-Hizb al-Watanī al-Dīmuqrātī* [The Memoirs of Kamil al-Chādirji and the History of the National Democratic Party] (Dar al-Tal'ia, 1970).

significance on the conjuncture in question, and which I have detailed in micro-histories in the previous chapters. In other words, one way to understand the *Wathba* is through the lens of the labour struggle against the material effects of semi-peripheral sovereignty on the lives of the ordinary Iraqi working classes. As Eric Davis has emphasised, workers provided 'the backbone' of the *Wathba*.[87] The Iraqi labour movement was making strides in their continuous struggles against their British employers of the colossal industrial enterprises of capitalist accumulation and extractivism. Before the *Wathba* exploded, labour strikes in these enterprises were rapidly becoming a concern for the British authorities.[88] Iraqi workers were not merely angered by their wretched conditions, but were also able, because of their unique location within the semi-colonial system of capitalist exploitation, to recognise a direct correlation between their immediate material conditions and the far-reaching issue of imperialism.

To understand the role of the labour movement in the *Wathba*, one must recall the organising efforts several years earlier of the railway, port and oil workers. During the years leading up to the *Wathba*, workers continuously developed extensive experiences in organisational tactics and strategies of strike action and anti-colonial protest, which made all the difference when they were on the ground, hand in hand with their Iraqi brethren fighting against the Portsmouth Treaty. Moreover, the workers' cognisance of the direct relationship between British imperialism and semi-colonialism, and the Iraqi state that they became gradually aware of during their labour struggles was *now* embedded into the overall national consciousness and 'common sense' of the majority of ordinary Iraqis. The working class were after all, as shown earlier, the class that was most affected by the implications of the treaty and 'semi-peripheral sovereignty' in their everyday lives.

An argument could therefore be made that the unique experiences of the workers and their movement contributed significantly to the momentum of the *Wathba*. If the students could be considered as those who ignited the *Wathba*, its organisational momentum was surely carried and maintained by the workers and their movement with the help of their lived experiences, for throughout the months after the 'Day of the Bridge' labour strikes intensified like never before. There was, in the words of Suʿād Khayrī, an 'awakening' within the labour movement.[89] The strikes were so potent that Nurī al-Saīd publicly remarked at the time that what he feared the most was not the actual demonstrations that led to the cancellation of the treaty, but rather the intensification of labour strikes, which he was afraid would lead to a great 'communist' revolution.[90] In that sense, the anti-colonial nationalist struggle shifted into the 'axis of labour',

[87] Davis, *supra*, 293.

[88] TNA. British Embassy, Baghdad to Foreign Office, 21 May 1948, enclosing minute on strikes at IPC [FO 371/68479].

[89] Khayrī, *supra*, 171, 173.

[90] *Ibid*.

turning strike action into the 'beating heart' of the *Wathba* movement.[91] Labour (economic) struggle and anti-colonial (political) struggle became precisely *one and the same* at this conjuncture. It was, after all, throughout these months that the massive successful Basra Port strike unfolded, and the legendary K3 pumping-station strike, which carried the 'liberationary [and solidarity] spirit of the *Wathba*,'[92] became a concrete reality. A state of emergency would ultimately be declared to violently repress these labour strikes. It is therefore not an overstatement to consider the *Wathba* as the wider reflection of a labour struggle against the semi-peripheral sovereignty that gave the juridical and ideological cover needed for the imposition of the capitalist economic structures over Iraq.

## X. THE WIDE IMPLICATIONS OF THE *WATHBA* AND ITS CONTRIBUTION TO THE CONJUNCTURE OF DECOLONISATION IN INTERNATIONAL LAW

Returning to the main analysis of TWAIL, inserting the social and juridical implications of the *Wathba* into my argument illustrates how scholars should begin the study of the conjuncture in the history of international law by connecting the 'micro-histories of resistance' from below to a broader and structural understanding of the conjuncture in question. This wide approach allows for an overarching understanding of revolutionary agency. Consequently, the conjunctural moment, which allowed anti-colonial and anti-imperial resistance to materialise in Iraq, cannot be explained without an attempt to understand the *wider* conjuncture of decolonisation in the region and the Global South. Decolonisation, as Mohammed Bedjaoui reminds us, is by its very definition a 'structural revolution *on a world scale*'.[93] For this reason, a conjunctural analysis must begin 'at the level of the international itself', ascertaining 'a dominant combination of causes' while evaluating 'the period characterised by the working out of that combination.'[94] It entails the necessity of simultaneously 'looking inwards to examine the detailed movement of a given period and outwards to locate that period in the longer historical process which it forms a part'.[95]

A conjunctural analysis of agency in its relation to international law, therefore, would have to be attentive to the organic movement within this wide scale while analysing agency, focusing on what Antonio Negri and Michael Hardt called the 'intersections' and the 'accumulation of struggles' against international law.[96] Although TWAIL scholars are generally familiar with such a wide

[91] *Ibid.*
[92] Nūʿamān, *supra*, 266.
[93] M Bedjaoui, *Towards A New International Economic Order: New Challenges to International Law*, (Holmes & Meier, 1979), 88.
[94] J Rosenberg quoted in Koivisto, 'Historical-Critical Dictionary of Marxism', 273.
[95] *Ibid.*
[96] M Hardt and A Negri, *Empire*, (Harvard University Press, 2000), 263.

historical analysis – one that Gramsci referred to as the study of the 'long waves' of history[97] (for instance Anghie's return to the thought of Francisco de Vitoria in the sixteenth century) – what is missing is how this connects to agency. The conjuncture, therefore, acts as a bridging device for one's analytic lens in relation to agency that could be used in tandem with the study of the imperial structures of international law. It is, nevertheless, not merely a matter of contextualisation, but rather about continuously being attentive to the question of agency or action in itself in one's overall analysis. Before moving to assess Iraqi working-class agency, I will first address the structural implications of the *Wathba* on various intersecting scales – the Iraqi, regional and international.

On the Iraqi scale, the *Wathba* contained the origins of the revolutionary process that culminated in the overthrow of the British-sponsored Hashemite monarchy by the 1958 July Revolution. It certainly inspired and stimulated the Free Officers to take matters into their own hands to defend the people, in the words of their leader Col. Abdul Karim Qassim, from 'the incubus of injustice that weighed upon them'.[98] I would go so far as to argue that the *Wathba* could be considered as the 'dress rehearsal' for the 1958 July Revolution, especially if one was to consider that the revolutionary process of struggle was sustained throughout the coming decade, resurfacing as mini-Wathbas – namely, the 1952 *Intifāda* and the 1956 Uprising. In many ways, it was the spark that started the process of the brewing and making of the July Revolution. It is in that sense that the *Wathba* and the July Revolution were a part of the same Iraqi conjuncture. The July Revolution was a genuine revolution that broke with the *ancien régime*. The Proclamation No. 1 that was read out on Baghdad Radio announced the establishment of a republic, promised that the Iraqi people would participate in shaping their own future, and established a neutralist foreign policy (explicitly referring to the 1955 Bandung Conference), ending its close alliance with the West.[99] The revolutionary processes began with the drafting of a Provisional Constitution barely two weeks after the revolution, frustrating the subjugating structures of the old Constitution or Organic Law, which limited popular sovereignty. Furthermore, the new Agrarian Reform law ended the 'semi-feudal' system that was the foundation of British policy and control, destroying the social power of the landed sheikhs by finally bringing the countryside under the purview of state law.[100] Finally, the positions of urban workers and the working class were significantly enhanced by the revision and enactment of an updated progressive labour law for the protection of workers' rights and their trade unions. As

[97] See M Finocchiaro. *Gramsci and the History of Dialectical Thought* (Cambridge University Press, 2002), 164.

[98] As quoted by Batatu, *supra*, 806.

[99] See J Romero, *The Iraqi Revolution of 1958: A Revolutionary Quest for Unity and Security.* (University Press of America, 2011).

[100] Marr, *supra*, 105.

for the anti-hegemonic impact of the *Wathba* on the region, it was apparent in how it inspired countless sympathy strikes and demonstrations in Beirut, Damascus, and Cairo. A revealing clipping from an Egyptian newspaper read, 'the Iraqi people did not only save itself, but saved the entire Arab world from remaining under Western colonial subjugation'.[101]

To situate the *Wathba* internationally, one needs to analyse how its revolutionary impetus was successful in striking at the heart of Western imperialism by preventing the imposition of a revised Anglo-Iraq Treaty. To do that, it is necessary to understand other regional and international events that rendered it the appropriate moment to attack (British) imperialism. Here, the weaving of other events of anti-colonial resistance against imperialism and the international legal order that happened in the Third World that year is necessary to grasp the vulnerability of British imperialism at that particular moment. Frank Furedi has detailed the historical conjuncture that emerged during the turbulent year of 1948 for anti-colonial and nationalist liberation struggles in the Third World.[102] He demonstrates how 1948 was a year of widespread panic in Whitehall as a crisis of imperial rule emerged unexpectedly where anti-colonial and anti-imperial resistance reached its utmost intensity: 'No part of the empire seemed immune from what appeared to be an epidemic of unrest'.[103] Twelve days before the *Wathba*, Burma rejected Commonwealth membership while February saw riots in Accra and in June emergency rule was established in Malaya.[104] Of course, regionally, 1948 was the year that the tragic Palestinian *Nakba* unfolded, and more than anything else this violent event represented the injustices of Zionist settler colonialism and Western imperialism for the Arab peoples. A focus on the manifestations of this conjuncture on the international scale can take all of these 'forces' into account in one's analysis of this particular moment of Iraqi agency against imperialism and its structures in international law.

The *Wathba* could also be situated in the conjuncture that was emerging within the international legal order and which manifested with the passing of the 1960 *Declaration on the Granting of Independence to Colonial Countries and Peoples* (GA Resolution 1514) by the UN General Assembly.[105] The significance of this document, sometimes referred to as the 'Magna Carta' of decolonisation, should not be understated.[106] The UN Charter of 1945 failed to clearly condemn

[101] *al-Nida' Newspaper*, (Cairo, February 5, 1948) as quoted in Ḥumaidī, *supra*, 546.
[102] F Furedi, *Colonial Wars and the Politics of Third World Nationalism*, (I.B. Tauris, 1994), 4, 88-108. Many thanks to John Reynolds for pointing out the significance of the year of 1948.
[103] *Ibid*, 89.
[104] *Ibid*.
[105] *Declaration on the Granting of Independence to Colonial Countries and Peoples* (1960), G.A. Res. 1514 (XV), UN GAOR, 15th sess., 947th plen. Mtg, UN Doc. A/RES/1514 (XV) (14 December 1960).
[106] Quayson-Sackey, as cited in C Quaye, *Liberation Struggles in International Law*, (Temple University Press, 1991), 111.

colonialism, and its imposition of a duty of administration on specific colonies could arguably be construed as recognising the legality of colonialism.[107] The fact that the Portsmouth Treaty, as I have shown, was technically drafted in a manner that fully conformed to the UN Charter is evidence of this limitation. The 1960 *Declaration* was, therefore, the first instrument in the history of international law in which colonialism and its many manifestation were deemed unlawful and in contravention of the UN Charter. As Christopher Quaye observed, the preamble of the *Declaration*, 'decried colonialism ... by observing the universal position against perpetuation of colonialism and expressing belief in liberation from anything that is colonial'.[108] In its words, the Declaration: '*Solemnly proclaims* the necessity of bringing a speedy and unconditional end to colonialism ***in all its forms and manifestations***'.[109] Despite its significance in international legal history, the *Declaration* did not fully accelerate the process of decolonisation at a pace corresponding to the hopes of the peoples under colonial rule, as its implementation had to be continuously fought for by the Afro-Asian Bloc over the next few years.[110]

Nevertheless, the contribution of the Iraqi anti-colonial struggle to this *Declaration* was indisputable. The *Wathba* and its revolutionary consequences on the Iraqi plane was only one event among a series of similar revolutionary events in other parts of the Third World that had a direct influence on the way the representatives of the Afro-Asian bloc in the U.N., adhering to the Bandung Spirit, were aggressively arguing for the drafting and liberal interpretation of this *Declaration*, while maintaining a firm anti-colonial stance.[111] It was clear that legal arguments were specifically made on the basis of 'the political weather outside the [U.N.] Headquarters'.[112] In other words, not only was (black letter) law rejected as a mechanism for dealing with the question of colonialism and imperialism, but also the social reality and the wave of events of decolonisation on the ground were considered as necessary *sources* for the drafting and moulding of international law and its instruments. The Afro-Asian Bloc continuously insisted that these anti-colonial struggles must be *unconditionally* recognised as legitimate – international 'law should be modified according to changed circumstances'.[113]

The Permanent Representative of the revolutionary government of Iraq in the U.N., Adnān Pāchachī took part in the drafting of the 1960 *Declaration*.[114]

[107] Quaye, *ibid*, 108-109.

[108] *Ibid*, 112.

[109] *Decelaration on the Granting.*

[110] DN Sharma. *Afro-Asian Group in the U.N.*, (Chaitanya Publishing, 1969), 205.

[111] *Ibid.*

[112] El-Ayouty, *supra*, 60.

[113] RP Anand, "Attitude of the Asian-African States Towards Certain Problems of international Law," in Snyder and Sathirathai (eds.), *Third World Attitudes Toward International Law: An Introduction*, (Martinus Nijhoff Publishers, 1987),14.

[114] A Pachachi, *Iraq's Voice at the United Nations 1959-69: A Personal Record*, (Quartet Books, 1991), 9.

The Iraqi delegation co-sponsored, together with a number of Asian and African states, the *Declaration* when it was presented to the General Assembly. In an impassioned and eloquent speech to the Assembly, the new Iraqi Foreign Minister, Hāshim Jawād, began by recounting the long history of colonialism in the Arab World, beginning with the first experience of European imperialism with the French conquest of Algeria in 1830, eventually referring to the Mandate system as 'a new form of colonialism' that was imposed on the peoples of the Middle East.[115] Jawād, accordingly, explicitly rejected the 'semi-peripheral sovereignty' that the Iraqi masses sought to abolish with their blood, sweat and tears during the *Wathba* and thereafter. He went on to state that although the Mandate in Iraq was terminated in 1932, it was replaced by a new relationship that retained for the former Mandatory Power great influence in the internal affairs of the country, stressing that 'it took another twenty-six years and our great July Revolution of 1958 for the people of Iraq to rid the country finally of the last vestiges of foreign domination and influence'.[116] Jawād then emphasised how he regarded all struggles for decolonisation as being interconnected by specifically referring to the Arab experience:

> I do not think I exaggerate when I say that few nations in the world have suffered as much as the Arab nation under colonial rule ... the Arab people have known colonialism in its worst forms and manifestations. They have experienced at first hand its oppression and treachery and have suffered from it physically, materially and spiritually as few others have. This is one of the reasons why we have such a deep sympathy and understanding for the struggle of the other nations for freedom and independence.[117]

He went on to make clear that it was the unique 'extensive' and 'tragic' experiences of semi-colonialism in the Arab world in general, and in Iraq in particular, that solidified his delegation's belief in the importance of an unequivocal anti-colonial wording in the *Declaration*.[118] The Iraqi contribution to the drafting of this document was, hence, in ensuring that the semi-peripheral sovereignty that was skilfully weaved into international law in Geneva and granted to Iraq in 1932, as a recognised form of 'independence', would be *unequivocally rejected* in the *Declaration*. International law should instead postulate *concrete* sovereignty and *complete* independence. N.M. Perrera, the representative for Ceylon (present-day Sri Lanka) plainly explained the meaning of this part of the *Declaration* when he emphasised that reference to the 'manifestations of colonialism' specifically referred to 'the various methods, procedures and legal figments which are used by colonial powers to cover the nakedness of rank colonialism'.[119] The semi-peripheral sovereignty described earlier and

[115] UN GAOR, 15th Sess., 937th plen., Mtg., UN Doc. A/PV 937 (6 December 1960), 120-138.
[116] *Ibid.*
[117] *Ibid.*
[118] *Ibid.*
[119] UN GAOR, 15th Sess., 926th plen. Mtg., UN Doc. A/PV 926 (28 November 1960), 1002.

which was a significant part of the Iraqi experience was one of these more sophisticated legal figments that were recognised under international law. It is in this way that the *Wathba* and its revolutionary consequences, in rejecting semi-peripheral sovereignty on the ground, could be linked through a conjunctural analysis to the wider changes within the international legal order and the decolonisation of international law.

## XI. THE ROLE OF LABOUR & WORKING-CLASS AGENCY TO THE CONJUNCTURE OF DECOLONISATION

The analysis above has shown how revolutionary agency emerges from within a particular conjuncture that materialises from the structures in question. TWAIL scholars would have arguably analysed the *Wathba* in isolation of these structures, concentrating on certain characteristics of agency as being external and not contingent to these structures (in particular its spontaneity, non-violence, and heterogeneity). However, this narrow approach differs from the broader conjunctural analysis that brings agency and structure into *one* fold, while it romanticises agency, approaching it as a form of resistance that is devoid of any revolutionary content. Many TWAIL scholars cannot conceive of emancipation without or beyond the law or the international legal order itself, despite it being the very target of their critique.[120] The *Wathba*, however, emerged for the very reason that the legal mechanisms of the state that were being manipulated by imperial instruments of international law were inept and completely dysfunctional. It eventually became (at least for the Iraqi left) about the subversion of the law rather than its mere reform. Furthermore, the *Wathba* demonstrated that the effectiveness of what I refer to as 'conjunctural agency' in the context of revolutionary action depends on its organisational capacity. It is not enough to put one's hopes on the spontaneity of action, for despite the unforeseen nature of the *Wathba*, the movement spurred into action at that particular moment because it was able to readily organise into effective steering committees. This was certainly possible because of some of its participants' past experiences in organising, especially those of the workers. In this manner, therefore, romanticising the spontaneity of agency ignores the fact that spontaneity and organisation must come *together* within a particular conjuncture to be effective.

I want to end by briefly returning to the significance of labour to the specific conjuncture in question. A focus on labour and working-class agency in this analysis demonstrates the strong affinity between capitalism, imperialism and international law, especially in the semi-periphery. This is what explains the

[120] See for example, L Eslava and S Pahuja, "Between Resistance and Reform: TWAIL and the Universality of International Law," 3(1) *Trade, Law and Development*, 103 (2011); BS Chimni. "Third World Approaches to International Law: A Manifesto," *International Community Law Review* 8: 3–27, (2006).

significant role of labour in countering the manifestations of the international legal order within the conjuncture in question. I have already shown how semi-peripheral sovereignty in the Iraqi context was manufactured as a mechanism to control the semi-colonial Middle East. The 'independence' of Iraq was more a mechanism to legalise the control of Iraqi oil and to regulate its transportation across the region. While the 1930 Anglo-Iraq Treaty maintained this control juridically, Iraqi labour was exploited to superintend the everyday functioning of this infrastructure of economic dominance. In this way, colonial and racial relations remained intact after Iraqi 'independence', especially in the colossal private enterprises and factories. The Anglo-Iraq treaty ensured British control of the most important economic sites of production and trade in the country. As I have shown, the framework for an 'independent Iraq' created an atmosphere of racism that was common elsewhere in the Empire. Iraqi workers, like their counterparts elsewhere in the Third World, embodied the contradictions of the racial capitalist system within the semi-colony, experiencing first hand the effects of imperialism and racism in their everyday lives, and so it should not be surprising that they would lead a significant role within the nationalist liberation movement.

Iraqi workers reconstituted the question of labour as being specifically an anti-colonial and anti-imperial question. This is why they found it necessary to connect their material conditions with the Anglo-Iraq Treaty, which they rejected, in turn rejecting the entire international legal and economic order imposed on the region. Fahad reveals the way the workers were thinking when he wrote: '… the working class did not separate the national [political] from the social [economic] content of liberation … [For them] national liberation is but a starting point of a fundamental change in the life of the people'.[121] The Iraqi labour movement *combined* claims of higher wages and better living conditions with anti-colonial demands of national liberation, ensuring its 'full integration into the national movement'.[122] This wide analytic lens was unique to the international conjuncture in question. It was prevalent at the time in other parts of the Global South.[123] Furedi characterised this conjuncture as a 'radical moment in anti-colonial politics', where there was a 'tendency of protests to acquire a more fundamental anti-systemic and anti-imperialist orientation, accompanied by increasing erosion of the boundaries between economic and political demands'.[124] This explains how 'relatively ordinary demands could mushroom into a major challenge to imperial authority'.[125] Iraqi workers, therefore, were

[121] Batatu, *supra*, 589.
[122] Farouk-Sluglett and Sluglett, 'The Social Classes and the Origins of the Revolution," in Fernea and Louis (eds.), *The Iraqi Revolution of 1958: The Old Social Classes Revisited*, (IB Tauris, 1991), 127–128.
[123] W Rodney, *supra*, 276.
[124] Furedi, *supra*, 38.
[125] *Ibid*.

unable to articulate their rejection of their social, living and working conditions without at the same time rejecting the entire international legal and economic order that was imposed upon them.

The British came to the conclusion that there needed to be an extensive development policy towards labour that would 'ameliorate the dire labour conditions' and 'fend off Communism'.[126] It is revealing that before the eruption of the *Wathba*, the British were in the process of advising the Iraqi government in drawing up 'regulations for the whole field of labour in Iraq' and in establishing an arbitration procedure that would address workers grievances.[127] It is this ultimately unsuccessful policy of development and conciliation that dominated British policy towards the region in the 1960s. In a similar vein, a development framework manifested within international law and its institutions. The International Labour Organization (ILO), for example, sent technical assistance missions to advise on labour and social issues in the Middle East. The ILO's technical assistance programs were conceived in the context of constricted notions of social and economic development with the aim of fighting the growing influence of communism.[128] Moreover, the 1961 *Declaration of the United Nations Development Decade* (GA Res. 1710) ensured that the effects of the 1960 *Declaration* would be limited in that it 'bound together decolonisation and development with a firm yoke'.[129] This maintained the subordination of society to the discipline of economics and led to the continuation of the development of underdevelopment.[130] Most importantly, this was what prevented the materialisation of an alternative international economic order from the 'salt-water' decolonisation that was won. In this way, the conjunctural shift did not ultimately produce the revolutionary changes that were sought after, whether it was within the international legal order or the Iraqi experience, where revolutionary processes were interrupted by a CIA-sponsored military coup in 1963.

## XII. CONCLUSION

The history of the *Wathba* recounted above is an illustration of how revolutionary action can be undertaken within a specific conjuncture to subvert the effects of the imperialism of international law. Although this affirms the transient and provisional nature of the foundations of international law, it is only

[126] TNA. FO 371/52406 British Embassy to Baghdad, to Rt Hon E. Bevin, Foreign Secretary, London, 2 July 1946, 'street demonstrations in Baghdad'.

[127] TNA. D.L. Busk, Baghdad, to Rt Hon E. Bevin, Foreign Secretary, London, 21, August 1946.

[128] D Maul, "The Morse Years: the ILO 1948-1970," in *ILO Histories: Essays on the International Labour Organization FO371/52456 and its impact on the World during the Twentieth Century*, (Peter Lang, 2010), 54.

[129] S Pahuja. "Decolonization and the eventness of international law," in F Johns; R Joyce; and S Pahuja (eds.), *Events: The Force of International Law*, (Routledge, 2011); 99.

[130] *Ibid.*

in relation to the structures in question that agency could be evaluated.[131] It is nevertheless important to recall Gramsci's warning that 'a common error … consists in an inability to find the correct relation between what is organic and what is conjunctural. This leads to … [either] … an excess of "economism" … [or] … an excess of "ideologism". In the first case there is an overestimation of mechanical causes, in the second an exaggeration of the voluntarist and individual element.'[132] It is necessary in the end to find an accurate correlation between the (organic) structure and (conjunctural) agency in one's analysis if one is to correctly evaluate how agency was (or is to be) deployed *within* the structural constraints of the international legal, political and economic order. It was after all, on the one hand, the overly weak hegemony of the Iraqi state and its corresponding semi-peripheral sovereignty that made it unable to maintain itself or permanently suppress the emerging counter-hegemonic movements and spaces that continued to arise despite being fractured again and again by the violent uses of emergency law. The counter-hegemonic, on the other hand, cannot be understood in isolation of the conditions that make agency possible (or at least that even contribute to an initially unsuccessful attempt at revolution, such as the *Wathba)*.

The prominent Iraqi poet Mohammed Mahdī al-Jawāhirī recited a celebrated poem eulogising those who died on the bridge during the *Wathba*, his brother amongst them. He begins with the following line: 'Are you aware or not, that the wounds of martyrs are a mouth?'[133] It is not only a matter of allowing this 'mouth' to speak in one's scholarship, but rather also to focus on the very conjunctures that allow those who take action to liberate themselves becoming 'wounded martyrs'. It is, in other words, the opening (or 'mouth') of the conjunctures that should be one's point of departure.

[131] S Marks. "False Contingency," (2010) 62 *Current Legal Problems* 1–22, 10.
[132] Gramsci, *supra*, 178.
[133] SK Jayyusi, *Trends and Movements in Modern Arabic Poetry*. (Brill, 1997). 199.

# *Conclusion*

## I. THE LINES OF EXPANSION AND THE CONTRACTION OF THE INTERNATIONAL LEGAL ORDER

To return to the image of drawing 'lines' on maps evoked in the introduction, what was laid out in this study is essentially a legal and social history of line-drawing, whether it be the carving of borderlines, the imposition of property lines, or the construction and protection of oil pipelines, railway lines, and shipping lanes. As Cornelia Vismann suggests, the law itself could be considered as a line or, in her words, 'the primordial scene of the *nomos* opens with drawing a line in the soil ... [the] very act [of which] initiates a specific concept of law, which derives order from the notion of space.'[1] This book shows how the straight lines of the law in all its scales – international, domestic, transnational, imperial, semi-colonial – produced and defined certain geopolitical spaces with the aim of controlling, regulating and exploiting the strategic sites and the natural resources of the semi-peripheral Middle East. The Iraqi state itself was established through an amalgamation of legal instruments, doctrines and methodologies until it was, contrary to the reality on the ground, proclaimed as an independent sovereign state. Retracing these lines of the law exposes how imperialism operated to obfuscate reality, while legitimising and expanding its order.

This book, however, also shows that no matter how straight a line is drawn and no matter how sophisticated a ruler is used to (violently) draw and impose its line, it could never fully dominate a surface, especially one that already contains other free-moving, organic living lines. Tim Ingold, who has written a fascinating anthropological history of lines, describes the sovereignty of the straight line drawn by a ruler. He writes,

> [a] ruler is a sovereign who controls and governs a territory. It is also an instrument for drawing straight lines. These two usages ... are closely connected. In establishing the territory as his to control, the ruler lays down guidelines for its inhabitants to follow. And in his political judgments and strategic decisions – his ruling – he plots the course of action they should take. As in the territory so also on the page, the ruler has been employed in drawing lines of all kinds.[2]

The analogy above is apt: to draw straight lines is a prerequisite for imperial control, but to do so, you need a 'ruler'. In other words, you need the

[1] C Vismann, "Starting from Scratch: Concepts of Order in No Man's Land" in H Bernd-Rudiger (ed) *War, Violence and the Modern Condition*. (Walter de Gruyter, 1997), 46.

[2] T Ingold. *Lines: A Brief History* (Routledge, 2007), 160.

law, but you also need to establish sovereignty. The British at the behest of international legal institutions drew straight lines on the maps of the Middle East – they installed a foreign ruler in Iraq and with the lines of the law developed a semi-peripheral sovereignty over this geostrategic territory, while maintaining their economic and political interests by carving up other lines of capitalist accumulation – that is, the infrastructural lines of oil pipelines and railways. Ingold contrasts the drawing of straight lines using a ruler with drawing by freehand, which he shows produces a life-like texture and contains an open-ended freedom as it is a movement along 'a path of observation' rather than the already defined sharp edges of the ruler.[3] The graceful organic lines of anti-colonial and anti-imperial agency – of the workers, students, peasants, squatters, activist lawyers, and the multitudes described in this book – move along these lines – that is, in a freehanded manner as they struggle to disentangle themselves from the sovereignty of the juridical straight lines. As they move, partly in an improvised and partly in an organised manner, they created their own alternative *nomos* with their very movements, with the aim of overthrowing the imperialism of the existing international legal order that was imposed on them. The analysis of the international conjuncture in international legal history presented in this study could accordingly be considered as a dialectical history of the lines of imperial authorities and anti-imperial movements – their coordination in relation to space and time, and their expansion and contraction. It is no doubt the most useful method to understand the manifestation and initiation of agency, and its counter-hegemonic spaces in relation to the structures of capitalism, imperialism and international law.

This book makes several contributions to the existing literature that go beyond just putting law at the centre of the history of modern Iraq. First, it substantiates the unique specificity of the semi-peripheral region of the Middle East in the history of international law. In other words, it shows that international law approached the semi-periphery differently than the periphery in the Third World. From this emerged new juridical formations of sovereignty in international law, such as the doctrine of semi-peripheral sovereignty. These new categories were in effect attempts to conceal the reality of imperial domination, colonialism and capitalist exploitation in the region. They were also threaded specifically for the Middle East, considering its importance in geostrategic thinking, as well as the valuable natural resources below its surface. By exploring European imperialism's development of unique legal techniques and formulations and their ensuing effects, international legal scholars would better appreciate the different (subtle) ways in which international law was deployed to obfuscate reality and to further imperial agendas. These hidden structures of the imperialism of international law are most interesting to study as their deconstruction illustrates how they are recycled and reformulated in the region today. Such a study would also add to the lesser-known histories

[3] *Ibid*, 166.

and genealogies of the concept of sovereignty in relation to the Third World. Secondly, this book contributes to the study of agency in relation to international law by proposing that with the use of a methodological approach that relies on the conjuncture, the history of agency can be better grasped within the making of international legal history. A broader and more open perspective that centres the agency of the ordinary peoples of the Third World illustrates that international law had concrete material effects not only on the state, but on those living under its guise. It also illustrates that the peoples' grassroots struggles against these forms of domination were a significant part of the history of international law and should be considered as such.

## II. THE FLEXIBLE FORMS OF SOVEREIGNTY IN INTERNATIONAL LAW AND THEIR RELATIONS TO CAPITALISM AND IMPERIALISM

I have recounted this social and legal history of Iraq not only to show that the law was central to the political and socio-economic transformations of the period in question, but also as an attempt to present a historical case for *how* imperialism and international law are *constitutive* of each other. Consequently, this book is not only a history of international law and its institutions (Chapter 2, 3, 7), but also an illustration of the simultaneous operations of (British) imperial law in its relation to tribal, customary law and property law (Chapter 1), international/transnational law of investment and municipal law (Chapters 2, 4), emergency law and criminal law (Chapter 6), and labour law (Chapters 3, 4, 5). It was generally with the foundational structures of international law and the construction of semi-peripheral sovereignty in Iraq through the Mandate process that these laws had the necessary scope to operate in the context of semi-colonialism. Moreover, it was international law, through the provisions of the 1930 Anglo-Iraq Treaty, which produced and maintained the spaces of capitalist accumulation – the extraterritorialised enclaves of the oil fields, railways and the port – described in this book, that allowed for imperialism to operate to maintain the flow of capital to and from this geo-strategic region.

The making of the doctrine of semi-peripheral sovereignty in Iraq was a significant event in that it was the first time that the necessary juridical ingredients were assembled to produce a unique non-European sovereignty through the Mandate process of international law that was reconciled (at least in theory) with the interwar international legal order, as it preserved the essential processes of imperialism and exploitation in the region. As I have shown, there was a spatial and economic specificity to the semi-periphery that made these legal techniques vital for controlling the Middle East as a whole, including its natural resources. Furthermore, from a regional and international perspective, this experiment with sovereignty was valuable in that it revealed how far a restrained non-European sovereignty could be extended without (legally or doctrinally) contradicting the main principles that underlie the emerging international legal order.[4] Semi-peripheral sovereignty in Iraq was in essence a form of sovereignty that ensured that Iraqi sovereignty was de jure complete under international law, but de facto fragmented – a fragmentation that was evident in the operations of the semi-autonomous and extraterritorialised enclaves of the IPC oil fields, the port of Basra and the Iraq State Railways, and which also included the two British (RAF) military bases that remained stationed on Iraqi soil.

At its crux, this book, therefore, uncovers the constitutive relationship between the juridical forms of sovereignty and capitalist social/economic relations of production and exploitation of Western imperialism in the Middle East region. Consequently, by tracing the effects of Iraqi semi-peripheral sovereignty to these relations, and how it relates to the open door principle, I have revealed exactly how these forms and processes were moulded to further the commercial and economic interests of the imperial powers and of capitalism in general. A close reading of the PMC deliberations on Iraq's readiness for independence, with those relating to the oil concessionary and pipeline agreements, suggests that Iraqi semi-peripheral sovereignty was in fact a juridical manifestation of the expansion and reproduction of capitalist relations in the region. The book consequently furthers the argument that sovereignty, as a core concept of international law, constitutively correlates with the structures of capitalism and imperialism. Sovereignty was in other words, not, as Anghie argues, primarily 'forged out of the confrontation between different cultures', which produced the 'dynamic of difference' but rather it was *already* embedded in the juridical forms of capitalism.[5] It is, in other words, primarily the economic rather than cultural dimensions of sovereignty and international law that should be underscored in its history. The understanding of the doctrine of semi-peripheral sovereignty and its evolution in Iraq will, it is hoped, explain its enduring characteristics, its continuities, and in turn its limitations as a category for the emerging Third World states in the post-colonial era.

This study of Iraq substantiates China Mieville's claim that, 'the imperialism of international law means more than just the global spread of an international legal order with capitalism – it means that the power dynamics of political imperialism are embedded within the very juridical equality of sovereignty.'[6] The social and economic transformation of Iraq described in this book is an illustration of how the legal form within the concept of sovereignty, as it was entrenched in the Anglo-Iraq Treaty, was used not only to uphold its military dominance, but also to maintain its corresponding capitalist structures and processes, ensuring its operation with a certain efficacy. While capitalist relations were solidified and

[4] I have shown that the legal arguments made by the PMC did at times contradict their own legal principles (especially of the open door), but the point is that it was as much about the *appearance* of reconcilement with international legal doctrine and legitimacy that anything else.

[5] Anghie, *supra*, 311.

[6] Mieville, *supra*, 270.

overcame the tribal structure of Iraqi society, as we saw in Chapter 1, extreme exploitation manifested within the industrialised spaces of oil production, railway communication and port apparatuses, as detailed in Chapters 4 and 5. By exposing the effects of the juridical forms of semi-peripheral sovereignty and how Iraqi workers were materially affected by these legal structures, not only does this study strive to further ground the history of international law, but in its explicit consideration of how anti-colonial and anti-imperial social and labour struggles shape the law, it also aims to move bottom-up to insert the agency of Third World peoples into its historiography. The hope is, as Upendra Baxi proposes, that 'international law [would no longer] be further understood merely as the history of the *law of nations* to the entire exclusion of the *law of peoples*'.[7] The actions of Third World peoples would finally be interpreted from the perspective of the global historiography of decolonisation and the transformation of the international order rather than being excluded from this realm.

## III. LEGALITY AS A QUESTION OF STRATEGY AND TACTICS IN REVOLUTIONARY STRUGGLES FOR DECOLONISATION

One theme that runs throughout this book concerns the manner by which counter-hegemonic movements appropriated the law and its language in their struggles for decolonisation. In Chapter 3, I showed how the labour movement was able to appropriate the 1936 Labour Law for its own advantage, using it as a reference point for its demands. Although the early labour movement had confidence in the principles of international law and its institutions (as its leaders were in direct contact with the ILO), its communist-led successor referred to the law (whether international law or the labour law of the state) only from the perspective of strategy and tactics. This did not mean that the law was unimportant for them, but rather they did not consider legal reform as sufficient for defeating the structures of the semi-colonial order nor for ending British imperialism in the country and the region.

The oil workers relentlessly referred to the 1936 Labour Law in their demands, in particular the right to form their own independent trade unions. However, they were aware that the limitations of the law and its application were due to the constricting structures of international and transnational law imposed on their country. Their experiences after the Gāwūrbāghī strike and massacre confirmed their views, as not one government or IPC official was held accountable under Iraqi law for the murder of oil workers. Similarly, the port workers explicitly fought for the inclusion of the right to strike into the labour law, which they argued was a part of their natural rights as workers. These legal demands

[7] U Baxi. 'What may the "Third World" expect from International Law' *Third World Quarterly*, Vol. 27, No. 5, pp.713–725, 2006; 720.

went unanswered and the workers were forced to move to more militant tactics of wild strike action and sabotage during the *Wathba* and beyond. The uses of law in the struggle had some advantages (whether as rhetorical tool or for its educative function), but it certainly also had its limits as the overall anti-colonial struggle itself was clearly waged and won outside the confines of law.

Does the law, then, and international law and its concept of sovereignty in particular, have an emancipatory potential for counter-hegemonic, anti-colonial and/or anti-imperialist movements? A central theme that emerges from this book is that the practical usefulness of law depends entirely on the historical conjuncture in question. It is a matter of strategy and tactics and should not be pursued for the simple reason that it is law or even a legal manifestation of a particular demand. Consequently, neither EP Thompson's claim that the rule of law is an 'unqualified human good' in its malleability as a recourse for the plebian, nor Ranajit Guha's categorical renunciation of this statement as a reflection of the 'hallucinatory effects of ideology', are accurate.[8] As Evgeny Pashukanis warned, 'legality is not an empty sack that can be filled with a new class content'.[9] In other words, the forms of bourgeois legality ensure its limited potential. Its usefulness, therefore, for any revolutionary movement is 'a mere question of tactics'.[10] International law, including human rights discourse, is not always a useful 'counter-hegemonic tool of resistance' as many critical legal scholars have implied.[11] The same could be said of the concept of sovereignty, for despite its inherently imperialistic juridical form, it could, provided the historical conjuncture is taken into account, contribute to a revolutionary struggle. A legal demand, including that of complete self-determination, in other words, could be made to further its revolutionary struggle, and this book has revealed how the Iraqi labour and nationalist movement did exactly that at certain critical conjunctures.

## IV. CONJUNCTURAL ANALYSIS AND THE WRITING OF HISTORY FOR THE PRESENT

It has already been mentioned that a conjunctural analysis of history is meant as a modus to grasp the *present* conjuncture (or in Lenin's 1917 expression, 'the Present Situation') so as to be able to formulate an organised plan of action

[8] EP Thompson, *supra*; and R Guha. *Dominance without Hegemony: History and Power in Colonial India*, (Harvard University Press, 1997), 67.

[9] E Pashukanis, "Lenin and the Problems of Law" in Piers Beirne & Robert Sharlet, eds, *Pashukanis: Selected Writings on Marxism and Law* (Academic Press, 1980), 143.

[10] G Lukacs, *History and Class Consciousness*, (MIT Press, 1990), 264. For an examination of this question in detail, see R Knox, "Marxism, International Law, and Political Strategy", *Leiden Journal of International Law*, 22 (2009), 413–436.

[11] B Rajagopal, "Counter-Hegemonic International Law: Rethinking Human Rights and Development as a Third World Strategy", 27(5) *Third World Quarterly*, 767–783.

today, which would be decisive. A conjunctural analysis, therefore, is not merely concerned with the elucidation of the historical past, but rather is meant to identify strategic and tactical sites of political action today. So the reader may wonder what was the purpose of undertaking a study and analysis on the early revolutionary history of Iraq? Why, for instance, are the past struggles of the oil, railway, and port workers significant to recall today? Why should we study their organised actions and strategies? How could the revolutionary history of the *Wathba* be useful for Iraqis and the peoples of the region today – in an age of US imperialism, and amidst the aftermath of the devastation of the 2003 US invasion, occupation, plunder and disintegration of Iraq and the region? One could argue that the legendary history of the *Wathba* and its vast and lost hopes that came with the 1958 July Revolution seem to hardly register in the memories of today's Iraqi youth – or even if so, are only considered as possibilities that were dashed by regional rivalries, left disorganisation and Western imperialism – a too brief and turbulent revolutionary interlude filled with optimism that has long gone. Although, I do not claim to have all the answers to these questions, it is certainly clear that the *Wathba* was a decisive moment in the modern history of Iraq, and that its effects reverberated beyond the 1958 July Revolution in many ways. As Hamit Bozarslan has argued, the Wathba's contemporary relevance to the post-1958 history of Iraq, including the Baʿathist period, and to the region was that it was 'the bearer of an unprecedented degree of radicalisation in the Arab world' and that it was precisely the continuation of this process well after 1958 that 'created a paradoxical situation and led to a radical bifurcation both in ideological and axiological terms'.[12] This 'radical bifurcation' in ideology between Iraqis who were staunchly anti-imperialist and who favoured concrete independence and non-alignment, and those who favoured a connection with the West became permanently entrenched, stirring continuous tensions, and arguably remained in place throughout the history of Iraq and the region to this day.

It is apparent then that without undertaking a re-examination of the past with the present in mind, it would be difficult to act to reconstruct an alternative future for the benefit of Iraq and the region. It is in this way that one should recollect how Iraqis developed creative and resourceful ways of organised resistance in their struggles against imperialism and its legal manifestations. What emerges, therefore, from this legal and historical study of Iraq is that ordinary working-class Iraqis were able to see through the obfuscation of the legal structures imposed on their country and at certain points in time organised successfully against them. The reality is that these experiences remain deeply (even if subconsciously) ingrained in the collective memories of the masses of

[12] H Bozarslan. "Rethinking the Ba'thist Period" in J Tejel, P Sluglett, R Bocco, H Bozarslan (eds.), *Writing the Modern History of Iraq: Historiographical and Political Challenges* (World Scientific Publishing), 144.

the region, and we know this because they tend to re-emerge without any warning as we saw happen with the 2011 Arab uprisings, and the 2019 October protest movement all over Iraq. Ordinary Iraqis continue to struggle against similar imperialist legal structures, organising in novel ways, despite their portrayals by the media as passive victims of dictatorship and imperial wars.[13] The oil workers and their contemporary trade unions, for instance, undoubtedly following their militant tradition, were at the forefront of an intense struggle against the imposition of an oil law in 2007 that intended to entirely open the oil industry to foreign investment, to sanction the interests of foreign companies (with the help of international investment law), and to completely reverse the process of oil nationalisation that started in 1972.[14]

I will end with a brief reflection on the value and the techniques of writing history, especially of international law. Anne Orford has highlighted the uniqueness of the uses of historical analysis by legal scholars, in particular TWAIL scholars.[15] She argues that legal scholars do not abide by the established methodology of historiography that rejects all forms of anachronism, emphasising that everything should be placed 'in the context of its own time.'[16] Historians, on the other hand, are expected to solely recover 'past meanings'.[17] Orford suggests that since law is inherently genealogical, depending on 'the movement of concepts, languages and norms across time and even space,' legal scholars are intuitively capable of breaking from this hallowed method through contextualising past concepts and by considering how these concepts remerge in the present.[18] In other words, legal scholars find it easier to use history and the past within the present context, as they do not abide by any stringent methodology.

Although, Orford is correct in pointing out the affinity between law and history and the constructive role of legal analysis in historical methodology, not

[13] See A Issa, *Against All Odds: Voices of Popular Struggle in Iraq* (Tadween Publishing, 2015).

[14] See G Muttitt, *Fuel on the Fire: Oil and Politics in Occupied Iraq*, (Bodley Head, 2011). Muttitt details the current struggles of the oil union and Iraqi civil society in organising against this law. On one of their strikes, he refers to their past militant history and experiences, 'The new oil union continued this tradition, demanding immediate improvements for the workers while raising the long-term structure of the industry and the economy', and an opportunity to have a say on the new oil law. Muttitt, 254.

[15] A Orford, "The past as law or history? The relevance of imperialism for modern international law," IILJ Working Paper 2012/2 (History and Theory in International Law Series), Finalised June 2012, (www.iilj.org). See A Orford. *International Law and the Politics of History* (CUP, 2021).

[16] *Ibid*, 6.

[17] *Ibid*.

[18] *Ibid*, 9. The methodological affinity between law and history in European thought could be traced back to at least the sixteenth century. François Baudouin and Jean Bodin, for example, argued that the jurist must be a historian if he is to avoid errors of interpretation and chronology, and the historian must be a jurist to set events in their proper political and social contexts. See A Grafton, *What was History? The art of history in early modern Europe* (Cambridge University press, 2007), 69.

all historians abide by this orthodox approach to historiography. In fact, many historians, especially of the left, see their craft as corresponding to the study of political action and its relation to the present. The writing of history is considered a political act – *making* of history and its production is, therefore, a technique to respond to the present, and is firmly rooted in the 'possibilities of making futures.'[19] Walter Rodney, for instance, believed that history was 'a way of ordering knowledge which could become an active part of the consciousness of an uncertified mass of ordinary people' and be utilised as 'an instrument of social change' to bring about an alternative future.[20] David Scott suggests a similar view in his rereading of *The Black Jacobins*, C. L. R. James's classic account of the only successful slave rebellion in the Caribbean, the Haitian Revolution of the 1790s:[21] 'The historical past', he writes, '… is never anachronistic […] [T]he past is [not] only available through the present […] but […] morally and politically what ought to be at stake in historical inquiry is a critical appraisal of the present itself, not the mere reconstruction of the past. The present, then, not the past, is what histories of the present are supposed to be about.'[22] In this way, Scott considers James's classic work as an 'exercise in writing a history of the present', suggesting that James 'directly challenges us to ask ourselves what kind of story might be best for the politico-historical *presents* within which we now live and write.'[23] It is revealing that James was, despite his silence on his initial intentions, it has been argued, motivated to begin writing *The Black Jacobins* when he arrived in London from his native Trinidad, by the US occupation of Haiti (1915-1934).[24] He was consciously weaving together a particular and even romantic history of the Haitian revolution while meditating on the underlying revolutionary potential of the peoples of the Caribbean, indirectly addressing US imperialism in his time, and its flaunting of Haitian sovereignty. His hope it seems was to inspire revolutionary action in the imaginations of the Caribbean people and to historically connect Caribbean anti-colonialism against US imperialism *with* the revolutionary struggle of Toussaint L'Overture and the Haitian Revolution for black liberation. It was, therefore, no coincidence that his classic study was written and published during that period, in 1938.

[19] B Schwarz, "'The people' in history: The Communist Party Historians' Group, 1946–56," *Making Histories: Studies in history-writing and politics*, R Johnson, (ed.) (Hutchinson & Co, 1983), 95.

[20] G Lamming's 'Forward' in W Rodney. *A History of the Guyanese Working People, 1881–1905*, (John Hopkins University Press, London, 1981), xvii.

[21] CLR. James, *The Black Jacobins: Toussaint L'Ouverture and the San Domingo Revolution*, (Vintage, 1989).

[22] D Scott, *Conscripts of Modernity: The Tragedy of Colonial Enlightenment*, (Duke University Press, 2004), 41.

[23] *Ibid*, 57.

[24] See R Dalleo, '"The Independence So Hardly Won has Been Maintained": C.L.R. James and the U.S. Occupation of Haiti,' *Cultural Critique* 87, Spring 2014, 38–59.

It is with a similar spirit that this history was written: as a reworking of the history and legacy of anti-colonial revolutionary struggle of Iraq *for* this present conjuncture of late US imperialism, following the 2003 invasion, occupation and domination of Iraq, the devastating effects of which linger to this day (not to mention the destruction of the Syrian state, the devastation of Lebanon, and the unrelenting Israeli genocide of the Palestinian people in Gaza and ethnic cleansing in the West Bank).

The British Ambassador to Iraq, John Troutbeck, once wrote in a dispatch to London that 'no country could owe more to imperialism than does Iraq'.[25] One should add that the imperialism that he was referring to was more specifically the imperialism of international law that we have detailed in this study. Iraq's experience with international law and its institutions could be said to be quite unique. It was a state that was established and granted a form of 'independence' through the mechanisms of the Mandate system and international law, so as to be exploited in 'peace' ('an organisation without occupation' as one member of the Indian civil service put it).[26] It would later become the target of US-backed coups; the recipient of an installed dictatorship; and be subject to acts of war, bombs, economic sanctions, invasion, plunder, looting and military occupation – all with the aim of its re-integration into the capitalist world economy and its subjugation into Western hegemony. Iraq's modern state and its institutions – once the pride of the international community of the interwar period – first developed through the mechanisms of international law, would be entirely destroyed seven decades later, all under the purview of the *same* international legal order. This may seem paradoxical indeed, but this study indicates otherwise. International law as the juridical manifestation of imperialism is predicated on 'civilising' violence. What is clear is that if Iraq were to ever gain its complete independence and its people their freedom, the *entire* semi-peripheral region of the Middle East (including and especially Palestine) would have to be liberated from the shackles of Western imperialism (and its most violent manifestation of Colonial Zionism), and this certainly means the imperialism of (Western) international law, or what is often referred to today as the US 'rules-based international order'.

[25] TNA, FO 371/110991. VQ 1015/82. J Troutbeck (British Embassy, Bagdad) to Anthony Eden (FO, London) December 9, 1954.

[26] See O Caroe, *Wells of Power: The Oilfields of South-Western Asia, A Regional and Global Study*, (Macmillan & Co, 1951).

# *Bibliography*


**I. Archival Sources:**

**Iraq Petroleum Company Records at the British Petroleum (BP) Archive, (Coventry, UK):**

File 135818.
File 135819.
File 162461.
File 4656.
File 60550.

**The National Archives of the United Kingdom (TNA), (London, UK):**

Records of Foreign Office: FO 371, 622, 624, 921, 925
Records of Colonial Office: CO 696, 730
Records of the Treasury: T 160
Records of the Ministry of Labour and successors: LAB 13
Records of the Cabinet: CAB 24

**Archives of the British Communist Party, (People's History Museum, Manchester):**

CP/CENT/INT/17/01, Workers of the Iraq Petroleum Co. go on strike, Baghdad, 5 Jul. 1946.
CP/CENT/INT/17/01.'The Slaughter of Kawer Baghi', 31 Oct, 1946.

**International Labour Organisation Records (ILO Headquarters, Geneva, Switzerland):**

D-600.
D-617.
ILO-BIT/ACD.

*Official Bulletin of the International Labour Office*, vol. XXXIX.

**League of Nations Minutes and Reports (UN Peace Palace Library, Geneva):**

*League of Nations Official Journal*

League of Nations. Permanent Mandates Commission: Minutes of the Seventh Session. Geneva: League of Nations, 1925.
League of Nations. Permanent Mandates Commission: Minutes of the Fourteenth Session. Geneva: League of Nations, 1928.
League of Nations. Permanent Mandates Commission: Minutes of the Sixteenth Session. Geneva: League of Nations, 1933.
League of Nations. Permanent Mandates Commission: Minutes of the Eighteenth Session. Geneva: League of Nations, 1930.
League of Nations. Permanent Mandates Commission: Minutes of the Nineteenth Session. Geneva: League of Nations, 1930.
League of Nations. Permanent Mandates Commission: Minutes of the Twentieth Session. Geneva: League of Nations, 1931.

League of Nations. Permanent Mandates Commission: Minutes of the Twenty-First Session. Geneva: League of Nations, 1932.

## II. Iraqi Laws

*Law Governing the Rights and Duties of Cultivators No. 28 of 1933*, Iraq Government Gazette no. 31(30 July 1933), pp. 315–323.
*Labour Law* No. 72, Iraq Government Gazette, No. 20, May 17,1936, p.278.
*Law Amending the Bagdad Penal Code No. 45 of 1936.*
*Ordinance for the Prevention of Harmful Propaganda No. 44 of 1937.*
*Law Supplemental to the Baghdad Penal Code No. 51.*
*Ordinance No. 17 of 1954 Supplemental to the Iraqi Nationality Law.*
*The Iraq Constitution (Organic Law)* – March 21, 1925, passed July 10, 1924, as amended July 29, 1925 and October 27, 1943.
*Ordinance for Martial Law Administration – No. 18 of 1935. Iraq Gazette*, No. 1420, 14-5-1935.
Law No. 36 of 1942 (Amendment to Labour Law No. 72 of 1936), *Al-Waqā'i' al-Iraqiyya* (Official Gazette), No. 2028, 31 May 1942.
Regulation (No. 63) of 1954 on Conciliation and Arbitration for the Settlement of Disputes between Employers and Workers.

## III. Treaties and Agreements

*Anglo-Iraq Treaty of 1930*, (Baghdad, June 30, 1930).
*Anglo-Iraq Treaty of Alliance, 1922, Cmd 2370.*
*Covenant of the League of Nations*, 28 April 1919, 13 (1919) *AJIL Sup*. 128.
Government of Iraq and Iraq Petroleum Company. *Supplementary Agreement to the Iraq Concession of 1925*. Baghdad, March 24, 1931. Included in *British and Foreign State Papers*, vol. 134. London: HMSO, 1941.
Great Britain and Iraq, *Agreement concerning the Port of Basrah and the Establishment of the Port Trust*, in *League of Nations – Treaty Series*, Vol. 35 (1925), No. 894, Article X.
Great Britain and Iraq. *Agreement between His Majesty in Respect of the United Kingdom and His Majesty the King of Iraq Regarding the Railway System of Iraq (including Transfer of the Railways to the Government of Iraq, with Exchange of Notes)*. Baghdad, March 31, 1936. Cmd. 5173. London: HMSO, 1936.
Iraq Government and Turkish Petroleum Company. *Concession for the Development of the Petroleum Resources of the State of Iraq*. Baghdad, March 14, 1925. Reprinted in *British and Foreign State Papers*, vol. 128. London: HMSO, 1935.
*The Sykes-Picot Agreement May 1916*, Oxford Public International Law.
*Treaty of Alliance between His Majesty in respect of the United Kingdom of Great Britain and His Majesty the King of Iraq*, Portsmouth, 15th January, 1948, Cmd. 7309.
*Treaty of Alliance between United Kingdom and Iraq*, PP 1929–1930, Cmd. 3627.
*Treaty with H.M. King Faisal*, 10 October 1922, Cmd 1757, 1922.

## IV. Newspapers, magazines and journals

*al-Thaqāfa al-Jadīda*
*Itiḥād al-Sha'ab*
*Ṭarīq al-Sha'ab*
*al-Zamān*
*Ṣawt al-Ahāli*

*al-Qā ʿida*
*al-Ḥiwār al-Mutamadin*
*Majala al-Ghadd*
*Basrah al-Ahāli*
*Ṣadā al-Ahāli*
*al-Nida'*
*al-Istiqlāl*

### V. Parliamentary Records/Papers

**Chamber of Deputies *(Iraq):***

***Taqrīr 'an a'māl al-lijān al-Dā'imah fī ijtimā'at Majlis al-Nuwāb*** [Reports of the Proceedings of the Standing Committees in the Sessions of the Iraqi Chamber of Deputies], (Baghdād : Majlis al-Nūwāb), [Accessed at the American University of Beirut Jafet Library, Beirut, Lebanon]: 1931; 1948; 1949; 1952; 1953.

**House of Commons (UK):**

HC Debate, 'Anglo-Iraq Treaty,' 18 February 1926, Vol 191 cc2167-289.

*Iraq: Papers Relating to the Application to Iraq of the Principles of Article 22 of the Covenant of the League of Nations, 1925*. Cmd. 2317. London: HMSO, 1925.

### VI. UN Records

**United Nations General Assembly.** *Official Records of the General Assembly, Fifteenth Session, 937th Plenary Meeting.* UN Doc. A/PV.937 (6 December 1960), 120–138.

**United Nations General Assembly.** *Official Records of the General Assembly, Fifteenth Session, 926th Plenary Meeting.* UN Doc. A/PV.926 (28 November 1960), 1002.

### VII. Official Reports

**Great Britain.** *Special Report on the Progress of Iraq, 1920–1931*. Colonial Office No. 58. London: H.M.S.O., 1931.

Dowson, Ernest. *An Inquiry into Land Tenure and Related Questions: Proposals for the Initiation of Reform,* (London: Garden City Press, 1931).

*Why Labour Leaves the Land: A Comparative Study of the Movement of Labour Out of Agriculture*, (Geneva: International Labour Office, 1960).

C.W.H. Weaver. "Impressions of a Visit to India, Iraq, Persia, and Turkey", *International Labour Review*, Vol.XXVIII, No.4, October 1933.

**Great Britain.** *Report by His Britannic Majesty's Government on the Administration of Iraq for the Period April 1923–December 1924*. Cmd. 2317. London: His Majesty's Stationery Office, 1925.

**Great Britain.** *Report by His Britannic Majesty's Government on the Administration of Iraq for the Period January–December 1924*. Cmd. 2318. London: His Majesty's Stationery Office, 1925.

Naval Intelligence Division. *Iraq and the Persian Gulf* (B.R. 524, Geographical Handbook Series, September 1944).

Iraq Petroleum Co. *An Account of the Construction in the years 1932 to 1934 of the Pipe-line of the Iraq Petroleum Company, limited, from its oilfield in the vicinity of Kirkuk, Iraq to the Mediterranean ports of Haifa (Palestine) and Tripoli (Lebanon)*, (London, St. Clements Press, 1934).

Iraqi State Railways. *Report on the Administration of the Railways*, 1945–46, (Baghdad: September 1st, 1947).

Iraq Police Reports, *A Secret Encyclopedia Concerning the Secret Iraqi Communist Party* (*Mawsu'a siriyya khāṣa bi'l hizb al-shuyu'ī al-'iraqī al-Sirī*); 1949 (Baghdad: Maktaba al-Nahda al-'Arabiya).

**VIII. Secondary Sources:**

'Abdul Hādī, Haydar. *Dirāsāt fi Qānūn al-Hūqūq al-Insān* [Studies in Human Rights Law], (Ammān: Dār al-Hamad, 2009).

Abdullah, Thabit. *Merchants, Mamluks, and Murder: The Political Economy of Trade in Eighteenth-Century Basra*, (New York: SUNY Press, 2001).

——, *Dictatorship, Imperialism and Chaos: Iraq since 1989*, (London: Zed Books, 2006).

Ahmed, Kamāl Mūzhir. *al-Tabaqa al-'umāliya al-'Iraqiyya: al-takkauwwn wa bidāyāt al-haraka* [The Iraqi Working Class: Its formation and the beginnings of its movement]; (Baghdad, Dar al-Rashid, 1981).

Alcock, Antony. *History of the International Labour Organisation* (London: Macmillan, 1971).

Alexandrowicz, C.H., *An Introduction to the History of the Law of Nations in the East Indies* (Oxford: Clarendon Press, 1967).

Alexandersson, Gunner and Norstrom, Goran. *World Shipping: An Economic Geography of Ports and Seaborne Trade* (New York: John Woley & Sons, 1963).

Althusser, Louis. *For Marx*, (London: Verso, 2005).

Anand, R.P. "Attitude of the Asian-African States Towards Certain Problems of international Law," in Snyder, FE and Sathirathai, S (eds.), *Third World Attitudes Toward International Law: An Introduction*, Dordrecht: Martinus Nijhoff Publishers, 1987).

Anghie, Antony. "The Evolution of International Law: colonial and postcolonial realities," *Third World Quarterly*, Vol. 27, (2008): 739–753.

——. 'Introduction to Symposium on the Many Lives and Legacies of Sykes-Picot', September 28, 2016, *AJIL Unbound*, https://www.asil.org/blogs/introduction-symposium-many-lives-and-legacies-sykes-picot.

——. *Imperialism, Sovereignty and the Making of International Law*, (Cambridge: Cambridge University Press, 2004).

——. '*The Heart of My Home*: Colonialism, Environmental Damage, and the Nauru Case', (1993) 34 *Harvard International Law Journal* No. 2, 445–506.

Antonius, George. *The Arab Awakening: The Story of the Arab National Movement* (New York: Capricorn Books, 1965).

Arrighi, Giovanni. *Semiperipheral Development: the politics of Southern Europe in the Twentieth Century*, (London: Sage, 1985).

Atabaki, Touraj. 'Chronicles of a Calamitous Strike Foretold: Abadan, July 1946' in Roth, Karl Heinz (ed.), *On the Road to Global Labour: A Festschrift for Marcel van der Linden* (Leiden: Brill, 2017), 93–128.

Atiyyah, Ghassan. *Iraq: 1908–1921. A Socio-Political Study*, (Beirut: The Arab Institute for Research and Publishing, 1973).

Azaria, Danae. *Treaties on Transit of Energy via Pipelines and Countermeasures* (Oxford: Oxford University Press, 2015).

al-Azzawi, Fadhil. *The Last of the Angels*, (tr. William M. Hutchins), (New York: Free Press, 2007).

Baali, Fuad. *Relation of the People to the Land in Southern Iraq*, (Gainesville: University of Florida Press, 1966).

Badre, Albert and Siksek, Simon. *Manpower and Oil in the Arab World*, (Westport: Hyperion Press, 1960).

al-Baharna, Hussein. *The Legal Status of the Arabian Gulf States*, (Manchester: Manchester University Press, 1968).

Bailey, Clinton. *Bedouin Law from Sinai & the Negev: Justice without Government*. (New Haven: Yale University Press, 2009).

Balfour-Paul, Glen. 'Britain's Informal Empire in the Middle East' in Brown and Louis, Wm Roger (eds.), *The Oxford History of the British Empire: Volume IV: The Twentieth, Judith Century* (Oxford: Oxford University Press, 1999), 490–514.

Bamberg, J.H. *The History of the British Petroleum Company: Volume 2, The Anglo-Iranian Years, 1928–1954*, (Cambridge: Cambridge University Press, 1994).

al-Barāzī, Nurī Khalīl. *Al-Badāwa wa al-Istiqrār fī al-ʿIraq* (The Bedouin and Settlement in Iraq), (Cairo: Mʿahad Biḥūth wa al-Dirāsāt al-ʿArabīya, 1969).

Barkey, Karen. "Aspects of Legal Pluralism in the Ottoman Empire," in Lauren Benton and Richard J. Ross (eds.), *Legal Pluralism and Empires, 1500–1850* (New York: New York University Press, 2013).

Barr, James. *A Line in the Sand: The Anglo-French Struggle for the Middle East*, (London: W.W. Norton & Co, 2012).

Barton, Sir William. *India's North-West Frontier*, (London: John Murray, 1939).

Bashkin, Orit. "A Patriotic Uprising: Baghdadi Jews and the Wathba," in Fuccaro, Nelida (ed.), *Violence and the City in the Modern Middle East*, (Stanford: Stanford University Press, 2016), 151–167.

Batatu, Hanna 'Of the Diversity of Iraqis, the Incohesiveness of their Society and their Progression …' in Hourani, Albert and Khoury, Philip S. (eds.), *The Middle East: A Reader*, (Berkley: University of California Press, 1993).

——. *The Old Social Classes and the Revolutionary Movements of Iraq: A Study of Iraq's Old Landed and Commercial Classes and of its Communists, Baʿthists and Free Officers*, (London: Saqi Books, 2004).

al-Bāzi, Hāmid. al-*Basrah fi Fatrah al-Muzlimah* [Basra in the Unjust Era] (Basrah: Dar Manshourāt al-Basrah, 1969).

Buchanan, George. *The Tragedy of Mesopotamia* (Edinburgh: William Blackwood, 1938).

al-Būti, Faʾq. *Mawsuʿa al-Saḥafīya al-ʿIraqīya* [The Encyclopedia of Iraqi Journalism], Baghdad: al-Mada, 2010).

Bunton, Martin (2023, August 10). Dowson, Sir Ernest MacLeod (1876–1950), colonial administrator and expert on land registration. *Oxford Dictionary of National Biography*. Retrieved 30 Jul. 2025, from https://www.oxforddnb.com/view/10.1093/ref:odnb/9780198614128.001.0001/odnb-9780198614128-e-54674.

——. "Inventing the Status Quo: Ottoman Land-Law during the Palestine Mandate, 1917–1936," *The International History Review*, 21:1, 28–56.

——. *Colonial Land Policies in Palestine 1917–1936* (Oxford: Oxford University Press, 2007).

Baxi, Upendra. 'What may the "Third World" expect from International Law' *Third World Quarterly*, (2006), Vol. 27, No. 5, pp.713–725.

al-Bayāti, ʿAbdul Rahmān. *Saīd al-Qazzāz wa Dourihū fī Sīyāsa al-ʿIraq* [Said al-Qazzaz and his role in Iraqi politics], (Beirūt: Muʾasasa al- ʿArabīya lil-Dirāsa wa al-Nashir, 2001).

Bedjaoui, Mohammed. *Towards A New International Economic Order: New Challenges to International Law*, (New York: Holmes & Meier, 1979).

Beer, George Louis. *African Questions at the Paris Peace Conference with Papers on Egypt, Mesopotamia, and the Colonial Settlement* (London: Macmillan, 1923).

Behal, Rana P. and Van der Linden, Marcel (eds.) *Coolies, Capital and Colonialism: Studies in Indian Labour History* (Cambridge: Cambridge University Press, 2006).

Bell, Morag; Butlin, Robin; and Heffernan, Michael (eds.). *Geography and Imperialism 1820–1940*, (Manchester: Manchester University Press, 1994).

Benjamin, Walter. 'Theses on the Philosophy of History,' in Arendt, Hannah (ed.), *Illuminations: Essays and Reflections*, (New York: Schocken, 1969).

Benney, Mark. 'Gramsci on law, morality, and power,' *International Journal of Sociology of Law*, 1983, 11(2), 205.

Benton, Lauren. "From International Law to Imperial Constitutions: The Problem of Quasi-Sovereignty, 1870–1900", *Law and History Review*, Vol. 26, issue 3, pp.595–619 (2008).

Benton, Lauren and Ford, Lisa. *Rage For Order: The British Empire and the Origins of International Law, 1800–1850* (Cambridge: Harvard University Press, 2016).

Bentwich, Norman. *The Mandates System*, (London: Longmans 1930).

——. "The Termination of the A Mandates', (Max-Planck Institut für ausländisches öffentliches Recht und Völkerrecht, 1933), http://www.zaoerv.de/03_1933/3_1933_1_a_176_191.pdf.

Berman, Nathaniel. *Passion and Ambivalence: Colonialism, Nationalism, and International Law* (Leiden: Martinus Nijhoff Publishers, 2011).

Berry, Willard. *Aspects of the Frontiers Crimes Regulation in Pakistan*, (Duke University Commonwealth Studies Center, Monograph number three, 1966).

Bet-Shlimon, Arbella. "The Politics and Ideology of Urban Development in Iraq's Oil City: Kirkuk, 1946–58," *Comparative Studies of South Asia, Africa and the Middle East*, Vol.33, No.1, 2013.

——. *City of Black Gold: Oil, Ethnicity and the Making of Modern Kikruk* (Stanford: Stanford University Press, 2019).

Bhandar, Brenna. *Colonial Lives of Property: Law, Land, and Racial Regimes of Ownership* (Durham: Duke University Press, 2018).

Biermann, Werner. *Tanganyika Railways – Carrier of Colonialism* (Münster: LIT Verlag, 1995).

Bishara, Fahad Ahmad. *A Sea of Debt: Law and Economic Life in the Western Indian Ocean 1780–1950* (Cambridge: Cambridge University Press, 2017).

Blomley, Nicholas. *Law, Space and the Geographies of Power* (New York: Guilford Press, 1994).

Bonné, Alfred. "The Concession for the Mosul-Haifa Pipe Line," *The Annals of the American Academy of Political and Social Science*, Vol. 164, Nov. 1932, 116–126.

Bonnie, Michael; Amanat, Abbas and Ezekiel, Michael Gasper (eds). *Is there a Middle East? The Evolution of a Geopolitical Concept*, (Stanford: Stanford University Press, 2012).

Borges, Marcelo J and Tores, Susana B. 'Company towns: Concepts, Historiography, and Approaches' in Borges and Tores (eds.), *Company Towns: Labor, Space, and Power Relations across Time and Continents* (Basingstoke: Palgrave Mcmillan, 2012).

Bozarslan, Hamit "Rethinking the Ba'thist Period" in Tejel, Jordi; Sluglett, Peter; Bocco, Riccardo; Bozarslan, Hamit (eds.), *Writing the Modern History of Iraq: Historiographical and Political Challenges* (Hackensack, NJ: World Scientific Publishing), 143–153.

Brown, L. Carl. *Diplomacy in the Middle East: The International Relations of Regional and Outside Powers* (London: I.B. Taurus, 2001).

Brown, Nathan. "Constitutionalism, Authoritarianism, and Imperialism in Iraq," *Drake Law Review*, Vol. 53 (2005).

Bruce, Colonel C.E. "The Sandeman Policy as Applied to Tribal Problems of To-day," (1932) *Journal of the Royal Central Asian Society*, 19:1, 45–67.

Buckel, S. and Fischer-Lescano, A. "Gramsci Reconsidered: Hegemony in Global Law," *Leiden Journal of International Law*, 22, (2009), 437–454.

Butlin, Robin A. *Geographies of Empire: European Empires and Colonies c. 1880–1960* (Cambridge, MA: Cambridge University Press, 2009).

Byford, Cecil. *The Port of Basrah Iraq*, (Published under the authority of the Port of Basrah Directorate, London: Waterlow & Sons, 1935).

Cain, Maureen. "Gramsci, The State and the Place of the Law" in Sugarman, David (ed.) *Legality, Ideology and the State* (London: Academic Press, 1983).

Capua, J.V. 'The Early History of Martial Law in England from the Fourteenth Century to the Petition of Right,' 36:1 *Cambridge Law Journal* (1977).

Caractacus (pseudonym). *Revolution in Iraq: An Essay in Comparative Public Opinion* (London: Gollancz, 1959).

Cardoso, Fernando H. and Faletto, Enrique. *Dependencia y desarrollo en America Latina* (Mexico City: Siglo XXI, 1979).

Caroe, Olaf. *Wells of Power: The Oilfields of South-Western Asia, A Regional and Global Study*, (London: Macmillan & Co, 1951).

Cattan, Henry. *The Evolution of Oil Concessions in the Middle East and North Africa*, (New York: Oceana Press, 1976).

Ceylan, Ebubekir. *The Ottoman Origins of Modern Iraq: Political Reform, Modernization and Development in the Nineteenth Century Middle East*, (London: IB Tauris, 2011).

Chādirjī, Rifʿat. *fī Haqq Mumārasa al-Sīyāsa wa al-Dīmuqrātīya: Iftītāhāt Jarīda al-Ahālī, 1944–1954* [The right to pursue politics & democracy: the openings of *al-Ahali* newspaper], 1944–1954), (Koln: al-Jamal, 2003).

al-Chādirjī, Kāmil. *Mudhakkirāt Kāmil al-Chādirjī wa Tārīkh al-Hizb al-Watanī al-Dīmuqrātī [The Memoirs of Kamil al-Chadirji and the History of the National Democratic Party]* (Beirut: Dar al-Ṭalīʿa, 1970).

Chakrabarty, Dipesh. "Subaltern Studies and Postcolonial Historiography," *Nepantla: Views from South* 1:1 (2000).

Chanock, Martin. *Law, Custom and Social Order: The Colonial Experience in Malawi and Zambia*, (Cambridge: Cambridge University Press, 1985).

Chimni, B.S. "Third World Approaches to International Law: A Manifesto," *International Community Law Review* 8, 3–27, (2006).

Chowdhuri, R.N. *International Mandates and Trusteeship Systems*, (The Hague: Martinus Nijhoff, 1955).

Clavin, Patricia. *Securing the World Economy: Securing the League of Nations, 1920–1946* (Cambridge: Cambridge University Press, 2015).

Clulow, Adam; Attwood, Bain; and Benton, Lauren (eds.). *Protection and Empire: A Global History* (Cambridge University Press, 2018).

Cooper, Fredrick. 'Dockworkers and labour history' in Sam Davies, Colin J. Davis, David de Vries, Lex Heerma van Voss, Lidewij Hesselink and Klaus Weinhauer (eds.), *Dock Workers: International Explorations in Comparative Labour History 1790–1970, Volume 1* (Basingstoke: Ashgate, 1970), pp. 423–541.

Collins, John M. *Martial Law and English Laws, c. 1500–c.1700* (Cambridge: Cambridge University Press, 2016).

Cowen, Deborah. 'Law as Infrastructure of Colonial Space: Sketches from Turtle Island' 117 *AJIL Unbound* (2023).

Critchley, A. Michael. "The Health of the Industrial Worker in Iraq," *British Journal of industrial Medicine* 12.1 (January 1955): 73–75.

Crook, Wilfrid H. *Communism and the General Strike* (London: Shoe String Press, 1960).

Cullinane, Michael Patrick; and Goodall, Alex. *The Open Door Era: United States Foreign Policy in the Twentieth Century* (Edinburgh: Edinburgh University Press, 2017).

Dalleo, Raphael. "The Independence So Hardly Won has Been Maintained": C.L.R. James and the U.S. Occupation of Haiti,' *Cultural Critique* 87, Spring 2014, pp. 38–59.

Daughton, JP. *In the Forest of No Joy: The Congo-Ocean Railway and the Tragedy of French Colonialism* (New York: W.W. Norton, 2021).

Davis, Eric. "History for the Many or History for the Few? The Historiography of the Iraqi Working Class," in *Workers and Working Classes in the Middle East*, Lockman, Z. (ed.), (New York: SUNY Press, 1994), 271–301.

Davis, Calrence B. and Wilburn, Kenneth E. Jr, with Robinson, Ronald E. (eds.), *Railway Imperialism* (Westport, CT: Greenwood Press, 1991).

DeNovo, John A. *American Interests and Policies in the Middle East 1900–1939* (Minneapolis: University of Minnesota Press, 1963).

Dewachi, Omar. *Ungovernable Life: Mandatory Medicine and Statecraft in Iraq* (Stanford, CA: Stanford University Press, 2017).

Dicey, A.V. *Introduction to the Study of the Law of the Constitution*, (8th ed. London: Macmillan, 1915).

Dietl, Gulshan. *The Global Game of Oil Pipelines* (London: Routledge, 2022).

Dietrich, Christopher. *Oil Revolution: Anticolonial Elites, Sovereign Rights and the Economic Culture of Decolonization* (Oxford: Oxford University Press, 2017).

Dodge, Toby. *Inventing Iraq: The Failure of Nation Building and a History Denied*, (New York: Columbia University Press, 2003).

Dunning, Thad and Wirpsa, Leslie. "Oil and the Political Economy of Conflict in Colombia and Beyond: A Linkage Approach" *Geopolitics*, Vol. 9, No. 1 (Spring 2004), 81–108.

Earle, Edward Mead. *Turkey, the Great Powers, and the Baghdad Railway: a Study in Imperialism*, (New York: Russell & Russell, 1966).

Ehasani, Kaveh. 'Social Engineering and the Contradictions of Modernization in Khuzestan's Company Towns: A Look at Abadan and Masjed-Soleyman' *International Review of Social History* Vol. 48, No. 3 (December 2003), 361–399.

El-Ayouty, Yasin. *The United Nations and Decolonization: The Role of Afro-Asia*, (The Hague: Martinus Nijhoff, 1971).

Elkins, Caroline. *Legacy of Violence: A History of The British Empire* (New York: Knopf, 2022).

Elm, Mostafa. *Oil, Power and Principle: Iran's Oil Natinalization and its Aftermath* (Syracuse, NY: Syracuse University Press, 1992).

Elwell-Sutton, EL. *Persian Oil: A Study in Power Politics* (London: Lawrence & Wishart, 1955).

Eslava, Luis and Pahuja, Sundhja. "Beyond the (Post)Colonial: TWAIL and the Everyday Life of International Law", *Journal of Law and Politics in Africa, Asia and Latin America – Verfassung und Recht in Übersee (VRÜ)*, Vol. 45(2), 2012.

——. "Between Resistance and Reform: TWAIL and the Universality of International Law," 3(1) *Trade, Law and Development*, 103 (2011).

Esmeir, Samera. "On Coloniality of Modern Law," *Critical Analysis of Law*, 2:1 (2015).

Fakhri, Michael. *Sugar and the Making of International Law* (Cambridge: Cambridge University Press, 2014).

Fanning, Leonard M. *Foreign Oil and the Free World* (New York: McGraw-Hill Book Co., 1954).

Farouk-Sluglett, Marion and Sluglett, Peter. "The Transformation of land Tenure and Rural Social Structure in Central and Southern Iraq, c. 1870–1958," *International Journal of Middle East Studies* 15 (1983), pp.491–505.

——. "The Social Classes and the Origins of the Revolution," in Robert Fernea and Roger Louis (eds.) *The Iraqi Revolution of 1958: The Old Social Classes Revisited*, (London: IB Tauris, 1991), pp. 118–142.

——. "Labor and National Liberation: the Trade Union Movement in Iraq, 1920–1958", *Arab Studies Quarterly*, 5, 2, 1983.

Fattah, Hala. *The Politics of Regional Trade in Iraq, Arabia, and the Gulf 1745–1900*, (New York: SUNY, 1997).

Fawaz, Leila Tarazi and Bayly, C.A. (eds.), *Modernity and Culture: From Mediterranean to the Indian Ocean* (New York: Columbia University Press, 2002).

Ferguson, James. "Seeing Like an Oil Company: Space, Security, and Global Capital in Neoliberal Africa," *American Anthropologist*, Vol 7, Issue, pp. 377–382.

Fernea, Robert. *Shaykh and Effendi: Changing Patterns of Authority Among El Shabana of Southern Iraq*, (1970) (Cambridge, MA: Harvard University Press).

Fields, Gary. *Enclosure: Palestinian Landscapes in a Historical Mirror* (Berkeley, CA: University of California Press, 2017).

Finocchiaro, Maurice. *Gramsci and the History of Dialectical Thought* (Cambridge: Cambridge University Press, 2002).

Fischbach, Michael R. *State, Society and Land in Jordan* (Leiden: Brill, 2000).

Fisher, John. *Curzon and British Imperialism in the Middle East 1916–19* (London: Frank Cass, 1999).

Fitzmaurice, Andrew. *Sovereignty, Property and Empire, 1500–2000* (Cambridge: Cambridge University Press, 2014).

Fitzpatrick, Peter. *Law and State in Papua New Guinea*, (London: Academic Press, 1980).

Fitzsimons, Matthew. *Empire by Treaty: Britain and the Middle East in the Twentieth Century* (Ann Arbor, MI: University of Michigan Press, 1964).

Fletcher, Robert S. G. *British Imperialism and 'The Tribal Question': Desert Administration and Nomadic Societies in the Middle East, 1919–1936* (Oxford: Oxford University Press, 2015).

Foliard, Daniel. *Dislocating the Orient: British Maps and the Making of the Middle East, 1854–1921* (Chicago: University of Chicago Press, 2017).
Forman, Geremy. "Settlement of Title in the Galilee: Dowson's Colonial Guiding Principles" *Israel Studies*, Fall 2002, Vol. 7, No. 3 (Fall, 2002), pp.61–83; 63.
Franzen, Johan. *Red Star Over Iraq: Iraqi Communism before Saddam* (London: Columbia/Hurst, 2011).
——. *Pride and Power: A Modern History of Iraq* (London: Hurst, 2020).
Fuccaro, Nelida. "Reading Oil as Urban Violence: Kirkuk and its Oil Conurbation, 1927–58," in Freitag, Ulrike; Fuccaro, Nelida; Ghrawi, Claudia & Lafi, Nora; (Eds.), *Urban Violence in the Middle East: Changing Cityscapes in the Transition from Empire into Nation State*, (New York: Berghahn, 2015), 222–242.
——. 'Arab Towns As Petro-Histories' in *Oil Spaces: Exploring the Global Petroleumscape* (London: Routledge, 2022), 129–144; 130.
Furedi, Frank. "Creating a Breathing Space: The Political Management of Colonial Emergencies," in Holland, Robert (ed.) *Emergencies and Disorder in the European Empires after 1945*, (London: Frank Cass, 1994).
——. *Colonial Wars and the Politics of Third World Nationalism*, (London: I.B. Tauris, 1994).
Garner, John (ed.), *The Company Town: Architecture and Society in the Early Industrial Age* (Oxford: Oxford University Press, 1992).
Gathii, James. "TWAIL: A Brief History of its Origins, its Decentralized Network, and a tentative Bibliography," 3(1) *Trade Law and Development*, (2011): 26.
Gerber, Haim. *The Social Origins of the Modern Middle East*, (London: Mansell Publishing, 1987).
Gerig, Benjamin. *The Open Door and the Mandate System: A Study of Economic Equality before and since the establishment of the Mandates System*, (London: George Allen & Unwin, 1930).
Getachew, Adom. *Worldmaking after Empire: The Rise and Fall of Self-Determination* (New Jersey: Princeton University Press, 2019).
Glanday, Daniel. 'Le Domaine Colonial: Class Formation in a Natural Resource Enclave,' *The Canadian Journal of Sociology* 9,2 (Spring 1984): 159–77.
Gordon, Robert W. "Critical Legal Histories", (1984) *Stanford Law Review*, 36:57.
Grafton, Anthony. *What was History? The art of history in early modern Europe*, (Cambridge: Cambridge University Press, 2007).
Gramsci, Antonio. *Selections from the Prison Notebooks*, Hoare, Q (ed.), (New York: International Publishers, 1971).
Grovogui, Siba N'zatioula. *Sovereigns, Quasi-Sovereigns, and Africans: Race and Self-Determination in International Law* (Minneapolis: University of Minnesota Press, 1996).
Guha, Ranajit. "Introduction," *Selected Subaltern Studies* (New York: Oxford University Press, 1988).
——. *A Rule of Property for Bengal: An Essay on the Idea of Permanent Settlement*, (New Dehli: Oreint Longman, 1982).
——. *Dominance without Hegemony: History and Power in Colonial India*, (Cambridge, MA: Harvard University Press, 1997).
Haider, Fayez. "Mehdi (Shanwar) Oūda : Qa'id ʿumālī Ṣalib wa Masīra Yathkurūhā al-Tārīkh" ('Mehdi (Shanwar) Ouda: A steadfast labour leader and a march remembered by history'), *al-Ḥiwār al-Mutamadin*, 2009/6/5, (http://www.ahewar.org/debat/show.art.asp?aid=174173).
Haj, Samira. "The problems of tribalism: the case of nineteenth-century Iraqi history," *Social History*, (1991) Vol. 16: No. 1, pp.45–58.
——. *The Making of Iraq 1900–1963*, (New York: SUNY Press, 1997).
al-Hājj, ʿAzīz. *Dafātir al-Shakhis al-Ākhir*, (Notebooks of the Other Person) (Beirut: Muʾsasa al-ʿArabiya li al-dirāsāt wa al-Nashir, 1985).
Hall, Duncan. *Mandates, Dependencies and Trusteeships* (Washington DC: Carnegie Endowment for International Peace, 1948).

Hammoudi. Ali. "International Order and Racial Capitalism: The Standardization of 'Free Labour' Exploitation in International Law" *Leiden Journal of International Law*; Volume 35, Number 4, December 2022, 779–799.

——. 'The International Law of Informal Empire and the "Question of Oman"' *TWAIL Review*, Issue 1 (2020) 121–151.

Hardt, Michael and Negri, Antonio. *Empire*, (Cambridge, MA: Harvard University Press, 2000).

Harvey, David. *The Limits of Capital*, (London: Verso, 1999).

——. *Spaces of Global Capitalism: A Theory of Uneven Geographical Development* (London: Verso, 2006).

al-Hasani, 'Abdul Razzāq. *Tārīkh al-Wīzārāt al-ʿIrāqīya* (The History of the Iraqi Cabinets), Vols. 3, 6, 7, 8 (Sidon: Matbaʿat al- ʿrfān, 1953).

Hast, Susanna. *Spheres of Influence in International Relations* (Oxford: Ashgate, 2014).

Hughes, Matthew. *Britain's Pacification of Palestine: The British Army, the Colonial State, and the Arab Revolt, 1936–1939* (Cambridge: Cambridge University Press, 2019).

Hazbun, Waleed. 'The Middle East Through the Lens of Critical Geopolitics' in Bonine, Michael; Amanat, Abbas & Gasper, Michael (eds.), *Is there a Middle East? The Evolution of a Geopolitical Concept* (Stanford, CA: Stanford University Press, 2012).

Head, Michael. *Emergency Powers: Theory and Practice* (Surrey: Ashgate, 2016).

Hein, Carola. 'Space, Time, and Oil: The Global Petroleumscape' in C Hein (ed.), *Oil Spaces: Exploring the Global Petroleumscape* (New York: Routledge, 2022).

Helmreich, Paul C. *From Paris To Sèvres: The Partition of the Ottoman Empire at the Peace Conference of 1919–1920* (Columbus: Ohio State University Press, 1974).

Hodge, Joseph Morgan. *Triumph of the Expert: Agrarian Doctrines of Development and the Legacies of British Colonies*, (Athens, OH: Ohio University Press, 2007).

Hoebel, E. Adamson. *The Law of Primitive Man: A Study in Comparative Legal Dynamics*, (Cambridge, MA: Harvard University Press, 1954).

Holland, RL (ed.). *Emergencies and Disorder in the European Colonies After 1945* (Abingdon, UK: Taylor and Francis, 2012).

Home, Robert. "Scientific survey and land settlement in British colonialism, with particular reference to land tenure reform in the Middle East 1920–1950" *Planning Perspectives*, 21:1, 1–22.

Hooper, C.A. *The Constitutional Law of Iraq*, (Baghdad: McKenzie & McKenzie, 1928).

Howell, E.B. "The Qanun Al Aradhi" (1922) in *Journal of The Royal Central Asian Society*, 9:1, 21–39.

Hopkins, Benjamin D. *Ruling the Savage Periphery: Frontier Governance and the Making of the Modern State* (Cambridge, MA: Harvard University Press, 2020).

Horowitz, Richard S. 'International Law and State Transformation in China, Siam, and the Ottoman Empire during the Nineteenth Century' (2004) 15 *J World Hist* 445.

Hoskins, Halford. *British Routes to India* (London: Longmans, Green & Co, 1928).

Hourani, George Fadlo. *Arab Seafaring in the Indian Ocean in Ancient and Early Medieval Times* (Princeton, NJ: Princeton University Press, 1951).

Howland, Douglas R. (2020) "State Title to Territory – The Historical Conjunction of Sovereignty and Property" *Beijing Law Review*, 11, 856–878.

Hughes, Hugh. *Middle East Railways* (Kenton: The Continental Railway Circle, 1981).

Hūmaīdī, Jaʿfar ʿAbbās. *Al-Taṭwūrāt al-Syāsīya fī al-ʿIraq, 1941–1953* ['The Political Developments in Iraq, 1941–1953'], (al-Najaf: Ma ṭbʿat al-Niʿmān, 1976).

al-Hūmeid, Shahāb Ahmed. *al-Thawra al-Ṣāmita: Idrāb Baghdad 1931* (The Silent Revolution: The Baghdad Strike of 1931), (Baghdad, n.d.).

Hurewitz, J.C. *Diplomacy in the Near and Middle East*, (New York: Van Nostrad, 1958).

Hūsayn, Muhammad Tawfīq. *Nihāyat al-Iqtāʿ fī al-ʿIraq:* (The End of Feudalism in Iraq: *A study of the conditions of the Iraqi peasant & the Agrarian Reform Law*), (Beirut: Dar al-ʿlim lil-malayeen, 1958).

Hussein, Nasser. *The Jurisprudence of Emergency: Colonialism and the Rule of Law*, (Ann Arbor: University of Michigan Press, 2003).

Hussein, Resān. Idhrāb Gāwūrbāghī: Mūthīra Nidhālīya Kabīra' ('The Gawurbaghi Strike: a great tragic struggle'), *Tarīq al-Sha'ab*, Issue 230, July 12, 2015.

Ibrahīm, 'Abdul Fatāh. *'Ala Ṭarīq al-Hind* [The Route to India], first published in 1935, (Dīmashq: Manshūrāt Wizarat al-Thaqāfa, 1991).

Ince, Godfrey. *The Ministry of Labour and National Service*, (London: George Allen & Unwin Ltd, 1960).

Ingold, Tim. *Lines: A Brief History* (London: Routledge, 2007).

Irby, Joseph K. "Aspects of *Musha* Land Tenure in Lebanon" *Yearbook of the Association of Pacific Coast Geographers*, Volume 33, 1971, 153–160.

Ireland, Phillip. *Iraq: A Study in Political Development* (New York: The McMillian Co, 1938).

Issa, Ali. *Against All Odds: Voices of Popular Struggle in Iraq* (Tadween Publishing, 2015).

Jamali, Mohammed Fadhil. *The New Iraq: Its Problem of Bedouin Education*, (New York City: The International Institute of Teachers College, Columbia University, 1934).

James, C.L.R. *The Black Jacobins: Toussaint L'Ouverture and the San Domingo Revolution* (New York: Vintage, 1989).

Jamīl, Hussein. *Al-Aḥkām al-'Urfiyya: Baḥith Fiqhī* [Martial Law: A Doctrinal Analysis], (Baghdad: Ma ṭba'a al-'Ani, 1953).

——. *Huqūq al-Insān wa al-Qānūn al-Jinā'i* [Human Rights and the Criminal Law], (Ma'ahad al-Bihūth wa al-Dirāsāt al-'Arabīya, 1972).

Jamīl, Maki. *T'alīqāt 'ala Nithām Di'āwy al-'ashā'ir wa T'adīlātahu* [A commentary on the Tribal Criminal and Civil Disputes Regulation and its amendments], (Baghdād: Matba'a al-Karakh, 1935).

Jayyusi, Salma Khadra. *Trends and Movements in Modern Arabic Poetry* (Leiden: Brill, 1997).

al-Jawāhiri, 'Imād Ahmad. *Tārīkh Mushkīlat al-'Arādi fī al-'Iraq wa Dirāsa fī Tatawurāt al-'Āma* [The history of land problems in Iraq c. 1914–1932], (Baghdad: Wizārat al-Thaqāfa wa al-Funūn, 1978).

Jenks, C. Wilfred. *Social Justice in the Law of Nations: The ILO Impact After Fifty Years* (Oxford: Oxford University Press, 1970).

Jenkins, Edward C. 'Economic Equality and the Mandates Commission' *Journal of Political Economy*, Vol. 37, No. 5 (Oct., 1929), 604–616.

Jones, Henry. (2019) "Property, territory, and colonialism: an international legal history of enclosures," *Legal Studies*, 39 (2), pp. 187–203.

Jones, Kevin M. "Unmaking the Middle Eastern working classes: labour and the politics of historiography", *Social History*, 2015, Vol. 40, No. 2, 145–156.

——. "A horizon lit with blood: public poetry and mass politics in Iraq," *Social History*, 2014, Vol. 39, No 4, 443–461.

——. *The Dangers of Poetry: Culture, Politics, and Revolution in Iraq* (Stanford: Stanford University Press, 2020).

Jouannet, Emmanuelle. *The Liberal-Welfarist Law of Nations: A History of International Law* (Cambridge, MA: Cambridge University Press, 2012).

Jwaideh, Albertine. "Aspects of land tenure and social change in lower Iraq during late ottoman times" in Tarif Khalidi (ed.), *Land Tenure and Social Transformation in the Middle East*, (Beirut: American University of Beirut, 1984).

——. "Midhat Pasha and the Land System of Lower Iraq,' (1963) in St. Antony's Papers Vol. XVI, *Middle Eastern Affairs* No. 3, pp. 106–137, London.

——. "Tribalism and Modern Society: Iraq, a Case Study" in R.M. Savory, ed., *Introduction to Islamic Civilization*, (Cambridge: Cambridge University Press, 1976).

Khalili, Laleh. *Sinews of War and Trade: Shipping and Capitalism in the Arabian Peninsula* (London: Verso, 2020).

Kamil, Mustafa. *Sharḥ al-Qānūn al-'Idāri al-'Iraqi* [A commentary on the administrative law of Iraq], (Baghdad: Matba' al-Najah, 1949).

Karuka, Manu. *Empire's Tracks: Indigenous Nations, Chinese Workers and the Transcontinental Railroad* (Berkeley, CA: University of California Press, 2019).
Kayaoglu, Turan. *Legal Imperialism: Sovereignty and Extraterritoriality in Japan, the Ottoman Empire and China*, (Cambridge: Cambridge University Press, 2015).
al-Kāzami, Nasīr Saīd [pseudonym for Aziz Sbāhī]. *Musāhama fī Kitabat Tarīkh al-Haraka al-ʿUmālīya fī al-ʿIraq hata 1958* (An attempt in writing the history of the workers' movement in Iraq until 1958), (Damascus: Centre for the Research of Socialist Studies in the Arab World, 1991).
Kedourie, Elie. *In the Anglo-Arab Labyrinth: the MacMahon-Husayn Correspondence and its Interpretations, 1914–1939* (London: Routledge, 2000).
Kennedy, William J. (ed.), *Secret History of the Oil Companies in the Middle East* (Salisbury, NC: Documentary Publications, 1979).
Kennedy, David. "A Move to Institutions," (1987) 8 *Cardozo Law Review* 841–988.
Kennedy, Duncan. "Antonio Gramsci and the Legal System," *American Legal Studies Forum*, (1982), 6(1), 32–37.
Kent, Marian. *Oil and Empire: British Policy and Mesopotamian Oil, 1900–1920*, (London: Macmillan, 1976).
Khayrī, Suʿād. *Min Tārīkh al-Ḥaraka al-Watanīya* [From the history of the Nationalist Movement], (Baghdad, 1975).
Khayrī, Zaki and Khayrī, Suʿād. *Dirāsāt fī Tārīkh al-Hizb al-Shīūʿi al-ʿIraqī*, [Studies in the history of the Iraqi Communist Party, Vol. 1], (Baghdad: al-Yūbil al-Thahabī, 1984).
Khayyat, Jaʿfar "al-Tatawur al-tārīkhi li-hiyazat al-ardh wa ʿlaqāt al-mūlkīya fi al-rīf al-ʿIraqi" [The historical development of landholding and ownership relations in rural Iraq], *Al-Iqtisādi* (Baghdad), 1970, Vol. 11, No. 2.
Khudayyir, Mohammed. *Basrayatha: Portrait of a City*, William Hutchins (tr), (Cairo: American University of Cairo Press, 2007).
Kingsbury, Benedict. "Introduction to the Symposium on the Infrastructuring of International Law" 117 *AJIL Unboud* (2023).
Kingston, Paul. *Britain and the politics of modernization in the Middle East, 1945–1958* (Cambridge: Cambridge University Press: 1996).
Kirasirova, Masha. "The Partisans of Peace in Lebanon and Syria: How Anti-Nuclear Acitivism in the 1950s Revitalized the Arab Left" *International Journal of Middle East Studies* (2023), 55, 650–674.
Klieman, Aaron. *Foundations of British Policy in the Arab World: The Cairo Conference of 1921.* (Baltimore, MD: John Hopkins Press, 1970).
Knox, Robert. "Marxism, International Law, and Political Strategy", *Leiden Journal of International Law*, 22 (2009), pp. 413–436.
Kohāri, Hirmuz. "Taḥiya Ijlal wa Kībār al-shūhadā' al-Ṭabaqa al-ʿUmalīya" [A homage to the great martyrs of the working class], in *al-Ḥīwār al-Mutamadin*, 5/3/2006 (http://m.ahewar.org/s.asp?aid=63746&r=0).
Koivisto, 'J., Lahtinen, M. "Historical-Critical Dictionary of Marxism: Conjuncture, politico-historical" *Historical Materialism* 20.1 (2012) 267–277.
Koskenniemi, Martii. *From Apology to Utopia: The Structure of International Legal Argument* (Cambridge: Cambridge University Press, 2006).
——. "Sovereignty, Property and Empire: Early Modern English Contexts" *Theoretical Inquiries in Law*, Vol. 18: 355 (2017); 389.
Kostal, R.W. *A Jurisprudence of Power: Victorian Empire and the Rule of Law*, (Oxford: Oxford University Press, 2005).
Kublock, Thomas Miller. *Contested Communities: Class, Gender, and Politics in Chile's El Teniente Copper Mines*, 1904–1951 (Durham: Duke University Press, 1998).
Lauterpacht, Hersch. *International Law: Being the Collected Papers of Hersch Lauterpacht, Volume 3, The Law of Peace*, (Cambridge: Cambridge University Press, 1977).
Lee, D. Campbell. *The Mandate for Mesopotamia and the Principle of Trusteeship in English Law*, (London: The League of Nations Union, 1921).

Lefebvre, Henri. *The Production of Space*, (Oxford: Willey, 1991).
Lenin, V.I. Letters from Afar, First Letter, "The First Stage of the First Revolution"', in *Lenin Collected Works* (Moscow: Progress Publishers, 1964).
——. "On Strikes," in *Lenin: Collected Works*, Volume 5 (Moscow: Progressive Publishers, 1960 [1899]), 310–19.
Linstrum. Erik. *Age of Emergency: Living with Violence at the End of the British Empire* (Oxford: Oxford University Press, 2023).
Liebesny, Herbret J. *The Law of the Near and Middle East: Readings, Cases and Materials*, (New York: State University of New York Press, 1975).
Lindley, M.F. *The Acquisition and Government of Backward Territory in International Law: Being a Treatise on the Law and Practice of Colonial Expansion*, (London: Longmans, Green & Co, 1926).
Linstrum. E. *Age of Emergency: Living with Violence at the End of the British Empire* (Oxford: Oxford University Press, 2023).
Litowitz, Douglas. "Gramsci, Hegemony, and the Law," *Brigham Young University Law Review*, 2000, No. 2, 515–551.
Little, Douglas. "Pipeline Politics: America, TAPLINE, and the Arabs," *Business History Review* (Vol. 64, Issue 2, 1990).
Lockman, Zachary. *Comrades and Enemies: Arab and Jewish Workers in Palestine, 1906–1948* (Berkley: University of California Press, 1996).
Lobban, Michael. *Imperial Incarceration: Detention Without Trial in the Making of British Colonial Africa* (Cambridge: Cambridge University Press, 2021).
Loevy, Karin. "The Sykes-Picot Agreement's Regional Moment: Drawing Lines of Development in a New and Open Space" Symposium on the Many Lives and Legacies of Sykes-Picot, *AJIL Unbound*, Vol.110, 2016, pp.120–126.
Longhurst, Henry. *Adventure in Oil: The Story of British Petroleum* (London: Sidgwick and Jackson, 1959).
Longrigg, Stephen and Stoakes, Frank. *Iraq* (London: Ernest Benn 1958).
Longrigg, Stephen. *Iraq 1900 to 1950: A Political, Social and Economic History*, (Oxford: Oxford University Press, 1953).
——. *Oil in the Middle East: Its Discovery and Development*, (Oxford: Oxford University Press, 1969).
Lorca, Arnulf Becker. *Mestizo International Law*, (Cambridge: Cambridge University Press, 2014).
Louis, Wm. Roger. *The British Empire in the Middle East 1945–1951: Arab Nationalism, the United States and Postwar Imperialism*, (Oxford: Oxford University Press, 1984).
——. "Great Britain and International Trusteeship: The Mandates System" in Robin W. Winks (ed.) *The Historiography of the British Empire-Commonwealth: Trends, Interpretations and Resources*, (Durham: Duke University Press, 1966), pp.296–311.
Ludden, David. "A Brief History of Subalternity," in Ludden, ed., *Reading Subaltern Studies* (London: Anthem Press, 2002).
Lukacs, György. *History and Class Consciousness*, (Boston: MIT Press, 1990).
Luxemburg, Rosa. "The Mass Strike, The Political Party, and the Trade Unions" in Helen Scott (ed.), *The Essential Rosa Luxemburg* (Chicago: Haymarket Press, 2008), 111–181.
Mahan, Alfred. "The Persian Gulf and International Relations" (1902) *The National Review*.
Mahdi, Kamil. *State and Agriculture in Iraq: modern development, stagnation and the impact of oil* (Reading, UK: Ithaca Press, 2000).
Mahmud, Tayyab. "Cheaper than a Slave: Indenture Labor, Colonialism, and Capitalism", *Whittier Law Review*, (2013), Vol. 34.2, 215–243.
——. "Law of Geography and the Geography of Law: A Post-Colonial Mapping" *Jurisprudence Review*, vol. 3.064, (2010).
Main, Ernest. *Iraq: From Mandate to Independence*, (London: George Allen & Unwin, 1935).
Mamdani, Mahmood. *Citizen and Subject: Contemporary Africa and the Legacy of Late Colonialism*, (New Jersey: Princeton University Press, 1996).

Mamlyuk, Boris N. 'Decolonization as Cold War Imperative: Bandung and the Soviets' in L Eslava; M Fakhri; V Nesiah (eds.), *Bandung, Global History and International Law: Critical Pasts and Pending Futures* (Cambridge: Cambridge University Press, 2017), 203.

Manjapra, Kris. *Colonialism in Global Perspective* (Cambridge: Cambridge University Press, 2020).

Mann, J.S. *An Administrator in the Making* (London: Macmillan & Co., 1921).

Mansūr, Shāb Tuma. *al-Wajīz fi Qānūn al-ʿAmal: Dirāsa Muqārana, al-Juzu' al-'Awal* (A brief comparative study of the labour law, volume one), (Baghdad: Sharīka al-Tibaʿa wa al-Nashir al-Ahlīya, 1965).

Mantena, Karuna. *Alibis of Empire: Henry Main and the Ends of Liberal Imperialism*, (New Jersey: Princeton University Press, 2010).

Margalith, Aaron. *The International Mandates*, (Baltimore, MD: John Hopkins Press, 1930).

Margolies, D; Özsu, U; Pal M and Tzouvala, N (eds), *The Extraterritoriality of Law: History, Theory, Politics* (Abingdon, UK: Routledge, 2019).

Marks, Susan. "False Contingency," (2010) 62 *Current Legal Problems* 1–22.

Marr, Phebe. *The Modern History of Iraq* (Oxford: Westview Press: 1985).

Marsden, Magnus and Hopkins, Benjamin. *Fragments of the Afghan Frontier* (New York: Columbia University Press, 2011).

Maul, Daniel. "The Morse Years: the ILO 1948–1970," in *ILO Histories: Essays on the International Labour Organization and its impact on the World during the Twentieth Century*, (Bern: Peter Lang, 2010), pp. 365–400.

——. *Human Rights, Development and Decolonization: The International Labour Organization, 1940–70* (Basingstoke, UK: Palgrave Macmillan, 2012).

Mazower, Mark. *No Enchanted Palace: The End of Empire and the Ideological Origins of the United Nations*, (Princeton: Princeton University Press, 2009).

McGillivary, Gillian *Blazing Cane: Sugar Communities, Class, and State Formation in Cuba, 1868–1959* (Durham: Duke University Press, 2009).

Meek, C.K. *Land Law and Custom in the Colonies*, (London: Frank Cass & Co, 1968).

Mejcher, Helmut, *The Imperial Quest for Oil: Iraq 1910–1928*, (Reading, UK: Ithaca Press, 1976).

Menon, Parvathi. "Negotiating Subjection: The Political Economy of Protection in the Iraq Mandate (1914–1932)" *TWAIL Review*, Issue 2, (2021).

Merry, Sally Engel. *Colonizing Hawaii: The Cultural Power of Law*, (New Jersey: Princeton University Press, 2000).

Mieville, China. *Between Equal Rights: A Marxist Theory of International Law*, (Chicago: Haymarket Books, 2006).

Miller, David Hunter. *My Diary at the Conference of Paris: Documents, Volume 4* (New York: Appeal Printing Company, 1924).

Mitchell, Timothy. *Carbon Democracy: Political Power in the Age of Oil*, (London: Verso, 2011).

Moore, Sally Falk. *Social Facts and Fabrications: "Customary" law on Kilimanjaro, 1880–1980*, (Cambridge: Cambridge University Press, 1986).

Moosa, Matti. "The Land Policy of Midhat Pasha in Iraq, 1869–1872," *Islamic Quarterly*, Jul 1, (1968); 12, 3, pp.146–159.

Morton, Michael Quentin. *In the Heart of the Desert: The Story of an Exploration Geologist and the Search for Oil in the Middle East*, (Aylesford: Green Mountain Press, 2007).

Morton, Stephen. *States of Emergency: Colonialism, Literature and Law*, (Liverpool: Liverpool University Press, 2003).

Muhammad Ali, Hasan. *Land Reclamation and Settlement in Iraq* (Baghdad: The Baghdad Printing Press, 1955).

Mūrūwwa, Karīm. *Karīm Mūrūwwa Yatathakar* [Karim Muruwwa Remembers], Saqir Abu Fakhir (ed.) (Damascus: al-Mada, 2002).

Muttitt, Greg. *Fuel on the Fire: Oil and Politics in Occupied Iraq*, (London: Bodley Head, 2011).

al-Nāṣirī, ʿAqīl. *Al-Jaysh wa al-Ṣulṭa fi al-ʿIraq al-Malaki*, 1921–1958 [The Military and Government in Monarchal Iraq], (Damascus: Dār al-Hassād li al-Nashir wa al-Tibāʿa wa al-Tawzīʿa, 2000).

Neilson, Keith. 'The Baghdad to Haifa railway: The culmination of railway planning for Imperial defence east of Suez,' in T.G. Otte and Keith Neilson (eds.) *Railways and International Politics: Paths of Empire, 1848–1945* (Abingdon, UK: Routledge, 2006), pp.156–172; 157.

Neocleous, Mark. "International Law as Primitive Accumulation; Or, the Secret of Systemic Colonization" *European Journal of International Law*, (2012) Vol. 23, no.4, 941–962.

al-Nū῾amān, Sālim. *Al-Hizb Al-Shīyu῾i al-῾Iraqi bi-qayādat Fahad* ('The Iraqi Communist Party under the Leadership of Fahad'), (Syria: Al-Mada, 2007).

Nurī, Baha᾽al-Dīn. *Muthākarāt Baha᾽al-Dīn Nurī*, (London: Dār al-Hikmāā, 2001).

Nuzzo, Luigi "The Birth of an Imperial Location: Comparative Perspectives on Western Colonialism in China" *Leiden Journal of International Law* (2018), 31, 569–596.

Oboosy, Mohammed Jawad. "A Study in the Theory of Economic Underdevelopment With Special Reference to Iraq," *Middle East Economic Papers*, 15:2 (Beirut: American University of Beirut, 1958).

Obregon, Liliana. "Completing Civilization: Creole Consciousness and International Law in Nineteenth-Century Latin America" in Orford, Anne (ed.), *International Law and Others* (Cambridge: Cambridge University Press, 2006).

Okafor, Obiora. "Newness, Imperialism and International Legal Reform in our Time: a TWAIL perspective," *Osgoode Hall Law Journal*, 43, No.1&2, (2005): 178.

Okoth-Ogendo, H.W.O. "The Imposition of Property Law in Kenya," in Sandra Burman and Barbara Harrell-Bond (eds). *The Imposition of Law* (New York: Academic Press, 1979).

Orakhelashvilli, Alexander. "Anglo-Iranian Oil Company", *Max Planck Encyclopedia of Public International Law* (October 2007).

Orford, Anne. "The past as law or history? The relevance of imperialism for modern international law," IILJ Working Paper 2012/2 (History and Theory in International Law Series), Finalized June 2012, (www.iilj.org).

——. *International Law and the Politics of History* (Cambridge: Cambridge University Press, 2021).

Oughlo, Najat Kawthar. *Safaḥāt Min Tarīkh Kirkuk minthū Fajir al-Tarīkh ila 1958* [Pages from the history of Kirkuk from the dawn of history until 1958], (London: Dar al-Hikma, 2015).

Özsu, Umut. *Formalizing Displacement: International Law and Population Transfers* (New York: Oxford University Press, 2015).

——. "From the 'semi-civilized state' to the emerging market': remarks on international legal history of the semi-periphery," in Ugo Mattei and John Haskell (eds.) *Research Handbook on Political Economy and Law* (Cheltenham: Edward Elgar, 2015), pp. 246–259.

——. "Sykes-Picot: the treaty that carved up the Middle East", *OUPBLOG* (May, 2016).

Ozyuksel, Murat. *Berlin-Baghdad Railway and the Ottoman Empire: Industrialization, Imperial Germany and the Middle East*, (London: I.B. Tauris, 2016).

Pachachi, Adnan. *Iraq's Voice at the United Nations 1959–69: A Personal Record*, (London: Quartet Books, 1991).

Pahuja, Sundhya. "Decolonization and the eventness of international law," in Johns, Fleur; Joyce, Richard; Pahuja, Sundhya (eds.). *Events: The Force of International Law*, (London: Routledge, 2011).

Pahuja, Sundhya and Storr, Cait. "Rethinking Iran and International Law: The Anglo-Iranian Oil Company Case Revisited' in Crawford, Koroma, Mahmoudi & Pellet (eds.), *The International Legal Order: Current Needs and Possible Responses, Essays in Honour of Djamchid Momtaz* (Leiden: Brill, 2017), 53–74.

Parmar, Pooja. *Indegeneity and Legal Pluralism in India: Claims, Histories, Meanings*, (Cambridge: Cambridge University Press, 2015).

Pashukanis, Evgeny. "Lenin and the Problems of Law" in Beirne, Piers & Sharlet, Robert eds. *Pashukanis: Selected Writings on Marxism and Law* (London: Academic Press, 1980).

Pederson, Susan. "Getting Out of Iraq – in 1932: The League of Nations and the Road to Normative Statehood," *American Historical Review*, (2010): 975–1000.

——. *The Guardians: The League of Nations and the Crisis of Empire*, (Oxford: Oxford University Press, 2015).

Penrose, Edith & Penrose, E.F. *Iraq: International Relations and National Development*, (London: Ernest Benn, 1978).

Phillips, Doris G. "Rural-to-Urban Migration in Iraq," *Economic Development and Cultural Change*, Jul., 1959, Vol. No. 4, 405–421.

Philippopoulos-Milhalopoulos, Andreas. "Law's Spatial Turn: Geography, Justice and a Certain Fear of Space" *Law, Culture and the Humanities* (2010), XX(X) 1–16.

Plata-Stenger, Veronique. *Social Reform, Modernization and Technical Diplomacy: The ILO Contribution to Development (1930–1946)*, (De Gruyter Oldenbourg, 2021).

Pool, David. "From Elite to Class: The Transformation of Iraqi Political Leadership," in Kelidar, Abbas (ed.), *The Integration of Modern Iraq* (London: Croom Helm, 1979).

Pratt, Wallace E, and Good, Dorothy (eds.), *World Geography of Petroleum* (New Jersey: Princeton University Press, 1950).

Pritt, D.N. *The Autobiography of D.N. Pritt*, (London: Lawrence & Wishart, 1965).

Pursley, Sara. "'Lines Drawn on an Empty Map': Iraq's Borders and the Legend of the Artificial State'", *Jadaliyya*, June 2 2015.

al-Qassāb, ʿAbdul Azīz. *Muthakarāt ʿAbdul Azīz al-Qassāb* [The memoirs of Abdul Aziz al-Qassab], (Amman: al-Mu'asasa al-'Arabīya li al-dirāsāt wa al-Nashir, 2007).

Quaye, Christopher. *Liberation Struggles in International Law*, (Philadelphia, PA: Temple University Press, 1991).

Rajagopal, Balakrishnan. "Counter-Hegemonic International Law: Rethinking Human Rights and Development as a Third World Strategy", 27(5) *Third World Quarterly* pp. 767–783.

——. *International Law from Below: Development, Social Movements and Third World Resistance*, (Cambridge: Cambridge University Press, 2007).

Ranger, Terence. "The Invention of Tradition in Colonial Africa," in *The Invention of Tradition*, (Cambridge: Cambridge University Press, 1983).

Renshaw. Patrick. *Nine Days That Shook Britain: The 1926 General Strike* (New York Anchor, 1976).

Rey, Matthieu. *When Parliments Ruled the Middle East: Iraq and Syria, 1946–63* (Cairo: American University of Cairo, 2022).

Reynolds, John. "The Long Shadow of Colonialism: The Origins of the Doctrine of Emergency in International Human Rights Law," (2010). *Comparative Research in Law & Political Economy*. Research Paper No. 19/2010, at 4. http://digitalcommons.osgoode.yorku.ca/clpe/86.

——. *Empire, Emergency and International Law*, (Cambridge: Cambridge University Press, 2017).

Rich, Paul (ed.), *A Voyage in the Gulf:* C.M. Cursetjee's *The Land of the Date* (1918) (Cambridge: Allborough, 1991).

Rodney, Walter. *A History of the Guyanese Working People, 1881–1905*, (Baltimore, MD: John Hopkins University Press, 1981).

——. *How Europe Underdeveloped Africa*, (London: Verso, 2018).

Rodriguez-Pinero, Luis. *Indigenous Peoples, Postcolonialism, and International Law: The ILO Regime (1919–1989)*, (Oxford: Oxford University Press, 2005).

Romero, Juan. *The Iraqi Revolution of 1958: A Revolutionary Quest for Unity and Security*. (Maryland: University Press of America, 2011).

Rubin, A. *Ottoman Nizamiye Courts: Law and Modernity*, (New York: Palgrave McMillan, 2001).

Rush, Dennis, and Priestland, David, eds. *Records of Iraq, Volume II: 1953–1956*. London: Archive Editions, 2001.

Rutledge, Ian. *Enemy on the Euphrates: The Battle for Iraq, 1914–1921* (London: Saqi Books, 2015).

al-Saffar, Samir. *al-Sheikh Mohammed Rida al-Sahabibi: Hayatahu wa Shirhu* [Sheikh Mohammed Rida al-Shabibi: His Life and Poetry] (Beirut: Dar al-Zahra, 1995).

Said, Edward W. *Orientalism*. (New York: Vintage, 1978).

al-Saīd, Ṣādiq Mahdī. *Munāzaʿāt al-ʿAmal al-Jamāʿya wa Hismaha* [Collective Labour Conflicts and their Resolution], (Baghdad: Mutabaʿa al-Maʿarif, 1961).

Said, Rosemarie Zahlan. *The Making of the Modern Gulf States* (London: Garnett, 1989).

Saksena, P. 'Jousting Over Jurisdiction: Sovereignty and International Law in Late Nineteenth-Century South Asia' *Law and History Review*, Issue 2, May 2020, 407–457.

Salim, Shakir. *Marsh Dwellers of the Euphrates Delta* (1962) (University of London: Athlon Press).

Samuel, Annie Tracy. 'The Open Door and U.S. Policy in Iraq between the World Wars' *Diplomatic History*, Vol. 38, No. 5 (2014).

Sassoon, Joseph. *Economic Policy in Iraq 1932–1950*, (London: Frank Cass, 1987).

Satia, Priya. *Spies in Arabia: The Great War and the Cultural Foundations of Britain's Convert Empire in the Middle East*, (Oxford: Oxford University Press, 2008).

Sbāhī, Azīz. *'Uqūd min Tārīkh al-Ḥizb al-Shīyū'ī al-'Irāqī, al-Juzu' al-Awal* [Decades from the History of the Communist Party of Iraq, volume 1], (Damascus: Manshourāt al-Thaqāfa al-Jadīda, 2002).

——. *'Uqūd min Tārīkh al-Ḥizb al-Shīyū'ī al-'Irāqī, al-Juzu' al-Thāni* [Decades from the History of the Communist Party of Iraq, volume 2], (Damascus: Manshourāt al-Thaqāfa al-Jadīda, 2003).

al-Sayyāb, Badir Shākir. *Kuntū Shū'īyan* [I was a Communist], (Cologne: Manshūrāt al-Jamal, 2007).

Schwarz, Bill. "'The people' in history: The Communist Party Historians' Group, 1946–56," Johnson, Richard et al (ed.), *Making Histories: Studies in history-writing and politics*, (London: Hutchinson & Co, 1983).

Scott, David. *Conscripts of Modernity: The Tragedy of Colonial Enlightenment*, (Durham: Duke University Press, 2004).

al-Sha'abān, 'Abdul Hussein. *Jithūr al-Tayyār al-Dimūqrātī fī al-'Iraq: Qira'a fī afkār Hussein Jamīl*, [The Roots of the Democratic Current in Iraq: A study in the thought of Hussein Jamil], (Beirut: Bīsān, 2007).

Sharma, D.N. *Afro-Asian Group in the U.N.* (Allahabad: Chaitanya Publishing, 1969).

Shwadran, Benjamin. *The Middle East, Oil and the Great Powers* (New York: Praeger, 1955).

Seccombe, Ian J. and Lawless, Richard I. *Work Camps and Company Towns: Settlement Patterns and the Gulf Oil Industry* (University of Durham. Centre for Middle Eastern and Islamic Studies, 1987).

Shabandar, Mūsa. *Dhikrayāt Baghdādiyya: al-Iraq Bayna al-Ihtilal wa al-Istiqlāl* [Baghdadi Memories: Iraq between Occupation and Independence] (London: Riad al-Rayyes, 1993).

Sheppard, Eric. "David Harvey and Dialectical SpaceTime", in Castree, Noel and Gregory, Derek (eds), *David Harvey: A Critical Reader*, (New York: Blackwell, 2006).

Shotwell, James T. "The International Labour Organization as an Alternative to Violent Revolution," *The Annals of the American Academy of Political and Social Science* 166 (1933), 18–25.

——. "ILO and the Tripartite System," *International Conciliation* 32 (1959), [iii]-448.

Shields, Sara. "Mosul Questions: Economy, Identity and Annexation," in Simon, Reeva and Tejirian, Eleanor (eds), *The Creation of Iraq, 1914–1921*, (New York: Columbia University of Press, 2004).

Shivji, Issa G. *Law, State, and the Working Class in Tanzania*, (Portsmouth: Heinemann, 1986).

Schofield, Richard N. *Evolution of the Shatt Al-'Arab Boundary Dispute* (Middle East and North African Studies Press, 1986).

Siksek, Simon. *The Legal Framework for Oil Concessions in the Arab World* (Beirut: The Middle East Research and Publishing Centre, 1960).

Silverfarb, Daniel. *Britain's Informal Empire in the Middle East: A Case Study of Iraq 1929–1941* (Oxford: Oxford University Press, 1986).

Simpson, Brian. *Human Rights and the End of Empire: Britain and the Genesis of the European Convention*, (Oxford: Oxford University Press, 2001).

Simpson, Gerry. *Great Powers and Outlaw States: Unequal Sovereigns in the International Legal Order*, (Cambridge: Cambridge University Press, 2004).

Sinclair, Guy Fiti. *To Reform the World: International Organizations and the Making of Modern States*, (Oxford: Oxford University Press, 2017).

Singh, Prabhakar. 'Of International Law, Semi-colonial Thailand, and Imperial Ghosts' (2019) 9 *Asian Journal of International Law* 46.

Sluglett, Peter. *Britain in Iraq: Contriving King and Country,* (New York: Columbia University Press, 2007).

Smith, Leonard V. *Sovereignty at the Paris Peace Conference* (Oxford University Press, 2018).

Smuts, Jan. *The League of Nations – A practical suggestion*, (London: Hodder and Stoughton, 1918).

Snyder, Francis G. "Colonialism and Legal Form: The Creation of 'Customary Law' in Senegal", in Sumner, Collin (ed.), *Crime, Justice and Underdevelopment*, (London: Macmillan & Co, 1982), pp.90–121.

Sornarajah, Muthucumaraswamy. *The International Law of Foreign Investment: Second Edition.* (Cambridge: Cambridge University Press, 2004).

Spear, Thomas. "Neo-Traditionalism and the Limits of Invention in British Colonial Africa," *Journal of African History*, 44 (2003), pp.3–27.

Statton, Morton B. 'British Railways and Motor Roads in the Middle East – 1918–1930, *Economic Geography*, Vol. 20, No. 2 (Apr., 1944), pp. 116–129.

Stewart, Desmond and Haylock, John. *New Babylon: A Portrait of Iraq* (London: Collins, 1956).

Stivers, William. *Supremacy and Oil: Iraq, Turkey and the Anglo-American World Order*, 1918–1930 (Ithaca: Cornell University Press, 1982).

Sūfwā, Najda Fatḥi. *Sālih Jabr: Sīra Syāsīya* [Salih Jabr: A Political Biography], (London: Dar al-Saqi, 2017).

Sykes, Mark. *The Caliphs' Last Heritage: A Short History of the Turkish Empire*, (London: Macmillan and Co, 1915).

Thorton, T.H. *Col. Sir Robert Sandeman: His Life and Work on Our Indian Frontier. A Memoir, with Selections from His Correspondence and Official Writings* (London: John Murray, 1895).

al-Ṭalibāni, Makram. 'Gawūrbāghī Malḥama Buṭūlīya', ["Gawurbaghi: a heroic epic of the working class"] *al-Thaqāfa al-Jadīda*, Issue 26, July 1971.

Tapper, Richard. "Anthropologists, Historians, and Tribespeople on Tribe and State Formation in the Middle East," in Khoury, Philip and Kostiner, Joseph (eds.), *Tribes and State Formation in the Middle East* (Berkley: University of California Press, 1990).

Taha, Mai. "Law, Class Struggle and Nervous Breakdowns," in K Greenman, A Orford, A Saunders, N Tzouvala (eds.) *Revolutions in International Law: The Legacies of 1917* (OUP, 2021), pp. 112–133.

——. "Reading 'Class' in International Law: The Labor Question in Interwar Egypt" (2016) *Social & Legal Studies*, Vol. 25(5), 567–589.

Taylor, Owen. "Reclaiming Revolution," *Finnish Yearbook of International Law* (Vol. 22, 2011), 259–292.

Thomas, Martin. *Violence and the Colonial Order: Police, Workers and Protest in the European Colonial Empires 1918–1940* (Cambridge: Cambridge University Press, 2012).

Thompson, E.P. *Whigs and Hunters: The Origin of the Black Act* (London: Penguin Books, 1975).

Thompson, Elizabeth F. *How the West Stole Democracy from the Arabs: The Syrian Arab Congress of 1920 and the Destruction of its Historic Liberal-Islamic Alliance* (New York: Atlantic Monthly Press, 2020).

Toynbee, Arnold. *Survey of International Affairs*, (London: Royal Institute of International Affairs, 1930).

Traverso, Enzo. *Revolution: An Intellectual History* (London: Verso, 2021).

Tripodi, Christian. *Edge of Empire: The British Political Officer and Tribal Administration on the North-West Frontier 1877–1947* (London: Ashgate, 2011).

Tucker, Eric and Fudge, Judy. *Labor Before the Law*, (Oxford: OUP, 2000).

Tuson, Penelope; Quick, Emma (eds.), *Arabian Treaties 1600–1960 Vols. 1–4* (London: Archive Editions, 1998).

Upthegrove, Campbell. *Empire by Mandate*, (New York: Bookman, 1954).

Valverde, Mariana. *Infrastructure: New Trajectories in Law* (Abingdon, UK: Routledge, 2022).

Vismann, Cornelia. "Starting from Scratch: Concepts of Order in No Man's Land" in Bernd-Rudiger Huppauf (ed) *War, Violence and the Modern Condition.* (Berlin: Walter de Gruyter, 1997).

Visser, Reider. *Basra, the Failed Gulf State* (Münster: LIT Verlag, 2005).

Vitalis, Robert. *America's Kingdom: Mythmaking on the Saudi Frontier*, (London: Verso, 2009).

al-Wa'ili, Ibrahim Harāj. *Thawarat al-'ishrin fī al-sh'ir al-'Iraqī* [The 1920 Revolution in Iraqi Poetry] (Baghdad: Al-Iman Press, 1968).

Wakely, A.V.T. *Some Aspects of Imperial Communications* (London: Sifton Praed & Co, 1924).

Wallerstein, Immanuel. *World-Systems Analysis: An Introduction*, (Durham: Duke University Press, 2004).

Wang, Dong. *China's Unequal Treaties: Narrating National History* (Lanham, MD: Lexington, 2005).

al-Wardi, 'Ali. *Shakhsīyāt al-Fard al-'Iraqi* [The Nature of the Iraqi Personality]. (Amman: Dar al-Warrāq, 2009).

——. *Lamahāt min Tārīkh al-'Iraq*. (Baghdad: al- Warrāq, 2007).

Warriner, Doreen. *Land Reform and* Development in the Middle East: A study of Egypt, Syria and Iraq, (Oxford: Oxford University Press).

——. *Land and Poverty in the Middle East*, (1948) (London: Royal Institute of International Affairs).

Watts, Michael J. "Securing Oil: Frontiers, Risk, and Spaces of Accumulated Insecurity," in Appel, Hannah; Mason, Arthur and Watts, Michael (eds.), *Subterranean Estates: Life Worlds of Oil and Gas*, (Ithaca: Cornell University Press, 2015), pp.211–236.

Weiss, Holger. *A Global Radical Waterfront: The International Propoganda Committee of Transport Workers and the International of Seamen and Harbour Workers, 1921–1937* (Leiden: Brill, 2021).

Wilson, Charles Morrow. *Oil Across the World: The American Saga of Pipel*ines (London: Longmans, Green and Co, 1946).

Williams, William A. *The Tragedy of America Diplomacy* (New York: W.W. Norton, 2009).

Williams, Raymond. 'Western' in *Keywords: A Vocabulary of Culture and Society* (Oxford: Oxford University Press, 1983) 333–334.

Wilmington, Martin W. *The Middle East Supply Centre* (New York: State University of New York, 1971).

Wolfe-Hunnicutt, Brandon. *The Paranoid Style in American Diplomacy: Oil and Arab Nationalization in Iraq* (Stanford: Stanford University Press, 2021).

Wratislaw, A.C. *A Consul in the East* (London: William Blackwood and Sons, 1924).

Wright, Quincy. "The Government of Iraq," (1926), 20(4) *The American Political Science Review*, 743.

——. 'The Mosul Dispute,' *American Journal of International Law* 20:3, July 1926: 453–64.

——. *The League of Nations*, (New York: Greenwood Press, 1930).

Wrytzen, Jonathan. *Worldmaking in the Long Great War: How Local and Colonial Struggles Shaped the Modern Middle East* (New York: Columbia University Press, 2022).

Quigley, John. *Britain and its Mandate over Palestine: Legal Chicanery on a World Stage* (London: Anthem Press, 2022).

Yazbak, Yūsuf Ibrahīm. *al-Nift Müst'abid al-Sh'wb* [*Oil, the Enslaver of Peoples*], (Damascus: Manshourāt Wizārat al-Thaqāfa, 1990).

Yergin, Daniel. *The Prize: The Epic Quest for Oil, Money and Power*, (New York: Simon & Schuster, 1991).

Young, Gabriel. 'Infrastructures of Empire and Sovereignty: The Port of Basra in Interwar Iraq,' *Journal of Arabian Studies* 9.2 (December 2019), 123–144.

Yūsuf Salmān Yūsuf. *Mu'alafāt al-Rafiq Fahad* ['The Works of Comrade Fahad'], (Baghdad: al-Thaqāfa al-Jadīda Press).

Yūsuf, Thamīna Nājī and Khālid, Nizār. *Salām Ādil: Sīra Mūnādil* [Salam Adil: The Story of a Resister] (Damascus: Dār al-Madā, 2001).

Zhu, Yuan Yi. 'Suzerainty, Semi-Sovereignty, and International Law' 10(2), *Asian Journal of International Law* 10/2 (2020), 293–320.

**IX. Unpublished Dissertations**

Alexander, Rachel Anne. 'Leadership in the National Movements of Egypt and Iraq 1945–1963', (PhD Dissertation, University of Exeter, 2007).

Gillick, Steven S. *Life and Labor in a Banana Enclave: Bananeros, the United Fruit Company, and the Limits of Trade Unionism in Guatemala, 1906 to 1931* (PhD, Tulane University, 1994).

Gupta, Huma. "Migrant *Sarifa* Settlements and State-building in Iraq" (PhD Dissertation, MIT, 2020).

Haider, Saleh. "Land Problems of Iraq", (PhD Thesis, University of London, 1942).

Kachim, M.N. *Reaction to Crime Under Tribal Law and Modern Codification in Iraq*, (D.Phil. Thesis, Oxford University, 1961).

Al-Khattab, Adil Abdullah. *Basra City: A Study in Urban Geography* (PhD Dissertation, SOAS, University of London, 1972).

Kamanda, Alfred. *A Study of the Legal Status of Protectorates in Public International Law* (University of Geneva, Thesis, 1961).

Najar, Basil Naim. "The Dynamics of Rural-Urban Migration and Assimilation in Iraq" (PhD, Wayne State University, 1976).

Stratton, Morton Brown. *British Communications in the Middle East 1885–1939*, (PhD, University of Pennsylvania, 1943).

Taha, Mai. *Nation and Class Subjectivity in International Law and its Institutions in the Middle East (1919–1939)*, (SJD Dissertation, University of Toronto, 2015).

Tellew, Fu'ad Hanna. "Labour Unions in Iraq." (M.A. Dissertation, University of Southern California, Los Angeles, 1954).

# Index

www.ingramcontent.com/pod-product-compliance
Ingram Content Group UK Ltd.
Pitfield, Milton Keynes, MK11 3LW, UK
UKHW020845290926
15470UKWH00004B/1555

9 781509 952878